P9-APY-953

POPULAR
MUSIC

Other Books by Nat Shapiro

Popular Music
An Annotated Index of American Popular Songs
Volume 1, 1950-1959
Volume 2, 1940-1949
Volume 3, 1960-1964

Hear Me Talkin' to Ya (Co-Editor)

The Jazz Makers (Co-Editor)

VOLUME 4

1930-1939

POPULAR
MUSIC

An Annotated Index of American Popular Songs

Edited by

NAT SHAPIRO

ADRIAN PRESS

** Brown·

First Edition
Copyright © 1968 by Adrian Press, Inc.

All rights reserved. No part of this book may be reproduced in any form, except for brief quotation in a review, without written permission from the publisher. All inquiries should be addressed to Adrian Press, Inc., 550 Fifth Avenue, New York, N.Y. 10036.

Library of Congress Catalog Card Number 64-23761

ML 120
, U555
ual. 4

BOSTON PUBLIC LIBRARY

Jacket designed by Robert Cato

Printed in the United States of America
by the Lerman Printing Co., New York, N.Y.

 426

Acknowledgments

The Editor is indebted to Carol Bridgman, Walter Evans, Elias Feilich, Lois Gold, Sara Kerber, Francia Luban, Philip Mahfouz, Betty Martone, Cora Martone, Sue Osen, Russell Sanjek, Amy L. Shapiro, Mark Sikelianos, Romano Tozzi, Saul Weinbaum; the Index Department of the American Society of Composers, Authors and Publishers (ASCAP); the Index Department of Broadcast Music, Inc. (BMI); and the numerous publishers, authors, and composers who took the time to remember, correspond, confirm, and correct. The Editor is particularly grateful to Miles Kreuger for his encyclopedic knowledge of theater and film music and his wit, taste, and hospitality; to Frank Driggs for his invaluable contribution in the area of discography and his deep concern for the accurate documentation of the works of jazz composers; and to Joe Charles Friedman for his very able and imaginative assistance with many aspects of the research. As with the earlier volumes of *Popular Music*, Dr. Vera Miller (Mrs. Nat Shapiro) was responsible for the design, organization, and production of the book. Her research training, editorial meticulousness, and enthusiasm for the project made it all possible.

Contents

About the Book and How To Use It

This volume is the fourth of a series, the aim of which is to set down in permanent and practical form a selective, annotated list of the significant popular songs of our times. Previous indexes of popular music have either dealt with special areas, such as jazz or theater and film music, or been concerned chiefly with songs which achieved a degree of popularity, as measured by the variably reliable music business trade indicators. And, unfortunately, the basic records kept by the active participants in the music business are often casual, inaccurate, and transitory.

There is no single source of comprehensive information about popular songs, and those sources which do exist do not publish complete material about even the musical works with which they are directly concerned. Two of the primary proprietors of basic information about our popular music are the major performing rights societies—the American Society of Composers, Authors and Publishers (ASCAP) and Broadcast Music, Inc. (BMI). Although each of these organizations has considerable information about the songs of its own writer and publisher members and has also issued indexes of its own songs, their files and published indexes are designed primarily for clearance identification by the commercial users of music. Their publications of annual or periodic lists of their "hits" necessarily include only a small fraction of their songs, and the facts given about these are also limited. Both ASCAP and BMI are, however, invaluable and indispensable sources of data about popular music. It is just that their data and special knowledge are not readily accessible to the researcher.

About the Book

Another basic source of information about musical compositions and their creators and publishers is the *Catalog of Copyright Entries* issued by the Copyright Office of The Library of Congress. Each year, two massive volumes are published by the Copyright Office, listing each published, unpublished, republished, and renewed copyright of songs registered with the Office. While these volumes are helpful in determining the precise date of the declaration of the original ownership of musical works, they contain no other information, are unwieldy, and, lacking a unified index, difficult to use. To complicate matters further, some authors, composers, and publishers have been known to employ rather makeshift methods of protecting their works legally, and there are several songs listed in *Popular Music* which are not to be found in The Library of Congress files.

In preparing this series, the Editor was faced with a number of separate problems. The first and most important of these was the basic one of selection. In this regard, the solution was determined by adherence to the stated aim of the project itself—to offer the user of the Index as comprehensive and accurate a listing of significant popular songs as possible. Significance was decided objectively and without any editorial prejudice for or against any type of popular music. It was not the Editor's intention to evaluate the importance or quality of show tunes, movie songs, jazz instrumentals, or novelties. Rather, it was the purpose of *Popular Music* to document those musical works which (1) achieved a substantial degree of popular acceptance, (2) were exposed to the public in especially notable circumstances, or (3) were accepted and given important performances by influential musical and dramatic artists.

Another problem was whether or not to classify the songs as to type. Most works of music are subject to any number of interpretations and, although it is possible to describe a particular performance, it is more difficult to give a musical composition a label applicable not only to its origin but to its subsequent musical history. In fact, the most significant versions of some songs are often quite at variance with their origins. It is believed, however, that the information in *Popular Music* for such songs indicates the important facts about not only their origins but also their subsequent lives.

About the Book

The principal sources of information for the titles, authors, composers, publishers, and dates of copyright of the songs in this volume were the Copyright Office of The Library of Congress, ASCAP, BMI, and individual writers and publishers. For the recording information; historical notes; anecdotes; information about foreign, folk, public domain, and classical origins; and identification of theatrical, film, and radio introducers of songs, the Editor relied upon his own and the New York Public Library's collection of record album notes, theater programs, sheet music, newspaper and magazine articles, and other material.

The information for each song in Volume 4, published in 1930-1939, is listed under the year of its original published copyright. The reader is, therefore, advised to consult the List of Titles to determine the year of the song's original published copyright. Songs are occasionally registered with the Copyright Office of The Library of Congress before publication, but, in almost all cases, the copyright year given in Volume 4 is that of the original *published* copyright and not the year of the original registration by the writer.

The primary listing for a song published in 1930-1939 includes, first of all, the full title and alternate title or titles, exactly as they appear on The Library of Congress copyright card or, in some cases, the sheet music. Since even a casual perusal of the List of Titles indicates considerable variation in spelling and punctuation, it should be noted that these are neither editorial nor typographical errors but the colloquialisms of the music trade. The title of a given song as it appears in this volume is, in almost all instances, the one under which it is legally registered.

In all cases, the primary listing reports the author or authors and the composer or composers. The reader will find variations in the spelling of a song writer's name. This results from the fact that some writers used different forms of their names at different times or in connection with different songs. In addition to this kind of variation in the spelling of writers' names, the reader will also notice that, in some cases, where the writer is also the performer, his name as a writer may differ from the form of the name he used as a performer.

About the Book

The publisher listed is the *current* publisher. Since *Popular Music* is designed as a practical reference work rather than an academic study, and since copyrights more than occasionally change hands, the current publisher is given instead of the original holder of the copyright. If a publisher has, for some reason, copyrighted a song more than once, the years of the significant copyrights, subsequent to the year of the original published copyright, are listed after the publisher's name.

If the song is of foreign origin, the primary listing indicates the country of origin after the title. Additional information about the original title, copyright date in country of origin (if other than copyright date in the United States), writers, publisher, and other facts about the adaptation are noted.

The primary listing includes also the musical, film, or other production in which the song was introduced and, where important, by whom it was introduced in the case of theater and film songs and those introduced on radio; any other performers identified with the song; first or best-selling recordings, indicating the performer and, where ascertainable, the record company; and other relevant data. The name of a performer may be listed differently in connection with different songs, especially over a period of years. The name listed is the form of the name given in connection with a particular performance or record. It should be noted that the designation, "best-selling record," does not mean that the record was a "hit." It means simply that the record or records noted as "best-selling" were the best-selling record or records of that particular song, in comparison with the sales of other records of the same song.

In all cases, if any fact about a song relates to a year other than the year of the original copyright, the year of such fact is noted in the primary listing. Cross-references to such songs appear under the other years in which there are significant facts for them. The one exception is that there are no cross-references to best-selling records appearing in the year immediately following the copyright year. Since many songs become popular in the year following the copyright year, such cross-references would have cluttered the book to the point of distracting the reader. The year of any annotation, including those of best-selling records, subsequent to the copyright year is, of course, noted in the primary listing. Cross-references for all important alternate titles of songs are also listed.

The List of Publishers, which is alphabetically arranged, includes the performing rights affiliation (ASCAP or BMI) and current address of each publisher of a song appearing in Volume 4.

Popular Music in the 1930's

The principal force that shaped the lives of Americans in the 1930's was the great economic depression that began on October 29, 1929 and continued until a measure of recovery and stability was achieved by the New Deal, under the guidance of President Franklin Delano Roosevelt. Coincidental with the breakdown of our industrial and economic machinery was a series of significant technological developments in the entertainment industry—primarily in motion pictures, commercial radio, and sound recording—which determined, to an important degree, the forms and the directions that our popular culture was to take.

Motion pictures were the major medium of mass entertainment. It was estimated that, during the decade, more than sixty million people went to motion picture theaters every week. Radio was the principal source of home entertainment, and, as the nation worked its way out of the depression, ballrooms and nightclubs, featuring dance orchestras, were widely attended. While vaudeville declined seriously with the advent of talking pictures, it revived in the late 1930's as the big bands began to be billed above tap dancers, juggling acts, and dialect comedians. The theater remained a stable factor, preserving its traditional appeal to those with the price of admission, but only in a very few metropolitan centers. The record industry, which waned drastically in the first years of the decade, began to recover in 1934 when lower-priced records by popular artists were introduced to the market. By 1939, records were again an important element in the entertainment field.

While unemployment, hunger, despair, and social and political unrest were reflected in literature, in the theater, in painting, and even in the dance, the popular, commercial areas of our cultural life—and popular music in particular—rarely

1

Popular Music in the 1930's

(and then, obliquely) recognized that something was happening "out there." In the era of breadlines, Hoovervilles, bonus marches, sit-down strikes, and the rise of Nazism in Germany, America's popular songs, hardly ever burdened by social responsibility or touched by an awareness of reality, continued to be preoccupied with their never-never world of love affairs consummated by a goodnight kiss and moons ever-full and ever-shining over exotic fairylands from Manakoora to Miami. There were, however, a few isolated concessions to the economic facts of life, and such songs as "Brother, Can You Spare a Dime?," "Remember My Forgotten Man," "Ten Cents a Dance," and "Hallelujah, I'm a Bum" did acknowledge the existence of folks who didn't wear a "Top Hat, White Tie and Tails."

Many of the most popular songs of the early 1930's reflected the fierce determination of song writers, music publishers, and film and musical comedy producers to be optimistic —almost desperately so. We were urged to "Smile, Darn Ya, Smile," and both major political parties insisted, in the Presidential election campaigns of 1932, that "Happy Days Are Here Again." Tin Pan Alley's philosophers asked their mass audiences to "Wrap Your Troubles in Dreams (and Dream Your Troubles Away)" and reminded them that life could be so sweet "On the Sunny Side of the Street." Money, after all, wasn't really that important, and radio listeners were advised that, since potatoes were cheaper and tomatoes were cheaper, "Now's the Time To Fall in Love." One could, they assured us, find a million dollar baby in a five and ten cent store and, although one had only a shanty in old shanty town, it was more than a palace or a millionaire's mansion. Above all, America, led by Walt Disney's plucky porkers, responded to the defiant rhetoric of "Who's Afraid of the Big Bad Wolf."

Although it was in 1927 that the painted, mock-minstrel lips of Al Jolson uttered the screen's first synchronized words, "You ain't heard nothin' yet, folks," in *The Jazz Singer*, it took more than a year for the film industry, theater owners, and movie audiences to adjust to the novelty not only of pictures that could speak but of pictures that could sing as well. Then, composers, lyricists, arrangers, conductors, and musicians clearly heard the sound of money and the challenging

2

ring of new problems issuing from Hollywood, and a new gold rush began. It seemed heaven sent. New York's Tin Pan Alley —with vaudeville in decline, the record business at its nadir, nightclubs in bankruptcy, and the musical theater in trouble— was wasting away. Suddenly, there was background music to be composed and scored and songs to be written, conducted, and performed for use in hundreds of feature films, short subjects, serials, and even newsreels. For all involved, it became well-paid, on-the-job training. No one, after all, knew quite what would and what wouldn't work. Sound equipment was primitive, and a whole new corps of recording and acoustical technicians had to be developed and schooled. It was all new; it was all exciting; and, for the first few years, film musicals were, on the whole, quite terrible.

There were exceptions. In 1929, King Vidor made an attempt, somewhat naive but extremely daring for its time, at a "folk opera" on film, *Hallelujah*, with an all-Negro cast. With typical Hollywood insensitivity, that well-known "folk composer," Irving Berlin, was engaged to write the score. In the same year, *Applause, Broadway, Broadway Babies, Broadway Melody, Broadway Scandals, Gold Diggers of Broadway*, and several other pictures began an apparently endless stream of "backstage" musicals, all of which, including those you've seen this year, had the same plot.

In 1930, the extraordinarily gifted French director, René Clair, taught Hollywood something about style and charm with his *Sous les Toits de Paris*, which was followed by *Le Million* and then by *A Nous la Liberté*, all of which made inventive use of music. Another European, Ernst Lubitsch, brought early distinction to the musical film with *The Love Parade* in 1929, an early triumph of sophistication starring Maurice Chevalier and Jeanette MacDonald. Lubitsch, in 1930, also directed Miss MacDonald in *Monte Carlo*, which was distinguished by a brilliant bit of musical cinematic magic in the presentation of "Beyond the Blue Horizon."

Generally, however, most of the film musicals of the early years of talking pictures were either clumsy attempts at photographing hit broadway musical comedies and operettas or vehicles for popular vaudeville, radio, theater, and other musical personalities. Songs, for the most part, were chosen

3

haphazardly and rarely had anything to do with the plots. In many cases, they were taken from the backlogs of material brought along by the army of song writers who had emigrated from New York to Hollywood.

One thing became certain in 1930. The movies most definitely had the power to create hits, and songs like "Three Little Words," "Cuban Love Song," "It Happened in Monterey," "Falling in Love Again," "My Ideal," "Puttin' on the Ritz," "Sing You Sinners," and "You Brought a New Kind of Love to Me," all introduced in films, became enormously popular.

By 1933, producers, directors, writers, composers, and lyricists had begun to find their way in the new medium. Rapid advances in sound recording equipment, the use of dubbing and prerecording, and new concepts of choreography for the camera brought the film musical to a point where it showed signs of becoming an art form in its own right. Warner Brothers brought forth three astonishing musicals, *Footlight Parade, Forty-Second Street,* and *Gold Diggers of 1933,* featuring gloriously extravagant, cinematically brilliant, and utterly ridiculous production numbers staged by Busby Berkeley. Also common to the three films was the presence of Ruby Keeler and Dick Powell, personalities possessing magnetic mediocrity, and the infectious, skillful songs of the team of Harry Warren and Al Dubin, among them "Shuffle Off to Buffalo," "Forty-Second Street," "You're Getting To Be a Habit with Me," "Shadow Waltz," "Remember My Forgotten Man," "The Gold Digger's Song (We're in the Money)," and "Shanghai Lil."

Another 1933 film, *Flying Down to Rio,* with a score by Vincent Youmans, was notable principally for its pairing of a young ingenue, dancer-comedienne Ginger Rogers, with the veteran Broadway star, Fred Astaire. This was the beginning of a series of musical films, featuring the as yet unsurpassed dancing of Astaire and Rogers, that was not only to add wit and style to the medium but also to utilize original and consistently excellent scores by America's leading composers and lyricists. *Top Hat* (1935), *Follow the Fleet* (1936), and *Carefree* (1938) had scores by Irving Berlin; the songs in *Swing Time* (1936) were written by Dorothy Fields and Jerome Kern; and *Shall We Dance?* (1937) had music and lyrics by George and Ira Gershwin.

As the decade moved along, as techniques sharpened, and as success patterns became evident, and even predictable, to the major studios, film musicals became more elaborate and Hollywood began to employ its own home-grown, film-oriented units of writers, composers, arrangers, and performers. Bing Crosby, who had served his apprenticeship as a band singer with Paul Whiteman and then as a radio performer, established himself as a superstar in *The Big Broadcast* in 1932 and continued, for more than two decades, to reign as Hollywood's principal hit maker. Such songs as "Please," "Temptation," "I'm an Old Cow Hand," "Pennies from Heaven," "Sweet Leilani," "I've Got a Pocketful of Dreams," "Small Fry," "May I?," "Love Thy Neighbor," "Love in Bloom," "June in January," "It's Easy To Remember," "Soon," and dozens of others were introduced by Crosby in his films. Among the many other film musical personalities who became identified with the most important songs of the 1930's were Alice Faye, Frances Langford, Martha Raye, Shirley Temple, Nelson Eddy and Jeanette MacDonald, Allan Jones, Charles "Buddy" Rogers, Dorothy Lamour, Shirley Ross, and Tony Martin.

Very early in the game, the film industry leaders recognized the enormous strategic and economic advantages in the ownership of its own musical establishment, and the major studios set about acquiring and building subsidiary music publishing companies. By the end of the decade, the great publishing firms of Harms, Remick, Witmark, Robbins, Feist, Miller, Famous, and several others were either partly or wholly owned and controlled by the film companies. In 1939, it was estimated that as much as sixty-five percent of the publishers' income derived from performances of popular music, collected by the American Society of Composers, Authors and Publishers, was going to companies owned by film interests.

Hundreds of song writers were signed to exclusive contracts by the motion picture companies, and a whole new group of composers and lyricists emerged to match Broadway and Tin Pan Alley as a source of popular song hits. Arthur Freed and Nacio Herb Brown, Mack Gordon and Harry Revel, Leo Robin and Ralph Rainger, Sam Coslow, Arthur Johnston, Johnny Burke, Johnny Mercer, Frederick Hollander, Louis Alter, John Green, Harold Adamson, Victor Young, Sidney D.

5

Popular Music in the 1930's

Mitchell and Lew Pollack, Frank Loesser, and Burton Lane are only a few of the song writers whose primary area of creativity during the 1930's was in Hollywood.

The quality of motion picture music was generally high during the first ten years of sound movies, and a great number of enduring songs were first heard in films. Most of them were a step above the routine output of the music publishing industry in New York but nowhere near the level of songs still being written for the theater.

The Broadway musical is traditionally the primary source of superior popular music in this country. In the 1930's—with 184 new musical comedies and revues opening in New York—it fulfilled its customary promise. Richard Rodgers and Lorenz Hart, with nine shows; Cole Porter, with eight; Irving Berlin, with two; George and Ira Gershwin, with six; and Jerome Kern, with four, managed to continue supplying the musical theater with songs of phenomenally consistent quality. The mere listing of such shows as *Girl Crazy, Of Thee I Sing, Porgy and Bess, Anything Goes, The Boys from Syracuse, Roberta, On Your Toes, Billy Rose's Jumbo, Babes in Arms, Music in the Air,* and *I Married an Angel*—and such songs as "Smoke Gets in Your Eyes," "I Got Rhythm," "Easter Parade," "Begin the Beguine," "Where or When," "Embraceable You," "This Can't Be Love," "Falling in Love with Love," "Little Girl Blue," "Heat Wave," and "Yesterdays"—is enough to evoke not only nostalgia but wonder as well.

In addition to the Grand Masters, Broadway heard songs by such newcomers as Harold Arlen, Kurt Weill, Arthur Schwartz and Howard Dietz, Harold Rome, E. Y. Harburg, and Vernon Duke, as well as scores from England's Noël Coward and by veterans B. G. De Sylva, Lew Brown, and Ray Henderson, Sigmund Romberg, and Vincent Youmans.

It was a fruitful decade for the musical theater but one marked by few innovations. The topical revue, influenced by intellectual and social ferment, did begin to touch—gently, to be sure—on "controversial issues." Such delightfully inoffensive shows as *As Thousands Cheer, Shoot the Works, The Band Wagon, Sing Out the News,* and *Pins and Needles* did, in varying degrees, mix mild social commentary with their songs and dances. But, for the most part, musical comedy remained just that, comedy with music. Apart from such theatrical experiments as Gershwin's *Porgy and Bess,* Kurt Weill's *Johnny Johnson,* and Marc Blitzstein's *The Cradle Will Rock,* almost no attempts were made to broaden the scope of the musical stage. That was to come in the 1940's.

As it was in the latter years of the 1920's—and as it was to be in the 1940's, 1950's, and 1960's—Duke Ellington's phenomenally fertile creative imagination was a significant factor in the musical life of America in the 1930's. This astonishing composer, possibly the greatest single figure in American music, recorded prolifically and appeared with his orchestra in theaters, nightclubs, and ballrooms, in films, in concerts, and on radio. His jazz compositions and popular songs were not only widely performed by popular singers and dance bands throughout the United States and in Europe but were the subject of scores of treatises, articles, and critical studies by music critics and students of popular culture.

Such compositions as "Sophisticated Lady," "Mood Indigo," "I Let a Song Go Out of My Heart," "It Don't Mean a Thing (If It Ain't Got That Swing)," "Prelude to a Kiss," "Lost in Meditation," "Caravan," "Azure," "Echoes of Harlem," "In a Sentimental Mood," "Solitude," "Drop Me Off in (at) Harlem," "Lazy Rhapsody," "Creole Rhapsody," "Rockin' in Rhythm," and dozens of others remain fresh and exciting to this day, and several, despite uninspired lyrics by Ellington's publisher, Irving Mills, are standards.

Significantly, the most serious critical appraisals of Duke Ellington's music were undertaken by Europeans. The United States, in the sometimes subtle, often brutal, grip of traditional racism, generally ignored the powerful cultural contributions being made by Negro artists, especially in jazz. Jazz musicians were entertainers, and jazz was still "vulgar"—except, of course, when it was presented by George Gershwin, Ferde Grofé, Morton Gould, or others in concert form. Jelly Roll Morton, James P. Johnson, and many other important composers in the jazz idiom were, for the most part, unrecognized except by musicians and a handful of avant-garde critics. The blues, an ever-flowing stream of folk songs, were heard mostly by the Negro populace but continued to influence and inspire the commercial popular and dance music of the day.

Despite its neglect by the intellectual community, jazz, in the 1930's, reached its peak of public acceptance as popular music through the medium of the dance band. Big band jazz, pioneered in the early years of the decade by Fletcher Henderson, The McKinney Cotton Pickers, The Casa Loma Orchestra, and others, became a dominant factor in popular music. As the country slowly emerged from economic blight, as theaters and dance halls reopened and the record industry, aided by both the availability of inexpensive, electrically-driven phonographs and the introduction of the low-priced (thirty-five cent) record, revived, music, and dance music in particular, began once more to take on the aspects of big business.

At some moment in the early 1930's, big band jazz became "swing music," and an era began. Perhaps it was when Duke Ellington informed us that "It Don't Mean a Thing (If It Ain't Got That Swing)," or, as one story has it, when England's staid BBC, looking for another word for the suspect "jazz," settled on "swing" as a descriptive title for one of its dance music programs. At any rate, it arrived, and Benny Goodman became King, and big band dance music, with a jazz beat, had itself a name. In its wake came new dances and new songs about the new dances. There was also a general classification for those who danced to the new music. Remember? "Jitterbugs" was what they were called. Among the dances, swing and non-swing, figments of song writers' imaginations and the real thing, were, to name a few, the Shag, the Big Apple, the Suzi-Q, the Continental, the Carioca, Truckin', the Yam, Posin', and, from England, the Lambeth Walk. In addition, dancers were "Stompin' at the Savoy," "Begin(ning) the Beguine," "Scattin' at the Kit Kat," and "Jumpin' at the Woodside." Actually, what almost everybody was really doing was the Lindy Hop.

Bands were making records again, traveling everywhere in the country playing one-night stands, and broadcasting regularly both on commercial network programs as well as on "remotes" from ballrooms, hotels, restaurants, and nightclubs. The dance orchestras, both swing and sweet, were instrumental in creating and promoting new songs, and a significant number of the important hits of the 1930's were introduced by them. In the sweet category, Guy Lombardo reigned supreme. But not far behind him in popularity were such favorites as Wayne King, Russ Morgan, Eddy Duchin, Kay Kyser, Leo Reisman, Ray Noble, Vincent Lopez, Hal Kemp, Shep Fields, Jan Garber, Sammy Kaye, Horace Heidt, and (even then) Lawrence Welk. In the swing category, the most important bands were led by Benny Goodman, Tommy Dorsey, Jimmy Dorsey, Glen Gray, Artie Shaw, Duke Ellington, Count Basie, Jimmie Lunceford, Fletcher Henderson, Harry James, Chick Webb, Andy Kirk, Earl Hines, Charlie Barnet, Bunny Berigan, Louis Armstrong, and Erskine Hawkins. Then, of course, there were the singing and "personality" band leaders—Rudy Vallée, Little Jack Little, Will Osborne, Ben Bernie, Art Jarrett, Cab Calloway, Bob Crosby, Woody Herman, and many, many more.

There were several hundred full-time traveling bands in the latter half of the decade, many of them recording, most of them broadcasting. A radio "plug" of a new song was of considerable importance to song writers and music publishers not only because of its promotional value but because fees derived from radio performances of popular music had become the principal source of writers' and publishers' income from ASCAP. Radio, therefore, became the primary area of exploitation for the music industry. Arrangements of new songs were often supplied to bands, free of charge, by music publishers; song pluggers worked with substantial expense accounts, "romancing" band leaders; and the word, "payola," was heard for the first time.

Because the record business had fallen off drastically in the early depression years, radio had become the major medium of home entertainment, and twenty million listeners to a popular program was not unusual. Broadcasting, however, was a means of communication rather than an art form, and, as far as music was concerned, offered no new creative paths to be explored by composers and lyricists. The musical theater, films, the big bands, and records continued to be the media for the *introduction* of new material. However, the *promotion* of new songs on radio was absolutely necessary to insure commercial success, and the most important indicator of popularity became the weekly radio show, *The Lucky Strike Hit Parade*. On this

Popular Music in the 1930's

program, which continued on radio and then on television into the 1950's, millions of Americans were, each week, kept abreast of the best-selling songs of the nation. The achievement of reaching "Number One" on *The Hit Parade* was of tremendous commercial value, and the show's listings were a reasonably accurate reflection of popular taste in music.

Apart from *The Hit Parade* and the nightly broadcasts by orchestras from their work locations, there were a number of music personalities with regular, prominently sponsored radio shows of their own during the 1930's who were, therefore, important to the music trades. Among them were Rudy Vallée, Eddie Cantor, Jessica Dragonette, Kate Smith, Bing Crosby, Paul Whiteman, Morton Downey, Russ Columbo, The Street Singer (Arthur Tracy), Lanny Ross, Ruth Etting, Fred Waring, Ben Bernie, Al Jolson, The Pickens Sisters, The Boswell Sisters, Frank Parker, James Melton, Jane Froman, Mildred Bailey, Julia Sanderson and Frank Crumit, and The Mills Brothers.

The economic depression almost destroyed the phonograph industry and the phonograph record industry throughout the world. While the record companies had, during the 1920's, been able to sell more than 100,000,000 records in a peak year, retail sales reached only 10,000,000 records in 1931. Until 1934, three companies accounted for almost all the record sales in the United States—Columbia, Victor, and Brunswick. Then, in 1934, financed by the English Decca Company, Decca Records was launched in this country. With the exceptionally popular Bing Crosby as its principal artist and a revolutionary price of thirty-five cents, Decca generated new energy into a moribund business, and, as economic recovery started to become evident, sales of popular records began a climb that has not—except for a few years during the Second World War—ceased yet.

Dance music led the field throughout the decade, and, apart from Crosby, Russ Columbo, and a very few other "crooners" and popular radio personalities, bands dominated the best-selling record lists. The arrival of swing stimulated great interest in music heretofore neglected by the record-buying public, the big band instrumental which most often featured solo passages by individual jazz musicians. Many of

10

the Duke Ellington compositions mentioned earlier, as well as such continually popular big and small band vehicles as "One o'Clock Jump," "South Rampart Street Parade," "Stompin' at the Savoy," "Cherokee," "In the Mood," "Undecided," "Don't Be That Way," "Yancey Special," and "Sing, Sing, Sing," became not only best-selling records but jazz classics as well, a great number of them still in the active catalogs of the record companies.

With the big band instrumental, a new group of idols came into being—the "sidemen." Thus, working band musicians like Harry James, Gene Krupa, Lionel Hampton, Tex Beneke, Glenn Miller, Bunny Berigan, and scores of others were soon to become popular in their own right as a result of their exposure to the public on records and in public appearances. Similarly, band vocalists of the 1930's, such as Perry Como, Frank Sinatra, Dick Haymes, Ella Fitzgerald, Eddy Howard, Helen Forrest, and Jo Stafford, were to become stars in the following decade when the popularity of big band music declined.

The 1930's offered very few innovations to the sound, form, or content of popular music. The decade did, however, supply us with a very large quantity of superlative songs. Each year produced dozens of durable melodies, songs that have given every indication of continuing to live on in all the varying contexts that time might shape for them.

While, in the light of the recent laudable tendencies to broaden the content of the popular lyric, 1930's songs may seem naive, trite, and trivial, many still retain their interest, and some of them, their beauty and power. With so much of the new poetry in popular songs being acclaimed at this writing, one wonders if this decade will produce writers with the wit of a Cole Porter or the charm of a Lorenz Hart—or one piece of work quite as beautiful as "September Song."

Let us hope so.

Nat Shapiro

March 1968

1930

1930

All the King's Horses
Words and music by Alex Wilder, Edward Brandt, and Howard
Dietz.
Harms, Inc.
Introduced by Margaret Lee in *Three's a Crowd* (revue).

Always in All Ways
Words by Leo Robin, music by Richard A. Whiting and W. Franke
Harling.
Famous Music Corp.
Introduced by Jack Buchanan and Jeanette MacDonald in
Monte Carlo (film).

Any Old Time
Words and music by Jimmie Rodgers.
Peer International Corp.
Introduced by Jimmie Rodgers (Victor). Best-selling record in
1956 by Webb Pierce (Decca)

Around the Corner
Words by Gus Kahn, music by Art Kassel.
Leo Feist, Inc.
Introduced by Art Kassel and his Orchestra.

Au Revoir, Pleasant Dreams
Words by Jack Meskill, music by Jean Schwartz.
De Sylva, Brown & Henderson, Inc.
Signature theme of Ben Bernie and his Orchestra.

Baby's Birthday Party
Words and music by Ann Ronell.
Famous Music Corp.
Popularized by Rudy Vallée and by Guy Lombardo and his
Royal Canadians.

Bench in the Park, A
Words by Jack Yellen, music by Milton Ager.
Advanced Music Corp.
Introduced by Paul Whiteman and his Orchestra, Jeanette Loff,
Stanley Smith, The Rhythm Boys, and The Brox Sisters in pro-
duction number in *King of Jazz* (film).

15

Betty Co-Ed
Words and music by J. Paul Fogarty and Rudy Vallée.
Carl Fischer, Inc.
Popularized by Rudy Vallée. Featured in *Betty Co-Ed* (film, 1947).

Beyond the Blue Horizon
Words by Leo Robin, music by Richard A. Whiting and W. Franke
Harling.
Famous Music Corp.
Introduced by Jeanette MacDonald in *Monte Carlo* (film). Sung by
Miss MacDonald in *Follow the Boys* (film, 1944).

Bidin' My Time
Words by Ira Gershwin, music by George Gershwin.
New World Music Corp.
Introduced by The Foursome (male quartet) in *Girl Crazy* (musical).
Featured in film version, 1943, *Rhapsody in Blue* (film, 1945), *The
Glenn Miller Story* (film, 1954), and *When the Boys Meet the Girls*
(film, 1965).

Blue Again
Words by Dorothy Fields, music by Jimmy McHugh.
Robbins Music Corp.
Introduced by Evelyn Hoey in *The Vanderbilt Revue* (revue).
Popularized by Guy Lombardo and his Royal Canadians.

Blue Is the Night
Words and music by Fred Fisher.
Robbins Music Corp.
Introduced by Norma Shearer in *Their Own Desire* (film).

Blue, Turning Gray over You
Words by Andy Razaf, music by Thomas "Fats" Waller.
Mayfair Music Corp./Anne-Rachel Music Corp.
First recording by Louis Armstrong and his Orchestra.

Body and Soul
Words by Edward Heyman, Robert Sour, and Frank Eyton, music
by John Green.
Harms, Inc.
Introduced by Libby Holman in *Three's a Crowd* (revue). First recording in United States by Leo Reisman and his Orchestra, featuring Eddy Duchin on piano. Introduced in England by Gertrude
Lawrence. First recording in England by Ambrose and his Orchestra. Sung by Ida Lupino in *The Man I Love* (film, 1946) and used
as theme for *Body and Soul* (film, 1947). Instrumental version
recorded by tenor saxophonist Coleman Hawkins in 1939 (Bluebird) a jazz classic.

Boy! What Love Has Done to Me
Words by Ira Gershwin, music by George Gershwin.
New World Music Corp.
Introduced by Ethel Merman in *Girl Crazy* (musical).

But Not for Me
Words by Ira Gershwin, music by George Gershwin.
New World Music Corp.
Introduced by Ginger Rogers, and reprised by Willie Howard, in
Girl Crazy (musical). Sung by Judy Garland in film version, 1943,
and by Harve Presnell and Connie Francis in *When the Boys Meet
the Girls* (film, 1965). Sung by Ella Fitzgerald on soundtrack and
theme of *But Not for Me* (film, 1959).

Button Up Your Heart
Words by Dorothy Fields, music by Jimmy McHugh.
Robbins Music Corp.
Introduced by Evelyn Hoey and Charles Barnes in *The Vanderbilt
Revue* (revue).

Bye Bye Blues
Words and music by Bert Lown, Chauncey Gray, David Bennett,
and Fred Hamm.
Bourne Co.
Introduced by and theme song of Bert Lown and his Hotel
Biltmore (New York) Orchestra.

Can This Be Love
Words by Paul James, music by Kay Swift.
Harms, Inc.
Introduced by Alice Boulden in *Fine and Dandy* (musical).

Cheerful Little Earful
Words by Ira Gershwin and Billy Rose, music by Harry Warren.
New World Music Corp.
Introduced by Hannah Williams and Jerry Norris in *Sweet and Low*
(musical).

Come Out of the Kitchen, Mary Ann
Words and music by James Kendis and Charles Bayha.
Bourne Co.

Cooking Breakfast for the One I Love
Words by Billy Rose, music by Henry H. Tobias.
Robbins Music Corp.
Introduced by Fanny Brice in *Be Yourself* (film).

Cottage for Sale, A
Words by Willard Robison, music by Larry Conley.
De Sylva, Brown & Henderson, Inc.
Introduced by Willard Robison and his Deep River Orchestra.

Could You Use Me
Words by Ira Gershwin, music by George Gershwin.
New World Music Corp.
Introduced by Allan Kearns and Ginger Rogers in *Girl Crazy*
(musical).

Crazy Feet
Words and music by Sidney D. Mitchell, Con Conrad, and Archie
Gottler.
De Sylva, Brown & Henderson, Inc.
Introduced by Dixie Lee in *Happy Days* (film).

Cryin' for the Carolines
Words by Sam H. Lewis and Joe Young, music by Harry Warren.
Remick Music Corp.
Introduced by Lawrence Gray in *Spring Is Here* (film). Popularized
by Guy Lombardo and his Royal Canadians.

Dancing on the Ceiling (He Dances on My Ceiling)
Words by Lorenz Hart, music by Richard Rodgers.
Harms, Inc.
Written for, but not used in, *Simple Simon* (musical). Introduced by
Jessie Matthews and Sonnie Hale in London in *Ever Green* (musi-
cal). Sung by Miss Matthews in film version, 1934.

Dancing with Tears in My Eyes
Words by Al Dubin, music by Joe Burke.
M. Witmark & Sons.
Written for, but not used in, *Dancing Sweeties* (film). Introduced on
radio by Rudy Vallée. Sung by John Payne in *Kid Nightingale*
(film, 1939).

Dark Night
Words by Clifford Grey, music by Herbert Stothart and Xavier
Cugat.
Robbins Music Corp.
Introduced by Ramon Novarro in *In Gay Madrid* (film).

Daughter of Peggy O'Neil, The
Words by Harry Pease and Harry Tobias, music by Charley Kisco.
Robbins Music Corp.

Don't Send My Boy to Prison
Words and music by Con Conrad.
Famous Music Corp.

Don't Tell Her What's Happened to Me
Words and music by B. G. De Sylva, Lew Brown, and Ray
Henderson.
De Sylva, Brown & Henderson, Inc./Anne-Rachel Music Corp.

18

Don't Tell Your Folks
Words by Lorenz Hart, music by Richard Rodgers.
Harms, Inc.
Introduced by Will Ahearn and Bobbe Arnst in *Simple Simon* (musical).

Double Check Stomp
Words and music by Albany "Barney" Bigard and Irving Mills.
Mills Music, Inc.
Introduced by Duke Ellington and his Orchestra.

Down the River of Golden Dreams
Words and music by John Klenner and Nathaniel Shilkret.
Leo Feist, Inc.

Dust
Words by Andy Rice, music by Fred Fisher.
Robbins Music Corp.
Introduced by May Boley in *Children of Pleasure* (film).

Eleven More Months and Ten More Days
Words and music by Arthur Fields and Fred Hall.
Piedmont Music Co., Inc.

Embraceable You
Words by Ira Gershwin, music by George Gershwin.
New World Music Corp.
Originally written in 1928 for unproduced musical, *East Is West*. Introduced by Allan Kearns and Ginger Rogers in *Girl Crazy* (musical). Sung by Eddie Quillan and Dorothy Lee in first film version, 1932; by Judy Garland in second film version, 1943; and by Harve Presnell in third film version (*When the Boys Meet the Girls*), 1965. Interpolated in *Rhapsody in Blue* (film, 1945), *Humoresque* (film, 1946), and *Always Leave Them Laughing* (film, 1949). Sung by Gene Kelly in *An American in Paris* (film, 1951) and by voice of Jane Froman, dubbed for Susan Hayward, in *With a Song in My Heart* (film, 1952).

Exactly Like You
Words by Dorothy Fields, music by Jimmy McHugh.
Shapiro, Bernstein & Co., Inc.
Introduced by Gertrude Lawrence and Harry Richman in *Lew Leslie's International Review* (revue).

Falling in Love Again (Can't Help It) (German)
English words by Sammy Lerner, music by Frederick Hollander.
Ufaton-Verlag, GmbH, Berlin, Germany/Famous Music Corp.
Introduced by Marlene Dietrich in *The Blue Angel* (film).

Falling in Love with You
Words by Gus Kahn, music by Victor Young and M. Neuman.
Leo Feist, Inc.
Theme song of *The Studebaker Champions* (radio show).

Fine and Dandy
Words by Paul James, music by Kay Swift.
Harms, Inc.
Introduced by Joe Cook and Alice Boulden in *Fine and Dandy* (musical).

Football Freddy (My Collegiate Man)
Words by Edgar Leslie, music by Con Conrad.
Remick Music Corp./Edgar Leslie.

For You
Words by Al Dubin, music by Joe Burke.
M. Witmark & Sons.
Best-selling record by Glen Gray and The Casa Loma Orchestra, vocal by Kenny Sargent. Interpolated in *Holy Terror* (film, 1931). Revived in 1964 with best-selling record by Rick Nelson (Decca).

"Free and Easy," The
Words by Roy Turk, music by Fred E. Ahlert.
Robbins Music Corp./Exeter Music, Inc.
Introduced by Buster Keaton in *Free and Easy* (film).

Froggy Bottom
Words and music by John Williams.
Leeds Music Corp.
Introduced by Andy Kirk and his Orchestra.

Georgia on My Mind
Words by Stuart Gorrell, music by Hoagy Carmichael.
Peer International Corp.
Introduced by Mildred Bailey. Revived in 1960-61 with best-selling record by Ray Charles (ABC-Paramount). Winner of National Academy of Recording Arts and Sciences Awards for "Best Rock and Roll Recording" and "Best Solo Vocal Performance — Male," 1960.

Get Happy
Words by Ted Koehler, music by Harold Arlen.
Remick Music Corp.
Harold Arlen's first published song. Introduced by Ruth Etting in *9:15 Revue* (revue). Sung by Judy Garland in *Summer Stock* (film, 1950) and by voice of Jane Froman, dubbed for Susan Hayward, in *With a Song in My Heart* (film, 1952).

Girl Trouble
Words and music by Fred Fisher.
Robbins Music Corp.
Introduced by Lawrence Gray in *Children of Pleasure* (film).

Give Me a Moment Please
Words by Leo Robin, music by Richard A. Whiting and W. Franke
Harling.
Famous Music Corp.
Introduced by Jack Buchanan and Jeanette MacDonald in *Monte
Carlo* (film). Theme song of violinist Rubinoff.

Go Home and Tell Your Mother
Words by Dorothy Fields, music by Jimmy McHugh.
Robbins Music Corp.
Introduced by Robert Montgomery and Dorothy Jordan in
Love in the Rough (film).

Good for You, Bad for Me
Words by B. G. De Sylva and Lew Brown, music by Ray Henderson.
De Sylva, Brown & Henderson, Inc./Anne-Rachel Music Corp.
Introduced by Pearl Osgood and Russ Brown in *Flying High*
(musical).

Goofus
Words by Gus Kahn, music by Wayne King and William Harold.
Leo Feist, Inc.
Introduced by Wayne King and his Orchestra.

Got a Man on My Mind (Worryin' Away)
Words by Dick Howard (pseudonym for Howard Dietz), music by
Ralph Rainger.
Famous Music Corp.
Introduced by Libby Holman.

Great Indoors, The
Words and music by Cole Porter.
Harms, Inc.
Introduced by Frances Williams in *The New Yorkers* (musical).

Hangin' Around with You
Words by Ira Gershwin, music by George Gershwin.
New World Music Corp.
Introduced by Gordon Smith and Doris Carson in *Strike Up the Band*
(musical).

Hangin' on the Garden Gate (Sayin' Good Night)
Words by Gus Kahn, music by Ted Fiorito.
M. Witmark & Sons.
Introduced by Ted Fiorito and his Orchestra.

Happy Feet
Words by Jack Yellen, music by Milton Ager.
Advanced Music Corp.
Introduced by Paul Whiteman, his Orchestra, and The Rhythm Boys
in *King of Jazz* (film).

Have a Little Faith in Me
Words by Sam M. Lewis and Joe Young, music by Harry Warren.
Remick Music Corp.
Introduced by Alexander Gray and Bernice Claire in *Spring Is Here* (film).

He Was Too Good to Me
Words by Lorenz Hart, music by Richard Rodgers.
Harms, Inc.
Introduced in *Simple Simon* (musical) but dropped from show before New York opening.

Here Comes the Sun
Words by Arthur Freed, music by Harry Woods.
Robbins Music Corp.
Introduced by Vincent Lopez and his Orchestra.

High Society Blues
Words by Joseph McCarthy, music by James F. Hanley.
Movietone Music Corp.
Introduced by Charles Farrell in *High Society Blues* (film).

Hittin' the Bottle
Words by Ted Koehler, music by Harold Arlen.
Remick Music Corp.
Introduced in eighth edition of *Earl Carroll Vanities* (revue).

Hooray for Captain Spaulding, see 1928.

I Am Only Human After All
Words by Ira Gershwin and E. Y. Harburg, music by Vernon Duke.
New World Music Corp.
Introduced by James Norris, Velma Vavra, and Imogene Coca in third edition of *The Garrick Gaieties* (revue). Vernon Duke's first Broadway show tune.

I Am the Words, You Are the Melody, see (I Am the Words), You Are the Melody.

I Got Rhythm
Words by Ira Gershwin, music by George Gershwin.
New World Music Corp.
Introduced by Ethel Merman in *Girl Crazy* (musical). Sung by Judy Garland in film version, 1943, and by Gene Kelly in *An American in Paris* (film, 1951). Used as theme for Gershwin's concert work, "Variations on I Got Rhythm," introduced by composer in 1934.

I Keep Remembering (Someone I Should Forget)
Words by Charles Newman, music by Isham Jones.
Leo Feist, Inc.
Introduced by Isham Jones and his Orchestra.

I Love You So Much
Words by Bert Kalmar, music by Harry Ruby.
Harms, Inc.
Introduced by Bert Wheeler in *The Cuckoos* (film).

I Mean To Say
Words by Ira Gershwin, music by George Gershwin.
New World Music Corp.
Introduced by Gordon Smith and Doris Carson in *Strike Up the Band* (musical).

I Still Believe in You
Words by Lorenz Hart, music by Richard Rodgers.
Harms, Inc.
Introduced by Ruth Etting in *Simple Simon* (musical).

I Still Get a Thrill (Thinking of You)
Words by Benny Davis, music by J. Fred Coots.
Words & Music, Inc.
Introduced by Hal Kemp and his Orchestra.

I Want a Little Girl
Words by Billy Moll, music by Murray Mencher.
Shapiro, Bernstein & Co., Inc.
Best-selling record by McKinney's Cotton Pickers, vocal by George Thomas (Victor).

If I Became the President
Words by Ira Gershwin, music by George Gershwin.
New World Music Corp.
Introduced by Blanche Ring and Bobby Clark in *Strike Up the Band* (musical).

If I Were King
Words by Leo Robin, music by Newell Chase and Sam Coslow.
Famous Music Corp.
Introduced by Dennis King in *The Vagabond King* (film).

I'll Still Belong to You
Words by Edward Eliscu, music by Nacio Herb Brown.
Leo Feist, Inc.
Introduced by Eddie Cantor in *Whoopee* (film).

I'm Confessin' (That I Love You)
Words by A. J. Neiburg, music by Doc Daugherty and Ellis Reynolds.
Bourne Co.
Originally introduced and recorded in 1929 by Fats Waller and his Buddies, with other lyrics and entitled "Lookin' for Another Sweetie." This version popularized by Rudy Vallée.

I'm Feelin' Blue ('Cause I Got Nobody)
Words by Dorothy Fields, music by Jimmy McHugh.
Shapiro, Bernstein & Co., Inc.
Introduced by Gertrude Lawrence in *Lew Leslie's International Review* (revue) but dropped before New York opening. Sung by Ethel Waters in Lew Leslie's *Rhapsody in Black* (revue, 1931).

I'm Getting Myself Ready for You
Words and music by Cole Porter.
Harms, Inc.
Introduced by Frances Williams, Barrie Oliver, Ann Pennington, and Maurice Lapue in *The New Yorkers* (musical).

I'm Glad I Waited
Words by Clifford Grey and Harold Adamson, music by Vincent Youmans.
The Vincent Youmans Co., Inc.
Introduced by Fred Astaire and Marilyn Miller in *Smiles* (musical).

I'm in the Market for You
Words by Joseph McCarthy, music by James F. Hanley.
Movietone Music Corp.
Introduced by Janet Gaynor and Charles Farrell in *High Society Blues* (film).

I'm Thinking Tonight of My Blue Eyes
Words and music by A. P. Carter.
Peer International Corp., 1930, 1942.
Introduced by The Carter Family. Revised in 1942, with additional lyrics by Don Marcotte. Reintroduced in 1942 by Bob Atcher (Okeh). Sung by Roy Rogers in *Man from Music Mountain* (film, 1943).

I'm Yours
Words by E. Y. Harburg, music by John Green.
Famous Music Corp.
Introduced in *Leave It to Lester* (film short). Interpolated and sung by Ruth Etting in *Simple Simon* (musical).

Into My Heart
Words by Roy Turk, music by Fred E. Ahlert.
Robbins Music Corp.
Introduced by Ramon Novarro in *In Gay Madrid* (film).

Is That Religion?
Words and music by Maceo Pinkard and Mitchell Parish.
Mills Music, Inc.
Popularized by Mildred Bailey.

It Happened in Monterey
Words by Billy Rose, music by Mabel Wayne.
Leo Feist, Inc.
Introduced by John Boles and Jeanette Loff in *King of Jazz* (film).

It Must Be True (You Are Mine, All Mine)
Words by Gus Arnheim and Gordon Clifford, music by Harry Barris.
Mills Music, Inc.
Introduced by Bing Crosby with The Rhythm Boys.

It Must Be You
Words by Roy Turk, music by Fred E. Ahlert.
Robbins Music Corp.
Introduced by Robert Montgomery in *Free and Easy* (film).

It Seems To Be Spring
Words by George Marion, Jr., music by Richard A. Whiting.
Famous Music Corp.
Introduced by Jeanette MacDonald and James Hall in *Let's Go Native* (film).

It's a Great Life (If You Don't Weaken)
Words by Leo Robin, music by Richard A. Whiting and Newell Chase.
Famous Music Corp.
Introduced by Maurice Chevalier in *Playboy of Paris* (film).

It's a Lonesome Old Town When You're Not Around
Words and music by Charles Kisco and Harry Tobias.
Bourne Co.
Theme song of Ben Bernie and his Orchestra.

I've Got a Crush on You
Words by Ira Gershwin, music by George Gershwin.
New World Music Corp.
Introduced by Mary Hay and Clifton Webb in *Treasure Girl* (musical, 1928). Song remained unpublished until reintroduced by Doris Carson and Gordon Smith in *Strike Up the Band* (musical, 1930).

Jungle Drums (Cuban)
English words by Carmen Lombardo and Charles O'Flynn, music by Ernesto Lecuona.
Edward B. Marks Music Corp.
Originally an instrumental published under title, "Canto Karabali," in 1929. English-language version introduced by Guy Lombardo and his Royal Canadians.

Just a Gigolo (Austrian)
English words by Irving Caesar, German words by Julius Brammer, music by Leonello Casucci.
Wiener Boheme Verlag, Vienna, Austria, 1929/De Sylva, Brown & Henderson, Inc./Anne-Rachel Music Corp.
Original German title, "Schöner Gigolo." Introduced in United States by Irene Bordoni. Popularized by Vincent Lopez and his Orchestra. Interpolated in *Lover, Come Back* (film, 1946).

Just a Little Closer
Words by Howard Johnson, music by Joseph Meyer.
Robbins Music Corp.
Introduced by Charles King in *Remote Control* (film).

Just an Idea, also known as **Mary's Idea**
Music by Mary Lou Williams.
Jewel Music Publishing Co., Inc.
Original title, "Mary's Idea." Introduced by Andy Kirk and his
Clouds of Joy Orchestra.

Just Like in a Story Book
Words by Joseph McCarthy, music by James F. Hanley.
Movietone Music Corp.
Introduced by Janet Gaynor in *High Society Blues* (film).

Keepin' Myself for You
Words by Sidney Clare, music by Vincent Youmans.
The Vincent Youmans Co., Inc.
Introduced by Polly Walker and Jack Oakie in *Hit the Deck* (film).
Sung in 1955 film version by Tony Martin, Ann Miller, and girls.

King's Horses (and the King's Men), The (English)
Words and music by Noel Gay (a pseudonym for Reginald
Armitage) and Harry Graham.
Lawrence Wright Music Co., Ltd., London, England/Leo Feist, Inc.

Kiss Waltz, The
Words by Al Dubin, music by Joe Burke.
M. Witmark & Sons.
Introduced by Sue Carol in *Dancing Sweeties* (film).

Kitty from Kansas City, see 1921.

Lady, Play Your Mandolin
Words by Irving Caesar, music by Oscar Levant.
Harms, Inc.
Introduced by Nick Lucas. Identified with Blossom Seeley.

Laughing at Life
Words by Nick Kenny and Charles Kenny, music by Cornell Todd
and Bob Todd.
M. Witmark & Sons.

Lazy Lou'siana Moon
Words and music by Walter Donaldson.
Bregman, Vocco & Conn, Inc.

Let Me Sing and I'm Happy
Words and music by Irving Berlin.
Irving Berlin Music Corp.
Introduced by Al Jolson in *Mammy* (film).

Let's Fly Away
Words and music by Cole Porter.
Harms, Inc.
Introduced by Charles King and Hope Williams in *The New Yorkers* (musical).

Let's Step Out
Words and music by Cole Porter.
Harms, Inc.
Introduced by Evelyn Hoey, Gertrude McDonald, and Reed and Duthers in *Fifty Million Frenchmen* (musical, 1929) after New York opening.

Like Ordinary People Do
Words by Lorenz Hart, music by Richard Rodgers.
Harms, Inc.
Introduced by Ben Lyon, Inez Courtney, and Ona Munson in *Hot Heiress* (film, 1931).

Linda
Words by Ted Koehler, music by Harold Arlen.
Arko Music Corp.
Introduced at Cotton Club (New York nightclub) in *Brown Sugar* (nightclub revue). Recorded by Harold Arlen, with Red Nichols and his Orchestra (Brunswick) and Benny Goodman and his Orchestra (Melotone).

Little Things in Life, The
Words and music by Irving Berlin.
Irving Berlin Music Corp.

Little White Lies
Words and music by Walter Donaldson.
Bregman, Vocco & Conn, Inc.
Introduced by Guy Lombardo and his Royal Canadians. Revived in 1948 with best-selling record by Dick Haymes (Decca).

Livin' in the Sunlight — Lovin' in the Moonlight
Words by Al Lewis, music by Al Sherman.
Famous Music Corp.
Introduced by Maurice Chevalier in *The Big Pond* (film).

Lonely
Words and music by Ramon Novarro, Herbert Stothart, and Clifford Grey.
Robbins Music Corp.
Introduced by Ramon Novarro in *Call of the Flesh* (film).

Looking at You
Words and music by Cole Porter.
Harms, Inc.
Introduced by Jessie Matthews and Dave Fitzgibbon in *Wake Up and Dream!* (musical, 1929).

Looking in the Window, Thinking of You
Words by Harry Richman and Al Bryan, music by M. K. Jerome.
M. Witmark & Sons.
Introduced by Harry Richman.

Love for Sale
Words and music by Cole Porter.
Harms, Inc.
Introduced by Kathryn Crawford, with June Shafer, Ida Pearson, and Arline Judge, in *The New Yorkers* (musical).

Love Is Like a Song
Words by J. Russel Robinson and George Waggner, music by Vincent Youmans.
The Vincent Youmans Co., Inc.
Introduced by Gloria Swanson in *What a Widow!* (film). First recording in 1966 by Ellie Quint (Evergreen).

Lucky Seven
Words by Howard Dietz, music by Arthur Schwartz.
Harms, Inc.
Introduced by Joey Ray in *The Second Little Show* (revue).

Mademoiselle in New Rochelle
Words by Ira Gershwin, music by George Gershwin.
New World Music Corp.
Introduced by Bobby Clark and Paul McCullough in *Strike Up the Band* (musical).

Man from the South (with a Big Cigar in His Mouth), The
Words and music by Rube Bloom and Harry Woods.
Skidmore Music Co., Inc.
Introduced by Ted Weems and his Orchestra.

March of Time, The
Words by Ted Koehler, music by Harold Arlen.
Remick Music Corp.
Introduced by Harry Stockwell and John Hale in eighth edition of *Earl Carroll Vanities* (revue).

Mary's Idea, see Just an Idea.

Memories of You
Words by Andy Razaf, music by Eubie Blake.
Shapiro, Bernstein & Co., Inc.
Introduced by Minto Cato in Lew Leslie's *Blackbirds of 1930* (revue). Best-selling record by Glen Gray and The Casa Loma Orchestra, featuring Sonny Dunham on trumpet (Decca). Theme song of Sonny Dunham and his Orchestra. Featured by The Benny Goodman Trio in *The Benny Goodman Story* (film, 1956).

Mia Cara (My Dear)
Words and music by Sammy Fain, Irving Kahal, and Pierre Norman Connor.
Famous Music Corp./Irving Kahal Music, Inc.
Introduced in *The Big Pond* (film).

Moment I Saw You, The
Words by Howard Dietz, music by Arthur Schwartz.
Harms, Inc.
Introduced by Clifton Webb in *Three's a Crowd* (revue).

Moon Is Low, The
Words by Arthur Freed, music by Nacio Herb Brown.
Robbins Music Corp.
Introduced by Cliff Edwards in *Montana Moon* (film).

Moonlight on the Colorado
Words by Billy Moll, music by Robert A. King.
Shapiro, Bernstein & Co., Inc.

More Than Ever
Words by Harold Adamson, music by Vincent Youmans.
The Vincent Youmans Co., Inc.
Introduced by Harriette Lake (Ann Sothern) in *Smiles* (musical), but dropped from show before New York opening.

My Baby Just Cares for Me
Words by Gus Kahn, music by Walter Donaldson.
Bregman, Vocco & Conn, Inc./Gus Kahn Music Co.
Introduced by Eddie Cantor in *Whoopee* (film).

My Future Just Passed
Words by George Marion, music by Richard A. Whiting.
Famous Music Corp.
Introduced by Charles "Buddy" Rogers in *Safety in Numbers* (film).

My Ideal
Words by Leo Robin, music by Richard A. Whiting and Newell Chase.
Famous Music Corp.
Introduced by Maurice Chevalier in *Playboy of Paris* (film).

My Mad Moment
Words by George Marion, Jr., music by Richard A. Whiting.
Famous Music Corp.
Introduced by Jeanette MacDonald and James Hall in *Let's Go Native* (film).

Mysterious Mose
Words and music by Walter Doyle.
M. Witmark & Sons.

Nina Rosa
Words by Irving Caesar, music by Sigmund Romberg.
Shubert Music Publishing Corp.
Introduced in *Nina Rosa* (musical).

(There's Something about an) Old Fashioned Girl
Words and music by B. G. De Sylva, Lew Brown, and Ray
Henderson.
De Sylva, Brown & Henderson, Inc./Anne-Rachel Music Corp.
Introduced by John Garrick in *Just Imagine* (film).

On the Sunny Side of the Street
Words by Dorothy Fields, music by Jimmy McHugh.
Shapiro, Bernstein & Co., Inc.
Introduced by Harry Richman in *Lew Leslie's International Review*
(revue). Interpolated in *Is Everybody Happy?* (film, 1943), *Two
Blondes and a Redhead* (film, 1947), and *This Earth Is Mine* (film,
1959). Sung by Frankie Laine in *On the Sunny Side of the Street*
(film, 1951). Played by Carmen Cavallero on soundtrack of *The
Eddy Duchin Story* (film, 1956) and by Benny Goodman and his
Orchestra in *The Benny Goodman Story* (film, 1956). Sung by
voice of Gogi Grant, dubbed for Ann Blyth, on soundtrack of
The Helen Morgan Story (film, 1957).

One More Waltz
Words by Dorothy Fields, music by Jimmy McHugh.
Robbins Music Corp.
Introduced in *Love in the Rough* (film).

Overnight
Words by Billy Rose and Charlotte Kent, music by Louis Alter.
Robbins Music Corp.
Introduced by Fanny Brice in *Sweet and Low* (revue). Popularized
by Helen Morgan.

Paper Doll
Words and music by Johnny Black.
Edward B. Marks Music Corp., 1930, 1942.
Written in 1915 but not published until 1930. Identified with
Tommy Lyman until best-selling record in 1942 by The Mills
Brothers (Decca).

Parlez-moi d'Amour, see Speak to Me of Love, 1932.

Please Don't Talk about Me When I'm Gone
Words by Sidney Clare, music by Sam H. Stept.
Remick Music Corp.
Popularized by Bee Palmer and by Kate Smith. Sung by Patricia
Neal in *The Breaking Point* (film, 1950) and featured in *Lullaby
of Broadway* (film, 1951).

Porter's Love Song to a Chambermaid, A
Words by Andy Razaf, music by James P. Johnson.
Mayfair Music Corp.
Theme song of Freddie Bergin and his Orchestra.

Practising Up on You
Words by Howard Dietz, music by Phil Charig.
Harms, Inc.
Introduced by Margaret Lee, Wally Coyle, and The California
    Collegians in *Three's a Crowd* (revue).

Puttin' on the Ritz
Words and music by Irving Berlin.
Irving Berlin Music Corp.
Introduced by Harry Richman in *Puttin' on the Ritz* (film).

Ragamuffin Romeo
Words and music by Harry De Costa and Mabel Wayne.
Leo Feist, Inc.
Introduced by Jeanie Lang in *King of Jazz* (film).

Reaching for the Moon
Words and music by Irving Berlin.
Irving Berlin Music Corp.
Introduced instrumentally in *Reaching for the Moon* (film, 1931).

Ring Dem Bells
Words and music by Edward Kennedy "Duke" Ellington and
    Irving Mills.
Harms, Inc./Tempo Music, Inc.
Introduced by Duke Ellington and his Orchestra.

Rockin' Chair
Words and music by Hoagy Carmichael.
Carmichael Music Publications, Inc.
Introduced by and theme song of Mildred Bailey.

Rogue Song, The
Words by Clifford Grey, music by Herbert Stothart.
Robbins Music Corp.
Introduced by Lawrence Tibbett in *The Rogue Song* (film).

Roses Are Forget-Me-Nots
Words and music by Al Hoffman, Charles O'Flynn, and Will
    Osborne.
M. Witmark & Sons.
Introduced by Will Osborne and his Orchestra.

St. James Infirmary
Words and music by Joe Primrose (pseudonym for Irving Mills).
Mills Music, Inc.
Adapted from traditional folk ballad. This version popularized
    by Cab Calloway.

Sam and Delilah
Words by Ira Gershwin, music by George Gershwin.
New World Music Corp.
Introduced by Ethel Merman in *Girl Crazy* (musical).

Send for Me
Words by Lorenz Hart, music by Richard Rodgers.
Harms, Inc.
Introduced by Doree Leslie, Alan Edwards, and chorus in
Simple Simon (musical).

She'll Love Me and Like It
Words by Leo Robin, music by Richard A. Whiting and W. Franke
Harling.
Famous Music Corp.
Introduced by Claude Allister in *Monte Carlo* (film).

Sing Something Simple
Words and music by Herman Hupfeld.
Harms, Inc.
Introduced by Ruth Tester, with Fay Brady and Arline Judge, in
The Second Little Show (revue).

Sing You Sinners
Words and music by Sam Coslow and W. Franke Harling.
Famous Music Corp.
Introduced by uncredited singer and chorus, and reprised by Lillian
Roth, in *Honey* (film). Sung by Billy Daniels in *Cruisin' down the
River* (film, 1953) and by Susan Hayward in *I'll Cry Tomorrow*
(film, 1957).

Skippy
Words by Benny Davis, music by Con Conrad.
Leo Feist, Inc.
Based on the popular comic-strip character created by Percy L.
Crosby.

(By the) Sleepy Lagoon (English)
Words by Jack Lawrence, music by Eric Coates.
Chappell & Co., Ltd., London, England/Chappell & Co., Inc.,
1930, 1940.
From a concert work by Coates. Lyrics added in 1940. First record-
ing of song version by Xavier Cugat and his Orchestra, vocal by
Buddy Clark (Columbia). Best-selling records in 1942 by Harry
James and his Orchestra (Columbia) and Tommy Dorsey and his
Orchestra (Victor). Featured in *Sleepy Lagoon* (film, 1943).

Sleepy Town Express
Words and music by Haven Gillespie.
Leo Feist, Inc.

So Beats My Heart for You
Words and music by Pat Ballard, Charles Henderson, and Tom Waring.
De Sylva, Brown & Henderson, Inc.
Introduced by Fred Waring's Pennsylvanians. Theme song of Freddie Rich and his Orchestra.

Someday I'll Find You (English)
Words and music by Noël Coward.
Chappell & Co., Ltd., London, England/Chappell & Co., Inc.
Introduced by Noël Coward and Gertrude Lawrence in *Private Lives* (play). First recording in 1931 by Gertrude Lawrence and Noël Coward (HMV). Theme song of *Mr. Keene, Tracer of Lost Persons* (radio detective series).

Something To Remember You By
Words by Howard Dietz, music by Arthur Schwartz.
Harms, Inc.
Melody originally used in London in *Little Tommy Tucker* (musical) under title, "I Have No Words To Say How Much I Love You." With present lyrics, introduced by Libby Holman in *Three's a Crowd* (revue). Sung by Janis Paige in *Her Kind of Man* (film, 1946). Featured in *Dancing in the Dark* (film, 1949) and *The Band Wagon* (film, 1953).

Somewhere in Old Wyoming
Words and music by Charlie Tobias and Peter De Rose.
Edwin H. Morris & Co., Inc.

Song of the Dawn
Words by Jack Yellen, music by Milton Ager.
Advanced Music Corp.
Introduced by John Boles in *King of Jazz* (film).

Soon
Words by Ira Gershwin, music by George Gershwin.
New World Music Corp.
Introduced by Jerry Goff and Margaret Schilling in *Strike Up the Band* (musical).

South
Words by Ray Charles, music by Bennie Moten and Thamon Hayes.
Peer International Corp., 1930, 1941.
Jazz instrumental, first recorded by Bennie Moten's Kansas City Orchestra in 1924. Lyrics written in 1941.

(Up on Top of a Rainbow) Sweepin' the Clouds Away
Words and music by Sam Coslow.
Famous Music Corp.
Introduced by Maurice Chevalier in *Paramount on Parade* (film).

Sweet and Hot
Words by Jack Yellen, music by Harold Arlen.
Advanced Music Corp.
Introduced by Lyda Roberti in *You Said It* (musical). Recorded by
Harold Arlen, with Red Nichols and his Orchestra (Brunswick).

Sweet Jennie Lee
Words and music by Walter Donaldson.
Bregman, Vocco & Conn, Inc.
Introduced by Guy Lombardo and his Royal Canadians.

Swingin' in a Hammock
Words by Tot Seymour and Charles O'Flynn, music by Pete
Wendling.
Bourne Co.
Popularized by Guy Lombardo and his Royal Canadians.

Take Me Back to Manhattan
Words and music by Cole Porter.
Harms, Inc.
Introduced by Frances Williams in *The New Yorkers* (musical).

Tango Della Gelosia, see Jealous of You, 1933.

Ten Cents a Dance
Words by Lorenz Hart, music by Richard Rodgers.
Harms, Inc.
Introduced by Ruth Etting in *Simple Simon* (musical). Sung by
Doris Day in *Love Me or Leave Me* (film, 1955).

Thank Your Father
Words and music by B. G. De Sylva, Lew Brown, and Ray
Henderson.
De Sylva, Brown & Henderson, Inc./Anne-Rachel Music Corp.
Introduced by Grace Brinkley and Oscar Shaw in *Flying High*
(musical).

Them There Eyes
Words and music by Maceo Pinkard, William Tracey, and Doris
Tauber.
Bourne Co.

There's Nothing Wrong in a Kiss
Words by Irving Caesar and Graham John, music by Oscar Levant.
Harms, Inc.
Introduced by Paula Stone and Eddie Foy, Jr. in *Ripples* (musical).

There's Something about an Old Fashioned Girl, see (There's Something about an) Old Fashioned Girl.

Three Little Words
Words by Bert Kalmar, music by Harry Ruby.
Harms, Inc.
Introduced by Duke Ellington and his Orchestra, with The Rhythm
Boys, featuring Bing Crosby, in *Check and Double Check* (film).
Popularized on radio by Rudy Vallée. Title song of film biography
of Kalmar and Ruby, *Three Little Words*, 1950.

Time on My Hands (You in My Arms)
Words by Harold Adamson and Mack Gordon, music by Vincent
Youmans.
Miller Music Corp.
Introduced by Marilyn Miller and Paul Gregory in *Smiles* (musical).
Introduced in London by Marion Harris. Theme of *The Chase and
Sanborn Hour* (radio variety series).

Train Whistle Blues
Words and music by Jimmie Rodgers.
Peer International Corp.
Introduced by Jimmie Rodgers (Victor).

Trav'lin All Alone
Words and music by J. C. Johnson.
Record Music Publishing Co.
Introduced by Ethel Waters.

Treat Me Rough
Words by Ira Gershwin, music by George Gershwin.
New World Music Corp.
Introduced by William Kent in *Girl Crazy* (musical).

Two Hearts in Three-Quarter Time (German)
English words by Joe Young, German words by W. Reisch and
A. Robinson, music by Robert Stolz.
Alrobi Musikverlag, GmbH, Berlin, Germany/Harms, Inc.
Original title, "Zwei Herzen im Dreivierteltakt," from German
film of same title.

Typical Self-Made American, A
Words by Ira Gershwin, music by George Gershwin.
New World Music Corp.
Introduced by Dudley Clements, Jerry Goff, and chorus in *Strike
Up the Band* (musical).

Walk Right In
Words by Gus Cannon, music by H. Woods.
Peer International Corp.
Introduced in 1929 by Gus Cannon's Jug Stompers (Victor). Re-
vived in 1963 with best-selling record by The Rooftop Singers
(Vanguard).

Walkin' My Baby Back Home
Words and music by Roy Turk and Fred E. Ahlert.
De Sylva, Brown & Henderson, Inc.
Introduced by Harry Richman. Revived in 1952 with best-selling
record by Johnnie Ray (Columbia). Sung by Donald O'Connor in
Walkin' My Baby Back Home (film, 1953).

Waltz You Saved for Me, The
Words by Gus Kahn, music by Emil Flindt and Wayne King.
Leo Feist, Inc.
Introduced by and theme song of Wayne King and his Orchestra.
Theme of *Lady Esther Serenade* (radio musical series).

Was I To Blame for Falling in Love with You
Words and music by Chester Conn, Victor Young, and Gus Kahn.
Leo Feist, Inc.
Theme song of The Casa Loma Orchestra.

Wasn't It Beautiful While It Lasted?
Words by B. G. De Sylva and Lew Brown, music by Ray
Henderson.
De Sylva, Brown & Henderson, Inc./Anne-Rachel Music Corp.
Introduced by Grace Brinkley and Oscar Shaw in *Flying High*
(musical).

When a Woman Loves a Man
Words by Billy Rose, music by Ralph Rainger.
Robbins Music Corp.
Introduced by Fanny Brice in *Be Yourself* (film).

When It's Harvest Time in Peaceful Valley
Words and music by Robert Martin and Raymond McKee.
Leeds Music Corp.
Sung in *Swing in the Saddle* (film, 1944).

When the Bloom Is on the Sage
Words and music by Fred Howard and Nat Vincent.
Southern Music Publishing Co., Inc.
Theme of *Tom Mix and His Straight-Shooters* (radio series).

When Your Hair Has Turned to Silver (I Will Love You Just the Same)
Words by Charles Tobias, music by Peter De Rose.
Edwin H. Morris & Co., Inc.
First recording by Russ Morgan and his Orchestra. Popularized
by Rudy Vallée.

Where Have You Been?
Words and music by Cole Porter.
Harms, Inc.
Introduced by Charles King and Hope Williams in *The New Yorkers*
(musical).

White Dove, The (Austrian)

English words by Clifford Grey, German words by Alfred Maria Willner and Robert Bodanzky, music by Franz Lehár.
Breitkopf and Härtel, New York, New York, 1908/W. Karczag, Vienna, Austria, 1924/Chappell & Co., Inc., 1911, 1930.
Introduced under original German title, "Ich Weiss Ein Rezept," in 1910 Viennese operetta, *Zigeunerliebe, (Gypsy Love)*. First English-language version, with lyrics by Harry B. Smith and Robert B. Smith and entitled "The Melody of Love," presented in 1911 American production of *Gypsy Love*. Clifford Grey's English-language version introduced by Lawrence Tibbett in *The Rogue Song* (film).

Whole Darned Thing's for You, The

Words by Roy Turk, music by Fred E. Ahlert.
Robbins Music Corp.
Introduced by Lawrence Gray in *Children of Pleasure* (film).

Without Love

Words by B. G. De Sylva and Lew Brown, music by Ray Henderson.
De Sylva, Brown & Henderson, Inc./Anne-Rachel Music Corp.
Introduced by Grace Brinkley, and reprised by Oscar Shaw and Kate Smith, in *Flying High* (musical). Sung by Sheree North in *The Best Things in Life Are Free* (film, 1956).

Would You Like To Take a Walk? (Sump'n Good'll Come from That)

Words by Mort Dixon and Billy Rose, music by Harry Warren.
Remick Music Corp.
Introduced by Hannah Williams and Hal Thompson in *Sweet and Low* (revue).

(I Am the Words), You Are the Melody

Words and music by B. G. De Sylva, Lew Brown, and Ray Henderson.
De Sylva, Brown & Henderson, Inc./Anne-Rachel Music Corp.
Introduced by John Garrick and Maureen O'Sullivan in *Just Imagine* (film). Sung in *Holy Terror* (film, 1931).

You Brought a New Kind of Love to Me

Words and music by Sammy Fain, Irving Kahal, and Pierre Norman Connor.
Famous Music Corp.
Introduced by Maurice Chevalier in *The Pig Pond* (film). Used as a theme for *A New Kind of Love* (film, 1963).

You Will Remember Vienna

Words by Oscar Hammerstein II, music by Sigmund Romberg.
Harms, Inc.
Introduced by Vivienne Segal and Alexander Gray in *Viennese Nights* (film). Sung by Helen Traubel in *Deep in My Heart* (film, 1954).

Your Smiles, Your Tears
Words by Irving Caesar, music by Sigmund Romberg.
Shubert Music Publishing Corp.
Introduced by Guy Robertson and Ethelind Terry in *Nina Rosa*
(musical).

You're Driving Me Crazy (What Did I Do?)
Words and music by Walter Donaldson.
Bregman, Vocco & Conn, Inc.
Introduced by Guy Lombardo and his Royal Canadians. Sung by
Adele Astaire, Eddie Foy, Jr., and chorus in *Smiles* (musical).

You're Lucky to Me
Words by Andy Razaf, music by Eubie Blake.
Shapiro, Bernstein & Co., Inc.
Introduced by Neeka Shaw and John Bubbles, and reprised by Ethel
Waters and Eubie Blake, in Lew Leslie's *Blackbirds of 1930* (revue).

You're Simply Delish
Words by Arthur Freed, music by Joseph Meyer.
Robbins Music Corp.
Introduced by Cliff Edwards and Fifi D'Orsay in *Those Three
French Girls* (film).

You're the One
Words by J. Russel Robinson and George Waggner, music by
Vincent Youmans.
Fred Fisher Music Co., Inc./The Vincent Youmans Co., Inc.
Introduced by Gloria Swanson in *What a Widow!* (film). First
recording in 1966 by Nolan Van Way (Evergreen).

You're the One I Care For
Words by Harry Link, music by Bert Lown and Chauncey Gray.
Anne-Rachel Music Corp.
Introduced by Bert Lown and his Orchestra.

1931

1931

Actions Speak Louder Than Words
Words by Rudy Vallée, music by Richard Himber and Ben Green
(pseudonym for Ben Bernie).
Mills Music, Inc.

Adios
Words by Eddie Woods, music by Enric Madriguera.
Peer International Corp.
Theme song of Enric Madriguera and his Orchestra.

All of Me
Words and music by Seymour Simons and Gerald Marks.
Bourne Co./Marlong Music Corp.
Introduced on radio by Belle Baker. Featured in *Careless Lady* (film,
1932). Sung by Frank Sinatra in *Meet Danny Wilson* (film, 1952)
and by Gloria De Haven in *Down among the Sheltering Palms*
(film, 1953).

As Time Goes By
Words and music by Herman Hupfeld.
Harms, Inc.
Introduced by Frances Williams in *Everybody's Welcome* (revue).
First recording by Rudy Vallée. Revived by Dooley Wilson in
Casablanca (film, 1942).

At Your Command
Words and music by Harry Tobias, Harry Barris, and Bing Crosby.
Robbins Music Corp.
Introduced by Bing Crosby.

Beautiful Love
Words by Haven Gillespie, music by Victor Young, Wayne King, and
Egbert Van Alstyne.
Movietone Music Corp.
Introduced by Wayne King and his Orchestra. Sung by Allan Jones
in *Sing a Jingle* (film, 1944).

Because, Because
Words by Ira Gershwin, music by George Gershwin.
New World Music Corp.
Introduced by Grace Brinkley and George Murphy in *Of Thee I Sing* (musical).

Begging for Love
Words and music by Irving Berlin.
Irving Berlin Music Corp.

Bend Down Sister
Words by Ballard MacDonald and Dave Silverstein, music by Con Conrad.
Mayfair Music Corp.
Introduced by Charlotte Greenwood in *Palmy Days* (film).

Between the Devil and the Deep Blue Sea
Words by Ted Koehler, music by Harold Arlen.
Arko Music Corp.
Introduced by Aida Ward at Cotton Club (New York nightclub) in *Rhythmania* (nightclub revue).

Blah-Blah-Blah
Words by Ira Gershwin, music by George Gershwin.
New World Music Corp.
Originally written as "Lady of the Moon" for unproduced 1928 musical, *East Is West*. Then, as "I Just Looked at You," with new lyrics by Ira Gershwin and Gus Kahn, scheduled for, but not used in, *Show Girl* (musical, 1929). Finally, with present title and lyrics, introduced by El Brendel in *Delicious* (film).

Blue Yodel No. 8, see Mule Skinner Blues.

Blues in My Heart
Words and music by Benny Carter and Irving Mills.
Mills Music, Inc.
Introduced by Fletcher Henderson and his Orchestra.

Business in F
Music by Archie Bleyer.
Peer International Corp.
Introduced by Fletcher Henderson and his Orchestra.

By Special Permission (of the Copyright Owners I Love You)
Words by Owen Murphy and Robert A. Simon, music by Lewis E. Gensler.
Harms, Inc.
Introduced by Ruth Tester and Jack McCauley in *The Gang's All Here* (musical).

By the River Sainte Marie
Words by Edgar Leslie, music by Harry Warren.
Robbins Music Corp.
Popularized by Kate Smith.

By the Sycamore Tree
Words by Haven Gillespie, music by Pete Wendling.
Bourne Co.

Call Me Darling (Call Me Sweetheart, Call Me Dear) (German)
English words by Dorothy Dick, German words and music by
Bert Reisfeld, Mart Fryberg, and Rolf Marbot.
Musikverlag "City," Leipzig, Germany/Anne-Rachel Music Corp.
Original German title, "Sag' Mir Darling." Popularized in United
States by Russ Columbo.

Can't We Talk It Over
Words by Ned Washington, music by Victor Young.
Remick Music Corp.
Popularized by Lee Wiley.

Casa Loma Stomp
Music by H. Eugene Gifford.
Mayfair Music Corp.
Introduced by The Casa Loma Orchestra.

C'est Pas Comme Ça (It's Not Like That) (French)
English words by Ned Washington, French words by René Nazelles,
music by Raoul Moretti.
Francis Salabert, Paris, France, 1930/Harms, Inc.
Introduced in French by Albert Prejean in *Sous les Toits de Paris*
(French film, 1930).

Charlie Cadet
Words and music by J. Paul Fogarty and Rudy Vallée.
Leo Feist, Inc.
Introduced by Rudy Vallée.

Cigarettes, Cigars
Words and music by Mack Gordon and Harry Revel.
Miller Music Corp./Harry Revel Music Corp.
Introduced by Ruth Etting in *Ziegfeld Follies of 1931* (revue).

Come to Me
Words and music by B. G. De Sylva, Lew Brown, and Ray Henderson.
De Sylva, Brown & Henderson, Inc./Anne-Rachel Music Corp.
Introduced by Gloria Swanson in *Indiscreet* (film).

Concentratin' (on You)
Words by Andy Razaf, music by Thomas "Fats" Waller.
Anne-Rachel Music Corp.
Introduced by Fats Waller.

Confession
Words by Howard Dietz, music by Arthur Schwartz.
Harms, Inc.
Introduced by "The Girls and The Boys" in *The Band Wagon*
(revue).

Creole Rhapsody
Music by Edward Kennedy "Duke" Ellington.
Mills Music, Inc., 1965.
Introduced by Duke Ellington and his Orchestra in 1931 but not
published until 1965.

Crosby, Columbo and Vallée
Words and music by Al Dubin and Joe Burke.
M. Witmark & Sons/Joe Burke Music Co.

Cuban Love Song
Words and music by Dorothy Fields, Jimmy McHugh, and
Herbert Stothart.
Robbins Music Corp.
Introduced by Lawrence Tibbett in *Cuban Love Song* (film).

Cute Little Things You Do, The
Words and music by James F. Hanley.
Movietone Music Corp.
Introduced by Fifi D'Orsay in *Young As You Feel* (film).

Dancing in the Dark
Words by Howard Dietz, music by Arthur Schwartz.
Harms, Inc.
Introduced by John Barker, to a dance by Tilly Losch, in *The Band
Wagon* (revue). Title song of and sung by Betsy Drake in *Dancing
in the Dark* (film, 1949) and danced to by Fred Astaire and Cyd
Charisse in *The Band Wagon* (film, 1953). Best-selling record in
1941 by Artie Shaw and his Orchestra (Victor).

Delishious
Words by Ira Gershwin, music by George Gershwin.
New World Music Corp.
Introduced by Raul Roulien in *Delicious* (film). First song hit by
the Gershwins written directly for films.

Do the New York
Words and music by J. P. Murray, Barry Trivers, and Ben Oakland.
Miller Music Corp.
Introduced by Harry Richman in *Ziegfeld Follies of 1931* (revue).

Don't Ask Me Why (German)
English words by Joe Young, German words by Walter Reisch and
Robinson A. Lackenbach, music by Robert Stolz.
Alrobi Musikverlag, GmbH, Berlin, Germany, 1930/Warock Corp./
Harms, Inc.
Original German title, "Das Leid Ist Aus." Featured by
Marlene Dietrich.

Draggin' My Heart Around
Words and music by Alex Hill.
Mayfair Music Corp.

Dream a Little Dream of Me
Words by Gus Kahn, music by Wilbur Schwandt and Fabian Andre.
Words & Music, Inc.
Introduced by Wayne King and his Orchestra. Popularized by
Kate Smith.

Drums in My Heart
Words by Edward Heyman, music by Vincent Youmans.
Miller Music Corp./The Vincent Youmans Co., Inc.
Introduced by Gregory Gaye in *Through the Years* (musical play).

Egyptian Ella
Words and music by Walter Doyle.
Skidmore Music Co., Inc.
Introduced by Ted Weems and his Orchestra.

Elizabeth (Austrian)
English words by Irving Caesar, German words by Robert Katscher
and G. Herczeg, music by Robert Katscher.
Ludwig Doblinger, Vienna, Austria, 1930/Harms, Inc.
Introduced in United States by Al Jolson in *The Wonder Bar*
(musical).

Fiesta
Words and music by Walter G. Samuels and Leonard Whitcup.
Crisscott Music Co./Anne-Rachel Music Corp.

Good Evening Friends (German)
English words by Irving Caesar, German Words by Karl Farkas and
Geza Herczeg, music by Robert Katscher.
Ludwig Doblinger (Bernhard Herzmansky), Vienna, Austria and
Leipzig, Germany, 1930/Harms, Inc.
Introduced in United States by Al Jolson in *The Wonder Bar*
(musical).

Goodnight Sweetheart (English)
Words and music by Ray Noble, James Campbell, and Reg Connelly;
"American version" by Rudy Vallée.
Campbell-Connelly Co., Ltd., London, England/Robbins Music Corp.
Introduced in London by Henry Hall's BBC Orchestra. Introduced in
United States by Rudy Vallée. Interpolated by Milton Watson and
Woods Miller in ninth edition of *Earl Carroll Vanities* (revue).
First United States recording by Wayne King and his Orchestra.
Performed by Ray Noble and his Orchestra in *Big Broadcast of
1936* (film, 1935). Sung by Rudy Vallée in *Palm Beach Story*
(film, 1942), by Gene Autry in *Stardust on the Sage* (film, 1942),
and by chorus in *You Were Meant for Me* (film, 1948).

Got a Date with an Angel (English)
Words by Clifford Grey and Sonny Miller, music by Jack Waller and
Joseph Tunbridge.
Chappell & Co., Inc./Anne-Rachel Music Corp.
Best-selling record by Hal Kemp and his Orchestra, vocal by
Skinnay Ennis. Theme song of Skinnay Ennis and his Orchestra.

Got the Bench, Got the Park (but I Haven't Got You)
Words and music by Al Lewis, Al Sherman, and Fred Phillips.
Bourne Co./Robert Music Corp.

Green Eyes (Cuban)
English words by E. Rivera and Eddie Woods, Spanish words by
Adolfo Utrera, music by Nilo Menendez.
Peer International Corp.
Original Spanish title, "Aquellos Ojos Verdes." Introduced by Don
Azpiazu and his Havana Casino Orchestra. Best-selling record in
1941-42 by Jimmy Dorsey and his Orchestra, vocal by Helen
O'Connell and Bob Eberly (Decca).

Guilty
Words and music by Gus Kahn, Harry Akst, and Richard A. Whiting.
Leo Feist, Inc./Whiting Music Corp.
Revived in 1947 with best-selling record by Margaret Whiting
(Capitol).

Half Caste Woman (English)
Words and music by Noël Coward.
Harms, Inc.
Introduced in London by Ada May in Charles B. Cochran's *1931
Revue* (revue). Introduced in United States by Helen Morgan in
Ziegfeld Follies of 1931 (revue).

Have a Heart
Words by Harold Adamson, music by Burton Lane.
Robbins Music Corp.
Introduced by Lillian Roth and Woods Miller in ninth edition of
Earl Carroll Vanities (revue).

Heartaches
Words by John Klenner, music by Al Hoffman.
Leeds Music Corp.
Introduced by Guy Lombardo and his Royal Canadians. Revived in
1947 with best-selling record by Ted Weems and his Orchestra
(Decca) and in 1961 with best-selling record by The Marcels
(Colpix).

Hello! Beautiful!
Words and music by Walter Donaldson.
Bregman, Vocco & Conn, Inc.
Introduced by Maurice Chevalier.

Hello, My Lover, Good-bye
Words by Edward Heyman, music by John Green.
Famous Music Corp.
Introduced by Frances Langford in *Here Goes the Bride* (musical).

Help Yourself to Happiness
Words and music by Mack Gordon, Harry Revel, and Harry Richman.
Fred Fisher Music Co., Inc./Miller Music Corp./Harry Revel
Music Corp.
Introduced by Harry Richman in *Ziegfeld Follies of 1931* (revue).

High and Low (I've Been Looking for You)
Words by Howard Dietz and Desmond Carter, music by Arthur
Schwartz.
Harms, Inc.
Introduced by Roberta Robinson and John Barker in *The Band
Wagon* (revue).

Home (When Shadows Fall)
Words and music by Peter Van Steeden, Harry Clarkson, and Jeff
Clarkson.
Mills Music, Inc.
Introduced on eight different radio programs on Thanksgiving Eve,
1931 by Kate Smith, Rudy Vallée, Russ Columbo, The Sisters of the
Skillet, and others. Theme song of Smith Ballew and his Orchestra.

Hoops
Words by Howard Dietz, music by Arthur Schwartz.
Harms, Inc.
Introduced by Fred Astaire and Adele Astaire in *The Band Wagon*
(revue).

Hour of Parting
Words by Gus Kahn, music by Mischa Spoliansky.
Harms, Inc.

How About It?
Words by Lorenz Hart, music by Richard Rodgers.
Harms, Inc.
Introduced by Inez Courtney and Jack Whiting, and reprised by
Jeanne Aubert, Gus Shy, Jack Whiting, and ensemble, in *America's
Sweetheart* (musical).

How Long Will It Last?
Words by Max Lief, music by Joseph Meyer.
Robbins Music Corp./Robert Music Corp./Sherwin Music, Inc.
Introduced by Joan Crawford in *Possessed* (film).

I Apologize
Words and music by Al Hoffman, Ed. G. Nelson, and Al Goodhart.
De Sylva, Brown & Henderson, Inc.
Introduced by Bing Crosby. Revived in 1951 with best-selling record
by Billy Eckstine (M-G-M).

I Don't Know Why (I Just Do)
Words by Roy Turk, music by Fred E. Ahlert.
Fred Ahlert Music Corp./Cromwell Music, Inc.

I Found a Million Dollar Baby (in a Five and Ten Cent Store)
Words by Billy Rose and Mort Dixon, music by Harry Warren.
Remick Music Corp.
Completely rewritten version of song with same title, written by
Billy Rose and Fred Fisher and published by Leo Feist, Inc. in
1926. Introduced by Ted Healy, Fanny Brice, Phil Baker, and Lew
Brice in *Billy Rose's Crazy Quilt* (revue). Interpolated in *Million
Dollar Baby* (film, 1935) and *Million Dollar Baby* (film, 1941).

I Happen To Like New York
Words and music by Cole Porter.
Harms, Inc.
Interpolated by Oscar "Rags" Ragland in *The New Yorkers*
(musical, 1930).

I Love a Parade
Words by Ted Koehler, music by Harold Arlen.
Harms, Inc.
Introduced by Cab Calloway at Cotton Club (New York nightclub) in
Rhythmania (nightclub revue). Popularized by Harry Richman.

I Love Louisa
Words by Howard Dietz, music by Arthur Schwartz.
Harms, Inc.
Introduced as production number with Fred Astaire and Adele Astaire
in *The Band Wagon* (revue). Sung by Betsy Drake in *Dancing in
the Dark* (film, 1949) and by Fred Astaire, assisted by Oscar
Levant, in *The Band Wagon* (film, 1953).

I Surrender, Dear
Words by Gordon Clifford, music by Harry Barris.
Mills Music, Inc.
Introduced and recorded by The Rhythm Boys, featuring Bing Crosby,
with Gus Arnheim's Orchestra. Popularized by Bing Crosby and
Russ Columbo. Theme song of Red Norvo and his Orchestra. Inter-
polated in *I Surrender Dear* (film, 1948).

I Want a Man
Words by Lorenz Hart, music by Richard Rodgers.
Harms, Inc.
Introduced by Jeanne Aubert in *America's Sweetheart* (musical).

I Want You for Myself
Words and music by Irving Berlin.
Irving Berlin Music Corp.

I Watch the Love Parade
Words by Otto Harbach, music by Jerome Kern.
T. B. Harms Co.
Introduced by George Meader and Flora Le Breton in *The Cat and the Fiddle* (musical). Sung by Jeanette MacDonald and Ramon Novarro in film version, 1934.

I Wouldn't Change You for the World
Words by Charles Newman, music by Isham Jones.
Leeds Music Corp./World Music, Inc.

I'll Be Glad When You're Dead, You Rascal You, see (I'll Be Glad When You're Dead), You Rascal You.

I'll Love You in My Dreams
Words and music by Abel Baer, Horace Heidt, and Benée Russell.
Leo Feist, Inc.
Theme song of Horace Heidt and his Musical Knights.

Illegitimate Daughter, The
Words by Ira Gershwin, music by George Gershwin.
New World Music Corp.
Introduced by Florenz Ames in *Of Thee I Sing* (musical).

I'm All Dressed Up with a Broken Heart
Words and music by Fred Fisher, Stella Unger, and Harold Stern.
Fred Fisher Music Co., Inc.

I'm Crazy 'bout My Baby (and My Baby's Crazy 'bout Me)
Words and music by Thomas "Fats" Waller and Alex Hill.
Mayfair Music Corp./Anne-Rachel Music Corp.
Introduced on records by Fats Waller, with Ted Lewis and his Band (Columbia).

I'm Keepin' Company
Words and music by Lu C. Bender, Vee Lawnhurst, and Dave Dreyer.
Bourne Co.

I'm One of God's Children (Who Hasn't Got Wings)
Words by Oscar Hammerstein II and Harry Ruskin, music by Louis Alter.
Harms, Inc.
Introduced by Janet Reade in *Ballyhoo* (musical, 1930).

I'm Sorry Dear
Words and music by Anson Weeks, Harry Tobias, and Johnnie Scott.
Robbins Music Corp.
Introduced by Anson Weeks and his Orchestra.

I'm Thru with Love
Words by Gus Kahn, music by Matt Malneck and Fud Livingston.
Robbins Music Corp.
Introduced by Mildred Bailey. Sung by Bobby Van in *The Affairs of Dobie Gillis* (film, 1953) and by Marilyn Monroe in *Some Like It Hot* (film, 1959).

I'm with You!
Words and music by Walter Donaldson.
Bregman, Vocco & Conn, Inc.
Introduced by Helen Morgan and Harry Richman in *Ziegfeld Follies of 1931* (revue).

In the Dark
Music by Leon "Bix" Beiderbecke.
Robbins Music Corp.
Introduced by Bix Beiderbecke at the piano.

In the Merry Month of Maybe
Words by Ira Gershwin and Billy Rose, music by Harry Warren.
New World Music Corp.
Introduced by Ethel Norris and Tom Monroe in Billy Rose's *Crazy Quilt* (revue).

It's Every Girl's Ambition
Words by Edward Heyman, music by Vincent Youmans.
Miller Music Corp./The Vincent Youmans Co., Inc.
Introduced by Martha Mason in *Through the Years* (musical).

It's the Darndest Thing
Words by Dorothy Fields, music by Jimmy McHugh.
Robbins Music Corp.
Introduced in *Singin' the Blues* (play with music).

It's the Girl
Words by Dave Oppenheim, music by Abel Baer.
Leo Feist, Inc.

I've Got Five Dollars
Words by Lorenz Hart, music by Richard Rodgers.
Harms, Inc.
Introduced by Jack Whiting and Harriette Lake (Ann Sothern) in *America's Sweetheart* (musical). Sung by Jane Russell and Scott Brady in *Gentlemen Marry Brunettes* (film, 1955).

Jalousie, see Jealousy.

Jazz Nocturne
Music by Dana Suesse.
Famous Music Corp.

Jealousy, also known as **Jalousie (**Danish**)**
English words by Vera Bloom, music by Jacob Gade.
Gade & Warny-Musikforlag, Copenhagen, Denmark, 1925/Éditions
Charles Brull, Paris, France, 1926/Harms, Inc.
Originally published in Denmark as instrumental composition en-
titled "Jalousie, a Tango Tzigane." Boston Pops Orchestra's re-
cording (Victor, 1938) possibly the first instrumental recording
of light music to reach, as it did by 1952, one million in sales.

Jimmie Brown, the Newsboy
Words and music by A. P. Carter.
Peer International Corp.
Introduced by The Carter Family. Revived in 1959 with best-selling
record by Mac Wiseman (Dot).

Just Friends
Words by Sam M. Lewis, music by John Klenner.
Robbins Music Corp.
Introduced by "Red" McKenzie.

Just One More Chance
Words by Sam Coslow, music by Arthur Johnston.
Famous Music Corp.
Introduced on radio by Bing Crosby. Best-selling record by
Russ Columbo.

Kathleen Mine
Words by Edward Heyman, music by Vincent Youmans.
The Vincent Youmans Co., Inc./Miller Music Corp.
Introduced by Natalie Hall and Michael Bartlett in *Through the
Years* (musical).

Katinkitschka
Words by Ira Gershwin, music by George Gershwin.
New World Music Corp.
Introduced by Janet Gaynor, El Brendel, and chorus in *Delicious*
(film).

Key to My Heart, The
Words by Ira Gershwin, music by Louis Alter.
New World Music Corp.
Introduced by Lenore Ulric in *The Social Register* (play).

Kickin' the Gong Around
Words by Ted Koehler, music by Harold Arlen.
Arko Music Corp.
Introduced by Cab Calloway. Performed by Calloway at Cotton Club
(New York night club) in *Rhythmania* (nightclub revue) and in
The Big Broadcast (film, 1932).

Lady Must Live, A
Words by Lorenz Hart, music by Richard Rodgers.
Harms, Inc.
Introduced by Jeanne Aubert in *America's Sweetheart* (musical).

Lady of Spain (English)
Words and music by Robert Hargreaves, Tolchard Evans, Stanley
J. Damerell, and Henry B. Tilsley.
The Peter Maurice Music Co., Ltd., London, England/Sam Fox
Publishing Co., Inc.
Introduced in England by Jack Payne and his Orchestra. Revived
in 1952 with best-selling record by Eddie Fisher (RCA Victor).

Lazy River
Words and music by Hoagy Carmichael and Sidney Arodin.
Peer International Corp.
Introduced on records by Hoagy Carmichael and his Orchestra. Sung
by Carmichael in *The Best Years of Our Lives* (film, 1946). Re-
vived in 1961 with best-selling record by Si Zentner (RCA Victor).
Winner of National Academy of Recording Arts and Sciences
Award for "Best Performance by an Orchestra," 1961.

Lies
Words by George E. Springer, music by Harry Barris.
Shapiro, Bernstein & Co., Inc.
Introduced by Russ Columbo.

Life Is Just a Bowl of Cherries
Words and music by Lew Brown and Ray Henderson.
De Sylva, Brown & Henderson, Inc.
Introduced by Ethel Merman in eleventh edition of *George White's
Scandals* (revue). Best-selling records by Bing Crosby and The
Boswell Sisters (Brunswick) and Rudy Vallée (Victor).

Lights of Paris (English)
Words and music by Erell Reaves, Tolchard Evans, and
Stanley J. Damerell.
Ed. Kassner Music Co., Ltd., London, England/Sam Fox Publishing
Co., Inc.

Little Girl
Words and music by Madeline Hyde and Francis Henry.
Leeds Music Corp.
Introduced and popularized by Guy Lombardo and his
Royal Canadians.

Love Came into My Heart
Words by Harold Adamson, music by Burton Lane.
Robbins Music Corp.
Introduced by Woods Miller and Milton Watson in ninth edition of
Earl Carroll Vanities (revue).

Love Is Like That (What Can You Do?)
Words and music by Benée Russell.
Leo Feist, Inc.
Introduced by Ruth Etting.

Love Is Sweeping the Country
Words by Ira Gershwin, music by George Gershwin.
New World Music Corp.
Introduced by George Murphy and June O'Dea in *Of Thee I Sing*
(musical). Melody previously written for, but dropped from,
Gershwin's unproduced *East Is West* (musical).

Love Letters in the Sand
Words by Nick Kenny and Charles Kenny, music by J. Fred Coots.
Bourne Co.
Introduced by Dolly Dawn. First recording by Russ Columbo. Theme
song of George Hall and his Orchestra. Sung by Pat Boone in
Bernadine (film, 1957). Best-selling record in 1957 by Pat Boone
(Dot).

Mad Dogs and Englishmen (English)
Words and music by Noël Coward.
Harms, Inc.
Introduced by Beatrice Lillie in *The Third Little Show* (revue).
Introduced by Romney Brent in London production of *Words and
Music* (revue, 1932).

Mama Don't Want No Peas an' Rice an' Cocoanut Oil
Words and music by L. Wolfe Gilbert and L. Charles (pseudonym
for Charlie Lofthouse).
Edward B. Marks Music Corp.
Adapted from popular song of the Bahamas. Interpolated in
It Happens Every Spring (film, 1949).

Mama Inez (Cuban)
English words by L. Wolfe Gilbert, music by Eliseo Grenet.
Edward B. Marks Music Corp.
Adapted from Cuban song, "Ay! Mama-Ines." Introduced in United
States by Maurice Chevalier.

Many Happy Returns of the Day
Words and music by Al Dubin and Joe Burke.
M. Witmark & Sons/Ahlert-Burke Corp./Joe Burke Music Co.

Maria, My Own (Cuban)
English words by L. Wolfe Gilbert, music by Ernesto Lecuona.
Edward B. Marks Music Corp.
Original title, "Maria-la-o"; from Cuban operetta of same title.

Marta (Cuban)

English words by L. Wolfe Gilbert, music by Moisés Simons.
Edward B. Marks Music Corp.
Theme song and radio signature of Arthur Tracy, "The Street Singer."

Me!

Words and music by Irving Berlin.
Irving Berlin Music Corp.

Minnie the Moocher (The Ho De Ho Song)

Words and music by Cab Calloway, Irving Mills, and Clarence Gaskill.
Mills Music, Inc.
Introduced by Cab Calloway at Cotton Club (New York nightclub).
Sung by Calloway in *The Big Broadcast* (film, 1932).

Mirabelle (Lover of My Dreams) (English)

Words and music by Noël Coward.
Chappell & Co., Ltd., London, England/Chappell & Co., Inc.
Introduced by Stella Wilson and Eric Purveur in London in *Cavalcade* (play). First recording in England by Noël Coward (HMV).

Mood Indigo

Words and music by Edward Kennedy "Duke" Ellington, Irving Mills, and Albany "Barney" Bigard.
Mills Music, Inc.
Introduced by Duke Ellington and his Orchestra in 1930 under the title, "Dreamy Blues."

(There Ought To Be a) Moonlight Saving Time

Words and music by Irving Kahal and Harry Richman.
Irving Kahal Music, Inc./Fred Fisher Music Co., Inc.
Introduced by Harry Richman.

Mule Skinner Blues, also known as New Mule Skinner Blues, also known as Blue Yodel No. 8

Words and music by Jimmie Rodgers and George Vaughn.
Peer International Corp.
Introduced by Jimmie Rodgers (Victor). Revived in 1960 with best-selling record by The Fendermen (Soma).

My Extraordinary Gal

Words and music by Terry Shand.
Leeds Music Corp.
Introduced on radio by Larry Funk and his Orchestra.

My Song

Words and music by Lew Brown and Ray Henderson.
De Sylva, Brown & Henderson, Inc.
Introduced by Ethel Merman and Rudy Vallée in eleventh edition of *George White's Scandals* (revue).

Nevertheless
Words and music by Bert Kalmar and Harry Ruby.
De Sylva, Brown & Henderson, Inc.
Popularized by Rudy Vallée and Bing Crosby. Sung by Anita Ellis, Fred Astaire, and Red Skelton in *Three Little Words* (film, 1950). Best-selling records in 1950 by The Mills Brothers (Decca) and Paul Weston and his Orchestra (Capitol).

New Love Is Old, A
Words by Otto Harbach, music by Jerome Kern.
T. B. Harms Co.
Introduced by Georges Metaxa in *The Cat and the Fiddle* (musical). Sung by Vivienne Segal, and reprised by Ramon Novarro and Jeanette MacDonald, in film version, 1934.

New Mule Skinner Blues, see Mule Skinner Blues.

New Sun in the Sky
Words by Howard Dietz, music by Arthur Schwartz.
Harms, Inc.
Introduced by Fred Astaire in *The Band Wagon* (revue). Sung by voice of India Adams, dubbed for Cyd Charisse, in *The Band Wagon* (film, 1953) and by Betsy Drake in *Dancing in the Dark* (film, 1949).

Night Was Made for Love, The
Words by Otto Harbach, music by Jerome Kern.
T. B. Harms Co.
Introduced by George Meader in *The Cat and the Fiddle* (musical). Sung by Ramon Novarro in film version, 1934.

Now That You're Gone
Words by Gus Kahn, music by Ted Fiorito.
Remick Music Corp.

Now You're in My Arms
Words and music by Allie Wrubel and Morton Downey.
Allison's Music, Inc./Remick Music Corp.
Introduced by Morton Downey.

Now's the Time To Fall in Love (Potatoes Are Cheaper — Tomatoes Are Cheaper)
Words and music by Al Sherman and Al Lewis.
De Sylva, Brown & Henderson, Inc.
Introduced by Eddie Cantor.

Of Thee I Sing
Words by Ira Gershwin, music by George Gershwin.
New World Music Corp.
Introduced by William Gaxton and Lois Moran in *Of Thee I Sing* (musical).

Oh, Donna Clara (Austrian)
English words by Irving Caesar, German words by Beda
(pseudonym for Beda Fritz Löhner), music by J. Petersburski.
Wiener Boheme Verlag, Vienna, Austria, 1930/Harms, Inc.
Introduced in United States by Al Jolson in *The Wonder Bar*
(musical).

Oh! Mo'nah!
Words and music by Ted Weems and "Country" Washburn.
Peer International Corp.
Introduced by Ted Weems and his Orchestra.

On Account of I Love You
Words by James Dyrenforth, music by Phil Charig.
Harms, Inc.
Introduced by Fay Wray, Douglass Montgomery, Nathaniel Wagner,
and Archie Leach (Cary Grant) in *Nikki* (play with music).

On Revival Day
Words and music by Andy Razaf.
George Simon, Inc.
Introduced by Bessie Smith.

One Moment Alone
Words by Otto Harbach, music by Jerome Kern.
T. B. Harms Co.
Introduced by Georges Metaxa in *The Cat and the Fiddle* (musical).
Sung by Ramon Novarro and Jeanette MacDonald in film version,
1934.

One More Hour of Love
Words by Clifford Grey, music by Oscar Straus.
Famous Music Corp.
Introduced by Maurice Chevalier in *The Smiling Lieutenant* (film).

Ooh That Kiss
Words by Mort Dixon and Joe Young, music by Harry Warren.
Harms, Inc./Warock Corp.
Introduced by Lawrence Gray, Jeanne Aubert, and ensemble in
The Laugh Parade (revue).

**Out of Nowhere, also known as You Came Along (from Out of
Nowhere)**
Words by Edward Heyman, music by John Green.
Famous Music Corp.
Introduced by Guy Lombardo and his Royal Canadians. Best-selling
record by Bing Crosby (Decca). Featured in *Dude Ranch* (film,
1931). Sung by Helen Forrest in *You Came Along* (film, 1945).

Paradise
Words by Gordon Clifford and Nacio Herb Brown, music by Nacio
    Herb Brown.
Leo Feist, Inc.
Introduced by Pola Negri in *A Woman Commands* (film, 1932).
    Theme song of Russ Columbo. Sung by Belita in *The Gangster*
    (film, 1947), by Gloria Grahame in *A Woman's Secret* (film, 1949),
    and by Valentina Cortesa in *Malaya* (film, 1949).

Penthouse Serenade (When We're Alone)
Words and music by Will Jason and Val Burton.
Famous Music Corp.

Poor Pierrot
Words by Otto Harbach, music by Jerome Kern.
T. B. Harms Co.
Introduced by Lucette Valsy and Peter Chambers in *The Cat and
    the Fiddle* (musical). Sung by Jeanette MacDonald in film version,
    1934.

Prisoner of Love
Words by Leo Robin, music by Russ Columbo and Clarence Gaskill.
Mayfair Music Corp./Sherwin Music, Inc.
Introduced by Russ Columbo. Revived in 1946 with best-selling
    record by Perry Como (Victor) and in 1963 with best-selling
    record by James Brown and The Famous Flames (King).

Put Your Little Arms around Me
Words and music by Gus Arnheim, Harry Tobias, and
    Charles N. Daniels.
Robbins Music Corp./Charles N. Daniels, Inc.

Quiérme Mucho, see Yours, 1937.

River Stay 'Way from My Door
Words by Mort Dixon, music by Harry Woods.
Shapiro, Bernstein & Co., Inc.
Introduced by Jimmy Savo in *Mum's the Word* (revue).

Rockin' in Rhythm
Music by Edward Kennedy "Duke" Ellington, Irving Mills, and
    Harry Carney.
Mills Music, Inc.
Introduced by Duke Ellington and his Orchestra.

Roll On, Mississippi, Roll On
Words and music by Eugene West, James McCaffrey, and
    Dave Ringle.
Shapiro, Bernstein & Co., Inc./Fred Fisher Music Co., Inc.

Running between the Raindrops
Words by James Dyrenforth, music by Carroll Gibbons.
Anne-Rachel Music Corp.

Save the Last Dance for Me
Words by Walter Hirsch, music by Frank Magine and Phil Spitalny.
Leo Feist, Inc./Musical Works.
Popularized by Arthur Tracy, "The Street Singer."

Shadrack (Shadrach)
Words and music by Robert MacGimsey.
Carl Fischer, Inc.
Best-selling record in 1938 by Louis Armstrong and his Orchestra
(Decca).

She Didn't Say "Yes"
Words by Otto Harbach, music by Jerome Kern.
T. B. Harms Co.
Introduced by Bettina Hall in *The Cat and the Fiddle* (musical).
Sung by Jeanette MacDonald in film version, 1934.

Singin' the Blues
Words by Dorothy Fields, music by Jimmy McHugh.
Robbins Music Corp.
Introduced in *Singin' the Blues* (play with music).

Smile, Darn Ya, Smile
Words by Charles O'Flynn and Jack Meskill, music by Max Rich.
De Sylva, Brown & Henderson, Inc./Fred Fisher Music Co., Inc.
Theme song of comedian Fred Allen's radio show.

Snuggled on Your Shoulder (Cuddled in Your Arms)
Words and music by Carmen Lombardo and Joe Young.
Leo Feist, Inc./Warock Corp.
Introduced by Guy Lombardo and his Royal Canadians. Popularized
by Bing Crosby.

Somebody from Somewhere
Words by Ira Gershwin, music by George Gershwin.
New World Music Corp.
Introduced by Janet Gaynor in *Delicious* (film). First recording
in 1955 by Shannon Bolin (Vanguard).

Sous les Toits de Paris (Under a Roof in Paree) (French)
English words by Irving Caesar, French words by René Nazelles,
music by Raoul Moretti.
Francis Salabert, Paris, France, 1930/Harms, Inc.
Introduced in French in *Sous les Toits de Paris* (French film, 1930).
English lyrics written in 1931.

Street Scene, see 1933.

Such Is Life, Such Is Love
Words by Mack Gordon, music by Harry Revel.
Miller Music Corp.
Introduced by Ruth Etting.

Sweet and Lovely
Words and music by Gus Arnheim, Harry Tobias, and Jules Lemare.
Robbins Music Corp./Charles N. Daniels, Inc.
Introduced by and theme song of Gus Arnheim and his Orchestra.
First recording by Gus Arnheim and his Orchestra, vocal by
Donald Novis. Popularized by Bing Crosby and by Russ Columbo.

Tabu
Words and music by Sam Coslow and W. Franke Harling.
Famous Music Corp.
Promotional song for *Tabu* (film).

Taking Off
Words by James Dyrenforth, music by Phil Charig.
Harms, Inc.
Introduced by Douglass Montgomery, Nathaniel Wagner, John
Brooke, and Archie Leach (Cary Grant) in *Nikki* (play with
music).

Tell Me with a Love Song
Words by Ted Koehler, music by Harold Arlen.
Advanced Music Corp.
Introduced by Kate Smith.

That's My Desire
Words and music by Carroll Loveday and Helmy Kresa.
Mills Music, Inc.
Introduced on radio by Lanny Ross. Revived in 1947 with
best-selling record by Frankie Laine (Mercury).

That's Why Darkies Were Born
Words and music by Lew Brown and Ray Henderson.
De Sylva, Brown & Henderson, Inc.
Introduction by Everett Marshall in eleventh edition of
George White's Scandals (revue).

There Ought To Be a Moonlight Saving Time, see (There Ought To Be a) Moonlight Saving Time.

There's Nothing Too Good for My Baby
Words and music by Eddie Cantor, Benny Davis, and Harry Akst.
Words & Music, Inc.
Introduced by Eddie Cantor in *Palmy Days* (film).

There's So Much More
Words by Lorenz Hart, music by Richard Rodgers.
Harms, Inc.
Introduced by Jeanne Aubert and Gus Shy in *America's Sweetheart*
(musical).

This Is the Missus
Words and music by Lew Brown and Ray Henderson.
De Sylva, Brown & Henderson, Inc.
Introduced by Rudy Vallée in eleventh edition of *George White's Scandals* (revue). Sung by Sheree North in *The Best Things in Life Are Free* (film, 1956).

Thrill Is Gone, The
Words and music by Lew Brown and Ray Henderson.
De Sylva, Brown & Henderson, Inc.
Introduced by Everett Marshall, Rudy Vallée, and Ross MacLean in eleventh edition of *George White's Scandals* (revue).

Through the Years
Words by Edward Heyman, music by Vincent Youmans.
Miller Music Corp.
Introduced by Natalie Hall and Michael Bartlett in *Through the Years* (musical).

Till the Real Thing Comes Along, see Until the Real Thing Comes Along, 1936.

Too Late
Words and music by Sam M. Lewis and Victor Young.
Remick Music Corp.
Introduced by Bing Crosby.

Toodle-oo, So Long, Good-Bye
Words and music by Rudy Vallée and Byron Gay.
Movietone Music Corp.
Introduced by Rudy Vallée.

Torch Song, The
Words by Mort Dixon and Joe Young, music by Harry Warren.
Harms, Inc./Warock Corp.
Introduced by Bartlett Simmons in *The Laugh Parade* (musical).

Travelin' Blues
Words and music by Jimmie Rodgers and Shelly Lee Alley.
Peer International Corp.
Introduced by Jimmie Rodgers (Victor). Revived in 1951 with best-selling record by Lefty Frizzell (Columbia).

Try To Forget
Words by Otto Harbach, music by Jerome Kern.
T. B. Harms Co.
Introduced by Doris Carson, Bettina Hall, and Eddie Foy, Jr. in *The Cat and the Fiddle* (musical). Sung by Jeanette MacDonald, and reprised by Ramon Novarro, in film version, 1934.

Twentieth Century Blues (English)
Words and music by Noël Coward.
Chappell & Co., Ltd., London, England/Chappell & Co., Inc.
Introduced by Binnie Barnes in London in *Cavalcade* (play). First
recording in England by New Mayfair Novelty Orchestra, vocal
by Al Bowlly (HMV).

Twenty One Years
Words and music by Bob Miller.
MCA, Inc.
New lyrics, by Frank Royal, added in 1961.

Two Little Blue Little Eyes
Words and music by Paul Francis Webster, John Jacob Loeb, and
Rudy Vallée.
Carl Fischer, Inc./John Jacob Loeb Co./Webster Music Corp.
Introduced by Rudy Vallée.

Two Loves Have I (French)
English words by J. P. Murray and Barry Trivers, French words by
Georges Koger and H. Varna, music by Vincent Scotto.
Francis Salabert, Paris, France, 1930/Miller Music Corp.
Original French title, "J'ai Deux Amours." Introduced in Paris by
Josephine Baker. Introduced in United States by Irene Bordoni.

Under a Roof in Paree, see Sous les Toits de Paris.

Wabash Moon
Words and music by Dave Dreyer, Morton Downey, and
Billy McKenny.
Bourne Co.
Introduced by and theme song of Morton Downey.

Was That the Human Thing To Do
Words by Joe Young, music by Sammy Fain.
Warock Corp./M. Witmark & Sons.
Introduced by Guy Lombardo and his Royal Canadians.

We'll Be the Same
Words by Lorenz Hart, music by Richard Rodgers.
Harms, Inc.
Introduced by Harriette Lake (Ann Sothern) and Jack Whiting,
and reprised by Jack Whiting and Gus Shy, in *America's Sweet-
heart* (musical).

When I Take My Sugar to Tea
Words and music by Sammy Fain, Irving Kahal, and
Pierre Norman Connor.
Famous Music Corp.
Interpolated in *Monkey Business* (film) and *The Mating Season*
(film, 1951).

When I'm the President
Words and music by Al Lewis and Al Sherman.
Al Sherman Music Co./Sherwin Music, Inc./Sovereign Music Corp.
Introduced by Eddie Cantor.

When It's Sleepy Time down South
Words and music by Leon René, Otis René, and Clarence Muse.
Mills Music, Inc./Sherwin Music, Inc.
Introduced by Clarence Muse. Theme of Louis Armstrong and
   his Orchestra.

When the Moon Comes over the Mountain
Words and music by Kate Smith, Harry Woods, and Harold Johnson.
Robbins Music Corp.
Introduced by and theme song of Kate Smith. Sung by Miss Smith
   in *The Big Broadcast* (film, 1932).

When We're Alone, see Penthouse Serenade.

When Your Lover Has Gone
Words and music by E. A. Swan.
Remick Music Corp.
Sung on soundtrack of *Blonde Crazy* (film).

When Yuba Plays the Rhumba on the Tuba
Words and music by Herman Hupfeld.
Harms, Inc.
Introduced by Walter O'Keefe in *The Third Little Show* (revue).
   Best-selling record by Rudy Vallée.

Where Can He Be?
Words by Howard Dietz, music by Arthur Schwartz.
Harms, Inc.
Introduced by Helen Broderick and chorus in *The Band Wagon*
   (revue).

Where the Blue of the Night (Meets the Gold of the Day)
Words and music by Roy Turk, Bing Crosby, and Fred E. Ahlert.
De Sylva, Brown & Henderson, Inc./Fred Ahlert Music Corp./
   Cromwell Music, Inc.
Introduced by Bing Crosby in *The Big Broadcast* (film, 1932).
   Also used by Crosby as his theme song.

While Hearts Are Singing
Words by Clifford Grey, music by Oscar Straus.
Famous Music Corp.
Introduced by Claudette Colbert in *The Smiling Lieutenant* (film).

Whistling in the Dark
Words by Allen Boretz, music by Dana Suesse.
Leeds Music Corp.

1931

Who Cares? (So Long As You Care for Me)
Words by Ira Gershwin, music by George Gershwin.
New World Music Corp., 1931, 1952.
Introduced by William Gaxton and Lois Moran in *Of Thee I Sing*
(musical). Slightly revised version sung by Jack Carson and Betty
Oakes in 1952 revival.

Who's Your Little Whoozis?
Words and music by Ben Bernie, Al Goering, and Walter Hirsch.
Famous Music Corp./World Music, Inc.
Introduced by Ben Bernie and his Orchestra.

Why Dance?
Words by Roy Turk, music by Fred E. Ahlert.
Fred Ahlert Music Corp./Cromwell Music, Inc.

Wintergreen for President
Words by Ira Gershwin, music by George Gershwin.
New World Music Corp.
Introduced by ensemble in *Of Thee I Sing* (musical).

Wrap Your Troubles in Dreams (and Dream Your Troubles Away)
Words by Ted Koehler and Billy Moll, music by Harry Barris.
Shapiro, Bernstein & Co., Inc.
Introduced by Bing Crosby.

You Call It Madness (but I Call It Love)
Words and music by Gladys Du Bois, Paul Gregory, Con Conrad, and
Russ Columbo.
Mayfair Music Corp./Sherwin Music, Inc.
Introduced by and theme song of Russ Columbo.

You Came Along (from Out of Nowhere), see Out of Nowhere.

You Can't Stop Me from Lovin' You
Words by Mann Holiner, music by Alberta Nichols.
Anne-Rachel Music Corp.
Interpolated by Ethel Waters and Blue McAllister in Lew Leslie's
Rhapsody in Black (revue).

You Didn't Have To Tell Me — I Knew It All the Time
Words and music by Walter Donaldson.
Bregman, Vocco & Conn, Inc.

You Forgot Your Gloves
Words by Edward Eliscu, music by Ned Lehac.
Robbins Music Corp.
Introduced by Constance Carpenter and Jerry Norris in
The Third Little Show (revue).

(I'll Be Glad When You're Dead), You Rascal You
Words and music by Sam Theard.
Mills Music, Inc.
Identified with Louis Armstrong.

You Said It
Words by Jack Yellen, music by Harold Arlen.
Advanced Music Corp.
Introduced by Mary Lawler and Stanley Smith in *You Said It* (musical). Recorded by Harold Arlen, with Red Nichols and his Orchestra (Brunswick).

You Try Somebody Else (We'll Be Back Together Again)
Words and music by B. G. De Sylva, Lew Brown, and
Ray Henderson.
De Sylva, Brown & Henderson, Inc./Anne-Rachel Music Corp.
Popularized by Russ Columbo. Sung by Sheree North in *The Best Things in Life Are Free* (film, 1956).

You'll Be Mine in Apple Blossom Time
Words by Charles Tobias, music by Peter De Rose.
Edwin H. Morris & Co., Inc.

You're Just a Dream Come True
Words by Charles Newman, music by Isham Jones.
Leo Feist, Inc.
Theme song of Isham Jones and his Orchestra.

You're My Everything
Words by Mort Dixon and Joe Young, music by Harry Warren.
Harms, Inc./Warock Corp.
Introduced by Jeanne Aubert and Lawrence Gray in *The Laugh Parade* (revue). Sung by Dan Dailey in *You're My Everything* (film, 1949).

Yours, see 1937.

Yours Is My Heart Alone (Austrian)
English words by Harry Bache Smith, German words by Ludwig
Herzer and Fritz Löhner, music by Franz Lehár.
W. Karczag, Vienna, Austria, 1929/Shubert Music Publishing Corp.
Original German title, "Dein Ist Mein Ganzes Herz." Introduced by Richard Tauber in Berlin in *Das Land des Lächelns (The Land of Smiles)* (operetta).

1932

1932

After All Is Said and Done
Words and music by Gus Arnheim, Henry Tobias, and Jules Lemare.
Bourne Co.

After Twelve o'Clock
Words by Joe Moore (pseudonym for Johnny Mercer), music by
   Hoagy Carmichael.
Southern Music Publishing Co., Inc.

After You
Words and music by Cole Porter.
Harms, Inc.
Introduced by Fred Astaire in *Gay Divorce* (musical).

All-American Girl
Words and music by Al Lewis.
Leo Feist, Inc.
Introduced by George Olsen and his Orchestra.

Alone Together
Words by Howard Dietz, music by Arthur Schwartz.
Harms, Inc.
Introduced by Jean Sargent, and danced to by Clifton Webb and
   Tamara Geva, in *Flying Colors* (revue).

Am I Wasting My Time?
Words by Jack Manus, music by Sanford Green.
Anne-Rachel Music Corp.

Amber Tresses Tied with Blue
Words and music by A. P. Carter.
Peer International Corp.
Introduced by The Carter Family.

And Love Was Born
Words by Oscar Hammerstein II, music by Jerome Kern.
T. B. Harms Co.
Introduced by Reinald Werrenrath in *Music in the Air* (musical).

67

(I Would Do) Anything for You
Words and music by Alex Hill, Bob Williams, and Claude Hopkins.
George Simon, Inc.
Introduced by and theme song of Claude Hopkins and his Orchestra.

April in Paris
Words by E. Y. Harburg, music by Vernon Duke.
Harms, Inc.
Introduced by Evelyn Hoey in *Walk a Little Faster* (revue). First
   recording by Marian Chase (Liberty). Sung by Doris Day, under
   titles, in *April in Paris* (film, 1953). Popular jazz version in 1955
   by Count Basie and his Orchestra (Verve).

As You Desire Me
Words and music by Allie Wrubel.
Words & Music, Inc.
Promotional song for *As You Desire Me* (film). Popularized in
   1940's by Tony Martin.

At the Close of a Long, Long Day
Words by Billy Moll, music by Johnny Marvin.
Shapiro, Bernstein & Co., Inc.

Auf Wiedersehn, My Dear
Words and music by Al Hoffman, Ed G. Nelson, Al Goodhart, and
   Milton Ager.
Advanced Music Corp.
Popularized by Russ Columbo.

Baby When You Ain't There
Words by Mitchell Parish, music by Edward Kennedy "Duke"
   Ellington.
Mills Music, Inc.
Introduced by Duke Ellington and his Orchestra, vocal by
   Cootie Williams.

Best Wishes
Words by Ted Koehler, music by Edward Kennedy "Duke" Ellington.
Mills Music, Inc.
Introduced by Duke Ellington and his Orchestra.

Black Jazz
Music by Eugene Gifford.
American Academy of Music, Inc.
Best-selling record by The Casa Loma Orchestra.

Brother, Can You Spare a Dime?
Words by E. Y. Harburg, music by Jay Gorney.
Harms, Inc.
Introduced by Rex Weber and chorus in *Americana* (revue).
   Popularized by Bing Crosby.

(In the Gloaming) By the Fireside (English)
Words and music by Ray Noble, Jimmy Campbell, and Reg Connelly.
Campbell-Connelly Co., Ltd., London, England, 1931/Robbins
  Music Corp.
Introduced in United States by Rudy Vallée.

Cabin in the Cotton
Words by Mitchell Parish, music by Frank Perkins.
Mills Music, Inc.

Chant of the Weed
Music by Don Redman.
Mills Music, Inc.
Theme song of Don Redman and his Orchestra.

Clouds Will Soon Roll By, The
Words and music by Harry Woods and Billy Hill.
Shapiro, Bernstein & Co., Inc.

Contented
Words and music by Roy Turk and Don Bestor.
Leo Feist, Inc./Cromwell Music, Inc.
Introduced by Don Bestor and his Orchestra. Theme song of the
  Carnation Milk radio show.

Corrine, Corrina
Words and music by J. M. Williams and Bo Chatman, with additional
  lyrics by Mitchell Parish.
Mills Music, Inc.
Best-known commercial adaptation of traditional folk blues. Identified with Cab Calloway. Revived in 1960 with best-selling record
  by Ray Peterson (Dunes).

Crazy People
Words and music by Edgar Leslie and James Monaco.
Leo Feist, Inc.
Introduced by The Boswell Sisters in *The Big Broadcast* (film).

(When It's) Darkness on the Delta
Words by Marty Symes and Al J. Neiburg, music by Jerry
  Livingston.
World Music, Inc./Anne-Rachel Music Corp.
Introduced by Mildred Bailey.

Dream Sweetheart
Words and music by Bud Green.
Holliday Publications.

Eadie Was a Lady
Words by B. G. De Sylva, music by Richard A. Whiting and
  Nacio Herb Brown.
Harms, Inc./Anne-Rachel Music Corp.
Introduced by Ethel Merman in *Take a Chance* (musical). Sung by
  Lillian Roth in film version, 1933.

España Cani (Spanish)
Spanish words and music by Pascual Marquina.
Morro Music Corp.
Popular pasadoble originally introduced at bull-fights in Madrid by band of Pascual Marquina. First recording made in Germany by Marek Weber and his Orchestra.

Ev'ryone Says "I Love You"
Words by Bert Kalmar, music by Harry Ruby.
Famous Music Corp.
Introduced by The Marx Brothers in *Horse Feathers* (film).

Fit As a Fiddle
Words and music by Arthur Freed, Al Hoffman, and Al Goodhart.
Leo Feist, Inc.
Introduced by Harry Richman in *George White's Music Hall Varieties* (revue). Sung by Gene Kelly and Donald O'Connor in *Singin' in the Rain* (film, 1952).

Forty-Second Street
Words by Al Dubin, music by Harry Warren.
M. Witmark & Sons.
Introduced by Ruby Keeler in *Forty-Second Street* (film, 1933).

Gamblin' Polka Dot Blues
Words and music by Jimmie Rodgers.
Peer International Corp.
Introduced by Jimmie Rodgers. Revived in 1949 with best-selling record by Tommy Duncan (Capitol).

(I Don't Stand) A Ghost of a Chance (with You)
Words by Bing Crosby and Ned Washington, music by Victor Young.
American Academy of Music, Inc.
Introduced by Bing Crosby.

Good-Bye Blues
Words and music by Jimmy McHugh, Dorothy Fields, and Arnold Johnson.
Robbins Music Corp.
Introduced by The Mills Brothers.

Got the South in My Soul
Words and music by Lee Wiley, Victor Young, and Ned Washington.
Harms, Inc.
Introduced by Lee Wiley, with Victor Young and his Orchestra.

Granada (Mexican)
English words by Dorothy Dodd, Spanish words and music by Augustin Lara.
Southern Music Publishing Co., Inc.
First and best-known adaptation in English.

Have You Forgotten?
Words by Leo Robin, music by Dana Suesse and Nathaniel Shilkret.
Harms, Inc.
Song version of instrumental composition by Suesse and Shilkret,
 entitled "Syncopated Love Song."

Here Lies Love
Words and music by Leo Robin and Ralph Rainger.
Famous Music Corp.
Introduced by Arthur Tracy, Bing Crosby, and Vincent Lopez and
 his Orchestra in *The Big Broadcast* (film).

How Deep Is the Ocean?
Words and music by Irving Berlin.
Irving Berlin Music Corp.
Popularized by Bing Crosby.

How'm I Doin? (Hey, Hey!)
Words and music by Lem Fowler and Don Redman.
Mills Music, Inc./Mayfair Music Corp.
Introduced by The Mills Brothers. Sung by The Mills Brothers in
 Twenty Million Sweethearts (film, 1934).

How's Your Romance?
Words and music by Cole Porter.
Harms, Inc.
Introduced by Erik Rhodes in *Gay Divorce* (musical).

I Am So Eager
Words by Oscar Hammerstein II, music by Jerome Kern.
T. B. Harms Co.
Introduced by Tullio Carminati and Natalie Hall in *Music in the Air*
 (musical).

I Can't Believe It's True
Words and music by Charles Newman, Ben Bernie, and Isham Jones.
Leo Feist, Inc./World Music, Inc.
Introduced by Ben Bernie and his Orchestra.

I Gotta Right To Sing the Blues
Words by Ted Koehler, music by Harold Arlen.
Harms, Inc.
Introduced by Lillian Shade in tenth edition of *Earl Carroll Vanities*
 (revue). Theme song of Jack Teagarden.

I Heard
Music by Don Redman.
Mayfair Music Corp.
Introduced by Don Redman and his Orchestra.

I Played Fiddle for the Czar
Words by Mack Gordon, music by Harry Revel.
De Sylva, Brown & Henderson, Inc.
Introduced by Ben Bernie and his Orchestra.

I Say It's Spinach
Words and music by Irving Berlin.
Irving Berlin Music Corp.
Introduced by J. Harold Murray and Katherine Carrington in
  Face the Music (musical).

I Wanna Be Loved
Words by Billy Rose and Edward Heyman, music by John Green.
Famous Music Corp., 1932, 1933, 1934.
Featured in *Casino de Paris* (nightclub revue, 1934). Revived in
  1950 with best-selling records by The Andrews Sisters (Decca)
  and Dinah Washington (Mercury).

I Want To Be with You
Words by B. G. De Sylva, music by Vincent Youmans.
Harms, Inc./Anne-Rachel Music Corp.
Written for, but not used in, *Take a Chance* (musical).

I Would Do Anything for You, see (I Would Do) Anything for You.

I Wouldn't Trade the Silver in My Mother's Hair (for All the Gold in the World)
Words and music by Little Jack Little and J. Fred Coots.
Bourne Co.
Introduced by Little Jack Little.

If I Love Again
Words by Jack Murray, music by Ben Oakland.
Harms, Inc.
Introduced by Ona Munsen and Stanley Smith in *Hold Your Horses*
  (musical). Best-selling record by Rudy Vallée and his Connecticut
  Yankees.

I'll Never Be the Same
Words by Gus Kahn, music by Matty Malneck and Frank Signorelli.
Robbins Music Corp.
Introduced by Mildred Bailey. First recorded instrumentally in 1931
  by Joe Venuti and Eddie Lang under its original title, "Little
  Buttercup." Also identified with Ruth Etting.

I'll Never Have To Dream Again
Words by Charles Newman, music by Isham Jones.
Leo Feist, Inc.

I'm Alone
Words by Oscar Hammerstein II, music by Jerome Kern.
T. B. Harms Co.
Introduced by Natalie Hall in *Music in the Air* (musical).

I'm Gettin' Sentimental over You
Words by Ned Washington, music by George Bassman.
Mills Music, Inc.
Theme song of Tommy Dorsey and his Orchestra.

I'm Making Hay in the Moonlight
Words by Tot Seymour, music by Jesse Greer.
M. Witmark & Sons.
Introduced by Dick Powell in *Blessed Event* (film).

I'm Playing with Fire
Words and music by Irving Berlin.
Irving Berlin Music Corp.

In a Shanty in Old Shanty Town
Words and music by Joe Young, John Siras, and Little Jack Little.
M. Witmark & Sons/Warock Corp.
Introduced by Little Jack Little. Sung by Teddy Joyce in *The Crooner* (film). First best-selling record by Ted Lewis and his Orchestra. Revived in 1940 with best-selling record by Johnny Long and his Orchestra.

In Egern on the Tegern See
Words by Oscar Hammerstein II, music by Jerome Kern.
T. B. Harms Co.
Introduced by Ivy Scott in *Music in the Air* (musical).

Is I in Love? I Is
Words by Mercer Cook, music by J. Russel Robinson.
De Sylva, Brown & Henderson, Inc./Venus Music Corp.

Isn't It a Pity?
Words by Ira Gershwin, music by George Gershwin.
New World Music Corp.
Introduced by George Givot and Josephine Houston in *Pardon My English* (musical, 1933).

Isn't It Romantic?
Words by Lorenz Hart, music by Richard Rodgers.
Famous Music Corp.
Introduced by Maurice Chevalier, Jeanette MacDonald, Bert Roach, Rolf Sedan, and Tyler Brook in *Love Me Tonight* (film). Title song of *Isn't It Romantic?* (film, 1948).

It Don't Mean a Thing (If It Ain't Got That Swing)
Words by Irving Mills, music by Edward Kennedy "Duke" Ellington.
Mills Music, Inc.
Introduced by Duke Ellington and his Orchestra, vocal by Ivie Anderson.

It Was So Beautiful
Words by Arthur Freed, music by Harry Barris.
De Sylva, Brown & Henderson, Inc.
Introduced by Harry Richman. Sung by Kate Smith in *The Big Broadcast* (film).

It's About Time
Words by John Mercer, music by Peter Tinturin.
Miller Music Corp.
Introduced by Ray Perkins.

It's Only a Shanty in Old Shanty Town, see In a Shanty in Old Shanty Town.

It's Over Because We're Through
Words and music by Willie Bryant and Leonard Reed.
Burke & Van Heusen, Inc.
Theme song of Willie Bryant and his Orchestra.

It's Wearin' Me Down
Words and music by J. C. Johnson and Fletcher Henderson.
Harms, Inc.
Introduced by Fletcher Henderson and his Orchestra.

I've Got the World on a String
Words by Ted Koehler, music by Harold Arlen.
Arko Music Corp.
Introduced by Aida Ward at Cotton Club (New York night club) in *Cotton Club Parade* (nightclub revue). Sung by June Haver and Gloria De Haven in *I'll Get By* (film, 1950).

I've Got To Be There
Words by Ira Gershwin, music by George Gershwin.
New World Music Corp.
Introduced by Carl Randall and Barbara Newberry in *Pardon My English* (musical, 1933).

I've Got You on My Mind
Words and music by Cole Porter.
Harms, Inc.
Introduced by Fred Astaire and Claire Luce in *Gay Divorce* (musical).

I've Told Every Little Star
Words by Oscar Hammerstein II, music by Jerome Kern.
T. B. Harms Co.
Introduced by Walter Slezak in *Music in the Air* (musical). Sung by Gloria Swanson in film version, 1934. Revived in 1961 with best-selling record by Linda Scott (Canadian-American).

Jazz Cocktail
Music by Benny Carter.
Mills Music, Inc.
Introduced by Benny Carter and his Orchestra.

Just an Echo in the Valley (English)
Words and music by Harry Woods, Jimmy Campbell, and
  Reg Connelly.
Campbell-Connelly Co., Ltd., London, England/Robbins Music Corp.
Introduced by Bing Crosby. Interpolated by Crosby in *Going
  Hollywood* (film, 1933).

Just Because You're You
Words and music by Cliff Friend.
Leeds Music Corp.

Keeping Out of Mischief Now
Words by Andy Razaf, music by Thomas "Fats" Waller.
Mayfair Music Corp.
Introduced by Fats Waller.

Kinda Like You
Words by Edward Heyman, music by Vincent Youmans.
Miller Music Corp./The Vincent Youmans Co., Inc.
Introduced by Martha Mason and Nick Long, Jr. in *Through the
  Years* (musical).

Lawd, You Made the Night Too Long
Words by Sam M. Lewis, music by Victor Young.
Shapiro, Bernstein & Co., Inc.
Parody version (1940), "Sam, You Made the Pants Too Long," with
  lyrics by Fred Whitehouse and Milton Berle, featured by comedian
  Joe E. Lewis. Revived in 1966 by Barbra Streisand.

Lazy Rhapsody
Words by Mitchell Parish, music by Edward Kennedy "Duke"
  Ellington.
Mills Music, Inc.
Introduced by Duke Ellington and his Orchestra, vocal by
  Cootie Williams.

Let's All Sing Like the Birdies Sing (English)
Words by Robert Hargreaves and Stanley J. Damerell, music by
  Tolchard Evans.
Campbell-Connelly Co., Ltd., London, England/Mills Music, Inc.
Introduced in England by Henry Hall and the BBC Orchestra.
  Popularized in United States by Ben Bernie.

Let's Call It a Day
Words by Lew Brown, music by Ray Henderson.
Elar Music Corp.
Introduced by Carolyn Nolte and Milton Watson in *Strick Me Pink*
  (musical).

Let's Have Another Cup of Coffee
Words and music by Irving Berlin.
Irving Berlin Music Corp.
Introduced by Katherine Carrington and J. Harold Murray in *Face the Music* (revue). Theme song of the *Maxwell House Show Boat* (radio show). Sung by Ethel Merman in *There's No Business Like Show Business* (film, 1954).

Let's Put Out the Lights (and Go to Sleep)
Words and music by Herman Hupfeld.
Harms, Inc.
Introduced by Rudy Vallée. Popularized by Ozzie Nelson and Harriet Hilliard. Interpolated by Harry Richman, Lili Damita, Bert Lahr, and chorus in *George White's Music Hall Varieties* (revue).

Let's Say Goodbye (English)
Words and music by Noël Coward.
Chappell & Co., Ltd., London, England/Chappell & Co., Inc.
Introduced in London by Rita Lyle and Edward Underdown in *Words and Music* (revue).

Little Street Where Old Friends Meet, A
Words and music by Gus Kahn and Harry Woods.
Edwin H. Morris & Co., Inc./Gus Kahn Music Co.

Lonesome Me
Words by Andy Razaf, music by Thomas "Fats" Waller and Con Conrad.
Gem Music Corp./Anne-Rachel Music Corp.
Introduced by George Hall and his Orchestra.

Lorelei
Words by Ira Gershwin, music by George Gershwin.
New World Music Corp.
Introduced in *Pardon My English* (musical, 1933). Sung by Lyda Roberti on the road and by Carl Randall and Barbara Newberry in New York.

Lost in Your Arms
Words by Sam M. Lewis, music by John Klenner.
Shapiro, Bernstein & Co., Inc.

Louisiana Hayride
Words by Howard Dietz, music by Arthur Schwartz.
Harms, Inc.
Introduced by Tamara Geva, Clifton Webb, chorus, and dancers in *Flying Colors* (revue). Sung by Nanette Fabray in *The Band Wagon* (film, 1953).

Love Me Tonight
Words by Bing Crosby and Ned Washington, music by Victor Young.
Robbins Music Corp.
Introduced by Bing Crosby.

Love Me Tonight
Words by Lorenz Hart, music by Richard Rodgers.
Famous Music Corp.
Introduced by Jeanette MacDonald and Maurice Chevalier in
   Love Me Tonight (film).

Love Me Tonight, see **Yours,** 1937.

Love, You Funny Thing
Words by Roy Turk, music by Fred E. Ahlert.
Fred Ahlert Music Corp./Cromwell Music, Inc.

Luckiest Man in the World
Words by Ira Gershwin, music by George Gershwin.
New World Music Corp.
Introduced by George Givot in *Pardon My English* (musical, 1933).

Lullaby of the Leaves
Words by Joe Young, music by Bernice Petkere.
Bourne Co./Rytvoc, Inc.
Introduced on radio by Freddie Berrens and his Orchestra.

Masquerade
Words by Paul Francis Webster, music by John Jacob Loeb.
Leo Feist, Inc.

Mimi
Words by Lorenz Hart, music by Richard Rodgers.
Famous Music Corp.
Introduced by Maurice Chevalier in *Love Me Tonight* (film). Sung
   by Chevalier in *Pepe* (film, 1960) and *A New Kind of Love* (film,
   1963).

Minnie the Moocher's Wedding Day
Words by Ted Koehler, music by Harold Arlen.
Arko Music Corp.
Introduced by Cab Calloway and his Orchestra at Cotton Club (New
   York nightclub) in *Cotton Club Parade* (nightclub revue).

Mister and Missus Fitch
Words and music by Cole Porter.
Harms, Inc.
Introduced by Luella Gear in *Gay Divorce* (musical).

Moon Song (That Wasn't Meant for Me)
Words by Sam Coslow, music by Arthur Johnston.
Famous Music Corp.
Introduced by Kate Smith in *Hello, Everybody!* (film, 1933).

Music, Music Everywhere (but Not a Song in My Heart)
Words by Ted Koehler, music by Harold Arlen.
De Sylva, Brown & Henderson, Inc.

My Cousin in Milwaukee
Words by Ira Gershwin, music by George Gershwin.
New World Music Corp.
Introduced by Lyda Roberti in *Pardon My English* (musical, 1933).

My Darling
Words by Edward Heyman, music by Richard Myers.
Harms, Inc.
Introduced by John Hale and Josephine Houston in tenth edition of
    Earl Carroll Vanities (revue).

My Lover
Words by B. G. De Sylva, music by Vincent Youmans.
Harms, Inc./Anne-Rachel Music Corp.
Written for, but not used in, *Take a Chance* (musical).

My Mom
Words and music by Walter Donaldson.
Bregman, Vocco & Conn, Inc.

My Romance
Words by Ned Washington, music by Victor Young.
American Academy of Music, Inc./Victor Young Publications, Inc.
Introduced by Arthur Tracy, "The Street Singer."

My Silent Love
Words by Edward Heyman, music by Dana Suesse.
Famous Music Corp.
Adapted from Suesse's instrumental composition, "Jazz Nocturne."

Neath the Silv'ry Moon
Words and music by Cliff Friend.
Robbins Music Corp.
Introduced by Arthur Jarrett.

New Orleans
Words and music by Hoagy Carmichael.
Southern Music Publishing Co., Inc.
Introduced by Hoagy Carmichael.

Night and Day
Words and music by Cole Porter.
Harms, Inc.
Introduced by Fred Astaire and Claire Luce in *Gay Divorce* (musi-
    cal). Sung and danced to by Fred Astaire and Ginger Rogers in
    The Gay Divorcee (film version, 1934). Sung by Deanna Durbin
    in *Lady on a Train* (film, 1945). Performed by Cary Grant and
    Alexis Smith in *Night and Day* (film, 1946).

Oh How I Long To Belong to You
Words by B. G. De Sylva, music by Vincent Youmans.
Harms, Inc./Anne-Rachel Music Corp.
Introduced by June Knight and Jack Whiting in *Take a Chance*
    (musical).

Old Man of the Mountain, The
Words by Billy Hill, music by Victor Young.
American Academy of Music, Inc.
Introduced by The Boswell Sisters.

On a Roof in Manhattan
Words and music by Irving Berlin.
Irving Berlin Music Corp.
Introduced by J. Harold Murray and Katherine Carrington in
Face the Music (revue).

(I'd Love To Spend) One Hour with You
Words by Leo Robin, music by Richard A. Whiting.
Famous Music Corp.
Introduced by Donald Novis, Maurice Chevalier, Jeanette MacDonald,
Charles Ruggles, and Genevieve Tobin in *One Hour with You*
(film). Signature theme of Eddie Cantor's radio show.

One More Dance
Words by Oscar Hammerstein II, music by Jerome Kern.
T. B. Harms Co.
Introduced by Tullio Carminati in *Music in the Air* (musical).

Organ Grinder, The
Words by Herb Magidson, music by Sam H. Stept.
M. Witmark & Sons/Magidson Music Co., Inc.

Out in the Great Open Spaces
Words by Sam Coslow, music by Arthur Johnston.
Famous Music Corp.
Introduced by Kate Smith in *Hello, Everybody!* (film, 1933).

Party's Over Now, The (English)
Words and music by Noël Coward.
Chappell & Co., Ltd., London, England/Chappell & Co., Inc.
Introduced in London by cast including John Mills, Doris Hare,
Steffi Duna, Joyce Barbour, Romney Brent, and Ivy St. Helier in
finale of *Words and Music* (revue). Used as signature theme by
Noël Coward in cabaret appearances.

Peanut Vendor, The (Cuban)
English words by Marion Sunshine and L. Wolfe Gilbert, music by
Moisés Simons.
Molina y Ca., Havana, Cuba, 1929/Edward B. Marks Music Corp.
Original Spanish title, "El Manisero." Introduced by Moisés Simons
and his Orchestra in *Cubanola* (Cuban revue). Introduced in
United States by Don Azpiazu and his Orchestra. Sung by Law-
rence Tibbett in *Cuban Love Song* (film, 1931) and by Judy Gar-
land in *A Star Is Born* (film, 1954).

Play, Fiddle, Play
Words by Jack Lawrence, music by Emery Deutsch and
Arthur Altman.
Edward B. Marks Music Corp.
Introduced by violinist and orchestra leader Emery Deutsch.

Please
Words and music by Leo Robin and Ralph Rainger.
Famous Music Corp.
Introduced by Bing Crosby in *The Big Broadcast* (film). Sung by
Jack Oakie in *From Hell to Heaven* (film, 1933).

Please Handle with Care
Words and music by F. D. "Pat" Ballard and Harry Stride.
Bibo Music Publishers, Inc.

Rain on the Roof
Words and music by Ann Ronell.
Famous Music Corp.
Introduced by Paul Whiteman and his Orchestra.

Rain, Rain, Go Away!
Words by Edward Heyman and Mack David, music by John Green.
Famous Music Corp.

Rainy Day, A
Words by Howard Dietz, music by Arthur Schwartz.
Harms, Inc.
Introduced by Clifton Webb in *Flying Colors* (musical).

Red Apple, also known as Wouldja for a Big Red Apple
Words and music by Henry Souvaine, Everett Miller, and Johnny
Mercer.
Shubert Music Publishing Corp.
Introduced by Peggy Cartwright, Gordon Smith, and girls in
Americana (revue).

Reefer Man
Words by Andy Razaf, music by J. Russel Robinson.
American Academy of Music, Inc./J. Russel Robinson, Inc.
Introduced by Don Redman and his Orchestra. Performed by Cab
Calloway and his Orchestra in *International House* (film, 1933).

Rise 'n Shine
Words by B. G. De Sylva, music by Vincent Youmans.
Harms, Inc./Anne-Rachel Music Corp.
Introduced by Ethel Merman in *Take a Chance* (musical). Sung by
Lillian Roth in film version, 1933.

Roll Along Kentucky Moon
Words and music by Bill Halley.
Southern Music Publishing Co., Inc.

Sam, You Made the Pants Too Long, see **Lawd, You Made the Night Too Long.**

Satan's L'il Lamb
Words by E. Y. Harburg and John Mercer, music by Harold Arlen.
Harms, Inc.
Introduced by Francetta Malloy and The Musketeers, and danced to by Doris Humphrey, José Limón, and Charles Weidman, in *Americana* (revue).

Say It Isn't So
Words and music by Irving Berlin.
Irving Berlin Music Corp.
Introduced by Rudy Vallée.

Scat Song, The (Scat 'n' Skeet 'n' Hi De Hi)
Words by Mitchell Parish, music by Frank Perkins and Cab Calloway.
Mills Music, Inc.
Introduced by Cab Calloway.

Sentimental Gentleman from Georgia
Words by Mitchell Parish, music by Frank Perkins.
Mills Music, Inc.
Popularized by The Boswell Sisters.

Seven Years with the Wrong Woman
Words and music by Bob Miller.
MCA, Inc.

She Came Rollin' down the Mountain
Words and adaptation of music by Arthur Lippman, Manning Sherwin, and Harry Richman.
De Sylva, Brown & Henderson, Inc./Fred Fisher Music Co., Inc.
Adapted from traditional song, "She'll Be Comin' 'round the Mountain." Introduced by Harry Richman.

Shine on Your Shoes, A
Words by Howard Dietz, music by Arthur Schwartz.
Harms, Inc.
Introduced by Buddy and Vilma Ebsen, Monette Moore, and Larry Adler in *Flying Colors* (revue). Sung by Fred Astaire in *The Band Wagon* (film, 1953).

Should I Be Sweet?
Words by B. G. De Sylva, music by Vincent Youmans.
Harms, Inc./Anne-Rachel Music Corp.
Introduced by June Knight in *Take a Chance* (musical) and sung by Miss Knight in film version, 1933.

Shuffle Off to Buffalo
Words by Al Dubin, music by Harry Warren.
M. Witmark & Sons.
Introduced by Ruby Keeler, Clarence Nordstrom, Ginger Rogers, and
Una Merkel in *Forty-Second Street* (film, 1933). Sung by Jack
Carson and Joan Leslie in *The Hard Way* (film, 1942).

Smile for Me
Words and music by Phil Baxter.
Leo Feist, Inc.
Theme song of *The Fitch Bandwagon* (radio series).

Smokin' Reefers
Words and music by Howard Dietz and Arthur Schwartz.
Harms, Inc.
Introduced by Jean Sargent and ensemble in *Flying Colors* (revue).

So At Last It's Come to This
Words by Gus Kahn, music by Matt Malneck and Frank Signorelli.
Robbins Music Corp.

So Do I
Words by B. G. De Sylva, music by Vincent Youmans.
Harms, Inc./Anne-Rachel Music Corp.
Introduced by Jack Whiting, June Knight, and ensemble in
Take a Chance (musical).

So What?
Words by Ira Gershwin, music by George Gershwin.
New World Music Corp.
Introduced by Josephine Houston, Jack Pearl, and "Guests" in
Pardon My English (musical, 1933).

Soft Lights and Sweet Music
Words and music by Irving Berlin.
Irving Berlin Music Corp.
Introduced by J. Harold Murray and Katherine Carrington in *Face
the Music* (revue).

Somebody Loves You
Words by Charles Tobias, music by Peter De Rose.
Edwin H. Morris & Co., Inc.
Introduced by Vincent Lopez and his Orchestra. Revived in 1961
with best-selling record by Skeeter Davis (RCA Victor).

Someone Stole Gabriel's Horn
Words and music by Irving Mills, Ned Washington, and
Edgar Hayes.
American Academy of Music, Inc.
Introduced by The Mills Blue Rhythm Band.

Someone To Care For
Words by Gus Kahn, music by Harry Warren.
Remick Music Corp.

Something To Do with Spring (English)
Words and music by Noël Coward.
Chappell & Co., Ltd., London, England/Chappell & Co., Inc.
Introduced in London by Joyce Barbour, John Mills, and ensemble
    in *Words and Music* (revue).

Song Is You, The
Words by Oscar Hammerstein II, music by Jerome Kern.
T. B. Harms Co.
Introduced by Tullio Carminati and Natalie Hall in *Music in the Air*
    (musical). Sung by John Boles in film version, 1934.

Speak to Me of Love, also known as Parlez-moi d'Amour
    (French)
English words by Bruce Siever, French words and music by
    Jean Lenoir.
Éditions Smyth, Paris, France, 1930/Harms, Inc./Southern Music
    Publishing Co., Inc.
Introduced in United States by Lucienne Boyer.

Speaking of Love
Words by E. Y. Harburg, music by Vernon Duke.
Harms, Inc.
Introduced by Donald Burr and Dave and Dorothy Fitzgibbon in
    Walk a Little Faster (revue).

Strange As It Seems
Words by Andy Razaf, music by Thomas "Fats" Waller.
American Academy of Music, Inc./Anne-Rachel Music Corp.
Introduced by Art Jarrett.

Strange Interlude
Words by Ben Bernie and Walter Hirsch, music by Phil Baker.
Miller Music Corp./World Music, Inc.
Introduced by Ben Bernie and his Orchestra.

Street of Dreams
Words by Sam Lewis, music by Victor Young.
Miller Music Corp.
Introduced by Morton Downey.

Sweethearts Forever
Words and music by Cliff Friend and Irving Caesar.
M. Witmark & Sons.
Introduced by David Manners in *The Crooner* (film).

Take Me in Your Arms (German)
English words by Mitchell Parish, German words and music by
Fritz Rotter and Alfred Markush.
Musikalienhandlung Alberti, GmbH, Berlin, Germany, 1931/
Mills Music, Inc.
Original German title, "Liebe Was Es Nie." Identified with
Ruth Etting.

Tell Me Why You Smile, Mona Lisa (German)
English words by Raymond B. Egan, German words by
Walter Reisch, music by Robert Stolz.
Alrobi Musikverlag, GmbH, Berlin, Germany, 1931/Leo Feist, Inc.
Original German title, "Warum Lächelst Du, Mona Lisa?" From
Der Raub der Mona Lisa (German film).

Thanksgivin'
Words by Johnny Mercer, music by Hoagy Carmichael.
Southern Music Publishing Co., Inc.

That Silver Haired Daddy of Mine
Words and music by Jimmy Long and Gene Autry.
Westpar Music Corp.
Introduced and best-selling record by Gene Autry.

That's What I Hate about Love
Words by Ted Koehler, music by Harold Arlen.
Arko Music Corp.
Introduced at Cotton Club (New York nightclub) in *Cotton Club
Parade* (nightclub revue).

This Is the Night
Words by Sam Coslow, music by Ralph Rainger.
Famous Music Corp.
Introduced in *This Is the Night* (film).

Three on a Match
Words by Raymond B. Egan, music by Ted Fiorito.
De Sylva, Brown & Henderson, Inc./World Music, Inc.
From *Blondie of the Follies* (film).

Three's a Crowd
Words by Al Dubin and Irving Kahal, music by Harry Warren.
M. Witmark & Sons.
Introduced by David Manners in *The Crooner* (film).

Tom Thumb's Drum (English)
Words and music by Leslie Sarony.
Lawrence Wright Music Co., Ltd., London, England, 1931/
Edward B. Marks Music Corp.
Identified with Rudy Vallée.

Tramps at Sea
Words and music by Herbert Stothart, Jimmy McHugh, and
Dorothy Fields.
Robbins Music Corp.
Introduced by Lawrence Tibbett in *Cuban Love Song* (film, 1931).

Try a Little Tenderness (English)
Words and music by Harry Woods, Jimmy Campbell, and
Reg Connelly.
Campbell-Connelly Co., Ltd., London, England/Robbins Music Corp.
Popularized by Ruth Etting.

Turn Out the Light
Words by B. G. De Sylva, music by Richard A. Whiting and
Nacio Herb Brown.
Harms, Inc./Anne-Rachel Music Corp.
Introduced by Sid Silvers, Jack Haley, June Knight, Jack Whiting,
and chorus in *Take a Chance* (musical).

Twenty Million People
Words by Sam Coslow, music by Arthur Johnston.
Famous Music Corp.
Introduced by Kate Smith in *Hello, Everybody!* (film, 1933).

Underneath the Harlem Moon
Words by Mack Gordon, music by Harry Revel.
De Sylva, Brown & Henderson, Inc.

Wail of the Reefer Man, The
Words by Ted Koehler, music by Harold Arlen.
Arko Music Corp.
Introduced by Cab Calloway at Cotton Club (New York nightclub) in
Cotton Club Parade (nightclub revue).

Waltzing in a Dream
Words by Bing Crosby and Ned Washington, music by Victor Young.
Leeds Music Corp.
Introduced by Bing Crosby.

We Just Couldn't Say Good-bye
Words and music by Harry Woods.
Words & Music, Inc.

We Will Always Be Sweethearts
Words by Leo Robin, music by Oscar Straus.
Famous Music Corp.
Introduced by Maurice Chevalier and Jeanette MacDonald in
One Hour with You (film).

What a Life Trying To Live without You
Words by Charlotte Kent, music by Louis Alter.
Harms, Inc.
Introduced by Helen Morgan.

What a Perfect Combination
Words by Bert Kalmar and Irving Caesar, music by Harry Ruby
and Harry Akst.
Harms, Inc.
Introduced by Eddie Cantor in *The Kid from Spain* (film).

When the Spring Is in the Air
Words by Oscar Hammerstein II, music by Jerome Kern.
T. B. Harms Co.
Introduced by Katherine Carrington and ensemble in *Music in the
Air* (musical).

Where Have We Met Before?
Words by E. Y. Harburg, music by Vernon Duke.
Harms, Inc.
Introduced by John Hundley, Sue Hicks, Donald Burr, and
Patricia Dorn in *Walk a Little Faster* (revue).

Where You Go, I Go
Words by Ira Gershwin, music by George Gershwin.
New World Music Corp.
Introduced by Lyda Roberti and Jack Pearl in *Pardon My English*
(musical, 1933).

Which Side Are You On
Words by Mrs. Sam Reece, music traditional.
Public domain.
Written by wife of Sam Reece, union organizer, during coal strike
in Harlan County, Kentucky in 1932. Music adapted from traditional Baptist hymn. First recorded by The Almanac Singers in
early 1940's.

Willow Weep for Me
Words and music by Ann Ronell.
Bourne Co.
Introduced by Paul Whiteman and his Orchestra, vocal by
Irene Taylor.

(I'm Still without a Sweetheart) With Summer Coming On
Words by Roy Turk, music by Fred E. Ahlert.
Fred Ahlert Music Corp./Cromwell Music, Inc.

Wooden Soldier and the China Doll, The
Words by Charles Newman, music by Isham Jones.
Leo Feist, Inc.

Wouldja for a Big Red Apple, see Red Apple.

You Are Too Beautiful
Words by Lorenz Hart, music by Richard Rodgers.
Harms, Inc.
Introduced by Al Jolson in *Hallelujah, I'm a Bum* (film, 1933).

You Can Depend on Me
Words and music by Charles Carpenter, Louis Dunlap, and
    Earl Hines.
Peer International Corp.
First recording by Louis Armstrong and his Orchestra (Columbia).
    Revived in 1961 with best-selling record by Brenda Lee (Decca).

You Can Make My Life a Bed of Roses
Words and music by Lew Brown and Ray Henderson.
De Sylva, Brown & Henderson, Inc.
Introduced by Buddy Rogers and June Knight in *Hot-cha!* (musical).

Young and Healthy
Words by Al Dubin, music by Harry Warren.
M. Witmark & Sons.
Introduced by Dick Powell in *Forty-Second Street* (film, 1933).

You're an Old Smoothie
Words and music by B. G. De Sylva, Richard A. Whiting, and
    Nacio Herb Brown.
Harms, Inc./Anne-Rachel Music Corp.
Introduced by Ethel Merman and Jack Haley in *Take a Chance*
    (musical). Theme song of Del Courtney and his Orchestra.

You're Blasé (English)
Words by Bruce Sievier, music by Ord Hamilton.
Chappell & Co., Ltd., London, England, 1931/Chappell & Co., Inc.
Introduced in London by Binnie Hale in *Bow Bells* (musical).

You're Everywhere
Words by Edward Heyman, music by Vincent Youmans.
Miller Music Corp./The Vincent Youmans Co., Inc.
Introduced by Natalie Hall and Michael Bartlett in *Through the
    Years* (musical).

You're Getting To Be a Habit with Me
Words by Al Dubin, music by Harry Warren.
M. Witmark & Sons.
Introduced by Bebe Daniels in *Forty-Second Street* (film, 1933).

You're in Love
Words and music by Cole Porter.
Harms, Inc.
Introduced by Fred Astaire, Claire Luce, and Erik Rhodes in
    Gay Divorce (musical).

1932

You've Got Me in the Palm of Your Hand!
Words by Cliff Friend and Edgar Leslie, music by James V. Monaco.
Bregman, Vocco & Conn, Inc.

You've Got What Gets Me
Words by Ira Gershwin, music by George Gershwin.
New World Music Corp.
Introduced by Dorothy Lee and Bert Wheeler in *Girl Crazy* (film).
First recording in 1959 by Ella Fitzgerald (Verve).

1933

1933

Adorable
Words by George Marion, Jr., music by Richard A. Whiting.
Movietone Music Corp.
Introduced by Henry Garat in *Adorable* (film).

After All You're All I'm After
Words by Edward Heyman, music by Arthur Schwartz.
Harms, Inc.
Introduced by John Beal in *She Loves Me Not* (play with music).

After Sundown
Words by Arthur Freed, music by Nacio Herb Brown.
Robbins Music Corp.
Introduced by Bing Crosby in *Going Hollywood* (film).

Ah, but Is It Love?
Words by E. Y. Harburg, music by Jay Gorney.
Harms, Inc.
Introduced by Roger Pryor and Lillian Miles in *Moonlight and Pretzels* (film).

Ah, the Moon Is Here
Words by Irving Kahal, music by Sammy Fain.
M. Witmark & Sons.
Introduced by Dick Powell, Frank McHugh, and girls in *Footlight Parade* (film).

Ain't-cha Glad?
Words by Andy Razaf, music by Thomas "Fats" Waller.
Words & Music, Inc.
Introduced by Fats Waller.

Annie Doesn't Live Here Anymore
Words by Joe Young and Johnny Burke, music by Harold Spina.
Bourne Co./Spina Music/Warock Corp.
Introduced by Fred Waring's Pennsylvanians.

Are You Makin' Any Money?
Words and music by Herman Hupfeld.
Harms, Inc.
Introduced by Lillian Miles in *Moonlight and Pretzels* (film).

Beautiful Girl
Words by Arthur Freed, music by Nacio Herb Brown.
Robbins Music Corp.
Introduced by Bing Crosby in *Going Hollywood* (film).

Beautiful Texas
Words and music by W. Lee O'Daniel.
Shapiro, Bernstein & Co., Inc.
O'Daniel subsequently became Governor of Texas and United
    States Senator from Texas.

Black Eyed Susan Brown
Words by Herb Magidson, music by Al Hoffman and Al Goodhart.
Miller Music Corp./Magidson Music Co., Inc.

Black Moonlight
Words and music by Arthur Johnston and Sam Coslow.
Famous Music Corp.
Introduced by Kitty Kelly in *Too Much Harmony* (film). Popularized
    by Bing Crosby.

Blue Hours
Words by Roy Turk, music by Wayne King and Jerry Castillo.
Leo Feist, Inc./Cromwell Music, Inc.
Introduced by Wayne King and his Orchestra.

Blue Prelude
Words and music by Joe Bishop and Gordon Jenkins.
World Music, Inc.
Introduced by Isham Jones and his Orchestra. Theme song of
    Woody Herman and his Orchestra.

Boulevard of Broken Dreams, The
Words by Al Dubin, music by Harry Warren.
Remick Music Corp.
Introduced by Constance Bennett in *Moulin Rouge* (film, 1934).

By a Waterfall
Words by Irving Kahal, music by Sammy Fain.
M. Witmark & Sons.
Introduced by Dick Powell and Ruby Keeler in *Footlight Parade*
    (film).

Calico Days
Words by Ted Koehler, music by Harold Arlen.
Arko Music Corp.
Introduced by George Dewey Washington at Cotton Club (New York
    night club) in twenty-second edition of *Cotton Club Parade*
    (nightclub revue).

Carioca
Words by Gus Kahn and Edward Eliscu, music by Vincent Youmans.
T. B. Harms Co.
Introduced by Etta Moten, and danced to by Fred Astaire and
    Ginger Rogers, in *Flying Down to Rio* (film). Nominated for
    Academy Award, 1934.

Cinderella's Fella
Words by Arthur Freed, music by Nacio Herb Brown.
Robbins Music Corp.
Introduced by Fifi D'Orsay, and reprised by Marion Davies, in
    Going Hollywood (film).

Close Your Eyes
Words and music by Bernice Petkere.
Miller Music Corp.
Identified with Ruth Etting.

Coffee in the Morning (and Kisses in the Night)
Words by Al Dubin, music by Harry Warren.
Remick Music Corp.
Introduced by Constance Bennett and Russ Columbo in *Moulin Rouge*
    (film, 1934).

Come Up and See Me Sometime
Words by Arthur Swanstrom, music by Louis Alter.
Harms, Inc.
Introduced by Lillian Roth in *Take a Chance* (film).

Count Your Blessings
Words by Irving Caesar (verse by Edgar A. Guest), music by
    Ferde Grofé.
T. B. Harms Co.
Introduced in *Palooka* (film, 1934).

Day You Came Along, The
Words and music by Arthur Johnston and Sam Coslow.
Famous Music Corp.
Introduced by Bing Crosby and Judith Allen in *Too Much Harmony*
    (film).

Deep Forest
Words by Andy Razaf, music by Reginald Foresythe and
    Earl Hines.
Mayfair Music Corp.
Introduced by and theme song of Earl Hines and his Orchestra.

Did You Ever See a Dream Walking?
Words by Mack Gordon, music by Harry Revel.
De Sylva, Brown & Henderson, Inc.
Introduced by Art Jarrett and Ginger Rogers in *Sitting Pretty*
    (film).

Dinner at Eight
Words by Dorothy Fields, music by Jimmy McHugh.
Robbins Music Corp.
Promotional song for *Dinner at Eight* (film). Introduced on radio
by Frances Langford.

Do Your Duty
Words and music by "Kid" Wesley "Sox" Wilson.
Northern Music Corp., 1933, 1962.
Introduced by Coot Grant and Sox Wilson. Best-selling record by
Bessie Smith (Columbia).

Doin' the Uptown Lowdown
Words by Mack Gordon, music by Harry Revel.
De Sylva, Brown & Henderson, Inc.
Introduced by Frances Williams in *Broadway thru a Keyhole* (film).

Don't Blame Me
Words by Dorothy Fields, music by Jimmy McHugh.
Robbins Music Corp.
Introduced in Chicago by Jeannette Loff in *Clowns in Clover* (revue,
1932). Promotional song for *Dinner at Eight* (film). Sung by
Freddie Stewart in *Freddie Steps Out* (film, 1946), by Betty Garrett in *Big City* (film, 1948), by Vic Damone in *The Strip* (film,
1951), and by Constance Towers in *Bring Your Smile Along*
(film, 1955).

Down the Old Ox Road
Words by Sam Coslow, music by Arthur Johnston.
Famous Music Corp.
Introduced by Richard Arlen, Lona Andre, Jack Oakie, Mary
Kornman, and Bing Crosby in *College Humor* (film).

Drop Me Off in Harlem, also known as Drop Me Off at Harlem
Words by Nick Kenny, music by Edward Kennedy "Duke"
Ellington.
Mills Music, Inc.
Introduced by Duke Ellington and his Orchestra.

Easter Parade
Words and music by Irving Berlin.
Irving Berlin Music Corp.
A rewritten version of a 1917 Berlin song entitled "Smile and Show
Your Dimple." Introduced by Clifton Webb and Marilyn Miller in
As Thousands Cheer (revue). Sung by Don Ameche in *Alexander's
Ragtime Band* (film, 1938), by Bing Crosby in *Holiday Inn* (film,
1942) and by Fred Astaire and Judy Garland in *Easter Parade*
(film, 1948). Best-selling records in 1942 by Harry James and his
Orchestra (Columbia) and in 1947 by Guy Lombardo and his
Royal Canadians (Decca).

Everything I Have Is Yours
Words by Harold Adamson, music by Burton Lane.
Robbins Music Corp.
Introduced by Joan Crawford and Art Jarrett in *Dancing Lady*
(film). Sung by Monica Lewis in *Everything I Have Is Yours*
(film, 1952).

Experiment
Words and music by Cole Porter.
Harms, Inc.
Introduced in London by Gertrude Lawrence in *Nymph Errant*
(musical).

Farewell to Arms
Words and music by Allie Wrubel and Abner Silver.
Allison's Music, Inc./Words & Music, Inc.
Promotional song for *A Farewell to Arms* (film).

Flying Down to Rio
Words by Gus Kahn and Edward Eliscu, music by Burton Lane.
T. B. Harms Co.
Introduced by Fred Astaire and chorus in *Flying Down to Rio* (film).

Fool in Love, A
Words by George McQueen, music by Sid Lippman.
Bourne Co.

Funnies, The
Words and music by Irving Berlin.
Irving Berlin Music Corp.
Introduced by Marilyn Miller in *As Thousands Cheer* (revue).

Gather Lip Rouge While You May
Words and music by B. G. De Sylva, Leo Robin, and Richard A.
Whiting.
Movietone Music Corp./Anne-Rachel Music Corp.
Introduced by Lilian Harvey in *My Weakness* (film).

Gimme a Pigfoot
Words and music by "Kid" Wesley "Sox" Wilson.
Northern Music Corp., 1933, 1962.
Best-selling record by Bessie Smith (Columbia).

Give Me Liberty or Give Me Love
Words by Leo Robin, music by Ralph Rainger.
Famous Music Corp.
Introduced by Claudette Colbert in *Torch Singer* (film).

Gold Digger's Song, The see **We're in the Money.**

Good Morning Glory
Words by Mack Gordon, music by Harry Revel.
De Sylva, Brown & Henderson, Inc.
Introduced by Jack Haley, Jack Oakie, Art Jarrett, The Pickens
    Sisters, and Ginger Rogers in *Sitting Pretty* (film).

Good Night Little Girl of My Dreams
Words and music by Charles Tobias and Joe Burke.
Edwin H. Morris & Co., Inc./Ahlert-Burke Corp./Joe Burke
    Music Co.

Guy What Takes His Time, A
Words and music by Ralph Rainger.
Famous Music Corp.
Introduced by Mae West in *She Done Him Wrong* (film).

Hallelujah, I'm a Bum
Words by Lorenz Hart, music by Richard Rodgers.
Harms, Inc.
Introduced by Al Jolson in *Hallelujah, I'm a Bum* (film).

Handful of Keys
Music by Thomas "Fats" Waller.
Anne-Rachel Music Corp.
Introduced by Fats Waller.

Happy As the Day Is Long
Words by Ted Koehler, music by Harold Arlen.
Arko Music Corp.
Introduced by Henry "Rubber Legs" Williams at Cotton Club (New
    York night club) in twenty-second edition of *Cotton Club Parade*
    (nightclub revue).

Harlem on My Mind
Words and music by Irving Berlin.
Irving Berlin Music Corp.
Introduced by Ethel Waters in *As Thousands Cheer* (musical).

Harlem Speaks
Music by Edward Kennedy "Duke" Ellington.
American Academy of Music, Inc.
Introduced by Duke Ellington and his Orchestra.

Have You Ever Been Lonely (Have You Ever Been Blue?)
Words by George Brown (pseudonym for Billy Hill), music by
    Peter De Rose.
Shapiro, Bernstein & Co., Inc.
Introduced by Paul Whiteman and his Orchestra.

Heat Wave
Words and music by Irving Berlin.
Irving Berlin Music Corp.
Introduced by Ethel Waters in *As Thousands Cheer* (revue). Sung
by Joan Caulfield in *Blue Skies* (film, 1946) and by Marilyn Monroe in *There's No Business Like Show Business* (film, 1954).

Hey, Young Fella, Close Your Old Umbrella
Words by Dorothy Fields, music by Jimmy McHugh.
Robbins Music Corp.
Introduced in Chicago by Walter Woolf (King) in *Clowns in Clover*
(revue, 1932). Sung by Miss Fields, with McHugh at the piano,
on opening program of Radio City Music Hall (New York, December 27, 1932). Sung by girls' chorus in *Dancing Lady* (film).

Hold Me
Words and music by Little Jack Little, Dave Oppenheim, and Ira
Schuster.
Robbins Music Corp./Anne-Rachel Music Corp./World Music, Inc.
Introduced by Little Jack Little.

Hold Your Man
Words by Arthur Freed, music by Nacio Herb Brown.
Robbins Music Corp.
Introduced by Jean Harlow in *Hold Your Man* (film). Sung by
Winnie Lightner in *Dancing Lady* (film).

Honestly
Words by Charles Newman, music by Isham Jones.
World Music, Inc.

Honeymoon Hotel
Words by Al Dubin, music by Harry Warren.
M. Witmark & Sons.
Introduced by Dick Powell and Ruby Keeler in *Footlight Parade*
(film).

How Could We Be Wrong
Words and music by Cole Porter.
Harms, Inc.
Introduced in London by Gertrude Lawrence in *Nymph Errant*
(musical).

How's Chances
Words and music by Irving Berlin.
Irving Berlin Music Corp.
Introduced by Marilyn Miller and Clifton Webb in *As Thousands
Cheer* (revue).

Hundred Years from Today, A
Words by Joe Young and Ned Washington, music by Victor Young.
Robbins Music Corp./Warock Corp.
Introduced by Kathryn Perry in Lew Leslie's *Blackbirds of 1933-34* (revue). Featured in *Girl from Missouri* (film, 1934).

I Can't Remember
Words and music by Irving Berlin.
Irving Berlin Music Corp.

I Cover the Waterfront
Words by Edward Heyman, music by John Green.
Harms, Inc.
Promotional song which, after achieving popularity, was used as title theme for *I Cover the Waterfront* (film, based on novel of same title by Max Miller). Introduced on radio by Ben Bernie and his Orchestra.

I Guess It Had To Be That Way
Words and music by Arthur Johnston and Sam Coslow.
Famous Music Corp.
Introduced by Bing Crosby in *Too Much Harmony* (film).

I Just Couldn't Take It, Baby
Words by Mann Holiner, music by Alberta Nichols.
Robbins Music Corp./Anne-Rachel Music Corp.
Introduced by Gretchen Branch, Phil Scott, Kathryn Perry, The Duncan Sisters, and Eloise Uggams in Lew Leslie's *Blackbirds of 1933-34* (revue).

I Like Mountain Music
Words by James Cavanaugh, music by Frank Weldon.
M. Witmark & Sons.
Introduced by Ethel Shutta.

I Like the Likes of You
Words by E. Y. Harburg, music by Vernon Duke.
Harms, Inc.
Introduced by Brice Hutchins and Judith Barron, and danced to by Vilma and Buddy Ebsen, in *Ziegfeld Follies of 1934* (revue, 1934).

I Wake Up Smiling
Words by Edgar Leslie, music by Fred E. Ahlert.
Fred Ahlert Music Corp./Bregman, Vocco & Conn, Inc.

I Want To Ring Bells
Words by Maurice Sigler, music by J. Fred Coots.
Mills Music, Inc.
Introduced by Guy Lombardo and his Royal Canadians.

I Want You — I Need You
Words and music by Ben Ellison and Harvey O. Brooks.
Famous Music Corp./Shapiro, Bernstein & Co., Inc.
Introduced by Mae West in *I'm No Angel* (film).

If I Forget You
Words and music by Irving Caesar.
Irving Caesar.
Introduced by James Melton.

If It's True
Words and music by Don Redman, Jule Penrose, and Gus Bently.
American Academy of Music, Inc.
Introduced by Don Redman and his Orchestra.

I'll Be Faithful
Words by Ned Washington, music by Allie Wrubel.
Allison's Music, Inc./Robbins Music Corp.

I'll Be Hard To Handle
Words by Bernard Dougall, music by Jerome Kern.
T. B. Harms Co.
Introduced by Lyda Roberti in *Roberta* (musical).

I'll Take an Option on You
Words by Leo Robin, music by Ralph Rainger.
Harms, Inc.
Introduced by Frank Fay and Betty Doree in *Tattle Tales* (revue).

I'm Down in the Dumps
Words and music by "Kid" Wesley "Sox" Wilson.
Northern Music Corp.
Best-selling record by Bessie Smith (Columbia).

I'm No Angel
Words and music by Gladys Du Bois, Ben Ellison, and Harvey O.
   Brooks.
Famous Music Corp./Shapiro, Bernstein & Co., Inc.
Introduced by Mae West in *I'm No Angel* (film).

I'm Satisfied
Words by Mitchell Parish, music by Edward Kennedy "Duke"
   Ellington.
Mills Music, Inc.
Introduced by Duke Ellington and his Orchestra.

In the Park in Paree
Words by Leo Robin, music by Ralph Rainger.
Famous Music Corp.
Introduced by Maurice Chevalier in *A Bedtime Story* (film).
   Sung by Chevalier in *A New Kind of Love* (film, 1963).

In the Valley of the Moon
Words and music by Charles Tobias and Joe Burke.
Edwin H. Morris & Co., Inc./Joe Burke Music Co./Ahlert-Burke
  Corp.

Inka Dinka Doo
Words by Ben Ryan, music by Jimmy Durante.
Bourne Co.
Introduced by Jimmy Durante in *Palooka* (film, 1934). Sung by
  Durante in *This Time for Keeps* (film, 1947) .

It Isn't Fair
Words by Richard Himber, music by Richard Himber, Frank
  Warshauer, and Sylvester Sprigato.
Words & Music, Inc.
Introduced by Richard Himber and his Orchestra. Revived in 1950
  with best-selling record by Don Cornell (Coral).

It Was a Night in June
Words and music by Mack Gordon and Harry Revel.
De Sylva, Brown & Henderson, Inc.

It's Only a Paper Moon
Words by Billy Rose and E. Y. Harburg, music by Harold Arlen.
Harms, Inc./Anne-Rachel Music Corp.
Introduced as "If You Believed in Me" by Claire Carleton in *The
  Great Magoo* (play, 1932). Sung by June Knight and Charles
  "Buddy" Rogers in *Take a Chance* (film). Best-selling records by
  The Mills Brothers (Decca) and Nat "King" Cole (Capitol).

It's Sunday Down in Caroline
Words by Marty Symes and Al J. Neiburg, music by Jerry
  Livingston.
Hallmark Music Co., Inc./World Music, Inc.

It's the Talk of the Town
Words by Marty Symes and Al J. Neiburg, music by Jerry
  Livingston.
Hallmark Music Co., Inc./World Music, Inc.
Popularized by The Casa Loma Orchestra.

I've Got To Pass Your House To Get to My House
Words and music by Lew Brown.
Elbee Music Co.
Introduced by Gertrude Niesen in *Paradise Revue* (nightclub revue).
  Popularized by Bing Crosby.

I've Got To Sing a Torch Song
Words by Al Dubin, music by Harry Warren.
Remick Music Corp.
Introduced by Dick Powell in *Gold Diggers of 1933* (film).

Jealous of You (Italian)
English words by Marjorie Harper, Italian words by Peppino
Mendes, music by Vittorio Mascheroni.
A & G Carisch & Co., Italy, 1930/Edward B. Marks Music Corp.
Original Italian title, "Tango Della Gelosia." Revived in 1951 with
best-selling record by Connie Francis (M-G-M).

Jimmy Had a Nickel
Words and music by Maurice Sigler, Al Goodhart, and Al Hoffman.
Shapiro, Bernstein & Co., Inc.

Jonny
Words by Edward Heyman, music by Frederick Hollander.
Famous Music Corp.
Introduced by Marlene Dietrich in *Song of Songs* (film).

Keep Young and Beautiful
Words by Al Dubin, music by Harry Warren.
M. Witmark & Sons.
Introduced by Eddie Cantor in *Roman Scandals* (film).

Last Round-Up, The
Words and music by Billy Hill.
Shapiro, Bernstein & Co., Inc.
Introduced by Joe Morrison at New York Paramount Theatre. Sung
by Don Ross in *Ziegfeld Follies of 1934* (revue). Best-selling
record by Bing Crosby (Decca). Sung by Gene Autry in *The
Singing Hill* (film, 1941) and by Roy Rogers in *Don't Fence Me
In* (film, 1945).

Lazybones
Words and music by Johnny Mercer and Hoagy Carmichael.
Southern Music Publishing Co., Inc.
Introduced by Mildred Bailey. Popularized by Rudy Vallée and
by Ben Bernie.

Learn To Croon
Words by Sam Coslow, music by Arthur Johnston.
Famous Music Corp.
Introduced by Bing Crosby in *College Humor* (film).

Let 'Em Eat Cake
Words by Ira Gershwin, music by George Gershwin.
New World Music Corp.
Introduced by William Gaxton and chorus in *Let 'Em Eat Cake*
(musical).

Let's Begin
Words by Otto Harbach, music by Jerome Kern.
T. B. Harms Co.
Introduced by George Murphy in *Roberta* (musical).

Let's Fall in Love
Words by Ted Koehler, music by Harold Arlen.
Bourne Co.
Introduced by Arthur Jarrett, and reprised by Ann Sothern, in *Let's Fall in Love* (film, 1934). Sung by Don Ameche and Dorothy Lamour in *Slightly French* (film, 1949), by Robert Cummings in *Tell It to the Judge* (film, 1949), by Judy Holliday and Jack Lemmon in *It Should Happen to You* (film, 1954), and played by Carmen Cavallero on soundtrack of *The Eddy Duchin Story* (film, 1956).

Let's Go Bavarian
Words by Harold Adamson, music by Burton Lane.
Robbins Music Corp.
Introduced by Joan Crawford and Fred Astaire in *Dancing Lady* (film).

Lonely Heart
Words and music by Irving Berlin.
Irving Berlin Music Corp.
Introduced by Harry Stockwell in *As Thousands Cheer* (revue).

Lonely Lane
Words by Irving Kahal, music by Sammy Fain.
Remick Music Corp.
Introduced by Dick Powell in *College Coach* (film).

Love Is the Sweetest Thing (English)
Words and music by Ray Noble.
Francis, Day & Hunter, Ltd., London, England, 1932/Harms, Inc.
Introduced in United States by Julia Sanderson. Originally introduced in *Say It with Music* (British film).

Love Is the Thing
Words by Ned Washington, music by Victor Young.
Mills Music, Inc./Victor Young Publications, Inc.
Popularized by Ethel Waters.

Love Locked Out (English)
Words by Max Kester (Dodgson), music by Ray Noble.
Victoria Music Publishing Co., Ltd., London, England/Harms, Inc.
Introduced by Ray Noble and his Orchestra.

Love Songs of the Nile
Words by Arthur Freed, music by Nacio Herb Brown.
Robbins Music Corp.
Introduced by Ramon Novarro in *The Barbarian* (film).

Lovely
Words by Edgar Leslie, music by Fred E. Ahlert.
Fred Ahlert Music Corp./Edgar Leslie.

Lover
Words by Lorenz Hart, music by Richard Rodgers.
Famous Music Corp.
Introduced, with special lyrics, by Jeanette MacDonald in *Love Me Tonight* (film, 1932). Revived in 1952 with best-selling record by Peggy Lee (Capitol). Sung by Peggy Lee in *The Jazz Singer* (film, 1953).

Lucky Fella
Words by Dorothy Fields, music by Jimmy McHugh.
Robbins Music Corp.
Introduced in *The Prizefighter and the Lady* (film).

Man on the Flying Trapeze, The (English)
Words and music by Walter O'Keefe.
Robbins Music Corp.
Based on English song, "The Flying Trapeze," written and introduced by English music-hall singer George Leybourne (Joe Saunders) in 1868. Current revised version introduced and featured by American comedian Walter O'Keefe.

Marching Along Together (English)
Words and music by Edward Pola and Franz Steininger; "American" words by Mort Dixon.
The Peter Maurice Music Co., Ltd., London, England, 1932/ Robbins Music Corp.
Introduced in United States by Kate Smith.

Maria Elena, see 1941.

Maybe It's Because (I Love You Too Much)
Words and music by Irving Berlin.
Irving Berlin Music Corp.
First recording by Fred Astaire, with Leo Reisman and his Orchestra (Victor).

Mine
Words by Ira Gershwin, music by George Gershwin.
New World Music Corp.
Introduced by William Gaxton and Lois Moran in *Let 'Em Eat Cake* (musical).

Moonlight and Pretzels
Words by E. Y. Harburg, music by Jay Gorney.
Harms, Inc.
Introduced as production number in *Moonlight and Pretzels* (film).

Moonstruck
Words by Sam Coslow, music by Arthur Johnston.
Famous Music Corp.
Introduced by Bing Crosby in *College Humor* (film).

Moten Swing
Music by Buster Moten and Bennie Moten.
Fred Fisher Music Co., Inc./Peer International Corp.
Introduced by Bennie Moten and his Orchestra.

Mother, the Queen of My Heart
Words and music by Hoyt Bryant and Jimmie Rodgers.
Peer International Corp.
Introduced by Jimmie Rodgers (Victor).

Muchacha
Words by Al Dubin, music by Harry Warren.
Remick Music Corp.
Introduced by Phil Regan, Dolores Del Rio, and chorus in
    In Caliente (film, 1935).

Music Makes Me
Words by Gus Kahn and Edward Eliscu, music by Vincent Youmans.
T. B. Harms Co.
Introduced by Ginger Rogers in *Flying Down to Rio* (film).

My Dancing Lady
Words by Dorothy Fields, music by Jimmy McHugh.
Robbins Music Corp.
Introduced by Art Jarrett, and danced to by Joan Crawford, in
    Dancing Lady (film).

My Happiness, see 1948.

My Hat's on the Side of My Head (English)
Words and music by Harry Woods and Claude Hulbert.
Campbell-Connelly Co., Ltd., London, England/Shapiro, Bernstein
    & Co., Inc.
Introduced by Jack Hulbert in *Jack Ahoy* (British film).

My Love
Words by Ned Washington, music by Victor Young.
Harms, Inc.
Introduced by Lee Wiley. Theme song of *Pond's Vanity Fair*
    (radio program).

My Moonlight Madonna
Words by Paul Francis Webster, adaptation of music by William
    Scotti.
Carl Fischer, Inc./Webster Music Corp.
Adapted from Fibich's "Poème." Introduced by Rudy Vallée.

New Deal Rhythm
Words by E. Y. Harburg, music by Roger Edens.
Harms, Inc.
Introduced in *Take a Chance* (film).

Night Owl
Words and music by Herman Hupfeld.
Harms, Inc.
Introduced by Cliff Edwards in *Take a Chance* (film).

No More Love
Words by Al Dubin, music by Harry Warren.
M. Witmark & Sons.
Introduced by Ruth Etting in *Roman Scandals* (film).

Not for All the Rice in China
Words and music by Irving Berlin.
Irving Berlin Music Corp.
Introduced by Marilyn Miller, Clifton Webb, and ensemble in *As Thousands Cheer* (revue). Sung by Bing Crosby in *Blue Skies* (film, 1946).

Old Man Harlem
Words and music by Rudy Vallée and Hoagy Carmichael.
Southern Music Publishing Co., Inc.
Introduced by Rudy Vallée.

Old Spinning Wheel, The
Words and music by Billy Hill.
Shapiro, Bernstein & Co., Inc.
Radio theme song of child singer Mary Small.

On and On and On
Words by Ira Gershwin, music by George Gershwin.
New World Music Corp.
Introduced by chorus in *Let 'Em Eat Cake* (musical).

On the Trail
Words by Harold Adamson, music by Ferde Grofé.
Robbins Music Corp., 1933, 1946.
From Grofé's orchestral suite, "Grand Canyon Suite." Introduced by Paul Whiteman and his Orchestra. Theme of the Philip Morris radio commercials. Lyrics by Adamson added in 1946.

One Minute to One
Words by Sam Lewis, music by J. Fred Coots.
Leo Feist, Inc./Cromwell Music, Inc.
Introduced by Harry Richman. Theme song of Gray Gordon and his Orchestra.

One Morning in May
Words by Mitchell Parish, music by Hoagy Carmichael.
Mills Music, Inc.
Introduced by Hoagy Carmichael.

Oodles of Noodles
Music by Jimmy Dorsey.
Robbins Music Corp., 1933, 1941.
Saxophone solo by Jimmy Dorsey, recorded by The Dorsey Brothers Orchestra. Developed into the composition, "Contrasts," in 1941 and used as a theme song by The Jimmy Dorsey Orchestra.

Oooh! Look-a-There, Ain't She Pretty?
Words and music by Clarence Todd and Carmen Lombardo.
MCA, Inc./Rytvoc, Inc.
Introduced by Guy Lombardo and his Royal Canadians.

Orchid to You, An
Words and music by Mack Gordon and Harry Revel.
De Sylva, Brown & Henderson, Inc.
Dedicated to newspaper columnist Walter Winchell.

Orchids in the Moonlight
Words by Gus Kahn and Edward Eliscu, music by Vincent Youmans.
T. B. Harms Co.
Introduced by Raul Roulien, and danced to by Fred Astaire and Dolores Del Rio, in *Flying Down to Rio* (film).

Our Big Love Scene
Words by Arthur Freed, music by Nacio Herb Brown.
Robbins Music Corp.
Introduced by Bing Crosby in *Going Hollywood* (film).

Peach Picking Time Down in Georgia
Words and music by Jimmie Rodgers and C. McMichen.
Peer International Corp.
Introduced by Jimmie Rodgers (Victor).

Pettin' in the Park
Words by Al Dubin, music by Harry Warren.
Remick Music Corp.
Introduced by Dick Powell and Ruby Keeler in *Gold Diggers of 1933* (film).

Physician, The
Words and music by Cole Porter.
Harms, Inc.
Introduced in London by Gertrude Lawrence in *Nymph Errant* (musical).

Pig Got Up and Slowly Walked Away, The
Words and music by Benjamin H. Burt.
Jerry Vogel Music Co., Inc.
Introduced by Fred Waring and his Pennsylvanians.

Queer Notions
Music by Coleman Hawkins.
Mills Music, Inc.
Introduced by Fletcher Henderson and his Orchestra, featuring
tenor saxophonist Coleman Hawkins.

Raisin' the Rent
Words by Ted Koehler, music by Harold Arlen.
Arko Music Corp.
Introduced at Cotton Club (New York night club) in twenty-second
edition of *Cotton Club Parade* (nightclub revue).

Remember My Forgotten Man
Words by Al Dubin, music by Harry Warren.
Remick Music Corp.
Introduced by Joan Blondell, Etta Moten, and chorus in *Gold
Diggers of 1933* (film).

Shadow Waltz
Words by Al Dubin, music by Harry Warren.
Remick Music Corp.
Introduced by Dick Powell and Ruby Keeler in *Gold Diggers of 1933*
(film).

Shame on You
Words by Edward Heyman, music by Harold Arlen.
Harms, Inc.

Shanghai Lil
Words by Al Dubin, music by Harry Warren.
M. Witmark & Sons.
Introduced by James Cagney, Ruby Keeler, and chorus in *Footlight
Parade* (film).

Sittin' on a Backyard Fence
Words by Irving Kahal, music by Sammy Fain.
M. Witmark & Sons.
Introduced by Ruby Keeler in *Footlight Parade* (film).

Sittin' on a Log (Pettin' My Dog)
Words and music by Byron Gay and Edward E. Confrey.
Robbins Music Corp.
Introduced by Jeanie Lang, with Jack Denny and his Orchestra.

Slippery Horn
Music by Edward Kennedy "Duke" Ellington.
Mills Music, Inc.
Introduced by Duke Ellington and his Orchestra.

Smoke Gets in Your Eyes
Words by Otto Harbach, music by Jerome Kern.
T. B. Harms Co.
Introduced by Tamara in *Roberta* (musical). Sung by Irene Dunne, and danced to by Fred Astaire, in film version, 1935, and sung by Kathryn Grayson in second film version, *Lovely To Look At*, 1952. Revived in 1958-59 with best-selling record by The Platters (Mercury).

Smoke Rings
Words by Ned Washington, music by H. Eugene Gifford.
American Academy of Music, Inc./Dorsey Bros. Music, Inc.
Introduced by and theme song of Glen Gray and The Casa Loma Orchestra.

Snowball
Words and music by Hoagy Carmichael.
Southern Music Publishing Co., Inc.
Introduced by Louis Armstrong.

Solomon
Words and music by Cole Porter.
Harms, Inc.
Introduced in London by Elisabeth Welch in *Nymph Errant* (musical).

Something Had To Happen
Words by Otto Harbach, music by Jerome Kern.
T. B. Harms Co.
Introduced by Lyda Roberti, Bob Hope, and Raymond Middleton in *Roberta* (musical).

Sophisticated Lady
Words by Mitchell Parish and Irving Mills, music by Edward Kennedy "Duke" Ellington.
Mills Music, Inc.
Introduced by Duke Ellington and his Orchestra.

Stay on the Right Side, Sister
Words by Ted Koehler, music by Rube Bloom.
Robbins Music Corp.
Identified with Ruth Etting. Sung by Doris Day in *Love Me or Leave Me* (film, 1955).

Stormy Weather
Words by Ted Koehler, music by Harold Arlen.
Arko Music Corp.
Written for Cab Calloway, but introduced and first recording by Leo Reisman and his Orchestra, vocal by Harold Arlen (Victor). Sung by Ethel Waters at Cotton Club (New York night club) in twenty-second edition of *Cotton Club Parade* (nightclub revue). Sung by Lena Horne in *Stormy Weather* (film, 1943) and Connee Boswell in *Swing Parade of 1946* (film, 1946).

Street Scene
Music by Alfred Newman.
Robbins Music Corp.
Theme from *Street Scene* (film, 1931).

Supper Time
Words and music by Irving Berlin.
Irving Berlin Music Corp.
Introduced by Ethel Waters in *As Thousands Cheer* (revue).

Sweet Madness
Words by Ned Washington, music by Victor Young.
Harms, Inc.
Introduced in *Murder at the Vanities* (musical).

Sweetheart Darlin'
Words by Gus Kahn, music by Herbert Stothart.
Robbins Music Corp.
Introduced by Marion Davies in *Peg o' My Heart* (film).

Swingy Little Thingy
Words and music by Bud Green and Sam H. Stept.
Mills Music, Inc.
Introduced by Audrey Christie, Max Hoffmann, Jr., and Lester Allen
    in *Shady Lady* (musical).

Take Me for a Buggy Ride
Words and music by "Kid" Wesley "Sox" Wilson.
Northern Music Corp., 1933, 1959.
Best-selling record by Bessie Smith (Columbia).

Temptation
Words by Arthur Freed, music by Nacio Herb Brown.
Robbins Music Corp.
Introduced by Bing Crosby in *Going Hollywood* (film). Revived in
    1953 with best-selling record by Perry Como (Victor). A comedy
    version, entitled "Timtayshun," successful in 1947 as recorded by
    Red Ingle and his Natural Seven, vocal by Cinderella G. Stump
    (pseudonym for Jo Stafford) (Capitol).

Thanks
Words and music by Arthur Johnston and Sam Coslow.
Famous Music Corp.
Introduced by Judith Allen and Bing Crosby in *Too Much Harmony*
    (film).

There's a Bluebird at My Window
Words by Mack Gordon, music by Harry Revel.
De Sylva, Brown & Henderson, Inc.
Introduced by Jack Oakie in *Sitting Pretty* (film).

There's a Cabin in the Pines
Words and music by Billy Hill.
Shapiro, Bernstein & Co., Inc.
Introduced by George Hall and his Orchestra, vocal by
Loretta Lee.

There's a Home in Wyomin'
Words by Billy Hill, music by Peter De Rose.
Shapiro, Bernstein & Co., Inc.
Sung in *Sunset in Wyoming* (film, 1941).

There's a Little Bit of You in Every Love Song
Words by E. Y. Harburg, music by Sammy Fain.
Harms, Inc.
Introduced by Roger Pryor in *Moonlight and Pretzels* (film).

There's Something about a Soldier (English)
Words and music by Noel Gay (pseudonym for Reginald M.
Armitage).
Lawrence Wright Music Co., Ltd., London, England/Mills Music,
Inc.
Introduced by Cicely Courtneidge in *Soldiers of the King*
(British film).

They Call Me Sister Honky Tonk
Words and music by Gladys Du Bois, Ben Ellison, and Harvey
O. Brooks.
Famous Music Corp./Shapiro, Bernstein & Co., Inc.
Introduced by Mae West in *I'm No Angel* (film).

This Little Piggie Went to Market
Words by Sam Coslow, music by Harold "Lefty" Lewis.
De Sylva, Brown & Henderson, Inc.
From *Eight Girls in a Boat* (film, 1934).

Throw Another Log on the Fire
Words and music by Charlie Tobias, Jack Scholl, and Murray
Mencher.
Leo Feist, Inc./Ched Music Co.
Popularized by Morton Downey.

Tony's Wife
Words by Harold Adamson, music by Burton Lane.
Bourne Co.
Identified with Gertrude Niesen. Sung by Lee Tracy in *Turn Back
the Clock* (film).

Touch of Your Hand, The
Words by Otto Harbach, music by Jerome Kern.
T. B. Harms Co.
Introduced by Tamara and William Hain in *Roberta* (musical).

Two Tickets to Georgia
Words and music by Joe Young, Charles Tobias, and J. Fred
Coots.
Bourne Co./Ched Music Co./Warock Corp.
Introduced by Ted Lewis. Popularized by The Pickens Sisters.

Under a Blanket of Blue
Words by Marty Symes and Al J. Neiburg, music by Jerry
Livingston.
World Music, Inc./Anne-Rachel Music Corp.
Introduced by Glen Gray and The Casa Loma Orchestra.

Underneath the Arches (English)
Words and music by Reginald Connelly, Bud Flanagan, and
Joseph McCarthy.
Campbell-Connelly Co., Ltd., London, England, 1952/Robbins
Music Corp.
Introduced in England by Flanagan and Allen, comedy team. Additional lyrics written in United States by McCarthy. Best-selling record in 1948 by Primo Scala's Banjo and Accordion
Orchestra (London) and The Andrews Sisters (Decca).

Wagon Wheels
Words and music by Billy Hill and Peter De Rose.
Shapiro, Bernstein & Co., Inc./Anne-Rachel Music Corp.
Introduced by Everett Marshall in *Ziegfeld Follies of 1934* (revue).
Best-selling record by George Olsen and his Orchestra (Columbia).

Water under the Bridge
Words by E. Y. Harburg, music by Vernon Duke.
Harms, Inc.
Introduced by Everett Marshall, and danced to by Patricia Bowman,
in *Ziegfeld Follies of 1934* (revue).

We'll Make Hay While the Sun Shines
Words by Arthur Freed, music by Nacio Herb Brown.
Robbins Music Corp.
Introduced by Bing Crosby and Marion Davies in *Going Hollywood*
(film).

We're in the Money (The Gold Digger's Song)
Words by Al Dubin, music by Harry Warren.
Remick Music Corp.
Introduced by Ginger Rogers in *Gold Diggers of 1933* (film).

What Is There To Say
Words by E. Y. Harburg, music by Vernon Duke.
T. B. Harms Co.
Introduced by Jane Froman and Everett Marshall in *Ziegfeld
Follies of 1934* (revue).

What More Can I Ask? (English)
Words by A. E. Wilkins, music by Ray Noble.
Lawrence Wright Music Co., Ltd., London, England, 1932/T. B.
Harms Co.
Introduced by Ray Noble and his Orchestra.

Whatever It Is I'm Against It
Words by Bert Kalmar, music by Harry Ruby.
Famous Music Corp.
Introduced by Groucho Marx in *Horse Feathers* (film, 1932).

When It's Lamp Lightin' Time in the Valley
Words and music by Joe Lyons, Sam C. Hart, and "The Vagabonds"
(Herald Goodman, Dean Upoon, and Curt Poulton).
Shapiro, Bernstein & Co., Inc.

When Love Comes Your Way
Words and music by Cole Porter.
Chappell & Co., Ltd., London, England/Harms, Inc.
Written for, but not used in, *Nymph Errant* (British musical). In-
troduced by Derek Williams and Margaret Adams in *Jubilee*
(musical, 1935).

When Tomorrow Comes
Words by Irving Kahal, music by Sammy Fain.
M. Witmark & Sons.
Introduced by Kay Francis in *Mandalay* (film, 1934).

White Jazz
Music by H. Eugene Gifford.
American Academy of Music, Inc.
Best-selling record by The Casa Loma Orchestra.

Who's Afraid of the Big Bad Wolf
Words and music by Frank E. Churchill, with additional lyrics
by Ann Ronell.
Bourne Co./Anne-Rachel Music Corp.
From *The Three Little Pigs* (cartoon film short).

Why Can't This Night Go On Forever
Words by Charles Newman, music by Isham Jones.
World Music, Inc.
Introduced by Jane Froman.

With a Feather in Your Cap
Words by Dorothy Fields, music by Jimmy McHugh.
Robbins Music Corp.
Introduced by Jeanie Lang on opening program at Radio City
Music Hall (New York, December 27, 1932).

Without That Certain Thing (English)
Words and music by Max Nesbitt and Harry Nesbitt.
Irwin Dash Music Co., Ltd., London, England/T. B. Harms Co.

Yesterdays
Words by Otto Harbach, music by Jerome Kern.
T. B. Harms Co.
Introduced by Fay Templeton in *Roberta* (musical).

You Gotta Be a Football Hero (To Get Along with the Beautiful Girls)
Words and music by Al Lewis, Al Sherman, and Buddy Fields.
Leo Feist, Inc./Sherwin Music, Inc.
Popularized by Ben Bernie and his Orchestra.

You Have Taken My Heart
Words by Johnny Mercer, music by Gordon Jenkins.
Anne-Rachel Music Corp.
Introduced by Lanny Ross.

Your Mother's Son-in-Law
Words by Mann Holiner, music by Alberta Nichols.
Anne-Rachel Music Corp.
Introduced by John Mason, Edith Wilson, Toni Ellis, Martha Thomas, Worthy and Thompson, and chorus in Lew Leslie's *Blackbirds of 1933-34* (revue). Debut recording of Billie Holiday, with Benny Goodman and his Orchestra (Columbia).

You're Devastating
Words by Otto Harbach, music by Jerome Kern.
T. B. Harms Co.
Introduced by Bob Hope and Tamara in *Roberta* (musical).

You're Gonna Lose Your Gal
Words by Joe Young, music by James V. Monaco.
International Pauline Corp.
Sung by Doris Day and Gordon MacRae in *Starlift* (film, 1951).

You're Mine, You!
Words by Edward Heyman, music by John Green.
Famous Music Corp.

You're My Past, Present and Future
Words by Mack Gordon, music by Harry Revel.
De Sylva, Brown & Henderson, Inc.
Introduced by Russ Columbo in *Broadway thru a Keyhole* (film).

You're Such a Comfort to Me
Words by Mack Gordon, music by Harry Revel.
De Sylva, Brown & Henderson, Inc.
Introduced by Ginger Rogers, Jack Oakie, Thelma Todd, and Jack Haley in *Sitting Pretty* (film).

You've Got Everything
Words by Gus Kahn, music by Walter Donaldson.
Robbins Music Corp.

You've Got Me Crying Again
Words by Charles Newman, music by Isham Jones.
World Music, Inc.
Popularized by Ruth Etting.

1934

1934

All I Do Is Dream of You
Words by Arthur Freed, music by Nacio Herb Brown.
Robbins Music Corp.
Introduced by Gene Raymond in *Sadie McKee* (film). Sung by Debbie
Reynolds in *Singin' in the Rain* (film, 1952) and by Debbie Reynolds and Bobby Van in *The Affairs of Dobie Gillis* (film, 1953).

All through the Night
Words and music by Cole Porter.
Harms, Inc.
Introduced by Bettina Hall and William Gaxton in *Anything Goes*
(musical). Featured by Bing Crosby in second film version, 1956.

Allá En El Rancho Grande, see **El Rancho Grande.**

Anything Goes
Words and music by Cole Porter.
Harms, Inc.
Introduced by Ethel Merman in *Anything Goes* (musical). Sung by
Miss Merman in first film version, 1936, and by Mitzi Gaynor in
second film version, 1956.

As Long As I Live
Words by Ted Koehler, music by Harold Arlen.
Arko Music Corp.
Introduced by Lena Horne and Avon Long at Cotton Club (New
York nightclub) in twenty-fourth edition of *Cotton Club Parade*
(nightclub revue).

Autumn in New York
Words and music by Vernon Duke.
Harms, Inc.
Introduced by J. Harold Murray in *Thumbs Up* (revue).

Baby, Take a Bow
Words by Lew Brown, music by Jay Gorney.
Movietone Music Corp.
Introduced by James Dunn, Shirley Temple, and Patricia Lee in
Stand Up and Cheer (film).

Be Still, My Heart!
Words and music by Allan Flynn and Jack Egan.
Broadway Music Corp.

Beat of My Heart, The
Words by Johnny Burke, music by Harold Spina.
Bourne Co.
Introduced by Paul Whiteman and his Orchestra.

Believe It, Beloved
Words by George Whiting and Nat Schwartz, music by J. C. Johnson.
Record Music Publishing Co.
Introduced by Fats Waller.

Beloved
Words and music by Victor Schertzinger.
Bourne Co.
Introduced in *Beloved* (film).

Big John's Special
Music by Horace Henderson.
American Academy of Music, Inc.
Swing instrumental, introduced by Fletcher Henderson and his Orchestra. Best-selling record by Benny Goodman and his Orchestra (Victor).

Blame It on My Youth
Words by Edward Heyman, music by Oscar Levant.
T. B. Harms Co.

Blow, Gabriel, Blow
Words and music by Cole Porter.
Harms, Inc.
Introduced by Ethel Merman in *Anything Goes* (musical). Sung by Mitzi Gaynor, Bing Crosby, Donald O' Connor, Jeanmaire, and chorus in second film version, 1956.

Blue Feeling
Music by Edward Kennedy "Duke" Ellington.
American Academy of Music, Inc.
Introduced by Duke Ellington and his Orchestra.

Blue Interlude
Words and music by Irving Mills, Manny Kurtz (Mann Curtis), and Benny Carter.
American Academy of Music, Inc.
Introduced by Benny Carter and his Club Harlem Orchestra.

Blue Lament (Cry for Me)
Words by Dave Franklin, music by Joe Bishop.
World Music, Inc.
Introduced by Isham Jones and his Orchestra, vocal by Eddie Stone.

Blue Moon
Words by Lorenz Hart, music by Richard Rodgers.
Robbins Music Corp.
Only successful Rodgers and Hart song not written especially for films, stage, or television. However, melody was written for never-completed film, *Hollywood Revue*, in which, under the title, "Prayer," it was to be sung by Jean Harlow. With still another lyric and entitled "The Bad in Every Man," melody was introduced by Shirley Ross in *Manhattan Melodrama* (film, 1934). Theme song of *Hollywood Hotel* (radio series). Sung by Mel Tormé in *Words and Music* (film, 1948), by Valentina Cortesa in *Malaya* (film, 1949), and by voice of Jane Froman, dubbed for Susan Hayward, in *With a Song in My Heart* (film, 1952). Best-selling records in 1961 by Elvis Presley (RCA Victor) and The Marcels (Colpix).

Bluebird of Happiness
Words by Edward Heyman, with additional lyrics by Harry Parr Davies, music by Sandor Harmati.
T. B. Harms Co., 1934, 1940.
Introduced at Radio City Music Hall (New York theater). Popularized by Jan Peerce. Best-selling record in 1948 by Art Mooney and his Orchestra (M-G-M).

Breakfast Ball
Words by Ted Koehler, music by Harold Arlen.
Arko Music Corp.
Introduced by Jimmie Lunceford and his Orchestra at Cotton Club (New York nightclub) in *Cotton Club Parade* (nightclub revue).

Breeze (That's Bringin' My Honey Back to Me), The
Words and music by Tony Sacco, Dick Smith, and Al Lewis.
Leeds Music Corp.
Best-selling record by Clarence Williams and his Orchestra (Vocalion).

Broadway's Gone Hill Billy
Words by Lew Brown, music by Jay Gorney.
Movietone Music Corp.
Introduced by Sylvia Froos in *Stand Up and Cheer* (film).

Buddie, Beware
Words and music by Cole Porter.
Harms, Inc.
Introduced by Ethel Merman in *Anything Goes* (musical).

Carry Me Back to the Lone Prairie
Words and music by Carson S. Robison.
Mills Music, Inc.
Adapted from American folk song first published in 1849 and entitled "The Ocean Burial." Subsequently known as "Bury Me Not

on the Lone Prairie" and "The Dying Cowboy." Above version
introduced by Carson Robison and sung by James Melton in *Stars
over Broadway* (film, 1935).

Cattle Call, The
Words and music by Tex Owens.
Forster Music Publishers, Inc.
Best-selling record in 1955 by Eddy Arnold (RCA Victor).

Champagne Waltz, The
Words and music by Con Conrad, Ben Oakland, and Milton Drake.
Famous Music Corp.
Introduced by Jack Denny and his Orchestra. Danced to by Veloz
and Yolanda in *The Champagne Waltz* (film, 1937).

Chime Bells
Words and music by Bob Miller and Elton Britt.
Leeds Music Corp.
Introduced by Elton Britt.

Cocktails for Two
Words and music by Arthur Johnston and Sam Coslow.
Famous Music Corp.
Introduced by Carl Brisson in *Murder at the Vanities* (film). Sung
by Miriam Hopkins in *She Love Me Not* (film). Best-selling record
in 1946 by Spike Jones and his City Slickers (Victor). Featured
by Jones in *Ladies' Man* (film, 1947).

College Rhythm
Words by Mack Gordon, music by Harry Revel.
De Sylva, Brown & Henderson, Inc.
Introdueed by Lyda Roberti and Jack Oakie in *College Rhythm*
(film).

Continental, The
Words by Herb Magidson, music by Con Conrad.
Harms, Inc.
Introduced by Ginger Rogers, danced to by Fred Astaire and Miss
Rogers, and reprised by Erik Rhodes and Lillian Miles in *The
Gay Divorcee* (film). First Academy Award-winning song, 1934.

Cross-Eyed Kelly (from Penn-syl-van-eye-ay)
Words and music by Al Sherman, Al Lewis, and Abner Silver.
Leo Feist, Inc.

Dames
Words by Al Dubin, music by Harry Warren.
Remick Music Corp.
Introduced by Dick Powell in *Dames* (film).

Daybreak Express
Music by Edward Kennedy "Duke" Ellington.
American Academy of Music, Inc.
Introduced by Duke Ellington and his Orchestra.

Deep Purple
Words by Mitchell Parish, music by Peter De Rose.
Robbins Music Corp., 1934, 1939.
Introduced by Paul Whiteman and his Orchestra on radio. Lyrics
by Parish added in 1939. Best-selling vocal version in 1939 by
Larry Clinton and his Orchestra, vocal by Bea Wain (Victor).
Revived in 1963 with best-selling record by Nino Tempo and
April Stevens (Atco). Winner of National Academy of Recording
Arts and Sciences Award for "Best Rock and Roll Recording,"
1963.

Don't Let It Bother You
Words by Mack Gordon, music by Harry Revel.
De Sylva, Brown & Henderson, Inc.
Introduced by unbilled singer, and danced to by Fred Astaire,
in *The Gay Divorcee* (film).

Don't Let Your Love Go Wrong
Words by George Whiting and Nat Schwartz, music by J. C. Johnson.
Record Music Publishing Co.
Introduced by Claude Hopkins and his Orchestra.

Don't Say Goodnight
Words by Al Dubin, music by Harry Warren.
M. Witmark & Sons.
Introduced by Dick Powell and chorus, and danced to by Ricardo
Cortez and Dolores Del Rio, in *Wonder Bar* (film).

Down t'Uncle Bill's
Words and music by Johnny Mercer and Hoagy Carmichael.
Southern Music Publishing Co., Inc.

Down Where Banjos Were Born
Words by Dave Oppenheim, music by Willard Robison and
Edmond Ruggieri.
La Salle Music Publishers, Inc.

Dream of You
Words and music by Sy Oliver, Jimmie Lunceford, and
Edward P. Moran.
Dorsey Bros. Music, Inc.
Introduced by Jimmie Lunceford and his Orchestra.

Earful of Music, An
Words by Gus Kahn, music by Walter Donaldson.
Robbins Music Corp.
Introduced by Ethel Merman in *Kid Millions* (film).

East of the Sun (and West of the Moon)
Words and music by Brooks Bowman.
Anne-Rachel Music Corp.
From the Princeton University Triangle Club production,
Stags at Bay (revue).

Easy Come, Easy Go
Words by Edward Heyman, music by John Green.
Harms, Inc.
Introduced instrumentally as background music in *Bachelor of Arts*
(film).

Ebony Rhapsody
Words and music by Arthur Johnston and Sam Coslow.
Famous Music Corp.
Based on Franz Liszt's "Second Hungarian Rhapsody." Introduced
by Duke Ellington and his Orchestra, vocal by Gertrude Michael,
in *Murder at the Vanities* (film).

(Allá En) El Rancho Grande (My Ranch) (Mexican)
English words by Bartley Costello, Spanish words by J. Del Moral,
music by Silvano R. Ramos.
Edward B. Marks Music Corp.
Best-selling record in United States by Bing Crosby (Decca). New
lyrics by Ben Raleigh added in 1958 for version entitled "El
Rancho Rock." Best-selling record in 1958 by The Champs (Chal-
lenge).

Emaline
Words by Mitchell Parish, music by Frank Perkins.
Mills Music, Inc.
Identified with Mildred Bailey.

Ending with a Kiss
Words by Harlan Thompson, music by Lewis E. Gensler.
Famous Music Corp.
Introduced by Lanny Ross in *Melody in Spring* (film).

Evenin'
Words by Mitchell Parish, music by Harry White.
Mills Music, Inc.
Introduced by Cab Calloway and his Orchestra.

Ev'ry Day
Words by Irving Kahal, music by Sammy Fain.
Remick Music Corp.
Introduced by Rudy Vallée in *Sweet Music* (film, 1935).

Fair and Warmer
Words by Al Dubin, music by Harry Warren.
M. Witmark & Sons.
Introduced by Dick Powell, with Ted Fiorito and his Orchestra, in
Twenty Million Sweethearts (film).

Fare Thee Well Annabelle
Words by Mort Dixon, music by Allie Wrubel.
Remick Music Corp.
Introduced by Rudy Vallée in *Sweet Music* (film, 1935).

Fare-Thee-Well to Harlem
Words by Johnny Mercer, music by Bernie Hanighen.
Southern Music Publishing Co., Inc.
Introduced on records by Paul Whiteman and his Orchestra,
    featuring Jack Teagarden and Johnny Mercer (Bluebird).

Feelin' High
Words by Howard Dietz, music by Walter Donaldson.
Robbins Music Corp.
Introduced by Shirley Ross and Harry Barris in *Hollywood Party*
    (film).

Flirtation Walk
Words and music by Mort Dixon and Allie Wrubel.
Remick Music Corp.
Introduced by Dick Powell and Ruby Keeler in *Flirtation Walk*
    (film).

For All We Know
Words by Sam M. Lewis, music by J. Fred Coots.
Leo Feist, Inc./Cromwell Music, Inc.
Introduced by Morton Downey.

Fun To Be Fooled
Words by Ira Gershwin and E. Y. Harburg, music by Harold Arlen.
New World Music Corp.
Introduced by Frances Williams and Bartlett Simmons in *Life
    Begins at 8:40* (revue).

Girl at the Ironing Board, The
Words by Al Dubin, music by Harry Warren.
Remick Music Corp.
Introduced by Joan Blondell in *Dames* (film).

Goin' to Heaven on a Mule
Words by Al Dubin, music by Harry Warren.
M. Witmark & Sons.
Introduced by Al Jolson in *Wonder Bar* (film).

Good Night Lovely Little Lady
Words and music by Mack Gordon and Harry Revel.
De Sylva, Brown & Henderson, Inc.
Introduced by Bing Crosby in *We're Not Dressing* (film).

Got the Jitters
Words by Billy Rose and Paul Francis Webster, music by
John Jacob Loeb.
Words & Music, Inc./Webster Music Corp.
Introduced by Ben Pollack and his Orchestra in revue at Casino
de Paris (New York nightclub).

Gypsy in Me
Words and music by Cole Porter.
Harms, Inc.
Introduced by Bettina Hall in *Anything Goes* (musical).

Ha-cha-cha
Words and music by Gus Kahn and Werner R. Heymann.
Movietone Music Corp.
Introduced in *Caravan* (film).

Hands across the Table
Words by Mitchell Parish, music by Jean Delettre.
Mills Music, Inc.
Introduced by Lucienne Boyer in *Continental Varieties* (revue).

Happy, I Am Happy
Words by Gus Kahn, music by Werner Richard Heymann.
Movietone Music Corp.
Introduced in *Caravan* (film).

Haunting Me
Words by Eddie De Lange, music by Joseph Myrow.
Mills Music, Inc.

Here Come the British (Bang! Bang!)
Words by Johnny Mercer, music by Bernard Hanighen.
Bourne Co.

Here Goes (a Fool)
Words by Ted Koehler, music by Harold Arlen.
Arko Music Corp.
Introduced by Jimmie Lunceford and his Orchestra at Cotton Club
(New York nightclub) in *Cotton Club Parade* (nightclub revue).

House Is Haunted (by the Echo of Your Last Goodbye), The
Words by Billy Rose, music by Basil G. Adlam.
Bregman, Vocco & Conn, Inc.
Introduced by Jane Froman in *Ziegfeld Follies of 1934* (revue).

How Was I To Know
Words by Eddie De Lange, music by Will Hudson.
American Academy of Music, Inc.

I Ain't Lazy, I'm Just Dreaming
Words and music by Dave Franklin.
World Music, Inc.
Introduced by Isham Jones and his Orchestra.

I Believe in Miracles
Words by Sam M. Lewis, music by Pete Wendling and
    George W. Meyer.
Leo Feist, Inc./Cromwell Music, Inc., 1962.

I Get a Kick out of You
Words and music by Cole Porter.
Harms, Inc.
Introduced by William Gaxton and Ethel Merman in *Anything Goes*
    (musical). Sung by Miss Merman in first film version, 1936; by
    Jeanmaire and male septet in second film version, 1956; and by
    Ginny Simms in *Night and Day* (film, 1946).

I Never Had a Chance
Words and music by Irving Berlin.
Irving Berlin Music Corp.

I Only Have Eyes for You
Words by Al Dubin, music by Harry Warren.
Remick Music Corp.
Introduced by Dick Powell and Ruby Keeler in *Dames* (film).
    Revived in 1956 with best-selling record by The Flamingos (End).

I Saw Stars
Words and music by Maurice Sigler, Al Goodhart, and Al Hoffman.
Robbins Music Corp.
Introduced by Paul Whiteman and his Orchestra.

I See Two Lovers
Words by Mort Dixon, music by Allie Wrubel.
M. Witmark & Sons.
Introduced by Helen Morgan in *Sweet Music* (film, 1935).

I Wish I Were Twins (So I Could Love You Twice As Much)
Words by Frank Loesser and Eddie De Lange, music by
    Joseph Meyer.
Bregman, Vocco & Conn, Inc.
Introduced by Fats Waller and his Rhythm (Victor).

I Woke Up Too Soon
Words and music by Dave Franklin.
De Sylva, Brown & Henderson, Inc.
Introduced by The Casa Loma Orchestra.

If (English)
Words by Robert Hargreaves and Stanley J. Damerell, music by
Tolchard Evans.
Sidney Bron Music Co., Ltd., London, England, 1934, 1950/Ed.
Kassner Music Co., Ltd., London, England, 1934, 1950/Shapiro,
Bernstein & Co., Inc.
Best-selling record in 1950 by Perry Como (Victor).

If Dreams Come True
Words by Irving Mills, music by Edgar Sampson and
Benny Goodman.
American Academy of Music, Inc.
Introduced by Benny Goodman and his Orchestra.

If I Had a Million Dollars
Words by Johnny Mercer, music by Matty Malneck.
Bourne Co.
Introduced by The Boswell Sisters in *Transatlantic Merry-Go-Round*
(film).

If There Is Someone Lovelier Than You
Words by Howard Dietz, music by Arthur Schwartz.
Harms, Inc.
Introduced by Conrad Thibault in *The Gibson Family* (radio series).
Sung by Georges Metaxa in *Revenge with Music* (musical).

I'll Follow My Secret Heart (English)
Words and music by Noël Coward.
Chappell & Co., Ltd., London, England/Chappell & Co., Inc.
Introduced in London by Noël Coward and Yvonne Printemps in
Conversation Piece (musical).

I'll String Along with You
Words by Al Dubin, music by Harry Warren.
M. Witmark & Sons.
Introduced by Dick Powell in *Twenty Million Sweethearts* (film).
Sung by Doris Day in *My Dream Is Yours* (film, 1949) and by
Danny Thomas in *The Jazz Singer* (film, 1953). Used as a theme
in *Battle Cry* (film, 1955).

Ill Wind (You're Blowin' Me No Good)
Words by Ted Koehler, music by Harold Arlen.
Arko Music Corp.
Introduced by Aida Ward at Cotton Club (New York nightclub)
in twenty-fourth edition of *Cotton Club Parade* (nightclub revue).

I'm a Black Sheep Who's Blue
Words and music by Ralph Rainger and Leo Robin.
Famous Music Corp.
Introduced by Dorothy Dell in *Little Miss Marker* (film).

I'm a Hundred Percent for You
Words and music by Irving Mills, Ben Oakland, and Mitchell Parish.
Mills Music, Inc.
Introduced at Cotton Club (New York nightclub) in *Cotton Club Parade* (nightclub revue).

I'm Hummin' — I'm Whistlin' — I'm Singin'
Words and music by Mack Gordon and Harry Revel.
De Sylva, Brown & Henderson, Inc.
Introduced by Bing Crosby in *She Loves Me Not* (film).

I'm Laughin'
Words and music by Lew Brown and Jay Gorney.
Movietone Music Corp.
Introduced by Nick (Dick) Foran, Tess Gardella (Aunt Jemima),
and ensemble in *Stand Up and Cheer* (film).

I'm on a See-Saw (English)
Words by Desmond Carter, music by Vivian Ellis.
Chappell & Co., Ltd., London, England/Chappell & Co., Inc.
Introduced in London in *Jill Darling* (musical).

I'm Popeye the Sailor Man
Words and music by Sammy Lerner.
Famous Music Corp.
Theme song of *Popeye the Sailor* (cartoon film series). Best-selling
record by Frank Luther (Decca).

In a Blue and Pensive Mood
Words and music by Al J. Neiburg, Marty Symes, and
Jerry Livingston.
Hallmark Music Co., Inc./World Music, Inc./Al J. Neiburg,
Music Publisher.

Isle of Capri (English)
Words by Jimmy Kennedy, music by Will Grosz.
The Peter Maurice Music Co., Ltd., London, England/T. B. Harms
Co./Alamo Music, Inc.
Introduced in England by Lew Stone and his Orchestra, vocal by
Nat Gonella. Introduced in United States by Guy Lombardo and
his Royal Canadians. First recording in United States by Xavier
Cugat and his Orchestra. Identified with and best-selling record
in 1935 by Joe "Wingy" Manone.

It's Dark on Observatory Hill
Words by Johnny Burke, music by Harold Spina.
Bourne Co.
Introduced by Ozzie Nelson and his Orchestra, vocal by
Harriet Hilliard.

It's Funny to Everyone but Me
Words by Dave Franklin, music by Isham Jones.
World Music, Inc.
Introduced by Isham Jones and his Orchestra.

It's the Animal in Me
Words and music by Mack Gordon and Harry Revel.
De Sylva, Brown & Henderson, Inc.
Originally introduced in *We're Not Dressing* (film) but deleted
before release of film. Introduced by Ethel Merman, with chorus
of elephants, in *The Big Broadcast of 1936* (film, 1935).

I've Got an Invitation to a Dance
Words and music by Marty Symes, Al J. Neiburg, and
    Jerry Livingston.
Hallmark Music Co., Inc./World Music, Inc.

I've Had My Moments
Words by Gus Kahn, music by Walter Donaldson.
Robbins Music Corp.
Introduced by Eddie Quillan, June Clyde, Jimmy Durante, and
    Polly Moran in *Hollywood Party* (film).

Jazznocracy
Music by Will Hudson.
American Academy of Music, Inc.
Introduced by Jimmie Lunceford and his Orchestra.

Jitter Bug
Words and music by Irving Mills, Cab Calloway, and Ed Swayze.
American Academy of Music, Inc.
First use of term, "jitter-bug," in popular song. Introduced by
    Cab Calloway and his Orchestra.

Judy
Words and music by Hoagy Carmichael and Sammy Lerner.
Southern Music Publishing Co., Inc.

June in January
Words and music by Leo Robin and Ralph Rainger.
Famous Music Corp.
Introduced by Bing Crosby and Kitty Carlisle in *Here Is My Heart*
    (film).

Jungle Fever
Words by Howard Dietz, music by Walter Donaldson.
Robbins Music Corp.
Introduced by The Mills Brothers in *Operator 13* (film).

Junk Man
Words by Frank Loesser, music by Joseph Meyer.
Bregman, Vocco & Conn, Inc.
Introduced by Mildred Bailey.

Keep On Doin' What You're Doin'
Words by Bert Kalmar, music by Harry Ruby.
Bourne Co.
Introduced by Bert Wheeler, Robert Woolsey, Dorothy Lee,
Thelma Todd in *Hips, Hips Hooray* (film).

Keep Romance Alive
Words by Bert Kalmar, music by Harry Ruby.
Bourne Co.
Introduced by Ruth Etting in *Hips, Hips Hooray* (film).

La Cucaracha (Mexican)
Spanish words and music traditional.
Public domain.
An adaptation by Juan Y. D'Lorah introduced in *La Cucaracha*
(film short).

Lamplight
Words and music by James Shelton.
Chappell & Co., Inc.
Introduced by composer in *New Faces of 1934* (revue). Best-selling
record by Hal Kemp and his Orchestra, vocal by Skinnay Ennis.

Let's Get Together
Music by Chick Webb.
American Academy of Music, Inc.
Introduced by and theme song of Chick Webb and his Orchestra.

Let's K-nock K-nees
Words by Mack Gordon, music by Harry Revel.
De Sylva, Brown & Henderson, Inc.
Introduced by Edward Everett Horton and Betty Grable in
The Gay Divorcee (film).

Let's Take a Walk around the Block
Words by Ira Gershwin and E. Y. Harburg, music by Harold Arlen.
New World Music Corp.
Introduced by Earl Oxford and Dixie Dunbar in *Like Begins at 8:40*
(revue).

Lights Are Low, (the Music Is Sweet), The
Words and music by Cliff Friend and Carmen Lombardo.
M. Witmark & Sons.
Introduced by Grace Hayes.

Like a Bolt from the Blue
Words and music by Irving Mills, Ben Oakland, and Mitchell Parish.
Mills Music, Inc.
Introduced at Cotton Club (New York nightclub) in *Cotton Club
Parade* (nightclub revue).

Lilacs in the Rain, see 1939.

Little Dutch Mill
Words by Ralph Freed, music by Harry Barris.
Anne-Rachel Music Corp.
Introduced by Bing Crosby.

Little Man, You've Had a Busy Day
Words by Maurice Sigler and Al Hoffman, music by Mabel Wayne.
T. B. Harms Co.

(Let Me) Live and Love Tonight
Words by Sam Coslow, music by Arthur Johnston.
Famous Music Corp.
Introduced by Carl Brisson and Kitty Carlisle in *Murder at the Vanities* (film).

Lonesome Nights
Words by Irving Mills, music by Benny Carter.
American Academy of Music, Inc.
Introduced by Benny Carter and his Orchestra.

'Long about Midnight
Words and music by Alex Hill and Irving Mills.
American Academy of Music, Inc.
Introduced by Ozzie Nelson and his Orchestra.

Lost in a Fog
Words by Dorothy Fields, music by Jimmy McHugh.
Robbins Music Corp.
Written as a theme for and introduced by The Dorsey Brothers Band, vocal by Jimmy McHugh, at Ben Marden's Riviera (nightclub). Interpolated in *Have a Heart* (film, 1935).

Lotus Blossom, see Marahuana.

Louise, Louise Blues
Words and music by Johnny Temple and J. Mayo Williams.
Leeds Music Corp.
Introduced by Johnny "Geechie" Temple.

Love in Bloom
Words and music by Leo Robin and Ralph Rainger.
Famous Music Corp.
Introduced by Kitty Carlisle and Bing Crosby in *She Loves Me Not* (film). Nominated for Academy Award, 1934. Best-selling record by Bing Crosby. Sung by Lynn Overman in *New York Town* (film, 1941) and by Judy Canova in *True to the Army* (film, 1942). Used by Jack Benny as theme and for comic violin solo.

Love Is Just around the Corner
Words and music by Leo Robin and Lewis Gensler.
Famous Music Corp.
Introduced by Bing Crosby in *Here Is My Heart* (film). Sung by Robert Cummings in *Millions in the Air* (film, 1935).

Love Me
Words by Ned Washington, music by Victor Young.
Words & Music, Inc.
Introduced by Lee Wiley.

Love Thy Neighbor
Words by Mack Gordon, music by Harry Revel.
De Sylva, Brown & Henderson, Inc.
Introduced by Bing Crosby in *We're Not Dressing* (film).

Low-Down Lullaby
Words and music by Ralph Rainger and Leo Robin.
Famous Music Corp.
Introduced by Dorothy Dell in *Little Miss Marker* (film).

Marahuana
Words and music by Sam Coslow and Arthur Johnston.
Famous Music Corp.
Introduced by Gertrude Michael in *Murder at the Vanities* (film).
  Retitled "Lotus Blossom" for version recorded in 1947 by Julia
  Lee (Mercury).

May I?
Words by Mack Gordon, music by Harry Revel.
De Sylva, Brown & Henderson, Inc.
Introduced by Bing Crosby in *We're Not Dressing* (film).

Milk Cow Blues
Words and music by Kokomo Arnold.
Leeds Music Corp.
Introduced by Kokomo Arnold.

Miss Otis Regrets (She's Unable To Lunch Today)
Words and music by Cole Porter.
Harms, Inc.
One of the few Porter songs not written originally for a musical or
  film. Sung by Monty Woolley in *Night and Day* (film, 1946).

(Thank You So Much), Missus Lowsborough-Goodby
Words and music by Cole Porter.
Harms, Inc.
Introduced on records by Cole Porter (Victor).

Mr. and Mrs. Is the Name
Words by Mort Dixon, music by Allie Wrubel.
M. Witmark & Sons.
Introduced by Dick Powell and Ruby Keeler in *Flirtation Walk*
  (film).

Moon Country (Is Home to Me)
Words and music by Hoagy Carmichael and Johnny Mercer.
Southern Music Publishing Co., Inc.
Introduced by Hoagy Carmichael.

Moon Was Yellow, The
Words by Edgar Leslie, music by Fred E. Ahlert.
Fred Ahlert Music Corp./Edgar Leslie.

Moonglow
Words and music by Will Hudson, Eddie De Lange, and Irving Mills.
Mills Music, Inc./Scarsdale Music Corp.
Introduced by The Hudson-De Lange Orchestra. Revived in *Picnic* (film, 1956) in medley with "Theme from Picnic." Best-selling records of medley in 1956 by Morris Stoloff and his Orchestra (Decca) and George Cates and his Orchestra (Coral).

My Old Flame
Words and music by Arthur Johnston and Sam Coslow.
Famous Music Corp.
Introduced by Mae West, accompanied by Duke Ellington and his Orchestra, in *Belle of the Nineties* (film).

My Shawl (Ombo)
English words by Stanley Adams, Spanish words by Pedro Berrios, music by Xavier Cugat.
Edward B. Marks Music Corp.
Theme song of Xavier Cugat and his Orchestra.

Nasty Man
Words by Jack Yellen and Irving Caesar, music by Ray Henderson.
Movietone Music Corp.
Introduced by Alice Faye in *George White's 1935 Scandals* (film, 1935).

Needle in a Haystack, A
Words by Herb Magidson, music by Con Conrad.
Harms, Inc.
Introduced by Fred Astaire in *The Gay Divorcee* (film).

Nevermore (English)
Words and music by Noël Coward.
Chappell & Co., Ltd., London, England/Chappell & Co., Inc.
Introduced in London by Yvonne Printemps in *Conversation Piece* (musical).

New Moon Is over My Shoulder, A
Words by Arthur Freed, music by Nacio Herb Brown.
Robbins Music Corp.
Introduced by Phil Regan in *Student Tour* (film).

(There Was a) Night on the Water
Words and music by Carmen Lombardo, George Clarke, Bert Clarke, and Ellery Rand.
Leeds Music Corp.
Introduced by Guy Lombardo and his Royal Canadians.

No! No! a Thousand Times No!
Words and music by Al Sherman, Al Lewis, and Abner Silver.
Leo Feist, Inc.

Object of My Affection, The
Words and music by Pinky Tomlin, Coy Poe, and Jimmy Grier.
Bourne Co.
Introduced by Pinky Tomlin, with Jimmy Grier and his Orchestra.
Interpolated in *Times Square Lady* (film, 1935) and *The Fabulous Dorseys* (film, 1947).

Okay Toots
Words by Gus Kahn, music by Walter Donaldson.
Robbins Music Corp.
Introduced by Eddie Cantor in *Kid Millions* (film).

Old Water Mill, An
Words and music by Charles Tobias, Jack Scholl, and
Murray Mencher.
Leo Feist, Inc.

Ole Faithful (English)
Words and music by Michael Carr and Joseph Hamilton Kennedy.
Irwin Dash Music Co., Ltd., London, England/ Shapiro, Bernstein
& Co., Inc.
Introduced on records in England by The Original Hillbillies
(Parlaphone).

On Accounta I Love You
Words by Bud Green, music by Sam H. Stept.
Movietone Music Corp.
Introduced by Shirley Temple in *Baby, Take a Bow* (film).

On the Good Ship Lollipop
Words and music by Sidney Clare and Richard A. Whiting.
Movietone Music Corp.
Introduced by Shirley Temple in *Bright Eyes* (film). Sung by Dan
Dailey and Shari Robinson in *You're My Everything* (film, 1949).

Once in a Blue Moon
Words by Mack Gordon, music by Harry Revel.
De Sylva, Brown & Henderson, Inc.
Introduced by Bing Crosby in *We're Not Dressing* (film).

Once in a Lifetime
Words by Gus Kahn, music by Walter Donaldson.
Robbins Music Corp.
Introduced by Marion Davies in *Operator 13* (film).

One Night of Love
Words by Gus Kahn, music by Victor Schertzinger.
Bourne Co.
Introduced by Grace Moore in *One Night of Love* (film) .

Out in the Cold Again
Words by Ted Koehler, music by Rube Bloom.
Anne-Rachel Music Corp.
Identified with Ruth Etting.

Out of Space
Words and music by Joe Bishop, Eugene Gifford, and Winston Collins Tharp.
Anne-Rachel Music Corp., 1934, 1939.
Used for a time as theme song by Jan Savitt and his Orchestra. Lyrics added in 1939. Best-selling record by Glenn Miller and his Orchestra, vocal by Ray Eberle.

Over Somebody Else's Shoulder (I Fell in Love with You)
Words and music by Al Lewis and Al Sherman.
Bregman, Vocco & Conn, Inc.
Introduced by Ozzie Nelson and his Orchestra.

P.S. I Love You
Words by Johnny Mercer, music by Gordon Jenkins.
Commander Publications/MCA, Inc.
Revived in 1953 with best-selling record by The Hilltoppers (Dot).

Pardon My Southern Accent
Words and music by Johnny Mercer and Matty Malneck.
Bourne Co.

Play to Me, Gypsy (Czech-English)
English words by Jimmy Kennedy, Czech words by Beda (pseudonym for Beda Fritz Löhner), music by Karel Vacek.
Wiener Operetten Verlag, Vienna, Austria/B. Feldman & Co., Ltd., London, England/Bourne Co.

Pop! Goes Your Heart
Words by Mort Dixon, music by Allie Wrubel.
M. Witmark & Sons.
Introduced by Dick Powell in *Happiness Ahead* (film).

Rain
Words by Billy Hill, music by Peter De Rose.
Shapiro, Bernstein & Co., Inc.
Introduced on radio by Major Bowes and his Capitol Theatre Family.

Regency Rakes (English)
Words and music by Noël Coward.
Chappell & Co., Ltd., London, England/Chappell & Co., Inc.
Introduced in London by Sidney Grammer, Antony Brian, George Sanders, and Pat Worsley in *Conversation Piece* (musical).

Rhythm of the Raindrops
Words by Gus Kahn, music by James F. Hanley.
De Sylva, Brown & Henderson, Inc.

Ridin' Around in the Rain
Words and music by Gene Austin and Carmen Lombardo.
Anne-Rachel Music Corp.
Introduced by Guy Lombardo and his Royal Canadians. Best-selling record by Bing Crosby (Decca).

Riptide
Words by Gus Kahn, music by Walter Donaldson.
Robbins Music Corp.
Promotional song for *Riptide* (film).

Rock and Roll
Words by Sidney Clare, music by Richard A. Whiting.
Bourne Co.
Introduced by The Boswell Sisters in *Transatlantic Merry-Go-Round* (film).

Roll Along Covered Wagon (English)
Words and music by Jimmy Kennedy.
The Peter Maurice Music Co., Ltd., London, England/Alamo Music, Inc.
Sung in *The Arizonian* (film, 1935) and by The King's Men in *Knights of the Range* (film, 1940).

Roses in the Rain
Words by William Conselman, music by Richard A. Whiting.
Movietone Music Corp.
Introduced in *Handy Andy* (film).

Rug Cutter's Swing
Music by Horace Henderson.
American Academy of Music, Inc.
Swing instrumental, introduced by Fletcher Henderson and his Orchestra.

Sail On, Little Girl, Sail On
Words and music by Amos Easton.
Leeds Music Corp.
Blues, introduced by Bumble Bee Slim (pseudonym for Amos Easton).

Sailors' Chanty (Lady Fair), see There'll Always Be a Lady Fair, 1936.

Sandman
Words by Ralph Freed, music by Bonnie Lake.
Mills Music, Inc.
A theme song of The Dorsey Brothers Orchestra.

Santa Claus Is Comin' to Town
Words and music by J. Fred Coots and Haven Gillespie.
Leo Feist, Inc.
Introduced by George Olsen and his Orchestra, vocal by Ethel Shutta.
    Popularized by Eddie Cantor.

Say When
Words by Ted Koehler, music by Ray Henderson.
T. B. Harms Co.
Introduced by Harry Richman in *Say When* (musical).

Serenade for a Wealthy Widow (English)
Words by Dorothy Fields and Jimmy McHugh, music by
    Reginald Foresythe.
Irwin Dash Music Co., Ltd., London, England/Robbins Music Corp.
Introduced instrumentally by pianist Reginald Foresythe.

(She Walks Like You — She Talks Like You) She Reminds Me of You
Words by Mack Gordon, music by Harry Revel.
De Sylva, Brown & Henderson, Inc.
Introduced by Bing Crosby in *We're Not Dressing* (film).

She's Way Up Thar
Words and music by Lew Brown.
Movietone Music Corp.
Introduced by Lew Brown in *Stand Up and Cheer* (film).

Shoein' the Mare
Words by Ira Gershwin and E. Y. Harburg, music by Harold Arlen.
New World Music Corp.
Introduced by Adrienne Matzenauer in *Life Begins at 8:40* (revue).

Sidewalks of Cuba
Words and music by Mitchell Parish, Irving Mills, and Ben Oakland.
Mills Music, Inc.
Introduced at Cotton Club (New York nightclub) in twenty-fifth
    edition of *Cotton Club Parade* (nightclub revue). Revived in 1946
    and featured instrumentally by Woody Herman and his Orchestra.

Sleepy Head
Words by Gus Kahn, music by Walter Donaldson.
Robbins Music Corp.
Introduced by The Mills Brothers in *Operator 13* (film).

So Help Me
Words and music by Irving Berlin.
Irving Berlin Music Corp.

Solitude
Words by Eddie De Lange and Irving Mills, music by Edward
  Kennedy "Duke" Ellington.
Mills Music, Inc./Scarsdale Music Corp.
Introduced by Duke Ellington and his Orchestra.

Song of the Blacksmith, Clang, Clang, Clang
Words and music by Peter De Rose and Al Stillman.
Famous Music Corp.

South American Joe
Words and music by Cliff Friend and Irving Caesar.
Harms, Inc.

Stand Up and Cheer
Words by Lew Brown, music by Harry Akst.
Movietone Music Corp.
Introduced in *Stand Up and Cheer* (film).

Stars Fell on Alabama
Words by Mitchell Parish, music by Frank Perkins.
Mills Music, Inc.
Identified with Jack Teagarden.

Stay As Sweet As You Are
Words by Mack Gordon, music by Harry Revel.
De Sylva, Brown & Henderson, Inc./Famous Music Corp.
Introduced by Lanny Ross in *College Rhythm* (film).

Stompy Jones
Music by Edward Kennedy "Duke" Ellington.
American Academy of Music, Inc.
Introduced by Duke Ellington and his Orchestra.

Straight from the Shoulder (Right from the Heart)
Words and music by Mack Gordon and Harry Revel.
De Sylva, Brown & Henderson, Inc.
Introduced by Bing Crosby and Kitty Carlisle in *She Loves Me Not*
  (film).

Suddenly
Words by E. Y. Harburg and Billy Rose, music by Vernon Duke.
Harms, Inc.
Introduced by Jane Froman and Everett Marshall in *Ziegfeld
  Follies of 1934* (revue).

Take a Lesson from the Lark
Words and music by Ralph Rainger and Leo Robin.
Famous Music Corp.
Introduced by Ben Bernie and his Orchestra in *Shoot the Works*
  (film).

Take a Number from One to Ten
Words by Mack Gordon, music by Harry Revel.
De Sylva, Brown & Henderson, Inc.
Introduced by Lyda Roberti in *College Rhythm* (film).

Thank You for a Lovely Evening
Words by Dorothy Fields, music by Jimmy McHugh.
Robbins Music Corp.
Introduced by Phil Harris and Leah Ray in revue at Ben Marden's
    Palais Royale (New York nightclub). Sung in *Have a Heart* (film,
    1934) and *Girl from Missouri* (film, 1934).

That's Love
Words by Lorenz Hart, music by Richard Rodgers.
Bourne Co.
Introduced by Anna Sten in *Nana* (film).

Then I'll Be Tired of You
Words by E. Y. Harburg, music by Arthur Schwartz.
Harms, Inc.

There Goes My Heart
Words by Benny Davis, music by Abner Silver.
Gladys Music, Inc./Leo Feist, Inc./Anne-Rachel Music Corp.
Sung by Lina Romay, with Xavier Cugat and his Orchestra, in
    The Heat's On (film, 1943).

There'll Always Be a Lady Fair, see 1936.

There's a House in Harlem for Sale
Words by James Van Heusen, music by Jerry Arlen.
Anne-Rachel Music Corp.
Introduced at Cotton Club (New York nightclub) in twenty-third
    edition of *Cotton Club Parade* (nightclub revue).

This Is Our Last Night Together
Words and music by Jay Gorney and Lew Brown.
Movietone Music Corp.
Introduced by John Boles and Sylvia Froos in *Stand Up and Cheer*
    (film).

Tired of It All
Words by Bert Kalmar, music by Harry Ruby.
Bourne Co.
Introduced by Ruth Etting in *Hips, Hips Hooray* (film).

Tonight Is Mine
Words by Gus Kahn, music by W. Franke Harling.
Bourne Co.
Introduced by Irene Dunne in *Stingaree* (film).

Too Beautiful for Words
Words and music by Bernie Grossman, Russ Columbo, and
Jack Stern.
Harms, Inc.
Introduced by Russ Columbo in *Wake Up and Dream* (film).

True
Words and music by Walter G. Samuels and Leonard Whitcup.
International Pauline Corp.

Trust in Me
Words by Ned Wever, music by Jean Schwartz and Milton Ager.
Advanced Music Corp.
Revived in 1961 with best-selling record by Etta James (Argo).

Try To See It My Way
Words by Mort Dixon, music by Allie Wrubel.
Remick Music Corp.
Introduced by Dick Powell and Joan Blondell in *Dames* (film).

Tumbling Tumbleweeds
Words and music by Bob Nolan.
Williamson Music, Inc./Sam Fox Publishing Co., Inc.
Adapted from "Tumbleweed Trails," poem written by Bob Nolan in
1927. Introduced by Gene Autry in *Tumbling Tumbleweeds* (film,
1935). Best-selling record in 1940 by Bing Crosby (Decca). Sung
by Autry in *Don't Fence Me In* (film, 1945), by Roy Rogers in
Silver Spurs (film, 1943), and by The Sons of the Pioneers in
Hollywood Canteen (film, 1944).

Two Cigarettes in the Dark
Words by Paul Francis Webster, music by Lew Pollack.
De Sylva, Brown & Henderson, Inc.
Introduced by Gloria Grafton in *Kill That Story* (play).

Under Your Spell
Words by Howard Dietz, music by Arthur Schwartz.
Harms, Inc./Movietone Music Corp.
Introduced on radio by Conrad Thibault. Sung by Lawrence Tibbett
in *Under Your Spell* (film, 1936).

Unless (English)
Words and music by Robert Hargreaves, Stanley J. Damerell,
Tolchard Evans, and Henry B. Tilsley.
Francis, Day & Hunter, Ltd., London, England/Bourne Co.
Introduced in England by Henry Hall and the BBC Orchestra. Re-
vived in 1951 with best-selling record by Guy Mitchell (Columbia).

Very Thought of You, The (English)
Words and music by Ray Noble.
Campbell-Connelly Co., Ltd., London, England/M. Witmark & Sons.
Introduced in United States by The Casa Loma Orchestra. Sung by
Doris Day in *Young Man with a Horn* (film, 1950).

Viper's Drag
Music by Thomas "Fats" Waller.
Anne-Rachel Music Corp./Mayfair Music Corp.
Solo jazz piano composition, introduced by Fats Waller.

Waitin' at the Gate for Katy
Words by Gus Kahn, music by Richard A. Whiting.
Movietone Music Corp.
Introduced by John Boles and chorus in *Bottoms Up* (film). Lyrics
unrelated to lyrics of 1927 song, "Waitin' for Katy," also written
by Gus Kahn, with music by Ted Shapiro.

Waltz down the Aisle
Words and music by Cole Porter.
Harms, Inc.
Dropped from *Anything Goes* (musical) and *Jubilee* (musical, 1935).

Were You Foolin'?
Words by Edgar Leslie, music by Fred E. Ahlert.
T. B. Harms Co.
Introduced by Grace Hayes and Newell Chase.

Were Your Ears Burning, Baby?
Words and music by Mack Gordon and Harry Revel.
De Sylva, Brown & Henderson, Inc.
Introduced by Ben Bernie and his Orchestra in *Shoot the Works*
(film).

What a Diff'rence a Day Made (Mexican)
English words by Stanley Adams, Spanish words and music by
Maria Grever.
Edward B. Marks Music Corp.
Original Spanish title, "Cuando Vuelva a Tu Lado." Revived in
1959 with best-selling record by Dinah Washington (Mercury).

What a Little Moonlight Can Do
Words and music by Harry Woods.
Campbell-Connelly Co., Ltd., London, England/Harms, Inc.
Introduced in *Roadhouse Nights* (British film). Identified with
Billie Holiday.

What Can You Say in a Love Song?
Words by Ira Gershwin and E. Y. Harburg, music by Harold Arlen.
New World Music Corp.
Introduced by Josephine Houston and Bartlett Simmons in
Life Begins at 8:40 (revue).

When a Woman Loves a Man
Words by Johnny Mercer, music by Bernard Hanighen and
Gordon Jenkins.
Anne-Rachel Music Corp.

When He Comes Home to Me
Words and music by Leo Robin and Sam Coslow.
Famous Music Corp.
Introduced by Helen Morgan in *You Belong to Me* (film).

When My Ship Comes In
Words by Gus Kahn, music by Walter Donaldson.
Robbins Music Corp.
Introduced by Eddie Cantor in *Kid Millions* (film).

When You Were a Smile on Your Mother's Lips (and a Twinkle in Your Daddy's Eye)
Words by Irving Kahal, music by Sammy Fain.
Remick Music Corp.
Introduced in *Dames* (film).

White Heat
Music by Will Hudson.
American Academy of Music, Inc.
Introduced by Jimmie Lunceford and his Orchestra.

Why Do I Dream Those Dreams
Words by Al Dubin, music by Harry Warren.
M. Witmark & Sons.
Introduced by Dick Powell in *Wonder Bar* (film).

Wild Honey
Words and music by George Hamilton, Harry Tobias, and
Neil Moret (pseudonym for Charles N. Daniels).
Robbins Music Corp.
Introduced by and theme song of George Hamilton and his
Orchestra.

Winter Wonderland
Words by Richard B. Smith, music by Felix Bernard.
Bregman, Vocco & Conn, Inc.
Best-selling record in 1950 by The Andrews Sisters (Decca).

With Every Breath I Take
Words and music by Leo Robin and Ralph Rainger.
Famous Music Corp.
Introduced by Bing Crosby in *Here Is My Heart* (film).

With My Eyes Wide Open, I'm Dreaming
Words by Mack Gordon, music by Harry Revel.
De Sylva, Brown & Henderson, Inc.
Introduced by Dorothy Dell and Jack Oakie in *Shoot the Works*
(film). Sung by Dean Martin in *The Stooge* (film, 1952).

Wonder Bar
Words by Al Dubin, music by Harry Warren.
M. Witmark & Sons.
Introduced by Al Jolson in *Wonder Bar* (film).

1934

World Owes Me a Living, The
Words by Larry Morey, music by Leigh Harline.
Bourne Co.
From *The Grasshopper and the Ants* (*Silly Symphony* cartoon film).

Wrappin' It Up (The Lindy Glide)
Music by Fletcher Henderson.
American Academy of Music, Inc.
Introduced by Fletcher Henderson and his Orchestra. Best-selling
record in 1938 by Benny Goodman and his Orchestra.

You and the Night and the Music
Words by Howard Dietz, music by Arthur Schwartz.
Harms, Inc.
Introduced on radio by Conrad Thibault. Sung by Libby Holman
and Georges Metaxa in *Revenge with Music* (musical).

You Oughta Be in Pictures
Words by Edward Heyman, music by Dana Suesse.
Harms, Inc.
Interpolated by Jane Froman in *Ziegfeld Follies of 1934* (revue).
Sung by Doris Day in *Starlift* (film, 1951).

Your Head on My Shoulder
Words by Harold Adamson, music by Burton Lane.
Robbins Music Corp.
Introduced by Ann Sothern and George Murphy in *Kid Millions*
(film).

You're a Builder-Upper
Words by Ira Gershwin and E. Y. Harburg, music by Harold Arlen.
New World Music Corp.
Introduced by Ray Bolger and Dixie Dunbar in *Life Begins at 8:40*
(revue).

You're Not the Only Oyster in the Stew
Words by Johnny Burke, music by Harold Spina.
Bourne Co.
Best-selling record by Fats Waller and his Rhythm.

You're the Top
Words and music by Cole Porter.
Harms, Inc.
Introduced by Ethel Merman and William Gaxton in *Anything Goes*
(musical). Sung by Miss Merman and Bing Crosby in first film
version, 1936 and by Crosby, Mitzi Gaynor, Donald O'Connor and
Jeanmaire in second film version, 1956. Sung by Ginny Simms and
Cary Grant in *Night and Day* (film, 1946).

1935

1935

About a Quarter to Nine
Words by Al Dubin, music by Harry Warren.
M. Witmark & Sons.
Introduced by Al Jolson in *Go into Your Dance* (film). Sung by
Jolson on soundtrack of *The Jolson Story* (film, 1946).

Accent on Youth
Words by Tot Seymour, music by Vee Lawnhurst.
World Music, Inc.
From *Accent on Youth* (film).

According to the Moonlight
Words by Jack Yellen and Herb Magidson, music by Joseph Meyer.
Movietone Music Corp.
Introduced by Alice Faye in *George White's 1935 Scandals* (film).

Alone
Words by Arthur Freed, music by Nacio Herb Brown.
Robbins Music Corp.
Introduced by Allan Jones and Kitty Carlisle in *A Night at the Opera*
(film). Sung by Judy Garland in *Andy Hardy Meets Debutante*
(film, 1940).

Alone at a Table for Two
Words and music by Billy Hill, Daniel Richman, and Ted Fiorito.
Shapiro, Bernstein & Co., Inc.
Introduced by Ted Fiorito and his Orchestra.

And Then Some
Words by Tot Seymour, music by Vee Lawnhurst.
World Music, Inc./Famous Music Corp.

Animal Crackers in My Soup
Words by Ted Koehler and Irving Caesar, music by Ray Henderson.
Movietone Music Corp.
Introduced by Shirley Temple in *Curly Top* (film).

145

Ballad in Blue
Words by Irving Kahal, music by Hoagy Carmichael.
Southern Music Publishing Co., Inc.

Barrelhouse Music
Words and music by Willard Robison.
Mayfair Music Corp.
Best-selling record by Mildred Bailey.

Beautiful Lady in Blue, A
Words by Sam H. Lewis, music by J. Fred Coots.
Chappell & Co., Inc.
Introduced on radio by Jan Peerce.

Begin the Beguine
Words and music by Cole Porter.
Harms, Inc.
Introduced by June Knight in *Jubilee* (musical). Popularized and best-selling record in 1938 by Artie Shaw and his Orchestra (Bluebird). Sung in *Broadway Melody of 1940* (film, 1940) and *Night and Day* (film, 1946).

Bess, You Is My Woman
Words by Du Bose Heyward and Ira Gershwin, music by George Gershwin.
Gershwin Publishing Corp./New Dawn Music Corp.
Introduced by Todd Duncan and Anne Brown in *Porgy and Bess* (opera). Sung by voice of Robert McFerrin, dubbed for Sidney Poitier, and by voice of Adele Addison, dubbed for Dorothy Dandridge, in film version, 1959.

Blue Lou
Words and music by Edgar Sampson and Irving Mills.
American Academy of Music, Inc.
Introduced by Chick Webb and his Orchestra. Best-selling record by Benny Goodman and his Orchestra (Victor).

Blues Serenade, A
Words and music by Frank Signorelli, Jimmy Lytell, and Vincent Grande; additional lyrics by Mitchell Parish.
Mills Music, Inc.
Theme song of Henry King and his Orchestra.

Breakin' In a Pair of Shoes
Words and music by Ned Washington, Dave Franklin, and Sammy Stept.
Leo Feist, Inc.
Introduced by Benny Goodman and his Orchestra.

Broadway Rhythm
Words by Arthur Freed, music by Nacio Herb Brown.
Robbins Music Corp.
Introduced by Frances Langford in *Broadway Melody of 1936* (film).

Broken Record, The
Words and music by Cliff Friend, Charles Tobias, and Boyd Bunch.
Chappell & Co., Inc.
Best-selling record by Guy Lombardo and his Royal Canadians
(Decca).

Cavernism
Music by James Mundy and Earl Hines.
American Academy of Music, Inc.
Introduced by Earl Hines and his Orchestra.

Change Your Mind
Words and music by Ray Noble.
Paramount Music Corp.
Introduced by Carl Brisson in *Ship Café* (film).

Chasing Shadows
Words by Benny Davis, music by Abner Silver.
De Sylva, Brown & Henderson, Inc.

Cheek to Cheek
Words and music by Irving Berlin.
Irving Berlin Music Corp.
Introduced by Fred Astaire, and danced to by Astaire and Ginger
Rogers, in *Top Hat* (film). Nominated for Academy Award, 1935.

Circus on Parade, The
Words by Lorenz Hart, music by Richard Rodgers.
T. B. Harms Co.
Introduced by Henderson's Singing Razorbacks in *Billy Rose's Jumbo*
(musical). Sung by Doris Day, Martha Raye, and Jimmy Durante
in film version, 1962.

Clouds
Words by Gus Kahn, music by Walter Donaldson.
Robbins Music Corp.

Cockeyed Mayor of Kaunakakai
Words by R. Alex Anderson and Al Stillman, music by R. Alex
Anderson.
Edward B. Marks Music Corp.
Popularized by Clara Inter ("Hilo Hattie"). Sung by Miss Inter in
Song of the Islands (film, 1942). Sung in *Tahiti Nights* (film, 1945).

Cosi Cosa
Words by Ned Washington, music by Bronislaw Kaper and Walter
Jurmann.
Robbins Music Corp.
Introduced by Allan Jones in *A Night at the Opera* (film). Sung by
Jones in *Everybody Sing* (film, 1938).

Curly Top
Words by Ted Koehler, music by Ray Henderson.
Movietone Music Corp.
Introduced by John Boles in *Curly Top* (film).

Dance, My Darlings
Words by Oscar Hammerstein II, music by Sigmund Romberg.
Chappell & Co., Inc.
Introduced by Nancy McCord in *May Wine* (musical).

Diavalo
Words by Lorenz Hart, music by Richard Rodgers.
T. B. Harms Co.
Introduced by Bob Lawrence and Henderson's Singing Razorbacks in
Billy Rose's Jumbo (musical).

Dinner for One Please, James (English)
Words and music by Michael Carr.
The Peter Maurice Music Co., Ltd., London, England/
Chappell & Co., Inc.
Introduced in England by Leslie "Hutch" Hutchinson. Popularized
in United States by Hal Kemp and his Orchestra.

Dixieland Band
Words by Johnny Mercer, music by Bernard Hanighen.
Miller Music Corp.
Introduced by Benny Goodman and his Orchestra (Victor).

Dodging a Divorcee
Music by Reginald Foresythe.
Robbins Music Corp.
Introduced by Reginald Foresythe and his Orchestra (Columbia).

(Shipmates Forever) Don't Give Up the Ship
Words by Al Dubin, music by Harry Warren.
Remick Music Corp.
Introduced by Dick Powell in *Shipmates Forever* (film). Adopted by
United States Naval Academy as one of its "official" songs.

Double Trouble
Words and music by Ralph Rainger, Leo Robin, and Richard A.
Whiting.
Famous Music Corp.
Introduced by Lyda Roberti, Jack Oakie, and Henry Wadsworth in
Big Broadcast of 1936 (film).

Down by the River
Words by Lorenz Hart, music by Richard Rodgers.
Famous Music Corp.
Introduced by Bing Crosby in *Mississippi* (film).

Down South Camp Meetin'
Words by Irving Mills, music by Fletcher Henderson.
American Academy of Music, Inc.
Introduced by Fletcher Henderson and his Orchestra. Best-selling
record by Benny Goodman and his Orchestra (Victor).

(Oh Suzanna) Dust Off That Old Pianna
Words and music by Irving Caesar, Sammy Lerner, and
Gerald Marks.
Samuel M. Lerner Publications/Marlong Music Corp./Irving Caesar.
Introduced by Ozzie Nelson and his Orchestra.

Dusty Road
Words and music by Leon René and Otis René.
Robbins Music Corp.
Sung by Nelson Eddy in *Let Freedom Ring* (film, 1939).

Echo of Spring
Words and music by Clarence Williams, Willie "The Lion" Smith,
and Tausha Hammed.
Leo Feist, Inc.
Introduced by pianist Willie "The Lion" Smith.

Eeny, Meeny, Meiny, Mo
Words and music by Johnny Mercer and Matt Malneck.
Bourne Co.
Introduced by Johnny Mercer in *To Beat the Band* (film). Intro-
duced on radio by Fred Astaire. First recording by Ginger Rogers
and Johnny Mercer (Decca).

Every Now and Then
Words and music by Al Sherman, Abner Silver, and Al Lewis.
T. B. Harms Co.

Farewell, My Lovely
Words by Howard Dietz, music by Arthur Schwartz.
Chappell & Co., Inc.
Introduced by Woods Miller and The Continentals, and danced to by
Paul Haakon and Nina Whitney, in *At Home Abroad* (musical).

Fatal Fascination
Words by Harlan Thompson, music by Lewis E. Gensler.
Paramount Music Corp.
Introduced by Eddie Davis, and reprised by Carl Brisson, in
Ship Café (film).

First You Have Me High (Then You Have Me Low)
Words by Lew Brown, music by Harold Arlen.
T. B. Harms Co.
Introduced by Ethel Merman in *Strike Me Pink* (film, 1936).

Flowers for Madame
Words and music by Charlie Tobias, Charles Newman, and
Murray Mencher.
Harms, Inc.

From the Top of Your Head to the Tip of Your Toes
Words by Mack Gordon, music by Harry Revel.
De Sylva, Brown & Henderson, Inc.
Introduced by Bing Crosby in *Two for Tonight* (film).

Give a Broken Heart a Break
Words by Dave Franklin, music by Isham Jones.
Leo Feist, Inc.
Introduced by Isham Jones and his Orchestra.

Go into Your Dance
Words by Al Dubin, music by Harry Warren.
M. Witmark & Sons.
Introduced by Al Jolson in *Go into Your Dance* (film).

Good Old Fashioned Cocktail (with a Good Old Fashioned Girl), A
Words by Al Dubin, music by Harry Warren.
M. Witmark & Sons.
Introduced by Ruby Keeler in *Go into Your Dance* (film).

Good-bye
Words and music by Gordon Jenkins.
La Salle Music Publishers, Inc.
Signature theme of Benny Goodman and his Orchestra.

Got a Bran' New Suit
Words by Howard Dietz, music by Arthur Schwartz.
Chappell & Co., Inc.
Introduced by Ethel Waters, and danced to by Eleanor Powell, in
At Home Abroad (revue).

Headin' Home
Words by Ned Washington, music by Herbert Stothart.
Robbins Music Corp.
Introduced by Harry Stockwell in *Here Comes the Band* (film).

(Lookie, Lookie, Lookie) Here Comes Cookie
Words and music by Mack Gordon.
De Sylva, Brown & Henderson, Inc.
Introduced by Gracie Allen in *Love in Bloom* (film).

Here's to Romance
Words by Herb Magidson, music by Con Conrad.
Movietone Music Corp.
Introduced by Nino Martini in *Here's to Romance* (film).

Hobo on Park Avenue
Music by Will Hudson.
Mills Music, Inc.
Introduced by and theme song of Will Hudson and his Orchestra.

Hooray for Love
Words by Dorothy Fields, music by Jimmy McHugh.
Bourne Co.
Introduced by Gene Raymond in *Hooray for Love* (film).

Hottentot Potentate, The
Words by Howard Dietz, music by Arthur Schwartz.
Chappell & Co., Inc.
Introduced by Ethel Waters in *At Home Abroad* (revue).

I Built a Dream One Day
Words by Oscar Hammerstein II, music by Sigmund Romberg.
Chappell & Co., Inc.
Introduced by Walter Slezak, Walter Woolf King, and Robert C.
   Fischer in *May Wine* (musical).

I Can't Get Started
Words by Ira Gershwin, music by Vernon Duke.
Chappell & Co., Inc.
Introduced by Bob Hope in *Ziegfeld Follies of 1936* (revue). Theme
   song of Bunny Berigan and his Orchestra.

I Couldn't Believe My Eyes
Words and music by Walter G. Samuels, Leonard Whitcup, and
   Teddy Powell.
Shapiro, Bernstein & Co., Inc.

I Dream Too Much
Words by Dorothy Fields, music by Jerome Kern.
T. B. Harms Co.
Introduced by Lily Pons in *I Dream Too Much* (film).

I Feel a Song Comin' On
Words and music by Jimmy McHugh, Dorothy Fields, and
   George Oppenheimer.
Robbins Music Corp.
Introduced by Harry Barris, and reprised by Alice Faye, Frances
   Langford, and Patsy Kelly, in *Every Night at Eight* (film).

I Feel Like a Feather in the Breeze
Words and music by Mack Gordon and Harry Revel.
Famous Music Corp.
Introduced by girls' chorus in *Collegiate* (film, 1936).

I Found a Dream
Words by Don Hartman, music by Jay Gorney.
Movietone Music Corp.
Introduced by John Boles and Dixie Lee in *Redheads on Parade*
(film).

I Got Love
Words by Dorothy Fields, music by Jerome Kern.
T. B. Harms Co.
Introduced by Lily Pons in *I Dream Too Much* (film).

I Got Plenty o' Nuttin'
Words by Du Bose Heyward and Ira Gershwin, music by George
  Gershwin.
Gershwin Publishing Corp./New Dawn Music Corp.
Introduced by Todd Duncan in *Porgy and Bess* (opera). Sung by
  voice of Robert McFerrin, dubbed for Sidney Poitier, in film ver-
  sion, 1959.

I Hope Gabriel Likes My Music
Words and music by Dave Franklin.
Robbins Music Corp.
Introduced by Louis Armstrong and his Orchestra.

I Loves You Porgy
Words by Du Bose Heyward and Ira Gershwin, music by
  George Gershwin.
Gershwin Publishing Corp./New Dawn Music Corp.
Introduced by Anne Brown in *Porgy and Bess* (opera). Sung by
  voice of Adele Addison, dubbed for Dorothy Dandridge, in film
  version, 1959. Best-selling record in 1959 by Nina Simone (Beth-
  lehem).

I Saw Her at Eight o'Clock
Words by Johnny Mercer, music by Matt Malneck.
Bourne Co.
Introduced by Johnny Mercer, Evelyn Poe, and Fred Keating in
  To Beat the Band (film).

I Sold My Heart to the Junk Man
Words and music by Otis J. René, Jr. and Leon T. René.
Mills Music, Inc.
Best-selling record in 1947 by The Basin Street Boys (Exclusive).

I Was Lucky (C'etait Écrit)
English words by Jack Meskill, French words by A. Hornez, music
  by Jack Stern.
Robbins Music Corp.
Introduced by Maurice Chevalier and Ann Sothern in *Folies Bergere*
  (film).

I Wish I Were Aladdin
Words and music by Mack Gordon and Harry Revel.
De Sylva, Brown & Henderson, Inc.
Introduced by Bing Crosby in *Two for Tonight* (film).

I Wished on the Moon
Words by Dorothy Parker, music by Ralph Rainger.
Famous Music Corp.
Introduced by Bing Crosby in *Big Broadcast of 1936* (film).

I Won't Dance
Words by Otto Harbach and Oscar Hammerstein II, music by
Jerome Kern.
T. B. Harms Co.
Introduced in London by Adele Dixon and Richard Dolman in *Three Sisters* (musical, 1934). Performed by Fred Astaire and Ginger Rogers in *Roberta* (film). Sung by Van Johnson and Lucille Bremer in *Till the Clouds Roll By* (film, 1946). Performed by Marge and Gower Champion in *Lovely To Look At* (film, 1952).

I'd Rather Listen to Your Eyes
Words by Al Dubin, music by Harry Warren.
Remick Music Corp.
Introduced by Dick Powell in *Shipmates Forever* (film).

If I Should Lose You
Words and music by Leo Robin and Ralph Rainger.
Famous Music Corp.
Introduced by Gladys Swarthout and John Boles in *Rose of the Rancho* (film, 1936).

If the Moon Turns Green
Words by Paul Coates, music by Bernard Hanighen.
Bourne Co.

If You Were Mine
Words by Johnny Mercer, music by Matt Malneck.
Bourne Co.
Introduced by Roger Pryor in *To Beat the Band* (film).

I'll Never Say "Never Again" Again
Words and music by Harry Woods.
Bregman, Vocco & Conn, Inc.

I'm Building Up to an Awful Let-Down
Words by Johnny Mercer, music by Fred Astaire.
Bourne Co.
Introduced by Fred Astaire. Popularized in 1938.

I'm Gonna Sit Right Down and Write Myself a Letter
Words by Joe Young, music by Fred E. Ahlert.
De Sylva, Brown & Henderson, Inc.
Introduced by Fats Waller. Revived in 1957 with best-selling record
by Bill Haley and his Comets (Decca).

I'm in the Mood for Love
Words and music by Jimmy McHugh and Dorothy Fields.
Robbins Music Corp.
Introduced by Frances Langford in *Every Night at Eight* (film).
Sung by Miss Langford behind titles of *Palm Springs* (film, 1936)
and by Gloria De Haven in *The Big Clock* (film, 1948).

I'm Livin' in a Great Big Way
Words and music by Jimmy McHugh and Dorothy Fields.
Bourne Co.
Introduced by Bill Robinson and Jeni Le Gon in *Hooray for Love*
(film).

I'm Shooting High
Words by Ted Koehler, music by Jimmy McHugh.
Robbins Music Corp.
Introduced by Shaw and Lee, Jack Oakie, Warner Baxter, and
Alice Faye in *King of Burlesque* (film).

I'm Sitting High on a Hilltop
Words by Gus Kahn, music by Arthur Johnston.
Robbins Music Corp.
Introduced by Dick Powell in *Thanks a Million* (film).

I'm the Echo (You're the Song That I Sing)
Words by Dorothy Fields, music by Jerome Kern.
T. B. Harms Co.
Introduced by Lily Pons in *I Dream Too Much* (film).

In a Little Gypsy Tearoom
Words by Edgar Leslie, music by Joe Burke.
Edwin H. Morris & Co., Inc.
Introduced by Jack Denny and his Orchestra.

In a Sentimental Mood
Words and music by Edward Kennedy "Duke" Ellington.
American Academy of Music, Inc.
Introduced by Duke Ellington and his Orchestra.

In the Evening (When the Sun Goes Down)
Words and music by Leroy Carr.
Leeds Music Corp.
Blues, introduced by Leroy Carr.

In the Middle of a Kiss
Words and music by Sam Coslow.
Famous Music Corp.
Introduced by Johnny Downs, and reprised by Wendy Barrie, in
  College Scandal (film).

Island in the West Indies
Words by Ira Gershwin, music by Vernon Duke.
Chappell & Co., Inc.
Introduced by Gertrude Niesen, and danced to by Josephine Baker,
  in *Ziegfeld Follies of 1936* (revue).

Isn't Love the Grandest Thing?
Words by Jack Scholl, music by Louis Alter.
Leo Feist, Inc.
Introduced by Bert Wheeler and Dorothy Lee in *The Rainmakers*
  (film).

Isn't This a Lovely Day
Words and music by Irving Berlin.
Irving Berlin Music Corp.
Introduced by Fred Astaire in *Top Hat* (film).

It Ain't Necessarily So
Words by Ira Gershwin, music by George Gershwin.
Gershwin Publishing Corp./New Dawn Music Corp.
Introduced by John W. Bubbles in *Porgy and Bess* (opera). Sung by
  Sammy Davis, Jr. in film version, 1959.

It Must Have Been a Dream
Words and music by Charles Lawrence, Les Hite, Al Stillman, and
  Marv Johnson.
Edward B. Marks Music Corp.
Introduced by and theme song of Les Hite and his Orchestra.

It Takes Two To Make a Bargain
Words and music by Mack Gordon and Harry Revel.
De Sylva, Brown & Henderson, Inc.
Introduced by Bing Crosby in *Two for Tonight* (film).

It's an Old Southern Custom
Words by Jack Yellen, music by Joseph Meyer.
Movietone Music Corp.
Introduced by Alice Faye, James Dunn, and Cliff Edwards in
  George White's 1935 Scandals (film).

It's Easy To Remember
Words by Lorenz Hart, music by Richard Rodgers.
Famous Music Corp.
Introduced by Bing Crosby in *Mississippi* (film).

I've Got a Feelin' You're Foolin'
Words by Arthur Freed, music by Nacio Herb Brown.
Robbins Music Corp.
Introduced by Robert Taylor and June Knight, and reprised by
 Frances Langford, in *Broadway Melody of 1936* (film). Sung by
 voice of Jane Froman on soundtrack of *With a Song in My Heart*
 (film, 1952).

I've Got a Pocketful of Sunshine
Words by Gus Kahn, music by Arthur Johnston.
Robbins Music Corp.
Introduced by Dick Powell in *Thanks a Million* (film).

I've Got My Fingers Crossed
Words by Ted Koehler, music by Jimmy McHugh.
Robbins Music Corp.
Introduced by Dixie Dunbar and Fats Waller in *King of Burlesque*
 (film).

I've Got To Get Hot
Words by Jack Yellen, music by Ray Henderson.
T. B. Harms Co.
Introduced by Gracie Barrie in *George White's Scandals* (revue).

Jockey on the Carousel, The
Words by Dorothy Fields, music by Jerome Kern.
T. B. Harms Co.
Introduced by Lily Pons in *I Dream Too Much* (film).

Just Once around the Clock
Words by Oscar Hammerstein II, music by Sigmund Romberg.
Chappell & Co., Inc.
Introduced by Walter Woolf King, Vera Van, and Leo G. Carroll in
 May Wine (musical).

Just One of Those Things
Words and music by Cole Porter.
Harms, Inc.
Introduced by June Knight and Charles Walters in *Jubilee* (musical).
 Sung by Ginny Simms in *Night and Day* (film, 1946), by Doris
 Day in *Lullaby of Broadway* (film, 1951), by Peggy Lee in *The
 Jazz Singer* (film, 1953), by Frank Sinatra in *Young at Heart*
 (film, 1955), and by Maurice Chevalier in *Can-Can* (film, 1960).

Kiss To Build a Dream On, A
Words and music by Bert Kalmar, Harry Ruby, and Oscar
 Hammerstein II.
Miller Music Corp.
Sung by Kay Brown and Louis Armstrong in *The Strip* (film, 1951).

Lady in Red, The
Words by Mort Dixon, music by Allie Wrubel.
Remick Music Corp.
Introduced by Wini Shaw, Edward Everett Horton, George Humbert,
and Judy Canova in *In Caliente* (film).

Let's Dance
Words by Fanny Baldridge, music by Gregory Stone and
Joseph Bonine.
Edward B. Marks Music Corp.
Theme song of Benny Goodman and his Orchestra.

Life Is a Song (Let's Sing It Together)
Words by Joe Young, music by Fred Ahlert.
Robbins Music Corp.
Introduced by Frank Parker.

Lights Out
Words and music by Billy Hill.
Shapiro, Bernstein & Co., Inc.
Introduced by Ozzie Nelson and Harriet Hilliard.

Little Bit Independent, A
Words by Edgar Leslie, music by Joe Burke.
Bregman, Vocco & Conn, Inc.

Little Brown Gal (Hawaiian)
Words and music by Lee Wood, Don McDiarmid, and Johnny Noble.
Bourne Co.

Little Girl Blue
Words by Lorenz Hart, music by Richard Rodgers.
T. B. Harms Co.
Introduced by Gloria Grafton in *Billy Rose's Jumbo* (musical). Sung
by Doris Day in film version, 1962.

Little Things You Used To Do, The
Words by Al Dubin, music by Harry Warren.
M. Witmark & Sons.
Introduced by Helen Morgan in *Go into Your Dance* (film).

Little White Gardenia, A
Words and music by Sam Coslow.
Famous Music Corp.
Introduced by Carl Brisson, and reprised by Mary Ellis, in *All the
King's Horses* (film).

Living on Velvet
Words by Al Dubin, music by Harry Warren.
Remick Music Corp.
Introduced in *Living on Velvet* (film).

Love and a Dime
Words and music by Brooks Bowman.
Anne-Rachel Music Corp.
Introduced in Princeton University Triangle Club production,
Stags at Bay (revue).

Love and Kisses
Words by George Whiting and Nat Schwartz, music by
J. C. Johnson.
Record Music Publishing Co.
Introduced by Wingy Manone and his Orchestra.

Love Is a Dancing Thing
Words by Howard Dietz, music by Arthur Schwartz.
Chappell & Co., Inc.
Introduced by male chorus in production number in *At Home
Abroad* (revue).

Love Me Forever
Words by Gus Kahn, music by Victor Schertzinger.
Bourne Co.
Introduced by Grace Moore in *Love Me Forever* (film).

Love Passes By
Words by Jack Scholl, music by Victor Schertzinger.
Anne-Rachel Music Corp.
Introduced by Tullio Carminati in *Let's Live Tonight* (film).

Lovely Lady
Words by Ted Koehler, music by Jimmy McHugh.
Robbins Music Corp.
Introduced by Kenny Baker in *King of Burlesque* (film).

Lovely To Look At
Words by Dorothy Fields and Jimmy McHugh, music by
Jerome Kern.
T. B. Harms Co.
Introduced by Irene Dunne in *Roberta* (film). Nominated for Academy Award, 1935. Sung by Howard Keel in second film version,
entitled *Lovely To Look At*, 1952.

Lullaby of Broadway
Words by Al Dubin, music by Harry Warren.
M. Witmark & Sons.
Introduced by Wini Shaw and Dick Powell in *Gold Diggers of
Broadway* (film). Academy Award-winning song, 1935. Sung by
Doris Day in *Lullaby of Broadway* (film, 1951).

Lulu's Back in Town
Words by Al Dubin, music by Harry Warren.
M. Witmark & Sons.
Introduced by Dick Powell and The Mills Brothers in *Broadway
Gondolier* (film).

Mad about the Boy (English)
Words and music by Noël Coward.
Chappell & Co., Inc.
Introduced by Joyce Barbour, Steffi Duna, Norah Howard, and
Doris Hare in *Words and Music* (revue).

March Winds and April Showers
Words and music by Walter G. Samuels, Leonard Whitcup, and
Teddy Powell.
La Salle Music Publishers, Inc.

Maybe
Words and music by Allan Flynn and Frank Madden.
Robbins Music Corp.

Me and Marie
Words and music by Cole Porter.
Harms, Inc.
Introduced by Melville Cooper and Mary Boland in *Jubilee* (musical).

Meet Miss America
Words by Johnny Mercer, music by Matt Malneck.
Bourne Co.
Introduced by Joy Hodges in *To Beat the Band* (film).

Merry-Go-Round
Music by Edward Kennedy "Duke" Ellington.
American Academy of Music, Inc.
Introduced by Duke Ellington and his Orchestra.

Midnight in Paris
Words and music by Con Conrad and Herb Magidson.
Movietone Music Corp.
Introduced by Nino Martini in *Here's to Romance* (film).

Miss Brown to You
Words and music by Leo Robin, Richard A. Whiting, and
Ralph Rainger.
Famous Music Corp.
Introduced by Ray Noble and his Orchestra and chorus, and danced
to by Bill Robinson and The Nicholas Brothers, in *The Big Broad-
cast of 1936* (film). Associated with Billie Holiday.

Mr. Bluebird
Words and music by Hoagy Carmichael.
Southern Music Publishing Co., Inc.

Mrs. Worthington (Don't Put Your Daughter on the Stage) (English)
Words and music by Noël Coward.
Chappell & Co., Ltd., London, England/Chappell & Co., Inc.
Introduced by Noël Coward.

Moon over Miami
Words by Edgar Leslie, music by Joe Burke.
Bourne Co.
Introduced by Ted Fiorito and his Orchestra. Theme song of
Dean Hudson and his Orchestra.

Moonburn
Words by Edward Heyman, music by Hoagy Carmichael.
Harms, Inc.
Introduced by Bing Crosby in *Anything Goes* (film, 1936).

Most Beautiful Girl in the World, The
Words by Lorenz Hart, music by Richard Rodgers.
T. B. Harms Co.
Introduced by Donald Novis and Gloria Grafton in *Billy Rose's Jumbo*
(musical). Sung by Stephen Boyd, and reprised by Jimmy Durante,
in film version, 1962. Theme song of Ted Straeter and his Orchestra.

Music Goes 'Round and Around, The
Words by "Red" Hodgson, music by Ed Farley and Mike Riley.
Anne-Rachel Music Corp.
Introduced by Riley and Farley and their Band. Sung by The Ritz
Brothers in *Sing, Baby, Sing* (film, 1936).

Music in My Heart
Words by Dorothy Fields, music by Jimmy McHugh.
Bourne Co.
Introduced by Joey Ray, Bert Wheeler, and Betty Grable in
Nitwits (film).

My Heart and I
Words by Leo Robin, music by Frederick Hollander.
Harms, Inc.
Introduced by Bing Crosby in *Anything Goes* (film, 1936).

My Heart Is an Open Book
Words and music by Mack Gordon.
De Sylva, Brown & Henderson, Inc.
Introduced by Joe Morrison in *Love in Bloom* (film).

My Man's Gone Now
Words by Du Bose Heyward, music by George Gershwin.
Gershwin Publishing Corp./New Dawn Music Corp.
Introduced by Ruby Elzy in *Porgy and Bess* (opera). Sung by voice
of Inez Matthews, dubbed for Ruth Attaway, in film version, 1959.

My Romance
Words by Lorenz Hart, music by Richard Rodgers.
T. B. Harms Co.
Introduced by Donald Novis and Gloria Grafton in *Billy Rose's Jumbo*
(musical). Sung by Doris Day in film version, 1962.

My Very Good Friend, the Milkman
Words by Johnny Burke, music by Harold Spina.
Anne-Rachel Music Corp.
Popularized by Fats Waller.

New O'leans, also known as **New Orleans**
Words by Gus Kahn, music by Arthur Johnston.
Robbins Music Corp.
Introduced by Ramona, with Paul Whiteman and his Orchestra, in
  Thanks a Million (film).

No Strings (I'm Fancy Free)
Words and music by Irving Berlin.
Irving Berlin Music Corp.
Introduced by Fred Astaire in *Top Hat* (film).

Nobody's Darlin' but Mine
Words and music by Jimmie Davis.
Leeds Music Corp.
Introduced by Jimmie Davis. Revived in 1949 with best-selling
  record by Bing Crosby (Decca).

Noche de Ronda, see **Be Mine Tonight,** 1951.

Now I'm a Lady
Words and music by Irving Kahal, Sam Coslow, and Sammy Fain.
Famous Music Corp.
Introduced by Mae West in *Goin' to Town* (film).

Oh Bess, Oh Where's My Bess
Words by Du Bose Heyward and Ira Gershwin, music by
  George Gershwin.
Gershwin Publishing Corp./New Dawn Music Corp.
Introduced by Todd Duncan in *Porgy and Bess* (opera).

On a Sunday Afternoon
Words by Arthur Freed, music by Nacio Herb Brown.
Robbins Music Corp.
Introduced by Vilma Ebsen and Buddy Ebsen in *Broadway Melody
  of 1936* (film).

On Treasure Island
Words by Edgar Leslie, music by Joe Burke.
Joe Burke Music Co./Ahlert-Burke Music Corp./Edgar Leslie.

Oregon Trail, The
Words by Billy Hill, music by Peter De Rose.
Shapiro, Bernstein & Co., Inc.

Outside of You
Words by Al Dubin, music by Harry Warren.
M. Witmark & Sons.
Introduced by Dick Powell in *Broadway Gondolier* (film).

1935

Over and Over Again
Words by Lorenz Hart, music by Richard Rodgers.
T. B. Harms Co.
Introduced by Bob Lawrence and Henderson's Singing Razorbacks in *Billy Rose's Jumbo* (musical). Sung by Doris Day and chorus in film version, 1962.

Page Miss Glory
Words by Al Dubin, music by Harry Warren.
Harms, Inc.
Introduced by Dick Powell and Marion Davies in *Page Miss Glory* (film).

Panamania
Words by Sam Coslow, music by Al Siegel.
Famous Music Corp.
Introduced by Dorothy Lamour in *Swing High, Swing Low* (film, 1937).

Paris in the Spring
Words by Mack Gordon, music by Harry Revel.
De Sylva, Brown & Henderson, Inc.
Introduced by Mary Ellis in *Paris in the Spring* (film).

Piccolino, The
Words and music by Irving Berlin.
Irving Berlin Music Corp.
Introduced by Ginger Rogers in *Top Hat* (film).

Picture of Me without You, A
Words and music by Cole Porter.
Harms, Inc.
Introduced by June Knight and Charles Walters in *Jubilee* (musical).

Play, Orchestra, Play (English)
Words and music by Noël Coward.
Chappell & Co., Ltd., London, England/Chappell & Co., Inc.
Introduced by Noël Coward in *Shadow Play*, one of ten short plays in *Tonight at 8:30* (plays with music) presented in London in 1935 and in New York in 1936.

Please Believe Me
Words by Larry Yoell, music by Al Jacobs.
Miller Music Corp.

Put On an Old Pair of Shoes
Words and music by Dedette Lee Hill and Billy Hill.
Shapiro, Bernstein & Co., Inc.
Introduced by Ozzie Nelson and Harriet Hilliard.

Reckless
Words by Oscar Hammerstein II, music by Jerome Kern.
T. B. Harms Co.
Introduced by voice of Virginia Verrill (dubbed for Jean Harlow),
Allan Jones, and Nina Mae McKinney in *Reckless* (film).

Red Headed Woman Makes a Choo Choo Jump Its Track, A
Words by Du Bose Heyward and Ira Gershwin, music by
George Gershwin.
Gershwin Publishing Corp./New Dawn Music Corp.
Introduced by Warren Coleman in *Porgy and Bess* (opera). Sung
by Brock Peters in film version, 1959.

Red Sails in the Sunset (English)
Words by Jimmy Kennedy, music by Hugh Williams (pseudonym
for Will Grosz).
The Peter Maurice Music Co., Ltd., London, England/Shapiro,
Bernstein & Co., Inc.
Introduced in United States by Ray Noble and his Orchestra. Inter-
polated by Phyllis Austen and company in *Provincetown Follies*
(revue).

Reminiscing in Tempo
Music by Edward Kennedy "Duke" Ellington.
American Academy of Music, Inc.
Introduced by Duke Ellington and his Orchestra.

Rhythm and Romance
Words by George Whiting and Nat Schwartz, music by J. C. Johnson.
Record Music Publishing Co.
Introduced by Fats Waller.

(If I Had) Rhythm in My Nursery Rhymes
Words by Sammy Cahn and Don Raye, music by Jimmie Lunceford
and Saul Chaplin.
Anne-Rachel Music Corp.
Introduced by Jimmie Lunceford and his Orchestra.

Rhythm Lullaby
Words by Andy Razaf, music by Paul Denniker.
American Academy of Music, Inc.
Introduced by Earl Hines and his Orchestra, vocal by The Palmer
Brothers Trio.

Rhythm of the Rain
Words by Jack Meskill, music by Jack Stern.
Robbins Music Corp.
Introduced by Maurice Chevalier and Ann Sothern in *Folies Bergere*
(film).

Roll Along Prairie Moon
Words and music by Ted Fiorito, Harry MacPherson, and
Albert Von Tilzer.
Robbins Music Corp.
Introduced by Harry Stockwell in *Here Comes the Band* (film).

Rose in Her Hair, The
Words by Al Dubin, music by Harry Warren.
M. Witmark & Sons.
Introduced by Dick Powell in *Broadway Gondolier* (film).

Rosetta
Words and music by Earl Hines and Henri Woode.
Mayfair Music Corp.
Written in 1928, but not published until 1935. Introduced by
Earl Hines and his Orchestra.

Saddest Tale
Words and music by Irving Mills and Edward Kennedy "Duke"
Ellington.
Mills Music, Inc.
Introduced by Duke Ellington and his Orchestra.

Sailor Beware
Words by Leo Robin, music by Richard A. Whiting.
Harms, Inc./Famous Music Corp.
Introduced by Bing Crosby in *Anything Goes* (film, 1936).

She Shall Have Music
Words and music by Maurice Sigler, Al Goodhart, and Al Hoffman.
Campbell-Connelly Co., Ltd., London, England/Chappell & Co., Inc.
From *She Shall Have Music* (film). Theme song of Jack Hylton
and his Orchestra.

She's a Latin from Manhattan
Words by Al Dubin, music by Harry Warren.
M. Witmark & Sons.
Introduced by Al Jolson in *Go into Your Dance* (film). Sung by
John Leslie and Jack Carson in *The Hard Way* (film, 1942).

Shipmates Forever, see (Shipmates Forever) Don't Give Up the Ship.

Showboat Shuffle
Music by Edward Kennedy "Duke" Ellington.
American Academy of Music, Inc.
Introduced by Duke Ellington and his Orchestra.

Simple Things in Life, The
Words by Ted Koehler, music by Ray Henderson.
Movietone Music Corp.
Introduced by Rochelle Hudson in *Curly Top* (film).

Sing an Old Fashioned Song (to a Young Sophisticated Lady)
Words by Joe Young, music by Fred Ahlert.
De Sylva, Brown & Henderson, Inc.

Sing before Breakfast
Words by Arthur Freed, music by Nacio Herb Brown.
Robbins Music Corp.
Introduced by Vilma and Buddy Ebsen, with Eleanor Powell, in
Broadway Melody of 1936 (film).

Somebody Ought To Be Told
Words by Oscar Hammerstein II, music by Sigmund Romberg.
Chappell & Co., Inc.
Introduced by Vera Van in *May Wine* (musical).

Something New Is in My Heart
Words by Oscar Hammerstein II, music by Sigmund Romberg.
Chappell & Co., Inc.
Introduced by Nancy McCord in *May Wine* (musical).

Song of the Open Road
Words and music by Albert Hay Malotte.
Bourne Co.
Introduced by John Carroll in *Hi Gaucho* (film).

Soon
Words by Lorenz Hart, music by Richard Rodgers.
Famous Music Corp.
Introduced by Bing Crosby in *Mississippi* (film).

Speaking Confidentially
Words and music by Jimmy McHugh and Dorothy Fields.
Robbins Music Corp.
Introduced by Alice Faye, Frances Langford, and Patsy Kelly in
Every Night at Eight (film).

Spreadin' Rhythm Around
Words by Ted Koehler, music by Jimmy McHugh.
Robbins Music Corp.
Introduced by Alice Faye in *King of Burlesque* (film).

Stuff Is Here (and It's Mellow), The
Words and music by Walter Bishop, William H. Smith, and
Clarence Williams.
MCA, Inc.
Best-selling record by Cleo Brown (Decca).

Sugar Plum
Words by Gus Kahn, music by Arthur Johnston.
Robbins Music Corp.
Introduced by Ann Dvorak and Patsy Kelly in *Thanks a Million*
(film).

Summertime
Words by Du Bose Heyward, music by George Gershwin.
Gershwin Publishing Corp./New Dawn Music Corp.
Introduced by Abbie Mitchell in *Porgy and Bess* (opera). Sung by
voice of Loulie Jean Norman, dubbed for Dorothy Dandridge, in
film version, 1959. Sung by Anne Brown in *Rhapsody in Blue*
(film, 1945). Theme song of the Bob Crosby Band.

Swamp-Fire
Music by Harold Mooney.
Leeds Music Corp. or Photo Play Music Co., Inc.
Swing instrumental, introduced by Ozzie Nelson and his Orchestra.
Version, with lyrics with Irving Taylor, copyrighted in 1953.

Symphony in Riffs
Words and music by Irving Mills and Benny Carter.
American Academy of Music, Inc.
Introduced by Benny Carter and his Orchestra. Featured in late
1930's by Gene Krupa and his Orchestra.

Take It Easy
Words by Dorothy Fields, music by Jimmy McHugh.
Robbins Music Corp.
Introduced by Alice Faye, Frances Langford, and Patsy Kelly in
Every Night at Eight (film).

Take Me Back to My Boots and Saddle
Words and music by Walter G. Samuels, Leonard Whitcup, and
Teddy Powell.
La Salle Music Publishers, Inc.
Introduced by Gene Autry.

Takes Two To Make a Bargain
Words and music by Mack Gordon and Harry Revel.
De Sylva, Brown & Henderson, Inc.
Introduced by Bing Crosby in *Two for Tonight* (film).

Taking Care of You
Words by Lew Brown, music by Harry Akst.
Bourne Co.
Introduced by Harry Richman in sequence subsequently deleted from
The Music Goes Round (film, 1936). Performed by The Chords in
Stars on Parade (film, 1944).

Tell Me That You Love Me (Italian)
English words by Al Stillman, Italian words by Ennio Neri, music
by Cesare A. Bixio.
Casa Editrice Musicale C.A. Bixio, Milan, Italy, 1933/Italian Book
Co., 1933/T. B. Harms Co.
Original Italian title, "Parlami d'Amore, Mariu." Introduced in
United States by Frank Parker.

Tender Is the Night
Words by Harold Adamson, music by Walter Donaldson.
Robbins Music Corp.
Introduced by Harry Stockwell and Virginia Bruce in *Here Comes the Band* (film).

Thanks a Million
Words by Gus Kahn, music by Arthur Johnston.
Robbins Music Corp.
Introduced by Dick Powell in *Thanks a Million* (film).

That Moment of Moments
Words by Ira Gershwin, music by Vernon Duke.
Chappell & Co., Inc.
Introduced by Gertrude Niesen and Rodney McLennan in *Ziegfeld Follies of 1936* (revue, 1936).

That's What I Want for Christmas
Words by Irving Caesar, music by Gerald Marks.
Irving Caesar.
Introduced by Shirley Temple in *Stowaway* (film, 1936).

That's What You Think
Words and music by Truman "Pinky" Tomlin, Raymond Jasper, and Coy Poe.
Bourne Co.
Introduced by Pinky Tomlin in *King Solomon of Broadway* (film).

Then (English)
Words and music by Noël Coward.
Chappell & Co., Ltd., London, England/Chappell & Co., Inc.
Introduced by Gertrude Lawrence and Noël Coward in *Shadow Play*, one of ten short plays in *Tonight at 8:30* (plays with music), presented in London in 1935 and in New York in 1936.

(If It Isn't Pain) Then It Isn't Love
Words and music by Leo Robin and Ralph Rainger.
Famous Music Corp.
Introduced by Marlene Dietrich in sequence subsequently deleted from *The Devil Is a Woman* (film, 1935). Re-introduced by Carole Lombard in *Swing High, Swing Low* (film, 1937).

Then You've Never Been Blue
Words by Sam Lewis and Joe Young, music by Ted Fiorito.
Remick Music Corp./Warock Corp.
Introduced by Frances Langford in *Every Night at Eight* (film).

There's a Boat Dat's Leavin' Soon for New York
Words by Ira Gershwin, music by George Gershwin.
Gershwin Publishing Corp./New Dawn Music Corp.
Introduced by John W. Bubbles in *Porgy and Bess* (opera). Sung by Sammy Davis, Jr. in film version, 1959.

These Foolish Things (Remind Me of You) (English)
Words by Holt Marvell (pseudonym for Eric Maschwitz), music by Jack Strachey and Harry Link.
Boosey & Co., Ltd., London, England/Bourne Co.
Originally written for British Broadcasting Company musical program. Reintroduced by Dorothy Dickson in London in *Spread It Abroad* (revue, 1936). First recording by Leslie Hutchinson. Interpolated in *A Yank in the R.A.F.* (film, 1941), *Ghost Catchers* (film, 1944), and *Tokyo Rose* (film, 1945).

Thief in the Night
Words by Howard Dietz, music by Arthur Schwartz.
Chappell & Co., Inc.
Introduced by Ethel Waters in *At Home Abroad* (revue).

This Time It's Love
Words by Sam M. Lewis, music by J. Fred Coots.
Leo Feist, Inc./Cromwell Music, Inc.

Tiny Little Fingerprints
Words and music by Charles Newman, Sam H. Stept, and Charles Tobias.
De Sylva, Brown & Henderson, Inc.

Top Hat, White Tie and Tails
Words and music by Irving Berlin.
Irving Berlin Music Corp.
Introduced by Fred Astaire in *Top Hat* (film).

Truckin'
Words by Ted Koehler, music by Rube Bloom.
Mills Music, Inc.
Introduced by Cora La Redd and ensemble at Cotton Club (New York nightclub) in twenty-sixth edition of *Cotton Club Parade* (nightclub revue).

Two for Tonight
Words and music by Mack Gordon and Harry Revel.
De Sylva, Brown & Henderson, Inc.
Introduced by Bing Crosby in *Two for Tonight* (film).

Two Together
Words by Gus Kahn, music by Arthur Johnston.
Robbins Music Corp.
Introduced by Ann Sothern and Roger Pryor in *The Girl Friend* (film).

Wail of the Winds
Music by Harry Warren.
M. Witmark & Sons.
Theme song of Red Nichols and his Orchestra.

'Way Back Home
Words and music by Al Lewis and Tom Waring.
Bregman, Vocco & Conn, Inc.
Introduced by Fred Waring and his Pennsylvanians.

What a Wonderful World
Words by Howard Dietz, music by Arthur Schwartz.
Chappell & Co., Inc.
Introduced by Eleanor Powell, Woods Miller, and The Continentals
in *At Home Abroad* (revue).

What's the Reason (I'm Not Pleasin' You)?
Words by Coy Poe and Jimmie Grier, music by Truman "Pinky"
Tomlin and Earl Hatch.
Bourne Co.
Introduced by Pinky Tomlin in *Times Square Lady* (film).

When a Gypsy Makes His Violin Cry
Words by Dick Smith, Frank Wine-Gar, and Jimmy Rogan, music by
Emery Deutsch.
Bregman, Vocco & Conn, Inc.
Introduced by and theme song of Emery Deutsch and his Orchestra.

When I Grow Too Old To Dream
Words by Oscar Hammerstein II, music by Sigmund Romberg.
Robbins Music Corp.
Introduced by Evelyn Laye and Ramon Novarro in *The Night Is
Young* (film). Sung by José Ferrer in *Deep in My Heart* (film,
1954).

When I Grow Up
Words by Edward Heyman, music by Ray Henderson.
Movietone Music Corp.
Introduced by Shirley Temple in *Curly Top* (film).

When Love Comes Your Way, see 1933.

When the Sun Goes Down
Words and music by Leroy Carr.
Leeds Music Corp.
Traditional blues, introduced by Leroy Carr.

Where Am I? (Am I in Heaven?)
Words by Al Dubin, music by Harry Warren.
Harms, Inc.
Introduced by James Melton in *Stars over Broadway* (film).

Whose Big Baby Are You
Words by Ted Koehler, music by Jimmy McHugh.
Robbins Music Corp.
Introduced by Alice Faye in *King of Burlesque* (film).

Why Dream?
Words and music by Ralph Rainger, Leo Robin, and Richard A. Whiting.
Famous Music Corp.
Introduced by Henry Wadsworth in *Big Broadcast of 1936* (film).

Why Shouldn't I
Words and music by Cole Porter.
Harms, Inc.
Introduced by Margaret Adams in *Jubilee* (musical).

Why Stars Come Out at Night
Words and music by Ray Noble.
Famous Music Corp.
Introduced by Ray Noble and his Orchestra.

With All My Heart
Words by Gus Kahn, music by Jimmy McHugh.
Leo Feist, Inc.
Introduced by Peggy Conklin in *Her Master's Voice* (film, 1936).

Without a Word of Warning
Words and music by Mack Gordon and Harry Revel.
De Sylva, Brown & Henderson, Inc.
Introduced by Bing Crosby in *Two for Tonight* (film).

Woman Is a Sometime Thing, A
Words by Du Bose Heyward, music by George Gershwin.
Gershwin Publishing Corp./New Dawn Music Corp.
Introduced by Edward Matthews in *Porgy and Bess* (opera). Sung by Leslie Scott in film version, 1959.

Words Are in My Heart, The
Words by Al Dubin, music by Harry Warren.
M. Witmark & Sons.
Introduced by Dick Powell in *Gold Diggers of 1935* (film).

World Is Mine (Tonight), The (English)
Words by Holt Marvell (pseudonym for Eric Maschwitz), music by George Posford.
Keith, Prowse & Co., Ltd., London, England/Sam Fox Publishing Co., Inc.
Introduced by Nino Martini in *The Gay Desperado* (film, 1936).

Worried Man Blues
Words and music by A. P. Carter.
Peer International Corp.
Introduced by The Carter Family.

You Are My Lucky Star
Words by Arthur Freed, music by Nacio Herb Brown.
Robbins Music Corp.
Introduced by Frances Langford in *Broadway Melody of 1936* (film).
Sung by Gene Kelly and Debbie Reynolds in *Singin' in the Rain*
(film, 1953). Theme song of Enoch Light and his Orchestra.

You Are So Lovely and I'm So Lonely
Words by Lorenz Hart, music by Richard Rodgers.
Harms, Inc.
Introduced by Walter Pidgeon in *Something Gay* (play).

You Hit the Spot
Words and music by Mack Gordon and Harry Revel.
Famous Music Corp.
Introduced by Mack Gordon, Frances Langford, and Jack Oakie in
Collegiate (film, 1936).

You Let Me Down
Words by Al Dubin, music by Harry Warren.
Harms, Inc.
Introduced by Jane Froman in *Stars over Broadway* (film).

You Took the Words Right Out of My Mouth
Words by Harold Adamson, music by Burton Lane.
Robbins Music Corp.
Introduced by Maurice Chevalier in *Folies Bergere* (film).

You Were There (English)
Words and music by Noël Coward.
Chappell & Co., Ltd., London, England/Chappell & Co., Inc.
Introduced by Gertrude Lawrence and Noël Coward in *Shadow Play,*
one of ten short plays in *Tonight at 8:30* (plays with music), pre-
sented in London in 1935 and in New York in 1936.

You're a Heavenly Thing
Words and music by Joe Young and Little Jack Little.
World Music, Inc./Warock Corp.
Introduced by Little Jack Little.

You're All I Need
Words by Gus Kahn, music by Bronislaw Kaper and Walter Jurmann.
Robbins Music Corp.
Introduced by Lorraine Bridges in *Escapade* (film).

You're an Angel
Words by Dorothy Fields, music by Jimmy McHugh.
Bourne Co.
Introduced by Ann Sothern and Gene Raymond in *Hooray for Love*
(film).

You're My Thrill
Words by Ned Washington, music by Burton Lane.
Robbins Music Corp.
Introduced by Ted Lewis in *Here Comes the Band* (film).

Zing Went the Strings of My Heart
Words and music by James Hanley.
Harms, Inc.
Introduced by Hal Le Roy and Eunice Healy in *Thumbs Up* (revue, 1934). Sung by Judy Garland in *Listen Darling* (film, 1938) and by Gene Nelson in *Lullaby of Broadway* (film, 1951).

1936

1936

Ah Still Suits Me, see **I Still Suits Me.**

Alabama Barbecue
Words and music by Benny Davis and J. Fred Coots.
Mills Music, Inc.
Introduced at Cotton Club (New York nightclub) in twenty-seventh
edition of *Cotton Club Parade* (nightclub revue).

All My Life
Words by Sidney Mitchell, music by Sammy Stept.
Sam Fox Publishing Co., Inc.
Introduced by Phil Regan in *Laughing Irish Eyes* (film).

Am I Gonna Have Trouble with You?
Words by Charles Tobias, music by Sammy Fain.
La Salle Music Publishers, Inc.

Are You My Love?
Words by Lorenz Hart, music by Richard Rodgers.
Chappell & Co., Inc.
Introduced by Steffi Duna in *Dancing Pirate* (film).

At the Codfish Ball
Words by Sidney Mitchell, music by Lew Pollack.
Movietone Music Corp.
Introduced by Shirley Temple and Buddy Ebsen in *Captain January*
(film).

Awake in a Dream
Words by Leo Robin, music by Frederick Hollander.
Famous Music Corp.
Introduced by Marlene Dietrich in *Desire* (film).

Balboa
Words by Sidney D. Mitchell, music by Lew Pollack.
Movietone Music Corp.
Introduced by Judy Garland, Dixie Dunbar, The Yacht Club Boys,
Betty Grable, Johnny Downs, Jack Haley, and Patsy Kelly in
Pigskin Parade (film).

Big Chief De Sota
Words and music by Andy Razaf and Fernando Arbelo.
Mayfair Music Corp.
Introduced by Fletcher Henderson and his Orchestra. Popularized by Fats Waller.

Blame It on the Rhumba
Words by Harold Adamson, music by Jimmy McHugh.
Leo Feist, Inc.
Introduced by Gertrude Niesen in *Top of the Town* (film, 1937).

Blue Prairie
Words and music by Bob Nolan and Vern (Tim) Spencer.
Valley Publishers, Inc./American Division of Elvis Presley Music, Inc. and Rumbalero Music, Inc.
Introduced by The Sons of the Pioneers.

Blue Rhythm Fantasy
Music by Teddy Hill and Chappie Willet.
American Academy of Music, Inc.
Theme song of Teddy Hill and his Orchestra.

Bojangles of Harlem
Words by Dorothy Fields, music by Jerome Kern.
T. B. Harms Co.
Introduced by Fred Astaire in *Swing Time* (film).

(There's a) Bridle Hangin' on the Wall
Words and music by Carson J. Robison.
Shapiro, Bernstein & Co., Inc.

But Definitely
Words and music by Mack Gordon and Harry Revel.
Robbins Music Corp.
Introduced by Shirley Temple, Alice Faye, and Jack Haley in *Poor Little Rich Girl* (film).

But Where Are You
Words and music by Irving Berlin.
Irving Berlin Music Corp.
Introduced by Harriet Hilliard in *Follow the Fleet* (film).

By Strauss
Words by Ira Gershwin, music by George Gershwin.
Chappell & Co., Inc.
Introduced by Gracie Barrie and Robert Shafter in *The Show Is On* (revue). Sung by Gene Kelly, Oscar Levant, and Georges Guetary in *An American in Paris* (film, 1951).

Bye Bye Baby
Words by Walter Hirsch, music by Lou Handman.
Bourne Co.

Christopher Columbus
Words by Andy Razaf, music by Leon Berry.
Mayfair Music Corp.
Introduced by and theme song of Fletcher Henderson and his
Orchestra.

Clarinet Lament
Music by Edward Kennedy "Duke" Ellington and Barney Bigard.
American Academy of Music, Inc.
Written for clarinet soloist Barney Bigard. Introduced by Duke
Ellington and his Orchestra.

Close to Me
Words by Sam M. Lewis, music by Peter De Rose.
T. B. Harms Co.

Cool Water
Words and music by Bob Nolan.
Valley Publishers, Inc./American Division of Elvis Presley Music,
Inc. and Rumbalero Music, Inc.
Introduced by The Sons of the Pioneers. Best-selling record in 1948
by Vaughn Monroe and The Sons of thePioneers (Victor).

Copper-Colored Gal
Words by Benny Davis, music by J. Fred Coots.
Mills Music, Inc.

Cross Patch
Words by Tot Seymour, music by Vee Lawnhurst.
Famous Music Corp.

Cuban Pete (English)
Words and music by José Norman (pseudonym for Norman
Henderson).
Ed. Kassner Music Co., Ltd., London, England/Sam Fox Publishing
Co., Inc.
Title song of and performed by Desi Arnaz and The King Sisters in
Cuban Pete (film, 1946).

Darling, Je Vous Aime Beaucoup (French-American)
Words and music by Anna Sosenko.
Publications Francis-Day, S.A., Paris, France, 1935/Chappell &
Co., Inc.
Introduced by Hildegarde. Sung by Simone Simon in Love and
Hisses (film, 1937). Revived in 1955 with best-selling record by
Nat "King" Cole (Capitol).

Dedicated to You
Words and music by Sammy Cahn, Saul Chaplin, and Hy Zaret.
De Sylva, Brown & Henderson, Inc.

Did I Remember?
Words by Harold Adamson, music by Walter Donaldson.
Leo Feist, Inc.
Introduced by voice of Virginia Verrill, dubbed for Jean Harlow, and Cary Grant in *Suzy* (film). Nominated for Academy Award, 1936.

Did Your Mother Come from Ireland? (English)
Words and music by Jimmy Kennedy and Michael Carr.
The Peter Maurice Music Co., Ltd., London, England/De Sylva, Brown & Henderson, Inc.

Does Your Heart Beat for Me?
Words by Mitchell Parish, music by Russ Morgan and Arnold Johnson.
Mills Music, Inc.
Introduced by and theme song of Russ Morgan and his Orchestra.

Doin' the Suzi-Q
Words and music by Benny Davis and J. Fred Coots.
Mills Music, Inc.
Introduced at Cotton Club (New York nightclub) in twenty-seventh edition of *Cotton Club Parade* (nightclub revue).

Down in the Depths, on the Ninetieth Floor
Words and music by Cole Porter.
Chappell & Co., Inc.
Introduced by Ethel Merman in *Red, Hot and Blue!* (musical).

Duerme, see Time Was, 1941.

Early Bird
Words by Sidney Mitchell, music by Lew Pollack.
Movietone Music Corp.
Introduced by Shirley Temple in *Captain January* (film).

Easy To Love
Words and music by Cole Porter.
Chappell & Co., Inc.
Introduced by James Stewart, danced to by Eleanor Powell, and reprised by Frances Langford in *Born To Dance* (film).

Echoes of Harlem
Music by Edward Kennedy "Duke" Ellington.
American Academy of Music, Inc.
Written for trumpet soloist "Cootie" Williams. Introduced by Duke Ellington and his Orchestra.

Empty Saddles
Words and music by Billy Hill, from a poem by J. Keirn Brennan.
Shapiro, Bernstein & Co., Inc.
Introduced by Bing Crosby in *Rhythm on the Range* (film).

Fancy Meeting You
Words by E. Y. Harburg, music by Harold Arlen.
Harms, Inc.
Introduced by Dick Powell and Jeanne Madden in *Stage Struck* (film).

Fine Romance, A
Words by Dorothy Fields, music by Jerome Kern.
T. B. Harms Co.
Introduced by Ginger Rogers and Fred Astaire in *Swing Time* (film).

Follow Your Heart
Words by Sidney D. Mitchell, music by Victor Schertzinger.
Sam Fox Publishing Co., Inc.
Introduced by Marion Talley and Michael Bartlett in *Follow Your Heart* (film).

Friendly Moon
Words and music by Benny Davis and J. Fred Coots.
Southern Music Publishing Co., Inc.

Frisco Flo
Words and music by Benny Davis and J. Fred Coots.
Mills Music, Inc.
Introduced by Cab Calloway at Cotton Club (New York nightclub) in twenty-seventh edition of *Cotton Club Parade* (nightclub revue).

Gay Ranchero, A, also known as Las Alteñitas (Mexican)
English words by Abe Tuvim and Francia Luban, Spanish words and music by J. J. Espinosa.
Edward B. Marks Music Corp.
Sung by Roy Rogers in *King of the Cowboys* (film, 1933) and *A Gay Ranchero* (film, 1948).

Gee! but You're Swell
Words by Charlie Tobias, music by Abel Baer.
Remick Music Corp.

Get Thee behind Me Satan
Words and music by Irving Berlin.
Irving Berlin Music Corp.
Originally introduced by Ginger Rogers in *Top Hat* (film, 1935) but deleted from film before release. Reintroduced by Harriet Hilliard in *Follow the Fleet* (film).

Glad To Be Unhappy
Words by Lorenz Hart, music by Richard Rodgers.
Chappell & Co., Inc.
Introduced by Doris Carson and David Morris in *On Your Toes* (musical).

1936

Gloomy Sunday (Hungarian)
English words by Sam M. Lewis, Hungarian words by László Jávor, music by Rezsó Seress.
Csárdás, Budapest, Hungary, 1933/Chappell & Co., Inc.
Original Hungarian title, "Szomoru Vasárnap." Advertised and promoted as "the suicide song." Introduced in United States by Paul Robeson. Best-selling record in 1941 by Billie Holiday. Composer committed suicide in 1968.

Glory of Love, The
Words and music by Billy Hill.
Shapiro, Bernstein & Co., Inc.
Featured in *Guess Who's Coming to Dinner* (film, 1967).

Gone
Words by Gus Kahn, music by Franz Waxman.
Leo Feist, Inc.
Introduced in *Love on the Run* (film).

Goodbye, Little Dream, Goodbye
Words and music by Cole Porter.
Chappell & Co., Inc.
Introduced by Ethel Merman in *Red, Hot and Blue!* (musical).

Goodnight Irene, see 1950.

Goodnight, My Love
Words by Mack Gordon, music by Harry Revel.
Robbins Music Corp.
Introduced by Shirley Temple, and reprised by Alice Faye, in *Stowaway* (film).

Goody-Goody
Words and music by Johnny Mercer and Matt Malneck.
Commander Publications/Malneck Music.
Best-selling record by Benny Goodman and his Orchestra (Victor).

Hawaiian War Chant (Hawaiian)
Words by Ralph Freed, music by Johnny Noble and Leleiohaku.
Miller Music Corp.
From a theme by Prince Leleiohaku, brother of King Kalakaua of Hawaii. Best-selling record in 1939 by Tommy Dorsey and his Orchestra (Victor).

He Hasn't a Thing except Me
Words by Ira Gershwin, music by Vernon Duke.
Chappell & Co., Inc.
Introduced by Fanny Brice in *Ziegfeld Follies of 1936* (revue).

Head over Heels in Love
Words by Mack Gordon, music by Harry Revel.
Campbell-Connelly Co., Ltd., London, England/Leo Feist, Inc.
Introduced by Jessie Matthews in *Head over Heels* (British film).

180

Heart Is Quicker Than the Eye, The
Words by Lorenz Hart, music by Richard Rodgers.
Chappell & Co., Inc.
Introduced by Luella Gear and Ray Bolger in *On Your Toes* (musical).

Here's Love in Your Eye
Words and music by Leo Robin and Ralph Rainger.
Famous Music Corp.
Introduced by Benny Fields in *The Big Broadcast of 1937* (film).

Hey, Babe, Hey! (I'm Nuts about You)
Words and music by Cole Porter.
Chappell & Co., Inc.
Introduced by James Stewart, Eleanor Powell, Una Merkel, and Buddy Ebsen in *Born To Dance* (film).

Hey, What Did the Bluebird Say?
Words by Ted Koehler, music by Jimmy McHugh.
Leo Feist, Inc.
Introduced by Shirley Temple in *Dimples* (film).

House Jack Built for Jill, The
Words and music by Leo Robin and Frederick Hollander.
Famous Music Corp.
Introduced by Bing Crosby in *Rhythm on the Range* (film).

I Can't Escape from You
Words and music by Leo Robin and Richard A. Whiting.
Famous Music Corp.
Introduced by Bing Crosby in *Rhythm on the Range* (film).

I Don't Want To Make History (I Just Want To Make Love)
Words and music by Leo Robin and Ralph Rainger.
Famous Music Corp.
Introduced by Frances Langford in *Palm Springs* (film).

I Have the Room Above
Words by Oscar Hammerstein II, music by Jerome Kern.
T. B. Harms Co.
Introduced by Allan Jones and Irene Dunne in *Show Boat* (film).

I Love To Sing-a
Words by E. Y. Harburg, music by Harold Arlen.
Remick Music Corp.
Introduced by Al Jolson and Cab Calloway in *The Singing Kid* (film).

I Still Suits Me, also known as Ah Still Suits Me
Words by Oscar Hammerstein II, music by Jerome Kern.
T. B. Harms Co.
Introduced by Paul Robeson and Hattie McDaniel in *Show Boat* (film).

I Wanna Go to the Zoo
Words and music by Mack Gordon and Harry Revel.
Robbins Music Corp.
Introduced by Shirley Temple in *Stowaway* (film).

I Want To Be a Cowboy's Sweetheart
Words and music by Patsy Montana.
Leeds Music Corp.
Introduced by Patsy Montana. Revived in 1946 with best-selling
record by Rosalie Allen (Victor).

I'd Be Lost Without You
Words by Bob Wright and Chet Forrest, music by Walter Donaldson.
Leo Feist, Inc.
Introduced by Eadie Adams in *Sinner Take All* (film).

I'd Rather Drink Muddy Water
Words and music by Eddie Miller.
Duchess Music Corp.
Blues, introduced by composer. Best-selling record in early 1940's
by The Cats and the Fiddle (Bluebird).

I'd Rather Lead a Band
Words and music by Irving Berlin.
Irving Berlin Music Corp.
Introduced by Fred Astaire in *Follow the Fleet* (film).

If You Love Me
Words and music by Ray Noble.
Chappell & Co., Inc.
Introduced by Ray Noble and his Orchestra.

I'll Sing You a Thousand Love Songs
Words by Al Dubin, music by Harry Warren.
Remick Music Corp.
Introduced by Robert Paige in *Cain and Mabel* (film).

I'm an Old Cow Hand (from the Rio Grande)
Words and music by Johnny Mercer.
Leo Feist, Inc.
Introduced by Bing Crosby in *Rhythm on the Range* (film). Sung by
Roy Rogers in *King of the Cowboys* (film, 1943).

I'm in a Dancing Mood
Words and music by Al Hoffman, Al Goodhart, and Maurice Sigler.
Campbell-Connelly Co., Ltd., London, England/De Sylva, Brown &
Henderson, Inc.
Introduced by Jack Buchanan and Elsie Randolph in *This'll Make
You Whistle* (British film).

I'm Putting All My Eggs in One Basket
Words and music by Irving Berlin.
Irving Berlin Music Corp.
Introduced by Fred Astaire and Ginger Rogers in *Follow the Fleet* (film).

In the Chapel in the Moonlight
Words and music by Billy Hill.
Shapiro, Bernstein & Co., Inc.
Best-selling record by Shep Fields and his Orchestra (Bluebird).
Revived in 1954 with best-selling record by Kitty Kallen (Decca) and in 1967 with best-selling record by Dean Martin (Reprise).

In Your Own Quiet Way
Words by E. Y. Harburg, music by Harold Arlen.
Harms, Inc.
Introduced by Dick Powell, and reprised by Jeanne Madden, in *Stage Struck* (film).

Is It True What They Say about Dixie?
Words and music by Irving Caesar, Sammy Lerner, and Gerald Marks.
Irving Caesar/Marlong Music Corp./Samuel M. Lerner Publications.
Popularized by Al Jolson.

Ise A-Muggin'
Words and music by "Stuff" Smith.
Anne-Rachel Music Corp.
Introduced by Stuff Smith at the Onyx Club (New York nightclub).

It's a Sin To Tell a Lie
Words and music by Billy Mayhew.
Bregman, Vocco & Conn, Inc.
Introduced by Kate Smith. Revived in 1955 with best-selling record by Something Smith and The Redheads (Epic).

It's D'Lovely, also known as It's De-lovely
Words and music by Cole Porter.
Chappell & Co., Inc.
Introduced by Ethel Merman and Bob Hope in *Red, Hot and Blue!* (musical). Sung by Donald O'Connor and Mitzi Gaynor in *Anything Goes* (film, 1956).

It's Got To Be Love
Words by Lorenz Hart, music by Richard Rodgers.
Chappell & Co., Inc.
Introduced by Ray Bolger and Doris Carson in *On Your Toes* (musical).

1936

It's Love I'm After
Words by Sidney D. Mitchell, music by Lew Pollack.
Movietone Music Corp.
Introduced by Judy Garland in *Pigskin Parade* (film).

I've Got You Under My Skin
Words and music by Cole Porter.
Chappell & Co., Inc.
Introduced by Virginia Bruce in *Born To Dance* (film). Nominated for Academy Award, 1936. Sung by Ginny Simms in *Night and Day* (film, 1946).

Knock, Knock, Who's There?
Words and music by Bill Tipton, Bill Davies, Johnny Morris, and Vincent Lopez.
Leo Feist, Inc.
Introduced by Vincent Lopez and his Orchestra.

Las Alteñitas, see A Gay Ranchero.

Last Night When We Were Young
Words by E. Y. Harburg, music by Harold Arlen.
Bourne Co.
Introduced by Lawrence Tibbett. Written for the Tibbett film, *Metropolitan* (1935) but vocal version deleted from film before release. Sung by Judy Garland in *In the Good Old Summertime* (film, 1949) and by Frank Sinatra in *Take Me Out to the Ball Game* (film, 1949), but deleted from both films before release.

Laughing Irish Eyes
Words by Sidney Mitchell, music by Sam H. Stept.
Sam Fox Publishing Co., Inc.
Introduced by Phil Regan in *Laughing Irish Eyes* (film).

Let Yourself Go
Words and music by Irving Berlin.
Irving Berlin Music Corp.
Introduced by Fred Astaire and Ginger Rogers in *Follow the Fleet* (film).

Let's Call a Heart a Heart
Words by Johnny Burke, music by Arthur Johnston.
Anne-Rachel Music Corp.
Introduced by Bing Crosby in *Pennies from Heaven* (film).

Let's Face the Music and Dance
Words and music by Irving Berlin.
Irving Berlin Music Corp.
Introduced by Fred Astaire, and danced to by Astaire and Ginger Rogers, in *Follow the Fleet* (film).

Let's Put Our Heads Together
Words by E. Y. Harburg, music by Harold Arlen.
Harms, Inc.
Introduced by Dick Powell in *Gold Diggers of 1937* (film).

Little Lady Make Believe
Words by Charles Tobias, music by Nat Simon.
Leeds Music Corp.

Little Old Lady
Words by Stanley Adams, music by Hoagy Carmichael.
Chappell & Co., Inc./M. Witmark & Sons.
Introduced by Mitzi Mayfair and Charles Walters in *The Show Is On*
(revue).

Little Skipper from Heaven Above, A
Words and music by Cole Porter.
Chappell & Co., Inc.
Introduced by Jimmy Durante and chorus in *Red, Hot and Blue!*
(musical).

Lost
Words and music by Phil Ohman, Johnny Mercer, and
Macy O. Teetor.
Robbins Music Corp.

Love Me, Love my Pekinese
Words and music by Cole Porter.
Chappell & Co., Inc.
Introduced by Virginia Bruce in *Born To Dance* (film).

Love Will Tell
Words by Jack Yellen, music by Lew Pollack.
Movietone Music Corp.
Introduced by Alice Faye in *Sing, Baby, Sing* (film).

Magnolias in the Moonlight
Words by Walter Bullock, music by Victor Schertzinger.
Sam Fox Publishing Co., Inc.
Introduced by Michael Bartlett in *Follow Your Heart* (film).

Manhattan Merry-Go-Round
Words and music by Gustave Haenschen and Pinky Herman.
Mayfair Music Corp.
Theme song of *Manhattan Merry-Go-Round* (radio program).

May I Have the Next Romance with You?
Words by Mack Gordon, music by Harry Revel.
Campbell-Connelly Co., Ltd., London, England/Leo Feist, Inc.
Introduced by Jessie Matthews and Louis Borrell in *Head over
Heels* (British film).

Me and the Moon
Words by Walter Hirsch, music by Lou Handman.
Anne-Rachel Music Corp.

Melody from the Sky, A
Words by Sidney D. Mitchell, music by Louis Alter.
Famous Music Corp.
Introduced by Fuzzy Knight in *The Trail of the Lonesome Pine* (film). Nominated for Academy Award, 1936.

Mickey Mouse's Birthday Party
Words and music by Charlie Tobias, Bob Rothberg, and Joseph Meyer.
Bourne Co.

Milkmen's Matinee, The
Words and music by Paul Denniker, Joe Davis, and Andy Razaf.
Mayfair Music Corp.
Theme song of *Milkman's Matinee*, all-night radio show on WNEW, New York.

Mister Deep Blue Sea
Words by Gene Austin, music by James P. Johnson.
Famous Music Corp.
Introduced by Mae West in *Klondike Annie* (film).

Mister Freddie Blues
Words and music by J. H. "Freddie" Shayne.
Leeds Music Corp., 1936, 1944, 1963.
Featured and recorded by blues pianist Jimmy Blythe in 1920's. Recorded by composer in 1935.

Mr. Ghost Goes to Town
Words by Irving Mills and Mitchell Parish, music by Will Hudson.
American Academy of Music, Inc.
Introduced by the Hudson-De Lange Orchestra.

Mr. Paganini, see (If You Can't Sing It) You'll Have To Swing It.

Mon Ami, My Friend
Words by Paul Green, music by Kurt Weill.
Chappell & Co., Inc.
Introduced by Paula Miller in *Johnny Johnson* (play with music).

Moonlight and Shadows
Words and music by Leo Robin and Frederick Hollander.
Paramount Music Corp.
Introduced by Dorothy Lamour in *Jungle Princess* (film).

Music in the Night (and Laughter in the Air)
Words by Oscar Hammerstein II, music by Erich Wolfgang
Korngold.
Famous Music Corp.
Introduced by Gladys Swarthout in *Give Us This Night* (film).

My Heart Is Singing
Words by Gus Kahn, music by Bronislaw Kaper and
Walter Jurmann.
Leo Feist, Inc.
Introduced by Deanna Durbin in *Three Smart Girls* (film, 1937).

My Kingdom for a Kiss
Words and music by Al Dubin, Harry Warren, and David Ormont.
M. Witmark & Sons.
Introduced by Dick Powell in *Hearts Divided* (film).

My Last Affair
Words and music by Haven Johnson.
Chappell & Co., Inc.
Introduced by Billie Haywood in *New Faces of 1936* (revue).

My Love Is Young
Words by S. Bickley Reichner, music by Irvin Graham.
Chappell & Co., Inc.
Introduced by Katharyn Mayfiield in *New Faces of 1936* (revue).

Never Gonna Dance
Words by Dorothy Fields, music by Jerome Kern.
T. B. Harms Co.
Introduced by Fred Astaire in *Swing Time* (film).

Night Is Young and You're So Beautiful, The
Words by Billy Rose and Irving Kahal, music by Dana Suesse.
Words & Music, Inc.
Introduced at Billy Rose's Casa Manana (Fort Worth, Texas
nightclub).

Nightfall
Words by Manny Kurtz (Mann Curtis), music by Benny Carter.
American Academy of Music, Inc.
Introduced by Benny Carter and his Orchestra.

(There Is) No Greater Love, also known as There Is No Greater Love
Words by Marty Symes, music by Isham Jones.
World Music, Inc.

No Regrets
Words by Harry Tobias, music by Roy Ingraham.
Miller Music Corp.
Introduced by The Casa Loma Orchestra.

Now
Words by Ted Fetter, music by Vernon Duke.
Chappell & Co., Inc.
Introduced by Gracie Barrie and Robert Shafter in *The Show Is On* (revue).

Now or Never
Words by Sam M. Lewis, music by Peter De Rose.
Shapiro, Bernstein & Co., Inc.

O, Heart of Love
Words by Paul Green, music by Kurt Weill.
Chappell & Co., Inc.
Introduced by Phoebe Brand in *Johnny Johnson* (play with music).

Occidental Woman
Words and music by Gene Austin.
Famous Music Corp.
Introduced by Mae West in *Klondike Annie* (film).

Oh, My Goodness!
Words by Mack Gordon, music by Harry Revel.
Robbins Music Corp.
Introduced by Shirley Temple in *Poor Little Rich Girl* (film).

Oh, the Rio Grande
Words by Paul Green, music by Kurt Weill.
Chappell & Co., Inc.
Introduced by Tony Kraber in *Johnny Johnson* (play with music).

On the Beach at Bali-Bali
Words and music by Al Sherman, Jack Meskill, and Abner Silver.
Edwin H. Morris & Co., Inc.

On Your Toes
Words by Lorenz Hart, music by Richard Rodgers.
Chappell & Co., Inc.
Introduced by Ray Bolger, Doris Carson, and David Morris in
On Your Toes (musical).

One Never Knows, Does One?
Words and music by Mack Gordon and Harry Revel.
Robbins Music Corp.
Introduced by Alice Faye in *Stowaway* (film).

One Rose (That's Left in My Heart), The (Hawaiian)
Words and music by Del Lyon and Lani McIntire.
Shapiro, Bernstein & Co., Inc.

One, Two, Button Your Shoe
Words by Johnny Burke, music by Arthur Johnston.
Anne-Rachel Music Corp.
Introduced by Bing Crosby in *Pennies from Heaven* (film).

Organ Grinder's Swing
Words by Mitchell Parish and Irving Mills, music by Will Hudson.
American Academy of Music, Inc.
Introduced by The Hudson-De Lange Orchestra. Best-selling record
by Chick Webb and his Orchestra, featuring Ella Fitzgerald.

Ours
Words and music by Cole Porter.
Chappell & Co., Inc.
Introduced by Dorothy Vernon, Thurston Crane, and The Hartmans
in *Red, Hot and Blue!* (musical).

Ozarks Are Calling Me Home, The
Words and music by Cole Porter.
Chappell & Co., Inc.
Introduced by Ethel Merman in *Red, Hot and Blue!* (musical).

Panic Is On, The
Words and music by George Clarke, Bert Clarke, and Winston Tharp.
Bourne Co.
Introduced by Fats Waller and his Rhythm.

Pennies from Heaven
Words and music by Johnny Burke and Arthur Johnston.
Anne-Rachel Music Corp.
Introduced by Bing Crosby in *Pennies from Heaven* (film). Nomi-
nated for Academy Award, 1936. Sung by Dick Haymes in *Cruisin'
down the River* (film, 1953).

Peter Piper
Words by Johnny Mercer, music by Richard A. Whiting.
Robbins Music Corp.

Pick Yourself Up
Words by Dorothy Fields, music by Jerome Kern.
T. B. Harms Co.
Introduced by Fred Astaire and Ginger Rogers in *Swing Time*
(film).

Picture Me without You
Words by Ted Koehler, music by Jimmy McHugh.
Leo Feist, Inc.
Introduced by Shirley Temple in *Dimples* (film).

Poinciana (Song of the Tree) (Cuban)
English words by Buddy Bernier, Spanish words by Manuel Lliso,
music by Nat Simon.
Edward B. Marks Music Corp./Anne-Rachel Music Corp.
Best-selling instrumental record in 1943 by David Rose and his
Orchestra (M-G-M); best-selling vocal record in 1944 by Bing
Crosby (Decca).

Quiet Night
Words by Lorenz Hart, music by Richard Rodgers.
Chappell & Co., Inc.
Introduced by Earl MacVeigh and ensemble in *On Your Toes*
(musical).

Rainbow on the River
Words by Paul Francis Webster, music by Louis Alter.
Leo Feist, Inc.
Introduced by Bobby Breen in *Rainbow on the River* (film).
Theme of *Dr. Christian* (radio dramatic series).

Rap Tap on Wood
Words and music by Cole Porter.
Chappell & Co., Inc.
Introduced by Eleanor Powell in *Born To Dance* (film).

Red, Hot and Blue
Words and music by Cole Porter.
Chappell & Co., Inc.
Introduced by Ethel Merman and chorus in *Red, Hot and Blue!*
(musical).

Rendezvous with a Dream
Words and music by Leo Robin and Ralph Rainger.
Famous Music Corp.
Introduced by Rochelle Hudson in *Poppy* (film).

Rhythm Saved the World
Words by Sammy Cahn, music by Saul Chaplin.
Anne-Rachel Music Corp.
First recording by Bunny Berigan and his Orchestra.

Ridin' High
Words and music by Cole Porter.
Chappell & Co., Inc.
Introduced by Ethel Merman in *Red, Hot and Blue!* (musical).

Right Somebody To Love, The
Words by Jack Yellen, music by Lew Pollack.
Movietone Music Corp.
Introduced by Shirley Temple in *Captain January* (film).

Robins and Roses
Words by Edgar Leslie, music by Joe Burke.
Bourne Co.
Introduced by Bing Crosby.

San Francisco
Words by Gus Kahn, music by Bronislaw Kaper and Walter Jurmann.
Robbins Music Corp.
Introduced by Jeanette MacDonald in *San Francisco* (film).

Saskatchewan
Words by Irving Caesar and Sammy Lerner, music by Gerald Marks.
Irving Caesar.
Popularized by violinist Dave Rubinoff and by Rudy Vallée.

Save Me, Sister
Words by E. Y. Harburg, music by Harold Arlen.
Remick Music Corp.
Introduced by Al Jolson, Cab Calloway, and Wini Shaw in
The Singing Kid (film).

(I've Been) Saving Myself for You
Words and music by Sammy Cahn and Saul Chaplin.
Harms, Inc.
Introduced at Grand Terrace (Chicago nightclub) in fifth edition of
Grand Terrace Revue (nightclub revue).

Say Si Si (Cuban)
English words by Al Stillman, Spanish words by Francia Luban,
music by Ernesto Lecuona.
Edward B. Marks Music Corp.
Original Spanish title, "Para Vigo Me Voy." Introduced by Xavier
Cugat and his Orchestra, vocal by Lina Romay. Best-selling record
in 1940 by The Andrews Sisters (Decca). Sung by Gene Autry in
Carolina Moon (film, 1940).

Seal It with a Kiss
Words by Edward Heyman, music by Arthur Schwartz.
Chappell & Co., Inc./De Sylva, Brown & Henderson, Inc.
Introduced by Lily Pons in *That Girl from Paris* (film).

Serenade in the Night (Italian)
English words and adaptation by Jimmy Kennedy, Italian words and
music by Cesare A. Bixio and B. Cherubini.
S.A.M. Bixio, Milan, Italy, 1934/Mills Music, Inc.
Original Italian title, "Violino Tzigano." Introduced in *Melodramma*
(Italian film).

Shoe Shine Boy
Words by Sammy Cahn, music by Saul Chaplin.
Laursteed Music, Inc./Dorsey Bros. Music, Inc.
Introduced by Louis Armstrong at Connie's Inn (New York
nightclub) in *Connie's Hot Chocolates of 1936* (nightclub revue).

Sing, Baby, Sing
Words by Jack Yellen, music by Lew Pollack.
Movietone Music Corp.
Introduced by Alice Faye in *Sing, Baby, Sing* (film).

191

Sing, Sing, Sing
Words and music by Louis Prima.
Robbins Music Corp.
Introduced by Louis Prima. Best-selling record by Benny Goodman
and his Orchestra (Victor).

Skeleton in the Closet
Words and music by Arthur Johnston and Johnny Burke.
Anne-Rachel Music Corp.
Introduced by Louis Armstrong in *Pennies from Heaven* (film).

Slaughter on Tenth Avenue
Music by Richard Rodgers.
Chappell & Co., Inc.
Danced to by Ray Bolger and Tamara Geva in *On Your Toes*
(musical).

Slave Song, The, see Until the Real Thing Comes Along.

Smoke Dreams
Words by Arthur Freed, music by Nacio Herb Brown.
Robbins Music Corp.
Introduced by Penny Singleton (Dorothy McNulty) in *After the
Thin Man* (film).

So Do I
Words by Johnny Burke, music by Arthur Johnston.
Anne-Rachel Music Corp.
Introduced by Bing Crosby in *Pennies from Heaven* (film).

Somebody Changed the Lock on My Door
Words and music by William Weldon.
Leeds Music Corp.
Best-selling record in 1945 by Louis Jordan and his Tympany Five
(Decca).

Song of the Woodman
Words by E. Y. Harburg, music by Harold Arlen.
Unpublished.
Introduced by Bert Lahr in *The Show Is On* (revue).

Sophisticated Swing
Words by Mitchell Parish, music by Will Hudson.
Mills Music, Inc.
Introduced by The Hudson-De Lange Orchestra.

Speaking of the Weather
Words by E. Y. Harburg, music by Harold Arlen.
Harms, Inc.
Introduced by Dick Powell in *Gold Diggers of 1937* (film).

Star Fell out of Heaven, A
Words by Mack Gordon, music by Harry Revel.
De Sylva, Brown & Henderson, Inc.
Introduced by Benny Fields.

Stars in My Eyes
Words by Dorothy Fields, music by Fritz Kreisler.
Chappell & Co., Inc./Charles Foley, Inc.
Adapted from "Who Can Tell," with lyrics by William Le Baron, from the 1919 Kreisler-Jacobi operetta, *Apple Blossoms*. New version introduced by Grace Moore in *The King Steps Out* (film).

Stealin' Apples
Words by Andy Razaf, music by Thomas "Fats" Waller.
American Academy of Music, Inc.
Introduced by Fletcher Henderson and his Orchestra.

Stompin' at the Savoy
Words by Andy Razaf, music by Benny Goodman, Chick Webb, and Edgar Sampson.
Robbins Music Corp.
First recorded in 1934, before publication, by Chick Webb and his Orchestra. Best-selling record by Benny Goodman and his Orchestra (Victor).

Summer Night
Words by Al Dubin, music by Harry Warren.
M. Witmark & Sons.
Introduced by James Melton in *Sing Me a Love Song* (film).

Swing, Brother, Swing
Words and music by Lewis Raymond, Walter Bishop, and Clarence Williams.
MCA, Inc.

Swingin' the Jinx Away
Words and music by Cole Porter.
Chappell & Co., Inc.
Introduced by Frances Langford in *Born To Dance* (film).

Swingtime in the Rockies
Music by Jimmy Mundy and Benny Goodman.
Robbins Music Corp.
Introduced by Benny Goodman and his Orchestra.

Take My Heart (and Do with It What You Please)
Words by Joe Young, music by Fred E. Ahlert.
Warock Corp./Fred Ahlert Music Corp.

Texas Tornado
Words by Sidney D. Mitchell, music by Lew Pollack.
Movietone Music Corp.
Introduced by Judy Garland in *Pigskin Parade* (film).

That Foolish Feeling
Words by Harold Adamson, music by Jimmy McHugh.
Leo Feist, Inc.
Introduced by Ella Logan in *Top of the Town* (film, 1937).

That's Life I Guess
Words by Sam M. Lewis, music by Peter De Rose.
De Sylva, Brown & Henderson, Inc.

There Is No Greater Love, see (There Is) No Greater Love.

There Isn't Any Limit to My Love
Words and music by Al Hoffman, Al Goodhart, and Maurice Sigler.
Campbell-Connelly Co., Ltd., London, England/Chappell & Co., Inc.
Introduced by Jack Buchanan in *This'll Make You Whistle*
(British film).

There'll Always Be a Lady Fair
Words and music by Cole Porter.
Harms, Inc.
Introduced by The Foursome as "Sailors' Chanty (Lady Fair)" in
Anything Goes (musical, 1934). Sung by Bing Crosby, Chill Wills,
and (two of) The Avalon Boys in first film version.

There's a Small Hotel
Words by Lorenz Hart, music by Richard Rodgers.
Chappell & Co., Inc.
Originally written for, but dropped from, *Billy Rose's Jumbo* (musi-
cal, 1935). Introduced by Doris Carson and Ray Bolger in *On Your
Toes* (musical). Sung by Betty Garrett in *Words and Music* (film,
1948) and by Frank Sinatra in *Pal Joey* (film, 1957).

There's No Two Ways about It
Words by Harold Adamson, music by Jimmy McHugh.
Leo Feist, Inc.
Introduced by Ella Logan in *Top of the Town* (film, 1937).

There's Something in the Air
Words by Harold Adamson, music by Jimmy McHugh.
Robbins Music Corp.
Introduced by Tony Martin in *Banjo on My Knee* (film).

There's That Look in Your Eyes
Words and music by Mack Gordon and Harry Revel.
Campbell-Connelly Co., Ltd., London, England/Leo Feist, Inc.
Introduced by Jessie Matthews in *Head over Heels* (British film).

Thinking of You
Words and music by Walter Donaldson and Paul Ash.
Leo Feist, Inc.
Theme song of Kay Kyser and his Orchestra.

This'll Make You Whistle
Words and music by Maurice Sigler, Al Goodhart, and Al Hoffman.
Campbell-Connelly Co., Ltd., London, England/Bourne Co.
Introduced by Jack Buchanan in *This'll Make You Whistle* (British film).

Thru the Courtesy of Love
Words by Jack Scholl, music by M. K. Jerome.
M. Witmark & Sons.
Introduced by Ross Alexander in *Here Comes Carter* (film).

To Love You and To Lose You
Words by Edward Heyman, music by Kurt Weill.
Chappell & Co., Inc.
Popular song version of "Johnny's Melody." Original version, with lyrics by Paul Green, introduced by Russell Collins in *Johnny Johnson* (play with music). First recording of popular song version by Ray Noble and his Orchestra.

To You Sweetheart, Aloha (Hawaiian)
Words and music by Harry Owens.
Anne-Rachel Music Corp.
Introduced by Harry Owens and his Royal Hawaiians.

Too Good for the Average Man
Words by Lorenz Hart, music by Richard Rodgers.
Chappell & Co., Inc.
Introduced by Luella Gear and Monty Woolley in *On Your Toes* (musical).

Top of the Town
Words by Harold Adamson, music by Jimmy McHugh.
Leo Feist, Inc.
Introduced by Gertrude Niesen in *Top of the Town* (film, 1937).

Tormented
Words and music by Will Hudson.
Mills Music, Inc.

Touch of God's Hand, The
Words and music by Bob Nolan.
Valley Publishers, Inc./American Division of Elvis Presley Music, Inc. and Rumbalero Music, Inc.
Introduced by The Sons of the Pioneers. Revived in 1953 with best-selling record by Johnnie Ray (Columbia).

1936

Touch of Your Lips, The (English)
Words and music by Ray Noble.
Anne-Rachel Music Corp.
Introduced by Ray Noble and his Orchestra, vocal by Al Bowlly.

Twilight on the Trail
Words by Sidney D. Mitchell, music by Louis Alter.
Famous Music Corp.
Introduced by Fuzzy Knight in *Trail of the Lonesome Pine* (film).

Twinkle, Twinkle, Little Star
Words by Herb Magidson, music by Ben Oakland.
Paramount Music Corp.
Introduced by Mae Clarke and John Payne in *Hats Off* (film).

(It Will Have To Do) Until the Real Thing Comes Along
Words and music by Sammy Cahn, Saul Chaplin, L. E. Freeman,
    Mann Holiner, and Alberta Nichols.
Chappell & Co., Inc./Anne-Rachel Music Corp.
Sometimes called "The Slave Song." An earlier version, entitled "Till
    the Real Thing Comes Along," published by Shapiro, Bernstein &
    Co., Inc. in 1931, credited to Mann Holiner and Alberta Nichols
    and introduced in Lew Leslie's *Rhapsody in Black* (revue). Best-
    selling record of revised version by Andy Kirk and his Clouds of
    Joy, vocal by Pha Terrell (Decca).

Until Today
Words by Benny Davis, music by J. Fred Coots and Oscar Levant.
Marlo Music Corp.

W.P.A. Blues
Words and music by Lester Melrose and William Weldon.
Leeds Music Corp.
Introduced by Casey Bill (pseudonym for William Weldon).

Wah-Hoo!
Words and music by Cliff Friend.
De Sylva, Brown & Henderson, Inc.
Sung by The Andrews Sisters in *Moonlight and Cactus* (film, 1944).

Wake Up and Sing
Words and music by Cliff Friend, Carmen Lombardo, and Charles
    Tobias.
Shapiro, Bernstein & Co., Inc.
Introduced by Guy Lombardo and his Royal Canadians.

Waltz in Swingtime
Words by Dorothy Fields, music by Jerome Kern.
T. B. Harms Co.
Danced to by Fred Astaire and Ginger Rogers in *Swing Time* (film).

Waltz Was Born in Vienna, A
Words by Earle Crooker, music by Frederick Loewe.
Chappell & Co., Inc.
Introduced in *The Illustrator's Show* (revue). Sung in *Salute to Spring* (musical, 1937), summer production of St. Louis Municipal Opera Company.

Waltzing Mathilda, see 1941.

Way You Look Tonight, The
Words by Dorothy Fields, music by Jerome Kern.
T. B. Harms Co.
Introduced by Fred Astaire in *Swing Time* (film). Academy Award-winning song, 1936.

We Saw the Sea
Words and music by Irving Berlin.
Irving Berlin Music Corp.
Introduced by Fred Astaire and male chorus in *Follow the Fleet* (film).

When Did You Leave Heaven
Words by Walter Bullock, music by Richard A. Whiting.
Robbins Music Corp.
Introduced by Tony Martin in *Sing, Baby, Sing* (film). Nominated for Academy Award, 1936.

When I'm with You
Words by Mack Gordon, music by Harry Revel.
Robbins Music Corp.
Introduced by Shirley Temple and Tony Martin, and reprised by Alice Faye, in *Poor Little Rich Girl* (film).

When It's Round-up Time in Heaven
Words and music by Jimmie Davis.
Peer International Corp.
Best-selling record by Gene Autry (Columbia).

When Lights Are Low
Words by Spencer Williams, music by Benny Carter.
The Peter Maurice Music Co., Ltd./Mills Music, Inc.
Introduced in England by Benny Carter and his Orchestra, vocal by Elizabeth Welch (English Decca).

When My Dreamboat Comes Home
Words and music by Cliff Friend and Dave Franklin.
M. Witmark & Sons.
Introduced by Guy Lombardo and his Royal Canadians.

When You Are Dancing the Waltz
Words by Lorenz Hart, music by Richard Rodgers.
Chappell & Co., Inc.
Introduced by Charles Collins and Steffi Duna in *Dancing Pirate* (film).

Where Are You ?
Words by Harold Adamson, music by Jimmy McHugh.
Leo Feist, Inc.
Introduced by Gertrude Niesen in *Top of the Town* (film, 1937).

Where Have You Been All My Life
Words by Herb Magidson, music by Ben Oakland.
Paramount Music Corp.
Introduced by Mae Clarke and John Payne in *Hats Off* (film).

Where the Lazy River Goes By
Words by Harold Adamson, music by Jimmy McHugh.
Robbins Music Corp.
Introduced by Barbara Stanwyck and Tony Martin in *Banjo on My Knee* (film).

Whiffenpoof Song, The
Original words and music by Meade Minnigerode, George S. Pomeroy, and Tod B. Galloway; revised version by Rudy Vallée.
Miller Music Corp.
Members of Yale University Glee Club adapted Rudyard Kipling's poem, "Gentleman Rankers" and adopted it as theme of The Whiffenpoof Society in 1909. First published version in *The New Yale Song Book* (G. Schirmer, Inc., 1918). Rudy Vallée brought his slightly revised version to attention of general public in 1935.

Who Minds about Me?
Words by Walter Bullock, music by Victor Schertzinger.
Sam Fox Publishing Co., Inc.
Introduced by Clarence Muse, with The Hall Johnson Choir, in *Follow Your Heart* (film).

Who's Afraid of Love
Words by Sidney D. Mitchell, music by Lew Pollack.
Movietone Music Corp.
Introduced by Don Ameche and Leah Ray in *One in a Million* (film).

Why Do You Pass Me By (French)
English words by Desmond Carter, French words by Charles Trenet, music by John Hess and Paul Misraki.
Éditions Vianelly, Paris, France/De Sylva, Brown & Henderson, Inc.
Original French title, "Vous Qui Passes Sans Me Voir." Introduced by Charles Trenet.

With a Banjo on My Knee
Words by Harold Adamson, music by Jimmy McHugh.
Robbins Music Corp.
Introduced by Buddy Ebsen and Walter Brennan in *Banjo of My Knee* (film).

With Plenty of Money and You
Words by Al Dubin, music by Harry Warren.
Harms, Inc.
Introduced by Dick Powell in *Gold Diggers of 1937* (film). Sung by Doris Day in *My Dream Is Yours* (film, 1949).

Words without Music
Words by Ira Gershwin, music by Vernon Duke.
Chappell & Co., Inc.
Introduced by Gertrude Niesen in *Ziegfeld Follies of 1936* (revue).

Would You
Words by Arthur Freed, music by Nacio Herb Brown.
Robbins Music Corp.
Introduced by Jeanette MacDonald in *San Francisco* (film). Sung by Debbie Reynolds in *Singin' in the Rain* (film, 1952).

Yearning for Love
Words by Mitchell Parish and Irving Mills, music by Edward Kennedy "Duke" Ellington.
American Academy of Music, Inc.
Introduced by Duke Ellington and his Orchestra.

You
Words by Harold Adamson, music by Walter Donaldson.
Leo Feist, Inc.
Introduced by The Ziegfeld Brides and Grooms in *The Great Ziegfeld* (film).

You Better Go Now
Words by Bickley Reichner, music by Irvin Graham.
Chappell & Co., Inc.
Introduced by Nancy Nolan and Tom Rutherford in *New Faces of 1936* (revue). First recording by Fairchild and Carroll and Orchestra, vocal by Rae Giersdorf (Liberty Music Shop). Revived in 1945 by Billie Holiday (Decca). Best-selling record by Jeri Southern (Decca).

You Can't Pull the Wool over My Eyes
Words and music by Milton Ager, Charles Newman, and Murray Mencher.
Advanced Music Corp.

You Do the Darndest Things, Baby
Words by Sidney D. Mitchell, music by Lew Pollack.
Movietone Music Corp.
Introduced by Jack Haley in *Pigskin Parade* (film).

You Dropped Me Like a Red Hot Penny
Words by Joe Young music by Fred E. Ahlert.
De Sylva, Brown & Henderson, Inc.

You Gotta S-M-I-L-E To Be H-A-Double P-Y
Words and music by Mack Gordon and Harry Revel.
Robbins Music Corp.
Introduced by Shirley Temple in *Stowaway* (film)

You Stayed Away Too Long
Words by George Whiting and Nat Schwartz, music by J. C. Johnson.
Record Music Publishing Co.
Introduced by Fats Waller.

You Turned the Tables on Me
Words by Sidney D. Mitchell, music by Louis Alter.
Movietone Music Corp./Anne-Rachel Music Corp.
Introduced by Alice Faye in *Sing, Baby, Sing* (film).

(If You Can't Sing It) You'll Have To Swing It, also known as Mr. Paganini
Words and music by Sam Coslow.
Famous Music Corp.
Introduced by Martha Raye in *Rhythm on the Range* (film).

Your Feet's Too Big
Words and music by Ada Benson and Fred Fisher.
Mayfair Music Corp.
Popularized by Fats Waller.

You're Not the Kind
Words and music by Will Hudson and Irving Mills.
Mills Music, Inc.

You're Slightly Terrific
Words by Sidney D. Mitchell, music by Lew Pollack.
Movietone Music Corp.
Introduced by Tony Martin and Dixie Dunbar in *Pigskin Parade* (film).

You're the Cure for What Ails Me
Words by E. Y. Harburg, music by Harold Arlen.
Remick Music Corp.
Introduced by Al Jolson, Sybil Jason, Edward Everett Horton, and Allen Jenkins in *The Singing Kid* (film).

You've Got Something
Words and music by Cole Porter.
Chappell & Co., Inc.
Introduced by Bob Hope and Ethel Merman in *Red, Hot and Blue!*
(musical).

You've Gotta Eat Your Spinach, Baby
Words and music by Mack Gordon and Harry Revel.
Robbins Music Corp.
Introduced by Shirley Temple, Alice Faye, and Jack Haley in
Poor Little Rich Girl (film).

1937

1937

Afraid To Dream
Words and music by Mack Gordon and Harry Revel.
Miller Music Corp.
Introduced by Don Ameche, and reprised by Tony Martin and
Alice Faye, in *You Can't Have Everything* (film).

After You
Words and music by Sam Coslow and Al Siegel.
Paramount Music Corp.
Introduced by Frances Faye, Martha Raye, Harry Barris, and
Bing Crosby in *Double or Nothing* (film).

Alabamy Home
Words and music by Dave Ringle and Edward Kennedy "Duke"
Ellington.
American Academy of Music, Inc.
Introduced by Duke Ellington and his Orchestra.

Alibi Baby
Words and music by Edward Heyman, Tot Seymour, and
Vee Lawnhurst.
Famous Music Corp.

All at Once
Words by Lorenz Hart, music by Richard Rodgers.
Chappell & Co., Inc.
Introduced by Mitzi Green and Ray Heatherton in *Babes in Arms*
(musical).

All Dark People
Words by Lorenz Hart, music by Richard Rodgers.
Chappell & Co., Inc.
Introduced by Harold Nicholas and Fayard Nicholas in *Babes in
Arms* (musical).

All God's Chillun Got Rhythm
Words by Gus Kahn, music by Bronislaw Kaper and Walter Jurmann.
Robbins Music Corp.
Introduced by Ivie Anderson in *A Day at the Races* (film).

All You Want To Do Is Dance
Words by John Burke, music by Arthur Johnston.
Anne-Rachel Music Corp.
Introduced by Bing Crosby in *Double or Nothing* (film).

Allegheny Al
Words by Oscar Hammerstein II, music by Jerome Kern.
T. B. Harms Co.
Introduced by Dorothy Lamour and Irene Dunne in *High, Wide and Handsome* (film).

Alligator Crawl
Words by Andy Razaf and Joe Davis, music by Thomas "Fats" Waller.
Anne-Rachel Music Corp./Mayfair Music Corp.
Composed in 1927 as jazz piano solo composition. Earlier titles were "House Party Stomp" and "Charleston Stomp." Introduced by Fats Waller.

Always and Always
Words by Bob Wright and Chet Forrest, music by Edward Ward.
Leo Feist, Inc.
Introduced by Joan Crawford in *Mannequin* (film). Nominated for Academy Award, 1938.

Am I in Love?
Words by Al Dubin, music by Harry Warren.
M. Witmark & Sons.
Introduced by Kenny Baker in *Mr. Dodd Takes the Air* (film).

Azure
Words by Irving Mills, music by Edward Kennedy "Duke" Ellington.
American Academy of Music, Inc.
Introduced by Duke Ellington and his Orchestra.

Babes in Arms
Words by Lorenz Hart, music by Richard Rodgers.
Chappell & Co., Inc.
Introduced by Mitzi Green, Ray Heatherton, and Alfred Drake in *Babes in Arms* (musical). Sung by Mickey Rooney, Judy Garland, Betty Jaynes, and Douglas McPhail in film version, 1939.

Be a Good Sport
Words and music by Mack Gordon and Harry Revel.
Leo Feist, Inc.
Introduced by The Brewster Twins in *Love and Hisses* (film).

206

(I've Got) Beginner's Luck
Words by Ira Gershwin, music by George Gershwin.
Gershwin Publishing Corp./Chappell & Co., Inc.
Introduced by Fred Astaire in *Shall We Dance?* (film).

Bei Mir Bist Du Schön (Means That You're Grand)
English words by Sammy Cahn and Saul Chaplin, Yiddish words by
Jacob Jacobs, music by Sholom Secunda.
Harms, Inc.
Introduced in Yiddish in New York by Aaron Lebedeff in *I Would
If I Could* (Yiddish musical, 1932) under the title, "Bei Mir Bistu
Shein." Originally published by the composer in 1933. Best-selling
record in 1937 by The Andrews Sisters (Decca). Sung by Priscilla
Lane in *Love, Honor and Behave* (film, 1938) and by Judy Gar-
land in sequence subsequently deleted from *Love Finds Andy
Hardy* (film, 1938).

Big Apple, The
Words by Buddy Bernier, music by Bob Emmerich.
De Sylva, Brown & Henderson, Inc.
Introduced by Tommy Dorsey and his Orchestra.

Black Butterfly
Words by Ben Carruthers and Irving Mills, music by Edward
Kennedy "Duke" Ellington.
American Academy of Music, Inc.
Introduced by Duke Ellington and his Orchestra.

Blame It on the Danube
Words and music by Harry Akst and Frank Loesser.
Marlo Music Corp.
Introduced by Ida Lupino (as nightclub ventriloquist in duet with
dummy), and reprised by John Boles, in *Fight for Your Lady*
(film).

Blossoms on Broadway
Words and music by Leo Robin and Ralph Rainger.
Famous Music Corp.
Introduced by Shirley Ross in *Blossoms on Broadway* (film).

Blue Hawaii
Words and music by Leo Robin and Ralph Rainger.
Famous Music Corp.
Introduced by Harry Owens and his Royal Hawaiian Orchestra in
Honolulu. Sung by Bing Crosby, and reprised by Crosby and
Shirley Ross, in *Waikiki Wedding* (film). Used as title song for
Elvis Presley film, *Blue Hawaii* (1961). Best-selling record in 1962
by Elvis Presley (RCA Victor).

Blue September
Words by Mitchell Parish, music by Peter De Rose.
Robbins Music Corp., 1937, 1940.
Based on a theme from De Rose's composition for piano,
"Royal Blue."

Blue Venetian Waters
Words by Gus Kahn, music by Bronislaw Kaper and Walter Jurmann.
Robbins Music Corp.
Introduced by Allan Jones in *A Day at the Races* (film).

Bob White (Whatcha Gonna Swing Tonight?)
Words by Johnny Mercer, music by Bernie Hanighen.
Remick Music Corp.
Introduced by Guy Lombardo and his Royal Canadians (Decca).
Best-selling record by Bing Crosby and Connee Boswell (Decca).

Boo-Hoo!
Words by Edward Heyman, music by Carmen Lombardo and
John Jacob Loeb.
Ahlert-Burke Corp./Flojan Music Publishing Co./Frank Music Corp.
Adapted from an earlier song by Carmen Lombardo entitled "Let's
Drink." Introduced by Guy Lombardo and his Royal Canadians.

Broadway Jamboree
Words by Harold Adamson, music by Jimmy McHugh.
Robbins Music Corp.
Introduced by Frances Hunt in *You're a Sweetheart* (film).

Broadway's Gone Hawaii
Words and music by Mack Gordon and Harry Revel.
Leo Feist, Inc.
Introduced by Ruth Terry, The Peters Sisters, and Ben Bernie and
his Orchestra in *Love and Hisses* (film).

Buds Won't Bud
Words by E. Y. Harburg, music by Harold Arlen.
Leo Feist, Inc.
Introduced by Hannah Williams in *Hooray for What!* (musical), but
dropped from show before New York opening. Sung by Judy Gar-
land in *Andy Hardy Meets Debutante* (film, 1940).

By Myself
Words by Howard Dietz, music by Arthur Schwartz.
De Sylva, Brown & Henderson, Inc.
Introduced by Jack Buchanan in *Between the Devil* (musical). Sung
by Fred Astaire in *The Band Wagon* (film, 1953) and by Judy
Garland in *I Could Go On Singing* (film, 1963).

Can I Forget You?
Words by Oscar Hammerstein II, music by Jerome Kern.
T. B. Harms Co.
Introduced by Irene Dunne in *High, Wide and Handsome* (film).

Caravan
Words by Irving Mills, music by Juan Tizol and Edward Kennedy "Duke" Ellington.
American Academy of Music, Inc.
Introduced by Duke Ellington and his Orchestra. Revived in 1953 with best-selling record by Ralph Marterie and his Orchestra (Mercury).

Chain Store Daisy
Words and music by Harold Rome.
Mills Music, Inc.
Introduced by Ruth Rubenstein in *Pins and Needles* (revue).

Close
Words and music by Cole Porter.
Chappell & Co., Inc.
Introduced by Nelson Eddy in *Rosalie* (film).

Dancing under the Stars (Hawaiian)
Words and music by Harry Owens.
Anne-Rachel Music Corp.

Danger — Love at Work
Words and music by Mack Gordon and Harry Revel.
Miller Music Corp.
Introduced by Louis Prima and Alice Faye in *You Can't Have Everything* (film). Sung by Ann Sothern and Jack Haley in *Danger — Love at Work* (film).

Diminuendo in Blue
Music by Edward Kennedy "Duke" Ellington.
American Academy of Music, Inc.
Introduced by Duke Ellington and his Orchestra.

Dipsy Doodle, The
Words and music by Larry Clinton.
Lincoln Music Corp.
Introduced by Tommy Dorsey and his Orchestra, vocal by Edythe Wright. Theme song of Larry Clinton and his Orchestra.

Doing the Reactionary
Words and music by Harold Rome.
Mills Music, Inc.
Introduced by Al Levy and Nettie Harary in *Pins and Needles* (revue).

Donkey Serenade, The
Words by Bob Wright and Chet Forrest, music by Rudolf Friml
and Herbert Stothart.
G. Schirmer, Inc., 1920, 1923, 1937.
First published as piano composition entitled "Chanson." Lyrics by
Dailey Paskman, Sigmund Spaeth, and Irving Caesar added in 1923
and title changed to "Chansonette." Present version, with addi-
tional music by Stothart and new lyrics, introduced by Allan
Jones in *The Firefly* (film).

Don't Say Goodbye If You Love Me
Words and music by Jimmie Davis and Bonnie Dodd.
Peer International Corp.

Down with Love
Words by E. Y. Harburg, music by Harold Arlen.
Chappell & Co., Inc.
Introduced by Jack Whiting, June Clyde, and Vivian Vance in
Hooray for What! (musical).

Dusk in Upper Sandusky
Music by Jimmy Dorsey and Larry Clinton.
Robbins Music Corp.
Introduced by Jimmy Dorsey and his Orchestra.

Dusk on the Desert
Words and music by Irving Mills and Edward Kennedy "Duke"
Ellington.
American Academy of Music, Inc.
Introduced by Duke Ellington and his Orchestra.

Everybody Sing
Words by Arthur Freed, music by Nacio Herb Brown.
Robbins Music Corp.
Introduced by Judy Garland in *Broadway Melody of 1938* (film).

Farewell to Dreams
Words by Gus Kahn, music by Sigmund Romberg.
Robbins Music Corp.
Introduced by Jeanette MacDonald and Nelson Eddy in sequence
subsequently deleted from *Maytime* (film).

Fifi
Words and music by Sam Coslow.
Famous Music Corp.
Introduced by Mae West in *Every Day's a Holiday* (film).

First Time I Saw You, The
Words by Allie Wrubel, music by Nathaniel Shilkret.
Anne-Rachel Music Corp.
Introduced by Frances Farmer in *The Toast of New York* (film).

Foggy Day, A
Words by Ira Gershwin, music by George Gershwin.
Gershwin Publishing Corp.
Introduced by Fred Astaire in *A Damsel in Distress* (film).

Folks Who Live on the Hill, The
Words by Oscar Hammerstein II, music by Jerome Kern.
T. B. Harms Co.
Introduced by Irene Dunne in *High, Wide and Handsome* (film).

Follow in My Footsteps
Words by Arthur Freed, music by Nacio Herb Brown.
Robbins Music Corp.
Introduced by Eleanor Powell, Buddy Ebsen, and George Murphy in
Broadway Melody of 1938 (film).

For Dancers Only
Words by Don Raye and Vic Schoen, music by Sy Oliver.
Leeds Music Corp., 1937, 1939.
Introduced by Jimmie Lunceford and his Orchestra.

Getting Some Fun out of Life
Words by Edgar Leslie, music by Joseph A. Burke.
Bregman, Vocco & Conn, Inc.

Girl on the Police Gazette, The
Words and music by Irving Berlin.
Irving Berlin Music Corp.
Introduced by Dick Powell, Alice Faye, and chorus in *On the Avenue*
(film). Sung by Frank Price (to Gypsy Rose Lee) in *Star and
Garter* (revue, 1942).

"Gone with the Wind"
Words by Herb Magidson, music by Allie Wrubel.
Bourne Co.

Good Mornin'
Words and music by Sam Coslow.
Famous Music Corp.
Introduced by Martha Raye in *Mountain Music* (film).

Good-bye Jonah
Words by Al Stillman, music by Arthur Schwartz.
Robbins Music Corp.
Introduced by John W. Bubbles in *Virginia* (musical).

Got a Pair of New Shoes
Words by Arthur Freed, music by Nacio Herb Brown.
Robbins Music Corp.
Introduced by Eleanor Powell in *Broadway Melody of 1938* (film),
but deleted before release. Reintroduced by Judy Garland in
Thoroughbreds Don't Cry (film).

Got My Mind on Music
Words and music by Mack Gordon and Harry Revel.
Robbins Music Corp.
Introduced by Alice Faye, Joan Davis, Marjorie Weaver, and The
Raymond Scott Quintet in *Sally, Irene and Mary* (film, 1938).

Great Speckled Bird, The
Words and music by Rev. Guy Smith.
Westpar Music Corp.

Greatest Mistake of My Life (English)
Words and music by James Netson.
Irwin Dash Music Co., Ltd., London, England/Mills Music, Inc.

Gypsy in My Soul, The
Words by Moe Jaffe, music by Clay Boland.
Words & Music, Inc.
Introduced in University of Pennsylvania Mask and Wig Club
production, *Fifty-Fifty* (revue).

Half Moon on the Hudson
Words by Walter Bullock, music by Harold Spina.
Robbins Music Corp.
Introduced by Alice Faye, The Brian Sisters, Joan Davis, and
Marjorie Weaver in *Sally, Irene and Mary* (film, 1938).

Harbor Lights (English)
Words by Jimmy Kennedy, music by Hugh Williams (pseudonym
for Will Grosz).
The Peter Maurice Music Co., Ltd., London, England/
Chappell & Co., Inc.
Best-selling record by Rudy Vallée. Used as background music for
The Long Voyage Home (film, 1940). Revived in 1950 with best-
selling record by Sammy Kaye and his Orchestra and in 1960 with
best-selling record by The Platters (Mercury).

Have You Got Any Castles, Baby?
Words by Johnny Mercer, music by Richard A. Whiting.
Harms, Inc.
Introduced by Priscilla Lane in *Varsity Show* (film).

Have You Met Miss Jones?
Words by Lorenz Hart, music by Richard Rodgers.
Chappell & Co., Inc.
Introduced by Joy Hodges and Austin Marshall in *I'd Rather Be
Right* (musical). Introduced in London by Bobby Howes in *All
Clear* (revue, 1940).

Havin' a Ball
Words and music by Andy Razaf and James P. Johnson.
Mayfair Music Corp.

He Ain't Got Rhythm
Words and music by Irving Berlin.
Irving Berlin Music Corp.
Introduced by Alice Faye, The Ritz Brothers, and girls' chorus in
On the Avenue (film).

Heaven Help This Heart of Mine
Words and music by Walter G. Samuels, Leonard Whitcup, and
Teddy Powell.
Chappell & Co., Inc.

High, Wide and Handsome
Words by Oscar Hammerstein II, music by Jerome Kern.
T. B. Harms Co.
Introduced by Irene Dunne in *High, Wide and Handsome* (film).

Home Town (English)
Words and music by Jimmy Kennedy and Michael Carr.
The Peter Maurice Music Co., Ltd., London, England/De Sylva,
Brown & Henderson, Inc.

Hooray for Hollywood
Words by Johnny Mercer, music by Richard A. Whiting.
Harms, Inc.
Introduced by Johnny "Scat" Davis, Frances Langford, and Benny
Goodman and his Orchestra in *Hollywood Hotel* (film). Sung by
Sammy Davis, Jr. in *Pepe* (film, 1960).

Horse with the Dreamy Eyes, The
Words by Chet Forrest and Bob Wright, music by Walter Donaldson.
Robbins Music Corp.
Introduced by Cliff Edwards, Una Merkel, Clark Gable, Hattie
McDaniel, and Jean Harlow in *Saratoga* (film).

How Could You?
Words by Al Dubin, music by Harry Warren.
Remick Music Corp.
Introduced by Ann Sheridan in *San Quentin* (film).

I Can Dream, Can't I?
Words by Irving Kahal, music by Sammy Fain.
Chappell & Co., Inc.
Introduced by Tamara in *Right This Way* (revue). Revived in
1949-50 with best-selling record by The Andrews Sisters (Decca).

I Can't Be Bothered Now
Words by Ira Gershwin, music by George Gershwin.
Gershwin Publishing Corp.
Introduced by Fred Astaire in *A Damsel in Distress* (film).

I Could Use a Dream
Words by Walter Bullock, music by Harold Spina.
Robbins Music Corp.
Introduced by Tony Martin and Alice Faye in *Sally, Irene and Mary* (film, 1938).

I Double Dare You
Words and music by Terry Shand and Jimmy Eaton.
Shapiro, Bernstein & Co., Inc.
Introduced by Freddy Martin and his Orchestra.

I Hit a New High
Words by Harold Adamson, music by Jimmy McHugh.
Robbins Music Corp.
Introduced by Lily Pons in *Hitting a New High* (film).

I Hum a Waltz
Words and music by Mack Gordon and Harry Revel.
Miller Music Corp.
Introduced by Barbara Stanwyck in *This Is My Affair* (film).

I Know Now
Words by Al Dubin, music by Harry Warren.
Remick Music Corp.
Introduced by Doris Weston in *The Singing Marine* (film).

I Live the Life I Love
Words and music by Clay Boland.
Words & Music, Inc.
Introduced in University of Pennsylvania Mask and Wig Club production, *Fifty-Fifty* (revue).

I See Your Face before Me
Words by Howard Dietz, music by Arthur Schwartz.
De Sylva, Brown & Henderson, Inc.
Introduced by Jack Buchanan, Evelyn Laye, and Adele Dixon in *Between the Devil* (musical).

I Still Love To Kiss You Goodnight
Words by Walter Bullock, music by Harold Spina.
Leo Feist, Inc.
Introduced by Pat Paterson in *Fifty-Second Street* (film).

I Wanna Be in Winchell's Column
Words and music by Mack Gordon and Harry Revel.
Leo Feist, Inc.
Introduced by Dick Baldwin in *Love and Hisses* (film).

I Want You for Christmas
Words by Charles Tobias, music by Sam H. Stept and
Ned Washington.
Harms, Inc.

I Wish I Were in Love Again
Words by Lorenz Hart, music by Richard Rodgers.
Chappell & Co., Inc.
Introduced by Grace McDonald and Rolly Pickert in *Babes in Arms*
(musical). Sung by Mickey Rooney and Judy Garland in *Words
and Music* (film, 1948).

I'd Rather Be Right
Words by Lorenz Hart, music by Richard Rodgers.
Chappell & Co., Inc., 1937, 1940.
Introduced by Austin Marshall, Joy Hodges, Mary Jane Walsh,
George M. Cohan, and ensemble in *I'd Rather Be Right* (musical).
An earlier version, dropped from show before New York opening,
with new lyrics and retitled "Now That I Know You," introduced
by Marie Nash and Earl Oxford in *Two Weeks with Pay* (revue,
1940).

If It's the Last Thing I Do
Words and music by Sammy Cahn and Saul Chaplin.
De Sylva, Brown & Henderson, Inc.

If My Heart Could Only Talk
Words and music by Walter G. Samuels, Leonard Whitcup, and
Teddy Powell.
Miller Music Corp.

I'll Take Romance
Words by Oscar Hammerstein II, music by Ben Oakland.
Bourne Co./Williamson Music, Inc.
Introduced by Grace Moore in *I'll Take Romance* (film).

I'm Bubbling Over
Words and music by Mack Gordon and Harry Revel.
Robbins Music Corp.
Introduced by Grace Bradley and The Brewster Twins in
Wake Up and Live (film).

I'm Feelin' Like a Million
Words by Arthur Freed, music by Nacio Herb Brown.
Robbins Music Corp.
Introduced by Eleanor Powell and George Murphy in *Broadway
Melody of 1938* (film).

I'm Gonna Move on the Outskirts of Town, also known as I'm Gonna Move to the Outskirts of Town

Words by William Weldon and Andy Razaf, music by William Weldon.
Leeds Music Corp., 1937, 1942.
Introduced by Casey Bill (pseudonym for William Weldon), under title "We Gonna Move (to the Outskirts of Town)." Additional lyrics by Razaf added in 1942. Best-selling records in 1942, under title "I'm Gonna Move to the Outskirts of Town," by Count Basie and his Orchestra, vocal by Jimmy Rushing (Columbia) and Louis Jordon and his Tympany Five (Decca).

I'm Wishing

Words by Larry Morey, music by Frank Churchill.
Bourne Co.
Introduced by voice of Adrienne Caselotti, as Snow White, in *Snow White and the Seven Dwarfs* (cartoon film).

In a Little Dutch Kindergarten (Down by the Zuider Zee) (Dutch)

English words by Al Bryan, Dutch words by Herre De Vos, music by L. Rosenstock.
J. Poeltuyn, Amsterdam, Holland/Sam Fox Publishing Co., Inc.

In a Little Hula Heaven

Words and music by Leo Robin and Ralph Rainger.
Famous Music Corp.
Introduced by Bing Crosby and Shirley Ross in *Waikiki Wedding* (film).

In the Shade of the New Apple Tree

Words by E. Y. Harburg, music by Harold Arlen.
Chappell & Co., Inc.
Introduced by Jack Whiting, Hugh Martin, Ralph Blane, Harold Cook, and John Smedburg in *Hooray for What!* (musical).

In the Still of the Night

Words and music by Cole Porter.
Chappell & Co., Inc.
Introduced by Nelson Eddy in *Rosalie* (film).

It Looks Like Rain in Cherry Blossom Lane

Words and music by Edgar Leslie and Joe Burke.
Edwin H. Morris & Co., Inc.
Introduced by Guy Lombardo and his Royal Canadians.

It Seems Like Old Times

Words and music by Charles Tobias and Sam H. Stept.
Anne-Rachel Music Corp.
Introduced by Guy Lombardo and his Royal Canadians. Theme of Arthur Godfrey's radio and television shows.

It's On, It's Off
Words and music by Sam Coslow and Al Siegel.
Paramount Music Corp.
Introduced by Martha Raye in *Double or Nothing* (film).

It's Raining Sunbeams
Words by Sam Coslow, music by Frederick Hollander.
Leo Feist, Inc.
Introduced by Deanna Durbin in *100 Men and a Girl* (film).

It's Swell of You
Words by Mack Gordon, music by Harry Revel.
Robbins Music Corp.
Introduced by voice of Buddy Clark, dubbed for Jack Haley, in
Wake Up and Live (film).

It's the Natural Thing To Do
Words by John Burke, music by Arthur Johnston.
Anne-Rachel Music Corp.
Introduced by Bing Crosby in *Double or Nothing* (film).

I've a Strange New Rhythm in My Heart
Words and music by Cole Porter.
Chappell & Co., Inc.
Introduced by Eleanor Powell in *Rosalie* (film).

I've Gone Romantic on You
Words by E. Y. Harburg, music by Harold Arlen.
Chappell & Co., Inc.
Introduced by Jack Whiting and June Clyde in *Hooray for What!*
(musical).

I've Got Beginner's Luck see (I've Got) Beginner's Luck.

I've Got My Love To Keep Me Warm
Words and music by Irving Berlin.
Irving Berlin Music Corp.
Introduced by E. E. Clive, Dick Powell, and Alice Faye in *On the
Avenue* (film). Revived in 1949 with best-selling record by Les
Brown and his Orchestra.

I've Got To Be a Rug Cutter
Words and music by Edward Kennedy "Duke" Ellington.
American Academy of Music, Inc.
Featured by Duke Ellington and his Orchestra, vocal by Rex Stewart,
Hayes Alvis, and Harry Carney, in *Hit Parade* (film).

I've Hitched My Wagon to a Star
Words by Johnny Mercer, music by Richard A. Whiting.
Harms, Inc.
Introduced by Dick Powell, with Raymond Paige and his Orchestra,
in *Hollywood Hotel* (film).

I've Taken a Fancy to You
Words by Sidney D. Mitchell, music by Lew Pollack.
Movietone Music Corp.
Introduced in *In Old Chicago* (film, 1938).

Johnny One Note
Words by Lorenz Hart, music by Richard Rodgers.
Chappell & Co., Inc.
Introduced by Wynn Murray in *Babes in Arms* (musical). Sung by
Judy Garland in *Words and Music* (film, 1948).

Joint Is Jumpin', The, see 1940.

Jolly Tar and the Milkmaid, The
Words by Ira Gershwin, music by George Gershwin.
Gershwin Publishing Corp./Chappell & Co., Inc.
Introduced by Fred Astaire, Jan Duggan, Mary Dean, Pearl
Amatore, Betty Rone, and chorus in *A Damsel in Distress* (film).

Josephine
Words by Gus Kahn, music by Wayne King and Bruce Bivens.
Leo Feist, Inc.
Introduced by Wayne King and his Orchestra.

Jubilee
Words by Stanley Adams, music by Hoagy Carmichael.
Famous Music Corp.
Introduced by Louis Armstrong in *Every Day's a Holiday* (film).

Just a Mood
Words by Spencer Williams, music by Benny Carter.
Mills Music, Inc./The Peter Maurice Music Co., Ltd.
Introduced in France by and theme song of Willie Lewis and his
Orchestra.

Just a Quiet Evening
Words by Johnny Mercer, music by Richard A. Whiting.
Harms, Inc.
Introduced by Ross Alexander in *Ready, Willing and Able* (film).

Just Another Rhumba
Words by Ira Gershwin, music by George Gershwin.
Gershwin Publishing Corp., 1937, 1959.
Composed for, but not used in, *Goldwyn Follies* (film, 1938).

Just Because
Words and music by Bob Shelton, Joe Shelton, and Sid Robin.
Leeds Music Corp.

Lady Is a Tramp, The
Words by Lorenz Hart, music by Richard Rodgers.
Chappell & Co., Inc.
Introduced by Mitzi Green in *Babes in Arms* (musical). Performed instrumentally in film version, 1939, by Lena Horne in *Words and Music* (film, 1948), and by Frank Sinatra in *Pal Joey* (film, 1957).

Lambeth Walk (English)
Words and music by Noel Gay (pseudonym for Reginald M. Armitage) and Douglas Furber.
Campbell-Connelly Co., Ltd., London, England/Mills Music, Inc.
Introduced in London by Lupino Lane in *Me and My Girl* (musical). Dance originated by Adele England.

Last Night I Dreamed of You
Words by Walter Hirsch, music by Lou Handman.
Anne-Rachel Music Corp.
Introduced by Frances Langford in *The Hit Parade* (film).

Leaning on the Lamp Post (English)
Words and music by Noel Gay (pseudonym for Reginald M. Armitage).
Campbell-Connelly Co., Ltd., London, England/Mills Music, Inc.
Introduced by George Formby in *Feather Your Nest* (British film). Revived in 1966 with best-selling record by Herman's Hermits (MGM).

Let's Call the Whole Thing Off
Words by Ira Gershwin, music by George Gershwin.
Gershwin Publishing Corp./Chappell & Co., Inc.
Introduced by Fred Astaire and Ginger Rogers in *Shall We Dance?* (film).

Let's Give Love Another Chance
Words by Harold Adamson, music by Jimmy McHugh.
Robbins Music Corp.
Introduced by Lily Pons in *Hitting a New High* (film).

Life Goes to a Party
Music by Harry James and Benny Goodman.
Robbins Music Corp.
Swing instrumental, introduced by Benny Goodman and his Orchestra.

Life's a Dance
Words by E. Y. Harburg, music by Harold Arlen.
Chappell & Co., Inc.
Introduced by Robert Shafer in *Hooray for What!* (musical).

Listen My Children and You Shall Hear
Words by Ralph Freed, music by Burton Lane.
Paramount Music Corp.
Introduced by Martha Raye in *Double or Nothing* (film).

Love Bug Will Bite You (If You Don't Watch Out), The
Words and music by Pinky Tomlin.
Anne-Rachel Music Corp.
Introduced by Pinky Tomlin.

Love Is Never out of Season
Words by Lew Brown, music by Sammy Fain.
Leo Feist, Inc.
Introduced by Harriet Hilliard and William Brady in *New Faces of 1937* (film).

Loveliness of You, The
Words by Mack Gordon, music by Harry Revel.
Miller Music Corp.
Introduced by Tony Martin in *You Can't Have Everything* (film).

Lovely One
Words by Frank Loesser, music by Manning Sherwin.
Leo Feist, Inc.
Introduced by The Wiere Brothers, Fred Lawrence, and Virginia Verrill in *Walter Wanger's Vogues of 1938* (film).

Make a Wish
Words by Louis Alter and Paul Francis Webster, music by Oscar Straus.
Leo Feist, Inc.
Introduced by Bobby Breen and Basil Rathbone in *Make a Wish* (film).

Me, Myself and I (Are All in Love with You)
Words and music by Irving Gordon, Allan Roberts, and Alvin S. Kaufman.
Words & Music, Inc.

Merry-Go-Round Broke Down, The
Words and music by Cliff Friend and Dave Franklin.
Harms, Inc.
Introduced by Guy Lombardo and his Royal Canadians.

Message from the Man in the Moon, A
Words by Gus Kahn, music by Bronislaw Kaper and Walter Jurmann.
Robbins Music Corp.
Introduced by Allan Jones in *A Day at the Races* (film).

Moanin' in the Mornin'
Words by E. Y. Harburg, music by Harold Arlen.
Chappell & Co., Inc.
Introduced by Vivian Vance and "The Singing Spies" in *Hooray for What!* (musical).

Mood That I'm In, The
Words and music by Abner Silver and Al Sherman.
Broadway Music Corp.

Moon Got in My Eyes, The
Words by Johnny Burke, music by Arthur Johnston.
Anne-Rachel Music Corp.
Introduced by Bing Crosby in *Double or Nothing* (film).

Moon of Manakoora, The
Words by Frank Loesser, music by Alfred Newman.
Frank Music Corp.
Introduced by Dorothy Lamour in *The Hurricane* (film).

Moonlight on the Campus
Words by Johnny Mercer, music by Richard A. Whiting.
Harms, Inc.
Introduced by Dick Powell in *Varsity Show* (film).

Music in My Heart
Words by Louis Alter and Paul Francis Webster, music by Oscar Straus.
Leo Feist, Inc.
Introduced by Marion Claire in *Make a Wish* (film).

My Dreams Have Gone with the Wind
Words and music by Milton Drake and Ben Oakland.
Bourne Co.
Introduced by Joyce Compton, and reprised by Irene Dunne, in *The Awful Truth* (film).

My Fine Feathered Friend
Words by Harold Adamson, music by Jimmy McHugh.
Robbins Music Corp.
Introduced by Alice Faye in *You're a Sweetheart* (film).

My First Impression of You
Words by Charles Tobias, music by Sam H. Stept.
Chappell & Co., Inc.

My Funny Valentine
Words by Lorenz Hart, music by Richard Rodgers.
Chappell & Co., Inc.
Introduced by Mitzi Green in *Babes in Arms* (musical). Interpolated by Jeanne Crain and Alan Young in *Gentlemen Marry Brunettes* (film, 1955) and interpolated in *Pal Joey* (film, 1957).

My Little Buckaroo
Words by Jack Scholl, music by M. K. Jerome.
M. Witmark & Sons.
Sung by Dick Foran in *Cherokee Strip* (film, 1940). Interpolated in
Ridin' Down the Canyon (film, 1942) and *Don't Fence Me In* (film,
1945).

Never in a Million Years
Words by Mack Gordon, music by Harry Revel.
Robbins Music Corp.
Introduced by voice of Buddy Clark, dubbed for Jack Haley, in
Wake Up and Live (film).

New Faces
Words and music by Charles Henderson.
Leo Feist, Inc.
Introduced in *New Faces of 1937* (film).

Nice Work If You Can Get It
Words by Ira Gershwin, music by George Gershwin.
Gershwin Publishing Corp./Chappell & Co., Inc.
Introduced by Jan Duggan, Mary Dean, Pearl Amatore, and
Fred Astaire in *A Damsel in Distress* (film).

Nightmare
Music by Artie Shaw.
Anne-Rachel Music Corp.
Theme song of Artie Shaw and his Orchestra.

Nobody Makes a Pass at Me
Words and music by Harold Rome.
Mills Music, Inc.
Introduced by Millie Weitz in *Pins and Needles* (revue).

Old Flame Never Dies, An
Words by Albert Stillman and Laurence Stallings, music by
Arthur Schwartz.
Robbins Music Corp.
Introduced by Anne Booth, and reprised by Miss Booth, Ronald
Graham, and Mona Barrie, in *Virginia* (musical).

Old King Cole
Words by Johnny Mercer, music by Richard A. Whiting.
Harms, Inc.
Introduced by Johnny "Scat" Davis in *Varsity Show* (film).

On the Sunny Side of the Rockies
Words and music by Roy Ingraham and Harry Tobias.
Sam Fox Publishing Co., Inc.
Introduced by Smith Ballew in *Roll Along Cowboy* (film).

On with the Dance
Words by Johnny Mercer, music by Richard A. Whiting.
Harms, Inc.
Introduced by Rosemary Lane in *Varsity Show* (film).

Once in a While
Words by Bud Green, music by Michael Edwards.
Miller Music Corp.
Introduced as instrumental by Tommy Dorsey and his Orchestra under the title, "Dancing with You." Vocal version also introduced by Dorsey, vocal by Jack Leonard. Featured in *I'll Get By* (film, 1950).

One Big Union for Two
Words and music by Harold Rome.
Mills Music, Inc.
Introduced by ensemble in *Pins and Needles* (revue).

One Song
Words by Larry Morey, music by Frank Churchill.
Bourne Co.
Introduced by voice of Harry Stockwell, as the Prince, in *Snow White and the Seven Dwarfs* (cartoon film).

Our Penthouse on Third Avenue
Words by Lew Brown, music by Sammy Fain.
Leo Feist, Inc.
Introduced by Harriet Hilliard and William Brady in *New Faces of 1937* (film).

Our Song
Words by Dorothy Fields, music by Jerome Kern.
T. B. Harms Co.
Introduced by Grace Moore in *When You're in Love* (film).

Paradise Isle (Hawaiian)
Words and music by Sam Koki.
Mills Music, Inc.
Introduced in *Paradise Isle* (film).

Peckin'
Words and music by Ben Pollack and Harry James.
Mills Music, Inc.
Introduced on records by Ben Pollack and his Orchestra, vocal by Harry James (Variety). Featured as grand finale in *New Faces of 1937* (film).

Please Pardon Us, We're in Love
Words and music by Mack Gordon and Harry Revel.
Miller Music Corp.
Introduced by Alice Faye in *You Can't Have Everything* (film).

Popcorn Man
Words and music by Will Hudson, Lou Klein, and Bill Livingston.
Mills Music, Inc.

Posin'
Words and music by Sammy Cahn and Saul Chaplin.
Chappell & Co., Inc.
Introduced by Fletcher Henderson's Orchestra at Grand Terrace
(Chicago nightclub) in *The New Grand Terrace Revue* (nightclub revue).

Powerhouse
Music by Raymond Scott.
Advanced Music Corp.
Introduced by The Raymond Scott Quintet.

Public Melody Number One
Words by Ted Koehler, music by Harold Arlen.
Famous Music Corp.
Introduced by Martha Raye and Louis Armstrong in *Artists and Models* (film).

Quaker City Jazz
Music by Jan Savitt and Jimmy Schultz.
Robbins Music Corp.
Theme song of Jan Savitt and his Top Hatters.

Remember Me?
Words by Al Dubin, music by Harry Warren.
M. Witmark & Sons.
Introduced by Kenny Baker in *Mr. Dodd Takes the Air* (film). Nominated for Academy Award, 1937. Best-selling record by Hal Kemp and his Orchestra, vocal by Skinnay Ennis. Sung by Errol Flynn and Eleanor Parker in *Never Say Goodbye* (film, 1946).

Roll 'Em
Music by Mary Lou Williams.
Robbins Music Corp.
Swing instrumental, introduced by Andy Kirk and his Orchestra. Best-selling record by Benny Goodman and his Orchestra (Victor).

Rollin' Plains
Words and music by Walter Samuels, Leonard Whitcup, and Teddy Powell.
La Salle Music Publishers, Inc.
Introduced by Tex Ritter in *Rollin' Plains* (film).

Rosalie
Words and music by Cole Porter.
Chappell & Co., Inc.
Introduced by Nelson Eddy in *Rosalie* (film).

Roses in December
Words and music by George Jessel and Ben Oakland.
Bourne Co.
Introduced by Gene Raymond and Harriet Hilliard in *Life of the Party* (film).

Sail Along, Silv'ry Moon
Words by Harry Tobias, music by Percy Wenrich.
Anne-Rachel Music Corp.
Revived in 1958 with best-selling record by Billy Vaughn and his Orchestra (Dot).

Sailboat in the Moonlight
Words and music by John Jacob Loeb and Carmen Lombardo.
De Sylva, Brown & Henderson, Inc.
Introduced by Guy Lombardo and his Royal Canadians.

Satan Takes a Holiday
Music by Larry Clinton.
Lincoln Music Corp.
Swing instrumental, introduced by Tommy Dorsey and his Orchestra.

Scattin' at the Kit Kat
Words by Irving Mills, music by Edward Kennedy "Duke" Ellington.
American Academy of Music, Inc.
Introduced by Duke Ellington and his Orchestra.

Sentimental and Melancholy
Words by Johnny Mercer, music by Richard A. Whiting.
Harms, Inc.
Introduced by Wini Shaw in *Ready, Willing and Able* (film).

September in the Rain
Words by Al Dubin, music by Harry Warren.
Remick Music Corp.
Introduced by James Melton in *Melody for Two* (film).

Seventh Heaven
Words by Sidney D. Mitchell, music by Lew Pollack.
Movietone Music Corp.
Introduced by chorus in *Seventh Heaven* (film).

Shag, The
Words and music by Al J. Neiburg, Jerry Livingston, and Milton Ager.
Advanced Music Corp.

Shall We Dance?
Words by Ira Gershwin, music by George Gershwin.
Gershwin Publishing Corp./Chappell & Co., Inc.
Introduced by Fred Astaire in *Shall We Dance?* (film).

Silhouetted in the Moonlight
Words by Johnny Mercer, music by Richard A. Whiting.
Harms, Inc.
Introduced by Rosemary Lane in *Hollywood Hotel* (film).

Sing Me a Song with Social Significance
Words and music by Harold Rome.
Mills Music, Inc.
Introduced by ensemble in *Pins and Needles* (revue).

Skrontch
Words and music by Henry Nemo, Irving Mills, and Edward
    Kennedy "Duke" Ellington.
Mills Music, Inc.
Introduced by Duke Ellington and his Orchestra, vocal by
    Ivie Anderson.

Slap That Bass
Words by Ira Gershwin, music by George Gershwin.
Gershwin Publishing Corp./Chappell & Co., Inc.
Introduced by Fred Astaire in *Shall We Dance?* (film).

Slumming on Park Avenue
Words and music by Irving Berlin.
Irving Berlin Music Corp.
Introduced by Alice Faye, The Ritz Brothers, and chorus in
    On the Avenue (film).

(You Know It All) Smarty
Words by Ralph Freed, music by Burton Lane.
Paramount Music Corp.
Introduced by Bing Crosby in *Double or Nothing* (film).

Snake Charmer, The
Words and music by Leonard Whitcup and Teddy Powell.
Piedmont Music Co., Inc.
Introduced by Teddy Powell and his Orchestra.

So Rare
Words by Jack Sharpe, music by Jerry Herst.
Robbins Music Corp.
Introduced by Jimmy Dorsey and his Orchestra. Revived in 1957
    with best-selling record by Jimmy Dorsey and his Orchestra
    (Fraternity).

Somebody Else Is Taking My Place
Words and music by Dick Howard, Bob Ellsworth, and Russ Morgan.
Shapiro, Bernstein & Co., Inc.
Introduced by Russ Morgan and his Orchestra. Best-selling record
    in 1941 by Benny Goodman and his Orchestra, vocal by Peggy Lee
    (Columbia).

Someday My Prince Will Come
Words and music by Larry Morey and Frank Churchill.
Bourne Co.
Introduced by voice of Adrienne Caselotti, as Snow White, in
  Snow White and the Seven Dwarfs (cartoon film).

Song of the Marines, The (We're Shovin' Right Off Again)
Words by Al Dubin, music by Harry Warren.
Remick Music Corp.
Introduced by Dick Powell in *The Singing Marine* (film).

Sophia, see Wake Up, Brother, and Dance.

Stardust on the Moon
Words and music by Emery Deutsch and Jimmy Rogan.
Edward B. Marks Music Corp.
Theme song of Emery Deutsch and his Orchestra.

Stiff Upper Lip
Words by Ira Gershwin, music by George Gershwin.
Gershwin Publishing Corp./Chappell & Co., Inc.
Introduced by Gracie Allen in *A Damsel in Distress* (film).

Stop! You're Breakin' My Heart
Words by Ted Koehler, music by Burton Lane.
Famous Music Corp.
Introduced by Judy Canova and Ben Blue in *Artists and Models*
  (film).

Study in Brown
Music by Larry Clinton.
Lincoln Music Corp.
Written for The Casa Loma Orchestra. First recording by Bunny
  Berigan and his Orchestra. Signature theme of Larry Clinton and
  his Orchestra.

Sunday in the Park
Words and music by Harold Rome.
Mills Music, Inc.
Introduced by ensemble in *Pins and Needles* (revue).

Susie Sapple
Words and music by Leo Robin and Ralph Rainger.
Paramount Music Corp.
Introduced in *Souls at Sea* (film).

Sweet As a Song
Words and music by Mack Gordon and Harry Revel.
Robbins Music Corp.
Introduced by Tony Martin in *Sally, Irene and Mary* (film, 1938).

Sweet Heartache
Words by Ned Washington, music by Sam H. Stept.
Anne-Rachel Music Corp.
Introduced by Frances Langford in *The Hit Parade* (film).

Sweet Is the Word for You
Words by Leo Robin, music by Ralph Rainger.
Famous Music Corp.
Introduced by Bing Crosby in *Waikiki Wedding* (film).

Sweet Leilani (Hawaiian)
Words and music by Harry Owens.
Anne-Rachel Music Corp.
Introduced by Bing Crosby in *Waikiki Wedding* (film). Academy
Award-winning song, 1937.

Sweet Sixty-Five
Words by Lorenz Hart, music by Richard Rodgers.
Chappell & Co., Inc.
Introduced by Joy Hodges and Austin Marshall in *I'd Rather Be
Right* (musical).

Sweet Someone
Words and music by Mack Gordon and Harry Revel.
Leo Feist, Inc.
Introduced by Simone Simon in *Love and Hisses* (film).

Swing High, Swing Low
Words by Ralph Freed, music by Burton Lane.
Famous Music Corp.
Introduced by Dorothy Lamour in *Swing High, Swing Low* (film).

Swing Is Here To Stay
Words and music by Mack Gordon and Harry Revel.
Robbins Music Corp.
Introduced by Jeni Le Gon and The Peters Sisters in *Ali Baba
Goes to Town* (film).

Take and Take and Take
Words by Lorenz Hart, music by Richard Rodgers.
Chappell & Co., Inc.
Introduced by Mary Jane Walsh in *I'd Rather Be Right* (musical).

Thanks for the Memory
Words and music by Leo Robin and Ralph Rainger.
Paramount Music Corp.
Introduced by Bob Hope and Shirley Ross in *Big Broadcast of 1938*
(film, 1938). Academy Award-winning song, 1938.

That Old Feeling
Words and music by Lew Brown and Sammy Fain.
Leo Feist, Inc.
Introduced by Virginia Verrill in *Walter Wanger's Vogues of 1938*
(film). Nominated for Academy Award, 1937. Sung by voice of
Jane Froman on soundtrack of *With a Song in My Heart* (film,
1952).

There's a Gold Mine in the Sky
Words and music by Charles Kenny and Nick Kenny.
Bourne Co.
Introduced by Gene Autry in *Gold Mine in the Sky* (film, 1938).
Best-selling record by Bing Crosby (Decca).

There's a Lull in My Life
Words by Mack Gordon, music by Harry Revel.
Robbins Music Corp.
Introduced by Alice Faye in *Wake Up and Live* (film).

They All Laughed
Words by Ira Gershwin, music by George Gershwin.
Gershwin Publishing Corp./Chappell & Co., Inc.
Introduced by Ginger Rogers in *Shall We Dance?* (film).

They Can't Take That Away from Me
Words by Ira Gershwin, music by George Gershwin.
Gershwin Publishing Corp.
Introduced by Fred Astaire in *Shall We Dance?* (film). Nominated
for Academy Award, 1937. Also sung by Astaire in *The Barclays
of Broadway* (film, 1949).

Things Are Looking Up
Words by Ira Gershwin, music by George Gershwin.
Gershwin Publishing Corp./Chappell & Co., Inc.
Introduced by Fred Astaire, and danced to by Astaire and Joan
Fontaine, in *A Damsel in Distress* (film).

Things I Want, The
Words by Oscar Hammerstein II, music by Jerome Kern.
T. B. Harms Co.
Introduced by Dorothy Lamour in *High, Wide and Handsome* (film).

This Never Happened Before
Words by Harold Adamson, music by Jimmy McHugh.
Robbins Music Corp.
Introduced by Lily Pons in *Hitting a New High* (film).

This Year's Kisses
Words and music by Irving Berlin.
Irving Berlin Music Corp.
Introduced by Alice Faye in *On the Avenue* (film).

Thrill of a Lifetime
Words and music by Frederick Hollander, Sam Coslow, and
Carmen Lombardo.
Chappell & Co., Inc.
Introduced by Dorothy Lamour, and reprised by Leif Erickson,
in *Thrill of a Lifetime* (film).

Tomorrow Is Another Day
Words by Gus Kahn, music by Bronislaw Kaper and Walter Jurmann.
Robbins Music Corp.
Introduced by Allan Jones in *A Day at the Races* (film).

Too Marvelous for Words
Words by Johnny Mercer, music by Richard A. Whiting.
Harms, Inc.
Introduced by Ross Alexander and Wini Shaw in *Ready, Willing and
Able* (film). Interpolated in *Dark Passage* (film, 1947) and sung
by Frankie Laine in *On the Sunny Side of the Street* (film, 1951).

Toy Trumpet, The
Words by Sidney D. Mitchell and Lew Pollack, music by
Raymond Scott.
Advanced Music Corp., 1937, 1938.
Introduced instrumentally by The Raymond Scott Quintet. Lyrics
added in 1938. Song version introduced by Shirley Temple, danced
to by Bill Robinson, and performed by The Raymond Scott
Quintet in *Rebecca of Sunnybrook Farm* (film, 1938).

Travelin' Light
Words by Sidney Clare, music by Harry Akst.
Movietone Music Corp.
Introduced by Anthony (Tony) Martin in *Sing and Be Happy* (film).

Triplets
Words by Howard Dietz, music by Arthur Schwartz.
De Sylva, Brown & Henderson, Inc.
Introduced by The Tune Twisters in *Between the Devil* (musical).
Sung by Fred Astaire, Nanette Fabray, and Jack Buchanan in
The Band Wagon (film, 1953).

True Confession
Words and music by Sam Coslow and Frederick Hollander.
Famous Music Corp.
From *True Confession* (film).

Turn Off the Moon
Words and music by Sam Coslow.
Paramount Music Corp.
Introduced by Kenny Baker in *Turn Off the Moon* (film).

Twilight in Turkey
Music by Raymond Scott.
Advanced Music Corp.
Introduced by The Raymond Scott Quintet. Featured in *Ali Baba Goes to Town* (film).

Vieni, Vieni (Corsican)
English words by Rudy Vallée, Italian-French words by George Koger and Henri Varna, music by Vincent Scotto.
Vincent B. Scotto, Paris, France, 1934/M. Witmark & Sons, 1934, 1937.
New arrangement, with added part-English chorus, popularized by Rudy Vallée.

Wake Up and Live
Words by Mack Gordon, music by Harry Revel.
Robbins Music Corp.
Introduced by Alice Faye in *Wake Up and Live* (film).

Wake Up, Brother, and Dance
Words by Ira Gershwin, music by George Gershwin.
Gershwin Publishing Corp.
Written for, but not used in, *Shall We Dance?* (film). With new title, "Sophia," and new lyrics copyrighted by Ira Gershwin in 1964, song introduced by Dean Martin in *Kiss Me Stupid* (film, 1964).

Was It Rain?
Words by Walter Hirsch, music by Lou Handman.
Anne-Rachel Music Corp.
Introduced by Frances Langford in *The Hit Parade* (film).

Way Out West (on West End Avenue)
Words by Lorenz Hart, music by Richard Rodgers.
Chappell & Co., Inc.
Introduced by Wynn Murray, Alex Courtney, Clifton Darling, James Gillis, and Robert Rounseville in *Babes in Arms* (musical).

We're Working Our Way through College
Words by Johnny Mercer, music by Richard A. Whiting.
Harms, Inc.
Introduced by Dick Powell and chorus in *Varsity Show* (film).

What a Beautiful Beginning
Words by Sidney Clare, music by Harry Akst.
Movietone Music Corp.
Introduced by Anthony (Tony) Martin in *Sing and Be Happy* (film).

What Good Is Love
Words and music by Harold Rome.
Mills Music, Inc.
Introduced by Nettie Harary in *Pins and Needles* (revue).

What Will I Tell My Heart
Words and music by Peter Tinturin, Jack Lawrence, and
  Irving Gordon.
De Sylva, Brown & Henderson, Inc.

When Love Is Young
Words by Harold Adamson, music by Jimmy McHugh.
Miller Music Corp.
Introduced by Virginia Bruce in *When Love Is Young* (film).

(Oh, How I'll Miss You) When Summer Is Gone
Words and music by Hal Kemp.
Morley Music Co., Inc.
Theme song of Hal Kemp and his Orchestra.

Where or When
Words by Lorenz Hart, music by Richard Rodgers.
Chappell & Co., Inc.
Introduced by Mitzi Green and Ray Heatherton in *Babes in Arms*
  (musical). Sung by Judy Garland in film version, 1939. Sung by
  Lena Horne in *Words and Music* (film, 1948). Used as theme in
  Gaby (film, 1956). Best-selling record in 1960 by Dion and The
  Belmonts (Laurie).

Whispers in the Dark
Words by Leo Robin, music by Frederick Hollander.
Famous Music Corp.
Introduced by Connee Boswell, with André Kostelanetz and his Or-
  chestra, in *Artists and Models* (film). Nominated for Academy
  Award, 1937.

Whistle While You Work
Words by Larry Morey, music by Frank Churchill.
Bourne Co.
Introduced by voice of Adrienne Caselotti, as Snow White, in
  Snow White and the Seven Dwarfs (cartoon film).

Whistling Boy, The
Words by Dorothy Fields, music by Jerome Kern.
T. B. Harms Co.
Introduced by Grace Moore in *When You're in Love* (film).

Who Knows?
Words and music by Cole Porter.
Chappell & Co., Inc.
Introduced by Nelson Eddy in *Rosalie* (film).

Why Did You Do It?
Words by Howard Dietz, music by Arthur Schwartz.
De Sylva, Brown & Henderson, Inc.
Introduced by Evelyn Laye and ensemble in *Between the Devil*
  (musical).

Why Should I Care?
Words and music by Cole Porter.
Chappell & Co., Inc.
Introduced in *Rosalie* (film).

Will You Marry Me Tomorrow, Maria?
Words by Oscar Hammerstein II, music by Jerome Kern.
T. B. Harms Co.
Introduced by William Frawley in *High, Wide and Handsome* (film).

With a Smile and a Song
Words by Larry Morey, music by Frank Churchill.
Bourne Co.
Introduced by voice of Adrienne Caselotti, as Snow White, in
  Snow White and the Seven Dwarfs (cartoon film).

Without Your Love
Words by Johnny Lange, music by Fred Stryker.
Miller Music Corp.
Introduced in *Pick a Star* (film).

You and I Know
Words by Albert Stillman and Laurence Stallings, music by
  Arthur Schwartz.
Robbins Music Corp.
Introduced by Anne Booth and Ronald Graham in *Virginia*
  (musical).

You Can't Have Everything
Words and music by Mack Gordon and Harry Revel.
Miller Music Corp.
Introduced by Alice Faye in *You Can't Have Everything* (film).

You Can't Stop Me from Dreaming
Words and music by Cliff Friend and Dave Franklin.
Remick Music Corp.
Introduced by Guy Lombardo and his Royal Canadians.

You Have Everything
Words by Howard Dietz, music by Arthur Schwartz.
De Sylva, Brown & Henderson, Inc.
Introduced by Charles Walters and Vilma Ebsen in *Between the
  Devil* (musical).

You Showed Me the Way
Words and music by Bud Green, Ella Fitzgerald, Teddy McRae, and
  Chick Webb.
Robbins Music Corp.
Introduced by Chick Webb and his Orchestra, vocal by Ella
  Fitzgerald.

You Took the Words Right Out of My Heart
Words and music by Leo Robin and Ralph Rainger.
Paramount Music Corp.
Introduced by Dorothy Lamour and Leif Erickson in *Big Broadcast of 1938* (film).

You're a Sweetheart
Words by Harold Adamson, music by Jimmy McHugh.
Robbins Music Corp.
Introduced by Alice Faye in *You're a Sweetheart* (film). Sung by Frank Sinatra in *Meet Danny Wilson* (film, 1952).

You're Laughing at Me
Words and music by Irving Berlin.
Irving Berlin Music Corp.
Introduced by Dick Powell in *On the Avenue* (film).

Yours (Cuban)
English words by Jack Sherr and Albert Gamse, Spanish words by Augustin Rodriguez, music by Gonzalo Roig.
Edward B. Marks Music Corp., 1931, 1932, 1937.
Original Spanish title, "Quiérme Mucho." First recording in Spanish by Tito Schipa (Victor). First English-language version, with lyrics by Carol Raven and entitled "Love Me Tonight," copyrighted in 1932. Present version sung by Gene Autry in *Sioux City Sue* (film, 1946). Best-selling records in 1941 by Jimmy Dorsey and his Orchestra (Decca) and in 1952 by Vera Lynn (London).

Yours and Mine
Words by Arthur Freed, music by Nacio Herb Brown.
Robbins Music Corp.
Introduced by Judy Garland, and reprised by Eleanor Powell, in *Broadway Melody of 1938* (film).

You've Got Something There
Words by Johnny Mercer, music by Richard A. Whiting.
Harms, Inc.
Introduced by Rosemary Lane and Dick Powell in *Varsity Show* (film).

1938

1938

April in My Heart
Words and music by Helen Meinard and Hoagy Carmichael.
Paramount Music Corp.
Introduced by Olympe Bradna in *Say It in French* (film).

Apurksady
Music by Gene Krupa and Chappie Willet.
Robbins Music Corp.
Theme song of Gene Krupa and his Orchestra.

At a Perfume Counter (on the Rue de la Paix)
Words by Edgar Leslie, music by Joe Burke.
Bregman, Vocco & Conn, Inc.
Introduced by Morton Downey and Wini Shaw at Billy Rose's Casa
  Manana (New York nightclub).

At Long Last Love
Words and music by Cole Porter.
Chappell & Co., Inc.
Introduced by Clifton Webb in *You Never Know* (musical).

At the Roxy Music Hall
Words by Lorenz Hart, music by Richard Rodgers.
Robbins Music Corp.
Introduced by Audrey Christie in *I Married an Angel* (musical).

At Your Beck and Call
Words and music by Eddie De Lange and Buck Ram.
Bourne Co./Scarsdale Music Corp.

A-Tisket A-Tasket
Words and music by Ella Fitzgerald and Al Feldman (also known as
  Van Alexander).
Robbins Music Corp.
Adapted from an American nursery song, which first appeared in
  print in 1879. Introduced and best-selling record by Ella Fitzger-
  ald, with Chick Webb and his Orchestra (Decca). Sung by Miss
  Fitzgerald in *Ride 'Em Cowboy* (film, 1942).

Bach Goes to Town
Music by Alec Templeton.
Leeds Music Corp.
Introduced by Benny Goodman and his Orchestra.

Be a Good Scout
Words by Harold Adamson, music by Jimmy McHugh.
Robbins Music Corp.
Introduced by Deanna Durbin in *That Certain Age* (film).

Between a Kiss and a Sigh
Words by Johnny Burke, music by Arthur Johnston.
Anne-Rachel Music Corp.

Bewildered
Words by Leonard Whitcup, music by Teddy Powell.
Miller Music Corp.
Best-selling records in 1949 by The Red Miller Trio (Bullet) and
    Amos Milburn (Aladdin).

Biggest Aspidastra in the World, The (English)
Words and music by James S. Hancock, W. G. Haines, and Tommie
    Connor.
Campbell-Connelly Co., Ltd., London, England/Robbins Music Corp.
Introduced by Gracie Fields.

Blue and Disillusioned
Words and music by Benny Davis and J. Fred Coots.
American Academy of Music, Inc.

Blue Light
Music by Edward Kennedy "Duke" Ellington.
American Academy of Music, Inc.
Introduced by Duke Ellington and his Orchestra.

Camel Hop
Music by Mary Lou Williams.
Robbins Music Corp.
Introduced by Andy Kirk and his Orchestra. Best-selling record by
    Benny Goodman and his Orchestra (Victor).

Cathedral in the Pines
Words and music by Charles Kenny and Nick Kenny.
Bourne Co.
First recording in 1957 by Pat Boone (Dot).

Change Partners
Words and music by Irving Berlin.
Irving Berlin Music Corp.
Introduced by Fred Astaire in *Carefree* (film). Nominated for
    Academy Award, 1938.

Chapel Bells
Words by Harold Adamson, music by Jimmy McHugh.
Robbins Music Corp.
Introduced by Deanna Durbin in *Mad about Music* (film).

Cherokee (English)
Music by Ray Noble.
The Peter Maurice Music Co., Ltd., London, England/Shapiro,
Bernstein & Co., Inc.
Introduced by Ray Noble and his Orchestra. Best-selling record in
1939 by Charlie Barnet and his Orchestra (Bluebird). Performed
by Charlie Barnet and his Orchestra in *Jam Session* (film, 1944).

Chimes of Arcady
Words by Harry Tobias, music by Percy Wenrich.
Tobey Music Corp.

Cinderella, Stay in My Arms (English)
Words and music by Jimmy Kennedy and Michael Carr.
The Peter Maurice Music Co., Ltd., London, England/Shapiro,
Bernstein & Co., Inc.

Cocoanut Grove (Hawaiian)
Words and music by Harry Owens.
Famous Music Corp.
Introduced by Harry Owens' Royal Hawaiian Orchestra in
Cocoanut Grove (film).

College Swing
Words by Frank Loesser, music by Hoagy Carmichael.
Famous Music Corp.
Introduced by Martha Raye, Betty Grable, and Skinnay Ennis in
College Swing (film).

Confidentially
Words by Al Dubin and Johnny Mercer, music by Harry Warren.
Harms, Inc.
Introduced by John Payne and Mabel Todd in *Garden of the Moon*
(film).

Could Be
Words by Johnny Mercer, music by Walter Donaldson.
Anne-Rachel Music Corp.

Cowboy and the Lady, The
Words by Arthur Quenzer, music by Lionel Newman.
Remick Music Corp.
Introduced in *The Cowboy and the Lady* (film). Nominated for
Academy Award, 1938.

Cowboy from Brooklyn
Words by Johnny Mercer, music by Harry Warren.
M. Witmark & Sons.
Introduced by Dick Powell in *Cowboy from Brooklyn* (film).

Cry, Baby, Cry
Words and music by Jimmy Eaton, Terry Shand, Remus Harris, and
Irving Melsher.
Shapiro, Bernstein & Co., Inc.
Best-selling record by Larry Clinton and his Orchestra (Victor).

Daydreaming (All Night Long)
Words by Johnny Mercer, music by Harry Warren.
Remick Music Corp.
Introduced by Rudy Vallée and Rosemary Lane in *Gold Diggers in
Paris* (film).

Dearest Love (English)
Words and music by Noël Coward.
Chappell & Co., Ltd., London, England/Chappell & Co., Inc.
Introduced in London by Muriel Barron and Max Oldaker, and re-
prised by Peggy Wood, in *Operette* (musical). Sung by Eva Ortega
and Hugh French in *Set to Music* (revue, 1939).

Deep in a Dream
Words by Eddie De Lange, music by Jimmy Van Heusen.
Harms, Inc.
Popularized by Guy Lombardo and his Royal Canadians and by
Russ Morgan and his Orchestra.

Did You Ever Get Stung?
Words by Lorenz Hart, music by Richard Rodgers.
Robbins Music Corp.
Introduced by Dennis Day, Vivienne Segal, and Charles Walters in
I Married an Angel (musical). Lyrics rewritten by Bob Wright
and Chet Forrest and song retitled "Little Work-a-day World" for
film version, 1942.

Dinner Music for a Pack of Hungry Cannibals
Music by Raymond Scott.
Advanced Music Corp.
Introduced by The Raymond Scott Quintet.

Do You Wanna Jump, Children?
Words and music by Al Donahue, Jimmy Van Heusen, Willie Bryant,
and Victor Selsman.
Advanced Music Corp.
Best-selling record by Count Basie and his Orchestra, vocal by
Jimmy Rushing (Decca).

Dog Town Blues
Music by Bob Haggart.
Leo Feist, Inc.
Introduced by Bob Crosby's Bobcats.

Don't Be That Way
Words by Mitchell Parish, music by Benny Goodman and Edgar
Sampson.
Robbins Music Corp.
Introduced instrumentally in 1934 by Chick Webb and his Orchestra
(Decca), with Edgar Sampson credited as composer. Best-selling
record in 1938 by Benny Goodman and his Orchestra (Victor).

Don't Cross Your Fingers, Cross Your Heart
Words and music by Johnny Marks, Al Donahue, and Larry Shay.
Advanced Music Corp.
Best-selling record by Henry Busse and his Orchestra (Decca).

Don't Let That Moon Get Away
Words by Johnny Burke, music by Jimmy Monaco.
Anne-Rachel Music Corp.
Introduced by Bing Crosby in *Sing You Sinners* (film).

Dreamy Hawaiian Moon (Hawaiian)
Words and music by Harry Owens.
Famous Music Corp.
Introduced by Harry Owens and his Royal Hawaiians in *Cocoanut
Grove* (film).

Dust
Words and music by Johnny Marvin.
Anne-Rachel Music Corp.
Introduced by Roy Rogers in *Under Western Stars* (film). Nominated
for Academy Award, 1938. Featured in *Under California Skies*
(film, 1948), "tenth anniversary" Rogers film.

Especially for You
Words and music by Orrin Tucker and Phil Grogan.
Shapiro, Bernstein & Co., Inc.
Introduced by Orrin Tucker and his Orchestra.

Every Tub
Music by William "Count" Basie and Ed Durham.
Bregman, Vocco & Conn, Inc.
Swing instrumental, introduced by Count Basie and his Orchestra.

F. D. R. Jones
Words and music by Harold Rome.
Florence Music Co., Inc.
Introduced by Rex Ingram in *Sing Out the News* (revue).

Falling in Love with Love
Words by Lorenz Hart, music by Richard Rodgers.
Chappell & Co., Inc.
Introduced by Muriel Angelus in *The Boys from Syracuse* (musical).
Sung by Allan Jones in film version, 1940.

Far, Far Away
Words and music by Cole Porter.
Chappell & Co., Inc.
Introduced by William Gaxton and Tamara in *Leave It to Me!*
(musical).

Fare Thee Honey, Fare Thee Well
Words and music by John Akers and J. Mayo Williams.
Leeds Music Corp.

Ferdinand the Bull
Words by Larry Morey, music by Albert Hay Malotte.
Bourne Co.
Introduced by voice of Sterling Holloway in *Ferdinand the Bull*
(cartoon film).

Flat Foot Floogie, The
Words and music by Slim Gaillard, Slam Stewart, and Bud Green.
Jewel Music Publishing Co., Inc.
Introduced by "Slim and Slam" (Slim Gaillard and Slam Stewart).

For No Rhyme or Reason
Words and music by Cole Porter.
Chappell & Co., Inc.
Introduced by Toby Wing and Charles Kemper in *You Never Know*
(musical).

Four Little Angels of Peace
Words and music by Harold Rome.
Mills Music, Inc.
Introduced by Hy Goldstein, Al Eban, Murray Modick, and Paul
Seymour in *Pins and Needles* (revue, 1937).

From Alpha to Omega
Words and music by Cole Porter.
Chappell & Co., Inc.
Introduced by Clifton Webb and Lupe Velez in *You Never Know*
(musical).

From Now On
Words and music by Cole Porter.
Chappell & Co., Inc.
Introduced by William Gaxton and Tamara in *Leave It to Me!*
(musical).

Funny Old Hills, The
Words and music by Leo Robin and Ralph Rainger.
Paramount Music Corp.
Introduced by Bing Crosby and Edward Everett Horton in *Paris Honeymoon* (film, 1939).

Garden of the Moon
Words by Al Dubin and Johnny Mercer, music by Harry Warren.
Harms, Inc.
Introduced by Mabel Todd in *Garden of the Moon* (film).

Get Out of Town
Words and music by Cole Porter.
Chappell & Co., Inc.
Introduced by Tamara in *Leave It to Me!* (musical).

Gin Mill Blues
Music by Joe Sullivan.
Leo Feist, Inc.
Introduced by jazz pianist Joe Sullivan in 1933. Featured by Bob Crosby and his Orchestra.

Girl Friend of The Whirling Dervish, The
Words by Johnny Mercer and Al Dubin, music by Harry Warren.
Harms, Inc.
Introduced by John Payne, Jerry Colonna, Johnnie Davis, Joe Venuti, and Ray Mayer in *Garden of the Moon* (film).

God's Country
Words by E. Y. Harburg, music by Harold Arlen.
Chappell & Co., Inc.
Introduced by Jack Whiting in *Hooray for What!* (musical, 1937). Performed by Mickey Rooney, Judy Garland, Douglas McPhail, Betty Jaynes, and chorus in *Babes in Arms* (film, 1939).

Good Morning Blues
Words and music by William "Count" Basie, Ed Durham, and James Rushing.
Bregman, Vocco & Conn, Inc.
Introduced by Count Basie and his Orchestra.

Gypsy without a Song
Words by Irving Gordon, music by Edward Kennedy "Duke" Ellington, Lou Singer, and Juan Tizol.
American Academy of Music, Inc.
Introduced by Duke Ellington and his Orchestra.

Harmony in Harlem
Words by Irving Mills, music by Edward Kennedy "Duke" Ellington and Johnny Hodges.
American Academy of Music, Inc.
Introduced by Duke Ellington and his Orchestra.

Havin' Myself a Time
Words and music by Leo Robin and Ralph Rainger.
Paramount Music Corp.
Introduced by Martha Raye in *Tropic Holiday* (film).

Hear My Song, Violetta (Austrian)
English words by Buddy Bernier and Bob Emmerich, German words
by Othmar Klose and Ermenegildo Carosio, music by Rudolf Luck-
esch and Othmar Klose.
Adolf Robitschek, Vienna, Austria, 1936/De Sylva, Brown &
Henderson, Inc., 1938, 1940.
Original German title, "Hor Mein Lied, Violetta." Introduced in
United States by Will Glahe and his Musette Orchestra (Victor).
Best-selling records in 1940 by Glenn Miller and his Orchestra
(Victor) and Tony Martin (Decca).

Heart and Soul
Words by Frank Loesser, music by Hoagy Carmichael.
Famous Music Corp.
Introduced by Larry Clinton and his Orchestra in *A Song Is Born*
(film short). Featured by Gene Krupa and his Orchestra in *Some
Like It Hot* (film, 1939).

Heavenly Party, A
Words by Dorothy Fields, music by Jerome Kern.
T. B. Harms Co.
Introduced by Irene Dunne, and reprised by Fuzzy Knight, in *Joy of
Living* (film).

Heigh-Ho (The Dwarfs' Marching Song)
Words by Larry Morey, music by Frank Churchill.
Bourne Co.
Introduced by the dwarfs in *Snow White and the Seven Dwarfs*
(cartoon film, 1937).

Hello Stranger
Words and music by A. P. Carter.
Peer International Corp.
Introduced by The Carter Family.

Hillbilly from Tenth Avenue
Words and music by M. K. Jerome and Jack Scholl.
M. Witmark & Sons.
Introduced by The Weaver Brothers and Elviry in *Swing Your
Lady* (film).

Hot Pretzels
Words and music by Will Glahe, Sam Ward, and W. A. Timm.
Southern Music Publishing Co., Inc.
Introduced by Will Glahe and his Musette Orchestra.

How Can You Tell an American?
Words by Maxwell Anderson, music by Kurt Weill.
De Sylva, Brown & Henderson, Inc.
Introduced by Richard Kollmar and Ray Middleton in *Knickerbocker Holiday* (musical).

How To Win Friends and Influence People
Words by Lorenz Hart, music by Richard Rodgers.
Robbins Music Corp.
Introduced by Audrey Christie, Charles Walters, and ensemble in *I Married an Angel* (musical).

Howdja Like To Love Me
Words by Frank Loesser, music by Burton Lane.
Famous Music Corp.
Introduced by Martha Raye and Bob Hope in *College Swing* (film).

Hurry Home
Words and music by Joseph Meyer, Buddy Bernier, and Bob Emmerich.
Larry Spier, Inc.

I Can't Face the Music (without Singing the Blues)
Words by Ted Koehler, music by Rube Bloom.
Remick Music Corp.

I Fall in Love with You Every Day
Words by Frank Loesser, music by Manning Sherwin and Arthur Altman.
Famous Music Corp.
Introduced by Florence George and John Payne in *College Swing* (film).

I Go for That
Words by Frank Loesser, music by Matt Malneck.
Famous Music Corp.
Introduced by The King's Men in *St. Louis Blues* (film, 1939).

I Hadn't Anyone till You
Words and music by Ray Noble.
Bourne Co.
Introduced by Ray Noble and his Orchestra.

I Have Eyes
Words and music by Leo Robin and Ralph Rainger.
Paramount Music Corp.
Introduced by Bing Crosby, Shirley Ross, and Franceska Gaal in *Paris Honeymoon* (film, 1939).

I Let a Song Go Out of My Heart
Words by Henry Nemo, John Redmond, and Irving Mills, music by
Edward Kennedy "Duke" Ellington.
Mills Music, Inc.
Introduced instrumentally by Duke Ellington and his Orchestra.
Vocal version introduced by Mildred Bailey.

I Love To Rhyme
Words by Ira Gershwin, music by George Gershwin.
Gershwin Publishing Corp.
Introduced by Phil Baker and Charlie McCarthy (Edgar Bergen) in
The Goldwyn Follies (film).

I Love To Walk in the Rain
Words by Walter Bullock, music by Harold Spina.
Robbins Music Corp.
Introduced by Shirley Temple in *Just Around the Corner* (film).

I Love To Whistle
Words by Harold Adamson, music by Jimmy McHugh.
Robbins Music Corp.
Introduced by Deanna Durbin, Christian Rub, Helen Parrish, and
Marcia Mae Jones in *Mad about Music* (film).

I Married an Angel
Words by Lorenz Hart, music by Richard Rodgers.
Robbins Music Corp.
Introduced by Dennis King in *I Married an Angel* (musical). Sung
by Nelson Eddy and Jeanette MacDonald in film version, 1942.

I Must See Annie Tonight
Words and music by Cliff Friend and Dave Franklin.
Bregman, Vocco & Conn, Inc.
Introduced by Guy Lombardo and his Royal Canadians.

I Used To Be Color Blind
Words and music by Irving Berlin.
Irving Berlin Music Corp.
Introduced by Fred Astaire in *Carefree* (film).

I Wanna Go Back to Bali
Words by Al Dubin, music by Harry Warren.
Remick Music Corp.
Introduced by Rudy Vallée in *Gold Diggers in Paris* (film).

I Want To Go Home
Words and music by Cole Porter.
Chappell & Co., Inc.
Introduced by Victor Moore in *Leave It to Me!* (musical).

I Was Doing All Right
Words by Ira Gershwin, music by George Gershwin.
Gershwin Publishing Corp./Chappell & Co., Inc.
Introduced by Ella Logan in *The Goldwyn Follies* (film).

If You Were in My Place (What Would You Do?)
Words by Irving Mills and Henry Nemo, music by Edward Kennedy
"Duke" Ellington.
Mills Music, Inc.
Introduced by Duke Ellington and his Orchestra at Cotton Club
(New York nightclub).

If You're a Viper
Words by Rosetta Howard, music by Horace Malcolm and Herbert
Moran.
Leeds Music Corp.
Introduced and best-selling record by Rosetta Howard (Decca).

I'll Be Seeing You
Words by Irving Kahal, music by Sammy Fain.
Williamson Music, Inc.
Introduced by Tamara in *Right This Way* (revue). Revived and
popularized in 1943-44. Used as theme for *I'll Be Seeing You* (film,
1944). Featured by Liberace in 1950's as closing theme on his radio
and television shows.

I'll Dream Tonight
Words by Johnny Mercer, music by Richard A. Whiting.
M. Witmark & Sons.
Introduced by Dick Powell and Priscilla Lane in *Cowboy from
Brooklyn* (film).

I'll Tell the Man in the Street
Words by Lorenz Hart, music by Richard Rodgers.
Robbins Music Corp.
Introduced by Vivienne Segal and Walter Slezak in *I Married an
Angel* (musical). Sung by Jeanette MacDonald and Nelson Eddy in
film version, 1942.

I'm Afraid the Masquerade Is Over, see (I'm Afraid) The Masquerade Is Over.

I'm Glad for Your Sake (but I'm Sorry for Mine)
Words and music by Peter Tinturin and Jack Lawrence.
De Sylva, Brown & Henderson, Inc.

I'm Gonna Lock My Heart (and Throw Away the Key)
Words and music by Jimmy Eaton and Terry Shand.
Shapiro, Bernstein & Co., Inc.

1938

I'm Prayin' Humble
Music by Bob Haggart.
Lincoln Music Corp.
Swing instrumental, introduced by Bob Crosby and his Orchestra.

I'm So Weary of It All (English)
Words and music by Noël Coward.
Chappell & Co., Inc.
Introduced by Beatrice Lillie in *Set to Music* (revue, 1939). Sung by
Miss Lillie in London in *All Clear* (revue, 1939).

In-Between
Words and music by Roger Edens.
Leo Feist, Inc.
Introduced by Judy Garland in *Love Finds Andy Hardy* (film).

Is That the Way To Treat a Sweetheart?
Words by Charles Tobias, music by Nat Simon.
Leeds Music Corp.

It Never Was You
Words by Maxwell Anderson, music by Kurt Weill.
De Sylva, Brown & Henderson, Inc.
Introduced by Jeanne Madden and Richard Kollmar in *Knickerbocker
Holiday* (musical). Sung by Judy Garland in *I Could Go On Singing*
(film, 1963).

It's a Low Down Dirty Shame
Words and music by Ollie Shepard.
Leeds Music Corp.
Blues, introduced by Ollie Shepard.

It's the Dreamer in Me
Words and music by Jimmy Dorsey and Jimmy Van Heusen.
Leo Feist, Inc.
Introduced by Jimmy Dorsey and his Orchestra.

I've Got a Date with a Dream
Words by Mack Gordon, music by Harry Revel.
Leo Feist, Inc.
Introduced by Arthur Jarrett, Buddy Ebsen, Joan Davis, and girls
in *My Lucky Star* (film).

I've Got a Pocketful of Dreams
Words by Johnny Burke, music by Jimmy Monaco.
Anne-Rachel Music Corp.
Introduced by Bing Crosby in *Sing You Sinners* (film).

Jeepers Creepers
Words by Johnny Mercer, music by Harry Warren.
M. Witmark & Sons.
Introduced by Louis Armstrong in *Going Places* (film). Nominated
for Academy Award, 1938.

248

Jeep's Blues
Music by Edward Kennedy "Duke" Ellington and Johnny Hodges.
American Academy of Music, Inc.
Introduced by Duke Ellington and his Orchestra. Best-selling record
by Johnny Hodges and his Orchestra (Vocalion).

Joe Hill
Words by Alfred Hayes, music by Earl Robinson.
Leeds Music Corp.
Popular song of the "left" and post-depression labor movement about
martyred IWW (Industrial Workers of the World) organizer.

Joobalai
Words and music by Leo Robin and Ralph Rainger.
Paramount Music Corp.
Introduced by Bing Crosby, Franceska Gaal, and chorus in *Paris
Honeymoon* (film, 1939).

Joseph! Joseph!
English words by Sammy Cahn and Saul Chaplin, Yiddish words and
music by Nellie Casman and Samuel Steinberg.
Harms, Inc.
English-language version introduced by The Andrews Sisters.

Jumpin' at the Woodside
Music by William "Count" Basie.
Bregman, Vocco & Conn, Inc.
Swing instrumental, introduced by Count Basie and his Orchestra.
Best-selling record by Benny Goodman and his Orchestra (Victor).

Just Let Me Look at You
Words by Dorothy Fields, music by Jerome Kern.
T. B. Harms Co.
Introduced by Irene Dunne in *Joy of Living* (film).

Kind'a Lonesome
Words and music by Leo Robin, Sam Coslow, and Hoagy Carmichael.
Famous Music Corp.
Introduced by Maxine Sullivan and The Hall Johnson Choir in
St. Louis Blues (film, 1939).

Lamp on the Corner, The
Words and music by Ned Washington and Agustin Lara.
Paramount Music Corp.
Introduced by Tito Guizar in *Tropic Holiday* (film).

Laugh and Call It Love
Words by John Burke, music by James V. Monaco.
Anne-Rachel Music Corp.
Introduced by Bing Crosby in *Sing You Sinners* (film).

Little Joe from Chicago
Words and music by Mary Lou Williams and Henry Wells.
Robbins Music Corp.
"Dedicated" to booking agent Joe Glaser. Introduced by Andy Kirk and his Clouds of Joy.

Little Kiss at Twilight
Words and music by Leo Robin and Ralph Rainger.
Paramount Music Corp.
Introduced by Martha Raye in *Give Me a Sailor* (film).

Little Rock Getaway
Music by Joe Sullivan.
Leo Feist, Inc., 1938, 1939, 1951.
Introduced as piano solo by Joe Sullivan in 1933. Jazz band instrumental version introduced by Bob Crosby and his Orchestra. Lyrics by Carl Sigman added in 1951.

Lost and Found
Words and music by Pinky Tomlin and Harry Tobias.
Anne-Rachel Music Corp.

Lost in Meditation
Words by Irving Mills, music by Edward Kennedy "Duke" Ellington, Juan Tizol, and Lou Singer.
American Academy of Music, Inc.
Introduced by Duke Ellington and his Orchestra.

Love Is Here To Stay
Words by Ira Gershwin, music by George Gershwin.
Gershwin Publishing Corp./Chappell & Co., Inc.
George Gershwin's last song. Introduced by Kenny Baker in *The Goldwyn Follies* (film). Sung by Gene Kelly to Leslie Caron in *An American in Paris* (film, 1951).

Love Is Where You Find It
Words by Al Dubin and Johnny Mercer, music by Harry Warren.
Harms, Inc.
Introduced by John Payne and Johnny "Scat" Davis in *Garden of the Moon* (film).

Love Like Ours, A
Words by Sidney D. Mitchell, music by Sam H. Stept.
American Academy of Music, Inc.

Love Walked In
Words by Ira Gershwin, music by George Gershwin.
Gershwin Publishing Corp./Chappell & Co., Inc.
Introduced by Kenny Baker in *The Goldwyn Follies* (film).

Lullaby in Rhythm
Words by Walter Hirsch, music by Benny Goodman, Edgar Sampson, and Clarence Profit.
Robbins Music Corp.
Introduced by Benny Goodman and his Orchestra.

Maria
Words and music by Cole Porter.
Chappell & Co., Inc.
Introduced by Clifton Webb in *You Never Know* (musical).

(I'm Afraid) The Masquerade Is Over
Words by Herb Magidson, music by Allie Wrubel.
Magidson Music Co., Inc./Allison's Music, Inc.

Meet the Beat of My Heart
Words and music by Mack Gordon and Harry Revel.
Leo Feist, Inc.
Introduced by Judy Garland in *Love Finds Andy Hardy* (film).

Merrily We Live
Words by Arthur Quenzer, music by Phil Charig.
Leo Feist, Inc.
Introduced in *Merrily We Live* (film). Nominated for Academy Award, 1938.

Mighty Like the Blues
Words and music by Leonard Feather.
American Academy of Music, Inc.
Introduced by Woody Herman and his Orchestra.

Mist over the Moon
Words by Oscar Hammerstein II, music by Ben Oakland.
Bourne Co.
Introduced by Lanny Ross in *The Lady Objects* (film). Nominated for Academy Award, 1938.

Moments Like This
Words by Frank Loesser, music by Burton Lane.
Famous Music Corp.
Introduced by Florence George in *College Swing* (film).

Most Gentlemen Don't Like Love
Words and music by Cole Porter.
Chappell & Co., Inc.
Introduced by Sophie Tucker in *Leave It to Me!* (musical). First recording by Mary Martin (Brunswick).

Music, Maestro, Please!
Words by Herb Magidson, music by Allie Wrubel.
Bourne Co.
Introduced in United States by Frank Parker and Frances Langford.
Introduced in London by Frances Day and Flanagan and Allen in
These Foolish Things (revue).

Mutiny in the Nursery
Words and music by Johnny Mercer.
M. Witmark & Sons.
Introduced by Louis Armstrong, Maxine Sullivan, Dick Powell, and
Anita Louise in *Going Places* (film).

My Heart Belongs to Daddy
Words and music by Cole Porter.
Chappell & Co., Inc.
Introduced by Mary Martin in *Leave It to Me!* (musical). Sung by
Mary Martin in *Love Thy Neighbor* (film, 1940) and *Night and
Day* (film, 1946) and by Marilyn Monroe in *Let's Make Love* (film,
1960).

My Heart Is Taking Lessons
Words by Johnny Burke, music by Jimmy Monaco.
Anne-Rachel Music Corp.
Introduced by Bing Crosby in *Doctor Rhythm* (film).

My Heart Is Unemployed
Words and music by Harold Rome.
Florence Music Co., Inc.
Introduced by Mary Jane Walsh and Michael Loring in *Sing Out
the News* (revue).

My Own
Words by Harold Adamson, music by Jimmy McHugh.
Robbins Music Corp.
Introduced by Deanna Durbin in *That Certain Age* (film). Nominated
for Academy Award, 1938.

My Reverie (French)
Words and adaptation of music by Larry Clinton.
Robbins Music Corp.
Based on Debussy's "Reverie," composed in 1890 but not published
until 1904. Best-selling record by Larry Clinton and his Orchestra,
vocal by Bea Wain (Victor).

My Walking Stick
Words and music by Irving Berlin.
Irving Berlin Music Corp.
Introduced by Ethel Merman in *Alexander's Ragtime Band* (film).

Never Again (English)
Words and music by Noël Coward.
Chappell & Co., Inc.
Introduced by Eva Ortega and Hugh French in *Set to Music* (revue, 1939).

Night Is Filled with Music, The
Words and music by Irving Berlin.
Irving Berlin Music Corp.
Introduced by Fred Astaire and Ginger Rogers in *Carefree* (film).

Now It Can Be Told
Words and music by Irving Berlin.
Irving Berlin Music Corp.
Introduced by Don Ameche, and reprised by Alice Faye, in *Alexander's Ragtime Band* (film). Nominated for Academy Award, 1938.

Oh, Diogenes!
Words by Lorenz Hart, music by Richard Rodgers.
Chappell & Co., Inc.
Introduced by Marcy Westcott in *The Boys from Syracuse* (musical).

Oh! Ma-Ma (The Butcher Boy) (Italian)
English words by Lew Brown and Rudy Vallée, Italian words and music by Paolo Citorello.
Italian Book Co., 1928/Shapiro, Bernstein & Co., Inc.
Based on Citorello's song, "Luna Mezzo Mare." English-language version introduced in United States by Rudy Vallée. Best-selling records by Rudy Vallée and his Connecticut Yankees (Bluebird) and The Andrews Sisters (Decca). "Lazy Mary," another English-language version, with lyrics by Lou Monte, published in 1958.

Ol' Man Mose
Words and music by Louis Armstrong and Zilner Randolph.
Anne-Rachel Music Corp.
Introduced by Louis Armstrong. Best-selling record by Eddy Duchin and his Orchestra, vocal by Patricia Norman.

Old Folks
Words by Dedette Lee Hill, music by Willard Robison.
Remick Music Corp.
Introduced by Mildred Bailey.

Old Straw Hat, An
Words by Mack Gordon, music by Harry Revel.
Leo Feist, Inc.
Introduced by Shirley Temple in *Rebecca of Sunnybrook Farm* (film).

On a Little Street in Singapore
Words by Billy Hill, music by Peter De Rose.
Shapiro, Bernstein & Co., Inc.

On the Bumpy Road to Love
Words and music by Al Hoffman, Al Lewis, and Murray Mencher.
Leo Feist, Inc.
Introduced by Judy Garland in *Listen, Darling* (film).

On the Sentimental Side
Words by Johnny Burke, music by James V. Monaco.
Anne-Rachel Music Corp.
Introduced by Bing Crosby and Mary Carlisle in *Doctor Rhythm* (film).

One o'Clock Jump
Music by William "Count" Basie.
Leo Feist, Inc.
Swing instrumental. Theme of Count Basie and his Orchestra. Best-selling record in 1941 by Harry James and his Orchestra (Columbia).

Patty Cake, Patty Cake (Baker Man)
Words and music by Andy Razaf, J. C. Johnson, and Thomas "Fats" Waller.
Sam Fox Publishing Co., Inc./Anne-Rachel Music Corp.
Introduced by Fats Waller.

Pavanne
Words by Gladys Shelley, music by Morton Gould.
Mills Music, Inc.
Song version adapted from Gould's "American Symphonette, No. 2," Second Movement.

Penny Serenade (English-Dutch)
Words by Hal Halifax, music by Melle Weersma.
The Peter Maurice Music Co., Ltd., London, England/Shapiro, Bernstein & Co., Inc.
Introduced in United States by Guy Lombardo and his Royal Canadians.

Please Be Kind
Words and music by Sammy Cahn and Saul Chaplin.
Harms, Inc.
Introduced by Mildred Bailey.

Please Forgive Me
Words by Irving Gordon and Irving Mills, music by Edward Kennedy "Duke" Ellington.
American Academy of Music, Inc.
Introduced by Duke Ellington and his Orchestra.

Prelude to a Kiss
Words by Irving Gordon and Irving Mills, music by Edward Kennedy "Duke" Ellington.
American Academy of Music, Inc.
Introduced by Duke Ellington and his Orchestra.

Pyramid
Words by Irving Gordon and Irving Mills, music by Edward Kennedy "Duke" Ellington and Juan Tizol.
American Academy of Music, Inc.
Introduced by Duke Ellington and his Orchestra.

(Listen to the) Rhythm of the Range
Words and music by Johnny Marvin and Gene Autry.
Anne-Rachel Music Corp.
Introduced by Gene Autry. Sung by Roy Rogers in *Under Western Stars* (film).

Ride, Tenderfoot, Ride
Words by Johnny Mercer, music by Richard A. Whiting.
M. Witmark & Sons.
Introduced by Dick Powell in *Cowboy from Brooklyn* (film).

Right Guy for Me, The
Words by Sam Coslow, music by Kurt Weill.
Famous Music Corp.
Introduced by Carol Paige in *You and Me* (film).

Rock It for Me
Words and music by Kay Werner and Sue Werner.
Words & Music, Inc.
Introduced by Ella Fitzgerald.

Room with a View, A
Words by Al Stillman, music by Einar Swan.
Bregman, Vocco & Conn, Inc.

Say It with a Kiss
Words by Johnny Mercer, music by Harry Warren.
M. Witmark & Sons.
Introduced by Maxine Sullivan in *Going Places* (film).

September Song
Words by Maxwell Anderson, music by Kurt Weill.
De Sylva, Brown & Henderson, Inc.
Introduced by Walter Huston in *Knickerbocker Holiday* (musical). Sung by Charles Coburn in film version, 1944. Best-selling record in 1946 by Bing Crosby (Decca). Sung by Maurice Chevalier in *Pepe* (film, 1960).

Serenade to the Stars, A
Words by Harold Adamson, music by Jimmy McHugh.
Robbins Music Corp.
Introduced by Deanna Durbin in *Mad about Music* (film).

Shortest Day of the Year, The
Words by Lorenz Hart, music by Richard Rodgers.
Chappell & Co., Inc.
Introduced by Ronald Graham and Dolores Anderson in *The Boys from Syracuse* (musical).

Silver on the Sage
Words and music by Leo Robin and Ralph Rainger.
Paramount Music Corp.
Introduced in *The Texans* (film).

Sing for Your Supper
Words by Lorenz Hart, music by Richard Rodgers.
Chappell & Co., Inc.
Introduced by Muriel Angelus, Marcy Westcott, and Wynn Murray in *The Boys from Syracuse* (musical). Sung by Martha Raye in film version, 1940.

Sixty Seconds Got Together
Words by Mack David, music by Jerry Livingston.
Anne-Rachel Music Corp.

Small Fry
Words and music by Frank Loesser and Hoagy Carmichael.
Famous Music Corp.
Introduced by Bing Crosby, Fred MacMurray, and Donald O'Connor in *Sing You Sinners* (film). Best-selling record by Bing Crosby and Johnny Mercer (Decca).

So Help Me (If I Don't Love You)
Words by Eddie De Lange, music by Jimmy Van Heusen.
Remick Music Corp.
Introduced by Lee Wiley. Popularized by Russ Morgan and his Orchestra.

South Rampart Street Parade
Words by Steve Allen, music by Ray Bauduc and Bob Haggart.
Leo Feist, Inc., 1938, 1952.
Introduced by Bob Crosby and his Orchestra. Lyrics added by Steve Allen in 1952.

Spring Again
Words by Ira Gershwin, music by Vernon Duke.
Chappell & Co., Inc.
Introduced by Kenny Baker in *The Goldwyn Follies* (film).

Spring Is Here
Words by Lorenz Hart, music by Richard Rodgers.
Robbins Music Corp.
Introduced by Dennis King and Vivienne Segal in *I Married an Angel* (musical).

Stately Homes of England, The (English)
Words and music by Noël Coward.
Chappell & Co., Ltd., London, England/Chappell & Co., Inc.
Introduced in London by Hugh French, Ross Landon, John Gatrell, and Kenneth Carten in *Operette* (musical, 1937). Sung by Hugh French, Angus Menzies, Kenneth Carten, and Anthony Pelissier in *Set to Music* (revue, 1939). Sung by chorus on soundtrack of *The Grass Is Greener* (film, 1961).

Steppin' into Swing Society
Words by Irving Mills and Henry Nemo, music by Edward Kennedy "Duke" Ellington.
American Academy of Music, Inc.
Introduced by Duke Ellington and his Orchestra.

Stop Beatin' 'round the Mulberry Bush
Words by Bickley Reichner, music by Clay Boland.
Bregman, Vocco & Conn, Inc.
Introduced by Tommy Dorsey and his Orchestra.

Stranger in Paree
Words by Al Dubin, music by Harry Warren.
Remick Music Corp.
Introduced by Rudy Vallée, Mabel Todd, Allen Jenkins, Gloria Dickson, Hugh Herbert, and Rosemary Lane in *Gold Diggers in Paris* (film).

Sunrise Serenade
Words by Jack Lawrence, music by Frankie Carle.
Jewel Music Publishing Co., Inc.
Introduced by Glen Gray and The Casa Loma Orchestra. Best-selling record by Glenn Miller and his Orchestra. Theme song of Frankie Carle and his Orchestra.

Swing Me an Old Fashioned Song
Words by Walter Bullock, music by Harold Spina.
Robbins Music Corp.
Introduced by Shirley Temple in *Little Miss Broadway* (film).

Ten Pins in the Sky
Words by Joseph McCarthy, music by Milton Ager.
Advanced Music Corp.
Introduced by Judy Garland in *Listen, Darling* (film).

Thanks for Ev'rything
Words and music by Mack Gordon and Harry Revel.
Robbins Music Corp.
Introduced by Tony Martin in *Thanks for Everything* (film).

That Certain Age
Words by Harold Adamson, music by Jimmy McHugh.
Robbins Music Corp.
Introduced by Deanna Durbin in *That Certain Age* (film).

That Week in Paris
Words by Oscar Hammerstein II, music by Ben Oakland.
Chappell & Co., Inc.
Introduced by Lanny Ross in *The Lady Objects* (film).

There's a Boy in Harlem
Words by Lorenz Hart, music by Richard Rodgers.
Harms, Inc.
Introduced by Jeni Le Gon in *Fools for Scandal* (film).

There's a Far Away Look in Your Eye
Words by Irving Taylor, music by Vic Mizzy.
World Music, Inc.

There's Nowhere To Go but Up
Words by Maxwell Anderson, music by Kurt Weill.
De Sylva, Brown & Henderson, Inc.
Introduced by Richard Kollmar and Clarence Nordstrom in
Knickerbocker Holiday (musical).

There's Something about an Old Love
Words by Irving Mills and Lupin Fein, music by Will Hudson.
American Academy of Music, Inc.

They Say
Words by Edward Heyman, music by Stephan Weiss and Paul Mann.
M. Witmark & Sons.
Introduced by Buddy Clark.

This Can't Be Love
Words by Lorenz Hart, music by Richard Rodgers.
Chappell & Co., Inc.
Introduced by Marcy Westcott and Eddie Albert in *The Boys from Syracuse* (musical). Sung by Rosemary Lane in film version, 1940.
Sung by Doris Day in *Jumbo* (film, 1962).

This Is My Night To Dream
Words by John Burke, music by James V. Monaco.
Anne-Rachel Music Corp.
Introduced by Bing Crosby in *Doctor Rhythm* (film).

Ti-Pi-Tin (Mexican)
English words by Raymond Leveen, Spanish words and music by
Maria Grever.
Leo Feist, Inc.
Introduced in United States by Horace Heidt and his Brigadiers.

Tomorrow
Words and music by Cole Porter.
Chappell & Co., Inc.
Introduced by Sophie Tucker and chorus in *Leave It to Me!*
(musical).

Tonight Will Live
Words and music by Ned Washington and Agustin Lara.
Paramount Music Corp.
Introduced by Dorothy Lamour and Elvira Rios, and reprised by
Tito Guizar, in *Tropic Holiday* (film).

Tutti-Frutti
Words and music by Doris Fisher and Slim Gaillard.
Anne-Rachel Music Corp.
Introduced by "Slim and Slam" (Slim Gaillard and Slam Stewart).

Twinkle in Your Eye, A
Words by Lorenz Hart, music by Richard Rodgers.
Robbins Music Corp.
Introduced by Vivienne Segal in *I Married an Angel* (musical).
Sung by Binnie Barnes and Jeanette MacDonald in film version,
1942.

Two Bouquets (English)
Words and music by Jimmy Kennedy and Michael Carr.
The Peter Maurice Music Co., Ltd., London, England/Shapiro,
Bernstein & Co., Inc.
Introduced in *Kickin' the Moon Around* (British film).

Two Sleepy People
Words by Frank Loesser, music by Hoagy Carmichael.
Famous Music Corp.
Introduced by Bob Hope and Shirley Ross in *Thanks for the
Memory* (film).

Umbrella Man, The
Words by James Cavanaugh, music by Vincent Rose and Larry Stock.
Harms, Inc.
Introduced in United States by Guy Lombardo and his Royal Ca-
nadians. Introduced in London by Flanagan and Allen in *These
Foolish Things* (revue).

Vol Vist Du Gaily Star
Words and music by Bulee "Slim" Gaillard and Bud Green.
Jewel Music Publishing Co., Inc.
Introduced by "Slim and Slam" (Slim Gaillard and Slam Stewart).

Wacky Dust
Words by Stanley Adams, music by Oscar Levant.
Robbins Music Corp.
Best-selling record by Ella Fitzgerald (Decca).

War Dance for Wooden Indians
Music by Raymond Scott.
Advanced Music Corp.
Introduced by The Raymond Scott Quintet. Performed by The Raymond Scott Quintet and The Condos Brothers in *Happy Landing* (film).

Weekend of a Private Secretary, The
Words by Johnny Mercer, music by Bernie Hanighen.
Remick Music Corp.
Introduced by Mildred Bailey, with Red Norvo and his Orchestra.

What Can You Do with a Man?
Words by Lorenz Hart, music by Richard Rodgers.
Chappell & Co., Inc.
Introduced by Wynn Murray and Teddy Hart in *The Boys from Syracuse* (musical).

What Goes On Here in My Heart
Words and music by Leo Robin and Ralph Rainger.
Paramount Music Corp.
Introduced by Betty Grable and Jack Whiting in *Give Me a Sailor* (film).

What Have You Got That Gets Me?
Words and music by Leo Robin and Ralph Rainger.
Famous Music Corp.
Introduced by The Yacht Club Boys, Joyce Comptom, Joan Bennett, and Jack Benny in *Artists and Models Abroad* (film).

What Is That Tune?
Words and music by Cole Porter.
Chappell & Co., Inc.
Introduced by Libby Holman in *You Never Know* (musical).

What Shall I Do?
Words and music by Cole Porter.
Chappell & Co., Inc.
Introduced by Lupe Velez in *You Never Know* (musical).

What's Good about Goodnight?
Words by Dorothy Fields, music by Jerome Kern.
T. B. Harms Co.
Introduced by Irene Dunne in *Joy of Living* (film).

What's the Use of Getting Sober
Words and music by Bubsy Meyers.
Leeds Music Corp., 1938, 1943.
Best-selling record in 1943 by Louis Jordan and his Tympany Five
(Decca).

What's Your Story, Morning Glory?
Words and music by Jack Lawrence, Paul Francis Webster, and
Mary Lou Williams.
Advanced Music Corp., 1938, 1940.
Introduced by Andy Kirk and his Clouds of Joy, featuring Mary
Lou Williams, pianist and arranger.

When They Played the Polka
Words by Lou Holzer, music by Fabian Andre.
Robbins Music Corp.
Introduced by Horace Heidt and his Brigadiers.

Where Are the Songs We Sung? (English)
Words and music by Noël Coward.
Chappell & Co., Ltd., London, England/Chappell & Co., Inc.
Introduced in London by Peggy Wood in *Operette* (musical).

Where in the World
Words and music by Mack Gordon and Harry Revel.
Leo Feist, Inc.
Introduced by Don Ameche in *Josette* (film).

While a Cigarette Was Burning
Words and music by Charles Kenny and Nick Kenny.
Bourne Co.
Introduced by Joan Edwards. Used as a theme for the Fred Waring
Chesterfield radio show.

Why Not String Along with Me?
Words by Lew Brown, music by Lew Pollack.
Robbins Music Corp.
Introduced by Ethel Merman in *Straight, Place and Show* (film).

Will You Remember Me?
Words by Maxwell Anderson, music by Kurt Weill.
De Sylva, Brown & Henderson, Inc.
Introduced by Richard Kollmar in *Knickerbocker Holiday* (musical).

With You on My Mind
Words by Lew Brown, music by Lew Pollack.
Robbins Music Corp.
Introduced by Ethel Merman in *Straight, Place and Show* (film).

Wrappin' It Up, see 1934.

Wynken, Blynken and Nod
Words (from a poem) by Eugene Field, music by Leigh Harline.
Bourne Co.
Introduced in *Wynken, Blynken and Nod* (*Silly Symphony* cartoon film).

Yam, The
Words and music by Irving Berlin.
Irving Berlin Music Corp.
Introduced by Fred Astaire and Ginger Rogers in *Carefree* (film).

Yancey Special
Words by Andy Razaf, music by Meade "Lux" Lewis.
Shapiro, Bernstein & Co., Inc.
Introduced by pianist Meade "Lux" Lewis. Dedicated to Jimmy Yancey, boogie-woogie pianist and composer. Featured by Bob Crosby and his Orchestra, with Bob Zurke on piano.

You Couldn't Be Cuter
Words by Dorothy Fields, music by Jerome Kern.
T. B. Harms Co.
Introduced by Irene Dunne in *Joy of Living* (film).

You Go to My Head
Words by Haven Gillespie, music by J. Fred Coots.
Remick Music Corp.
Introduced by Glen Gray and The Casa Loma Orchestra. First recording by Larry Clinton and his Orchestra, vocal by Bea Wain (Victor). Theme song of Mitchell Ayres and his Orchestra.

You Have Cast Your Shadow on the Sea
Words by Lorenz Hart, music by Richard Rodgers.
Chappell & Co., Inc.
Introduced by Marcy Westcott and Eddie Albert in *The Boys from Syracuse* (musical).

You Leave Me Breathless
Words by Ralph Freed, music by Frederick Hollander.
Famous Music Corp.
Introduced by Fred MacMurray in *Cocoanut Grove* (film).

You Must Have Been a Beautiful Baby
Words by Johnny Mercer, music by Harry Warren.
Remick Music Corp.
Introduced by Dick Powell in *Hard To Get* (film). Sung by Doris
Day in *My Dream Is Yours* (film, 1949). Revived in 1961 with
best-selling record by Bobby Darin (Atco).

You Never Know
Words and music by Cole Porter.
Chappell & Co., Inc.
Introduced by Libby Holman in *You Never Know* (musical).

You're a Natural
Words by Frank Loesser, music by Manning Sherwin.
Famous Music Corp.
Introduced by Gracie Allen in *College Swing* (film).

You're a Sweet Little Headache
Words and music by Leo Robin and Ralph Rainger.
Paramount Music Corp.
Introduced by Bing Crosby in *Paris Honeymoon* (film, 1939).

You're As Pretty As a Picture
Words by Harold Adamson, music by Jimmy McHugh.
Robbins Music Corp.
Introduced by Deanna Durbin in *That Certain Age* (film).

You're So Desirable
Words and music by Ray Noble.
Bregman, Vocco & Conn, Inc.
Introduced by Ray Noble and his Orchestra.

You're the Only Star (in My Blue Heaven)
Words and music by Gene Autry.
Shapiro, Bernstein & Co., Inc.
Introduced by Gene Autry in *The Old Barn Dance* (film).

1939

1939

Address Unknown
Words and music by Carmen Lombardo, Dedette Lee Hill, and
Johnny Marks.
Leeds Music Corp.
Best-selling record by The Ink Spots (Decca).

All Dressed Up (Spic and Spanish)
Words by Lorenz Hart, music by Richard Rodgers.
Chappell & Co., Inc.
Introduced by Diosa Costello in *Too Many Girls* (musical). Sung by
Desi Arnaz in film version, 1940.

All I Remember Is You
Words by Eddie De Lange, music by James Van Heusen.
Remick Music Corp.
Introduced by Tommy Dorsey and his Orchestra.

All in Fun
Words by Oscar Hammerstein II, music by Jerome Kern.
T. B. Harms Co.
Introduced by Frances Mercer and Jack Whiting in *Very Warm for
May* (musical).

All the Things You Are
Words by Oscar Hammerstein II, music by Jerome Kern.
T. B. Harms Co.
Introduced by Hiram Sherman, Frances Mercer, Hollace Shaw, and
Ralph Stuart in *Very Warm for May* (musical). Featured in
Broadway Rhythm (film, 1944); sung by Tony Martin in *Till the
Clouds Roll By* (film, 1946); and featured in *Because You're Mine*
(film, 1952).

All This and Heaven Too
Words by Eddie De Lange, music by Jimmy Van Heusen.
Remick Music Corp.
Promotional song for *All This and Heaven Too* (film, 1940).

Am I Proud
Words and music by Teddy Powell and Leonard Whitcup.
MCA, Inc.

Anatole (of Paris)
Words and music by Sylvia Fine.
Sylvia Fine.
Introduced by Danny Kaye in *The Straw Hat Revue* (revue). Sung
by Kaye in *The Secret Life of Walter Mitty* (film, 1947).

And the Angels Sing
Words by Johnny Mercer, music by Ziggy Elman.
Bregman, Vocco & Conn, Inc.
Introduced as instrumental, entitled "Fralich in Swing," by Ziggy
Elman and his Orchestra (Bluebird). Vocal version introduced by
Benny Goodman and his Orchestra, featuring Ziggy Elman on
trumpet, vocal by Martha Tilton (Victor). Featured in *The Benny
Goodman Story* (film, 1956).

Angel in Disguise
Words by Kim Gannon, music by Paul Mann and Stephan Weiss.
M. Witmark & Sons.
Introduced in *It All Came True* (film, 1940). Best-selling record
in 1940 by Dick Todd (Bluebird).

Apple for the Teacher, An
Words by Johnny Burke, music by James V. Monaco.
Anne-Rachel Music Corp.
Introduced by Bing Crosby and Linda Ware in *The Star Maker*
(film). Sung by Gene Autry in *The Last Round-Up* (film, 1947).

Are You Havin' Any Fun?
Words by Jack Yellen, music by Sammy Fain.
De Sylva, Brown & Henderson, Inc.
Introduced by Ella Logan in *George White's Scandals of 1939*
(revue).

Army Air Corps Song, see The U.S. Air Force (The Wild Blue Yonder).

At the Balalaika (English)
Original words by Eric Maschwitz, new words by Bob Wright and
Chet Forrest, original music by George Posford, adapted by
Herbert Stothart.
Keith, Prowse Co., Ltd., London, England, 1936/Leo Feist, Inc./
Sam Fox Publishing Co., Inc.
New version introduced by Ilona Massey and The Russian Art Choir
in *Balalaika* (film).

Babalú (Cuban)
English words by S. K. Russell, Spanish words and music by
Margarita Lecuona.
Peer International Corp., 1939, 1942.
Introduced by Xavier Cugat and his Orchestra. English lyrics
written in 1942.

Baby, Don't Tell on Me
Words and music by James Rushing, William "Count" Basie, and
Lester Young.
Bregman, Vocco & Conn, Inc.
Introduced by Count Basie and his Orchestra, vocal by
Jimmy Rushing.

Back Bay Shuffle
Music by Teddy McRae and Artie Shaw.
Robbins Music Corp.
Swing instrumental, introduced and best-selling record by
Artie Shaw and his Orchestra (Bluebird).

Back to Back
Words and music by Irving Berlin.
Irving Berlin Music Corp.
Introduced by Mary Healy in *Second Fiddle* (film).

Beer Barrel Polka (Roll Out the Barrel) (Czechoslovakian)
English words by Lew Brown, Czech words by Vasek Zeman and
Wladimir A. Timm, music by Jaromír Vejvoda.
Jana Hoffmanna Vva., Prague, Czechoslovakia, 1934/Shapiro,
Bernstein & Co., Inc.
Original Czech title, "Skoda Lásky" ("Lost Love"). Introduced in
United States by Will Glahe and his Musette Orchestra (Victor).
Best-selling record by The Andrews Sisters (Decca). Interpolated
by The Minute Men from Lexington in *Yokel Boy* (musical).

Between 18th and 19th on Chestnut Street
Words and music by Will Osborne and Dick Rogers.
Leeds Music Corp.
Best-selling record by Bing Crosby and Connee Boswell (Decca).

Between You and Me
Words and music by Cole Porter.
De Sylva, Brown & Henderson, Inc.
Introduced by George Murphy in *Broadway Melody of 1940*
(film, 1940).

Blame It on My Last Affair
Words and music by Henry Nemo and Irving Mills.
Mills Music, Inc.
Popularized by Mildred Bailey.

269

Blue and Sentimental
Words and music by Count Basie, Jerry Livingston, and
  Mack David.
Bregman, Vocco & Conn, Inc., 1939, 1947.
First recorded as an instrumental in 1938 by Count Basie and his
  Orchestra (Decca). Lyrics added in 1947.

Blue Evening
Words and music by Gordon Jenkins and Joe Bishop.
Miller Music Corp.
Introduced by Woody Herman and his Orchestra.

Blue Nightfall
Words by Frank Loesser, music by Burton Lane.
Famous Music Corp.
Introduced by Lloyd Nolan and Dorothy Lamour in *St. Louis Blues*
  (film).

Blue Orchids
Words and music by Hoagy Carmichael.
Famous Music Corp.
Best-selling record by Glenn Miller and his Orchestra (Victor).

Blue Rain
Words by Johnny Mercer, music by Jimmy Van Heusen.
Burke & Van Heusen, Inc.
Theme song of Alvino Rey and his Orchestra.

Bolero at the Savoy
Words and music by Gene Krupa, Ray Biondi, James Mundy, and
  Charles Carpenter.
Robbins Music Corp.
Best-selling record by Gene Krupa and his Orchestra, vocal by
  Anita O'Day (Brunswick).

Boomps-a-Daisy (English)
Words and music by Annette Mills.
Lawrence Wright Music Co., Ltd., London, England/Marlo
  Music Corp.
Introduced in England by Monsieur Pierre and Miss Doris Lavelle.
  In United States, interpolated in *Hellzapoppin'* (revue, 1940).

Boy Meets Horn
Words by Irving Mills, music by Edward Kennedy "Duke" Ellington
  and Rex Stewart.
American Academy of Music, Inc., 1939, 1940.
Swing instrumental, introduced in 1938 by Duke Ellington and his
  Orchestra, featuring Rex Stewart on trumpet (Columbia). Lyrics
  added in 1940.

Boys in the Back Room, The
Words by Frank Loesser, music by Frederick Hollander.
Robbins Music Corp.
Introduced by Marlene Dietrich in *Destry Rides Again* (film).

Brazil, see 1942.

But in the Morning, No!
Words and music by Cole Porter.
Chappell & Co., Inc.
Introduced by Bert Lahr and Ethel Merman in *Du Barry Was a Lady* (musical).

Careless
Words and music by Lew Quadling, Eddy Howard, and Dick Jurgens.
Bourne Co.
Introduced by Dick Jurgens and his Orchestra, vocal by Eddy Howard.

Chew-Chew-Chew (Chew Your Bubble Gum)
Words and music by Buck Ram, Chick Webb, and Ella Fitzgerald.
American Academy of Music, Inc.
Introduced by Chick Webb and his Orchestra, vocal by Ella Fitzgerald.

Ciribiribin (They're So in Love) (Italian)
English words and adaptation of music by Harry James and Jack Lawrence.
Paramount Music Corp.
Based on Italian song with lyrics by Carlo Tiochet and music by Albert Pestalozza, published in Italy in 1898. Best-selling record by Harry James and his Orchestra.

Come On In
Words and music by Cole Porter.
Chappell & Co., Inc.
Introduced by Ethel Merman in *Du Barry Was a Lady* (musical).

Comes Love
Words and music by Sam H. Stept, Charles Tobias, and Lew Brown.
Chappell & Co., Inc.
Introduced by Judy Canova, and danced to by Dixie Dunbar, in *Yokel Boy* (musical).

Concert in the Park
Words and music by Cliff Friend and Dave Franklin.
M. Witmark & Sons.

Crescendo in Blue
Music by Edward Kennedy "Duke" Ellington.
American Academy of Music, Inc.
Introduced by Duke Ellington and his Orchestra.

Cuckoo in the Clock
Words by Johnny Mercer, music by Walter Donaldson.
Bourne Co.

Darn That Dream
Words by Eddie De Lange, music by Jimmy Van Heusen.
Bregman, Vocco & Conn, Inc.
Introduced by Maxine Sullivan, Louis Armstrong, Bill Bailey, The
    Dandridge Sisters, The Rhythmettes, and The Deep River Boys in
    Swingin' the Dream (musical).

Day In — Day Out
Words by Johnny Mercer, music by Rube Bloom.
Bregman, Vocco & Conn, Inc.
Introduced by Bob Crosby and his Orchestra, vocal by Helen Ward.

Deep Purple, see 1934.

Ding-Dong! the Witch Is Dead
Words by E. Y. Harburg, music by Harold Arlen.
Leo Feist, Inc.
Introduced by The Singer Midgets, Judy Garland, and Billie Burke
    in *The Wizard of Oz* (film).

Do I Love You?
Words and music by Cole Porter.
Chappell & Co., Inc.
Introduced by Ethel Merman and Ronald Graham in *Du Barry Was
    a Lady* (musical). Sung by Gene Kelly in film version, 1943, and
    by Ginny Simms in *Night and Day* (film, 1946).

Don't Worry 'bout Me
Words by Ted Koehler, music by Rube Bloom.
Mills Music, Inc.
Introduced by Cab Calloway at Cotton Club (New York nightclub)
    in *Cotton Club Parade* (nightclub revue).

Don't You Miss Your Baby
Words and music by Ed Durham, William "Count" Basie, and
    James Rushing.
Bregman, Vocco & Conn, Inc.
Introduced by Count Basie and his Orchestra, vocal by
    Jimmy Rushing.

Drummin' Man
Words and music by Tiny Parham and Gene Krupa.
Robbins Music Corp.
Introduced by Gene Krupa and his Orchestra, vocal by Irene Daye
    (Brunswick).

East Side of Heaven
Words by Johnny Burke, music by James V. Monaco.
Anne-Rachel Music Corp.
Introduced by Bing Crosby in *East Side of Heaven* (film).

Ev'ry Day a Holiday
Words and music by Cole Porter.
Chappell & Co., Inc.
Introduced by Charles Walters and Betty Grable in *Du Barry Was a Lady* (musical).

Faithful Forever
Words and music by Leo Robin and Ralph Rainger.
Famous Music Corp.
Introduced by voices of Jessica Dragonette and Lanny Ross in *Gulliver's Travels* (cartoon film). Nominated for Academy Award, 1939.

Fidgety Joe
Words by Frank Loesser, music by Matt Malneck.
Famous Music Corp.
Introduced by Betty Grable and Phil Harris in *Man about Town* (film).

Flyin' Home
Words and music by Lionel Hampton, Benny Goodman, and Sid Robin.
Regent Music Corp.
Introduced by The Benny Goodman Sextet. Theme of Lionel Hampton and his Orchestra.

Frenesi, see 1941.

Friendship
Words and music by Cole Porter.
Chappell & Co., Inc.
Introduced by Ethel Merman and Bert Lahr in *Du Barry Was a Lady* (musical). Sung by Red Skelton, Lucille Ball, Gene Kelly, Virginia O'Brien, Rags Ragland, Zero Mostel, and Tommy Dorsey in film version, 1943. Best-selling record in 1940 by Kay Kyser and his Orchestra (Columbia).

Gal from Joe's, The
Words by Irving Mills, music by Edward Kennedy "Duke" Ellington.
American Academy of Music, Inc.
Introduced by Duke Ellington and his Orchestra.

Gaucho Serenade, The
Words and music by James Cavanaugh, John Redmond, and
Nat Simon.
Remick Music Corp.
Introduced by Sammy Kaye and his Orchestra. Featured in
It All Came True (film, 1940).

Give Him the Oo-La-La
Words and music by Cole Porter.
Chappell & Co., Inc.
Introduced by Ethel Merman in *Du Barry Was a Lady* (musical).

Give It Back It Back to the Indians
Words by Lorenz Hart, music by Richard Rodgers.
Chappell & Co., Inc.
Introduced by Mary Jane Walsh in *Too Many Girls* (musical).

God Bless America
Words and music by Irving Berlin.
Irving Berlin Music Corp.
Originally written for, but not used in, *Yip, Yip, Yaphank* (soldier
revue, 1918). Introduced by Kate Smith on Armistice Day, 1938.
All income from song donated by composer to Boy Scouts and
Girl Scouts of America. In national poll in late 1950's, voted second
to "The Star-Spangled Banner" as most popular patriotic song.

Good for Nothin' (but Love)
Words by Eddie De Lange, music by Jimmy Van Heusen.
M. Witmark & Sons.
Introduced by Guy Lombardo and his Royal Canadians.

Good Morning
Words by Arthur Freed, music by Nacio Herb Brown.
Chappell & Co., Inc.
Introduced by Judy Garland and Mickey Rooney in *Babes in Arms*
(film). Sung by Debbie Reynolds, Gene Kelly, and Donald O'Connor
in *Singin' in the Rain* (film, 1952).

Goody Goodbye
Words and music by James Cavanaugh and Nat Simon.
Leeds Music Corp.

Grievin'
Words by Billy Strayhorn, music by Edward Kennedy "Duke"
Ellington.
Robbins Music Corp.
Introduced by Duke Ellington and his Orchestra.

Hang Your Heart on a Hickory Limb
Words by Johnny Burke, music by James V. Monaco.
Anne-Rachel Music Corp.
Introduced by Bing Crosby in *East Side of Heaven* (film).

Have Mercy
Words by Buck Ram and Chick Webb, music by Buck Ram.
American Academy of Music, Inc.
Introduced by Chick Webb and his Orchestra, vocal by
    Ella Fitzgerald.

Heaven Can Wait
Words by Eddie De Lange, music by Jimmy Van Heusen.
Remick Music Corp.
Introduced by Tommy Dorsey and his Orchestra, vocal by
    Jack Leonard (Victor).

Heaven in My Arms
Words by Oscar Hammerstein II, music by Jerome Kern.
T. B. Harms Co.
Introduced by Jack Whiting, Frances Mercer, and Hollace Shaw in
    Very Warm for May (musical).

Hey, Good Looking
Words by Frank Loesser, music by Matt Malneck.
Miller Music Corp.
Introduced by Mary Carlisle in *Hawaiian Nights* (film). Not to be
    confused with "Hey, Good-Lookin'" by Cole Porter (1942) or
    "Hey, Good Lookin' " by Hank Williams (1951).

Hold Tight — Hold Tight (Want Some Sea Food Mama)
Words and music by Leonard Kent, Edward Robinson, Leonard Ware,
    Jerry Brandow, and Willie Spottswood.
American Academy of Music, Inc.
Best-selling record by The Andrews Sisters, with Jimmy Dorsey
    and his Orchestra (Decca).

Hong Kong Blues
Words and music by Hoagy Carmichael.
Larry Spier, Inc.
Introduced by Hoagy Carmichael. Sung by Carmichael in *To Have
    and Have Not* (film, 1945).

Honky Tonk Train
Music by Meade "Lux" Lewis.
Shapiro, Bernstein & Co., Inc.
Introduced by Meade "Lux" Lewis. Best-selling record by Bob
    Crosby and his Orchestra, with Bob Zurke on piano.

Honolulu
Words by Gus Kahn, music by Harry Warren.
Bregman, Vocco & Conn, Inc./Leo Feist, Inc.
Introduced by Gracie Allen in *Honolulu* (film).

(I'm in Love with) The Honorable Mr. So and So
Words and music by Sam Coslow.
Leo Feist, Inc.
Introduced by Virginia Bruce in *Society Lawyer* (film).

Hooray for Spinach
Words by Johnny Mercer, music by Harry Warren.
Remick Music Corp.
Introduced by Ann Sheridan in *Naughty but Nice* (film).

How Strange
Words by Gus Kahn, adaptation of music by Herbert Stothart and
   Earl Brent.
Leo Feist, Inc.
Adapted from "Kak Stranno" by B. A. Prozorovsky. Introduced by
   Norma Shearer in *Idiot's Delight* (film).

Huckleberry Duck
Words by Jack Lawrence, music by Raymond Scott.
Advanced Music Corp.
Introduced by Raymond Scott and his Orchestra.

Hut Sut Song
Words and music by Leo V. Killion, Ted McMichael, and Jack Owens.
Brenner Music, Inc.
Nonsense song, popularized by Freddy Martin and his Orchestra.
   Sung by The Merry Macs in *San Antonio Rose* (film, 1941).

I Concentrate on You
Words and music by Cole Porter.
De Sylva, Brown & Henderson, Inc.
Introduced by Douglas McPhail, and danced to by Fred Astaire and
   Eleanor Powell, in *Broadway Melody of 1940* (film, 1940).

I Didn't Know What Time It Was
Words by Lorenz Hart, music by Richard Rodgers.
Chappell & Co., Inc.
Introduced by Marcy Westcott and Richard Kollmar in *Too Many
   Girls* (musical). Sung by Lucille Ball, Eddie Bracken, Hal Le Roy,
   and Desi Arnaz in film version, 1940. Sung by Frank Sinatra in
   Pal Joey (film, 1957).

I Get Along without You Very Well (except Sometimes)
Words (from a poem) by Mrs. Jane Brown Thompson, music by
   Hoagy Carmichael.
Famous Music Corp.
Composed by Carmichael several years after being given Mrs.
   Thompson's unsigned poem by a student at Indiana University.
   After an extensive search, the author was located, but she died
   the night before song was introduced by Dick Powell on a network
   radio show. Sung by Hoagy Carmichael and Jane Russell in *The
   Las Vegas Story* (film, 1952).

I Like To Recognize the Tune
Words by Lorenz Hart, music by Richard Rodgers.
Chappell & Co., Inc.
Introduced by Eddie Bracken, Marcy Westcott, Mary Jane Walsh,
Richard Kollmar, and Hal Le Roy in *Too Many Girls* (musical).
Sung by June Allyson, Vaughn Monroe, Virginia O'Brien, Ziggy
Talent, and chorus in *Meet the People* (film, 1944).

I Never Knew Heaven Could Speak
Words and music by Mack Gordon and Harry Revel.
Robbins Music Corp.
Introduced by Alice Faye in *Rose of Washington Square* (film).

I Poured My Heart into a Song
Words and music by Irving Berlin.
Irving Berlin Music Corp.
Introduced by Tyrone Power, and reprised by Rudy Vallée, in
Second Fiddle (film). Nominated for Academy Award, 1939.

I Thought about You
Words by Johnny Mercer, music by Jimmy Van Heusen.
Burke & Van Heusen, Inc.
Introduced and first recorded by Benny Goodman and his Orchestra,
vocal by Mildred Bailey (Victor).

I Want My Mama, also known as Mama Yo Quiero (Brazilian)
English words by Al Stillman, Portuguese words and music by
Jararaca and Vincente Paiva, Spanish words by George Negrette.
Robbins Music Corp., 1939, 1940.
From the Brazilian song, "Mamãe Eu Quero." Popularized by Car-
men Miranda. Sung by Mickey Rooney in *Babes on Broadway*
(film, 1941).

I Went to a Marvelous Party (English)
Words and music by Noël Coward.
Chappell & Co., Inc.
Introduced by Beatrice Lillie in *Set to Music* (revue).

If I Didn't Care
Words and music by Jack Lawrence.
Chappell & Co., Inc.
Best-selling record by The Ink Spots (Decca).

If I Had My Life To Live Over
Words and music by Henry Tobias, Larry Vincent, and Moe Jaffe.
General Music Publishing Co., Inc.
First recording in 1947 by Larry Vincent (Pearl).

If I Knew Then (What I Know Now)
Words and music by Dick Jurgens and Eddy Howard.
Chappell & Co., Inc.
Introduced by Dick Jurgens and his Orchestra, vocal by
    Eddy Howard.

If I Only Had a Brain (Scarecrow Dance)
Words by E. Y. Harburg, music by Harold Arlen.
Leo Feist, Inc.
Introduced by Ray Bolger in *The Wizard of Oz* (film).

I'll Keep On Loving You
Words and music by Floyd Tillman.
Peer International Corp.
Introduced by Floyd Tillman (Victor).

I'll Never Smile Again (Canadian)
Words and music by Ruth Lowe.
MCA, Inc.
Introduced on radio in Canada by Percy Faith and his Orchestra.
    Best-selling record by Tommy Dorsey and his Orchestra, vocal by
    Frank Sinatra.

I'll Pray for You (English)
Words by Roy King (pseudonym for H. Robinson Cleaver), music by
    Stanley Hill (a pseudonym for Reginald M. Armitage, also known
    as Noel Gay).
Noel Gay Music Co., Ltd., London, England/Mills Music, Inc.
Popularized in England by Vera Lynn. Sung by The Andrews Sis-
    ters, Jane Frazee, and Gloria Jean in *What's Cooking?* (film,
    1942).

I'm Checking Out Goombye
Words and music by Billy Strayhorn and Edward Kennedy "Duke"
    Ellington.
Robbins Music Corp.
Introduced by Duke Ellington and his Orchestra, vocal by Ivie
    Anderson and Sonny Greer.

I'm Happy about the Whole Thing
Words by Johnny Mercer, music by Harry Warren.
Remick Music Corp.
Introduced by Dick Powell and Gale Page in *Naughty but Nice*
    (film).

I'm Sorry for Myself
Words and music by Irving Berlin.
Irving Berlin Music Corp.
Introduced by Mary Healy in *Second Fiddle* (film).

In a Moment of Weakness
Words by Johnny Mercer, music by Harry Warren.
Remick Music Corp.
Introduced by Ann Sheridan and Gale Page in *Naughty but Nice* (film).

In an Eighteenth Century Drawing Room
Words by Jack Lawrence, music by Raymond Scott.
Advanced Music Corp.
Based on Mozart's "Sonata in C," K. 525. Introduced by The Raymond Scott Quintet.

In Other Words, Seventeen
Words by Oscar Hammerstein II, music by Jerome Kern.
T. B. Harms Co.
Introduced by Grace McDonald and Donald Brian, and reprised by Eve Arden, in *Very Warm for May* (musical).

In the Heart of the Dark
Words by Oscar Hammerstein II, music by Jerome Kern.
T. B. Harms Co.
Introduced by Hollace Shaw, and reprised by Frances Mercer, in *Very Warm for May* (musical).

In the Mood
Words by Andy Razaf, music by Joe Garland.
Shapiro, Bernstein & Co., Inc.
Originally introduced and recorded in 1938 by Edgar Hayes and his Orchestra (Decca). Best-selling record in 1940 by Glenn Miller and his Orchestra (Bluebird). Featured in *Sun Valley Serenade* (film, 1941) and *The Glenn Miller Story* (film, 1954).

Indian Summer
Words by Al Dubin, music by Victor Herbert.
Harms, Inc.
From a Victor Herbert piano composition composed in 1919. Popularized by Frank Sinatra.

It Makes No Difference Now
Words and music by Floyd Tillman.
Peer International Corp.
Introduced by Jimmie Davis. Sung by Tex Ritter in *Down the Wyoming Trail* (film).

It Was Written in the Stars
Words and music by Cole Porter.
Chappell & Co., Inc.
Introduced by Ronald Graham in *Du Barry Was a Lady* (musical).

It's a Blue World
Words and music by Bob Wright and Chet Forrest.
Bourne Co.
Introduced by Tony Martin in *Music in My Heart* (film, 1940).
Nominated for Academy Award, 1940.

It's a Lovely Day Tomorrow
Words and music by Irving Berlin.
Irving Berlin Music Corp.
Introduced by Irene Bordoni in *Louisiana Purchase* (musical, 1940).

It's a Wonderful World
Words by Harold Adamson, music by Jan Savitt and Johnny Watson.
Robbins Music Corp.
Introduced by and a theme song of Jan Savitt and his Orchestra.

It's Funny to Everyone but Me
Words and music by Jack Lawrence.
M. Witmark & Sons.
Best-selling record in 1955 (recorded in 1939) by Harry James and
his Orchestra, vocal by Frank Sinatra (Columbia).

I've Got My Eyes on You
Words and music by Cole Porter.
De Sylva, Brown & Henderson, Inc.
Introduced by Fred Astaire in *Broadway Melody of 1940* (film).
Sung by Kathryn Grayson in *Andy Hardy's Private Secretary*
(film, 1941).

Jazz Pizzicato
Music by Leroy Anderson.
Mills Music, Inc.

Jiminy Cricket
Words by Ned Washington, music by Leigh Harline.
Bourne Co.
Promotional song for *Pinocchio* (cartoon feature film, 1940).

Jitterbug, The
Words by E. Y. Harburg, music by Harold Arlen.
Leo Feist, Inc.
Introduced by Ray Bolger, Jack Haley, Bert Lahr, and Judy Garland
in sequence subsequently deleted from *The Wizard of Oz* (film).
First recording by Judy Garland (Decca).

John Silver
Music by Ray Krise and Jimmy Dorsey.
Bregman, Vocco & Conn, Inc.
Swing instrumental, introduced by Jimmy Dorsey and his Orchestra.
Featured by Dorsey and his Orchestra in *Lost in a Harem* (film,
1944).

John's Idea
Music by William "Count" Basie and Ed Durham.
Bregman, Vocco & Conn, Inc.
Swing instrumental, introduced by Count Basie and his Orchestra.

Jumpin' Jive
Words and music by Cab Calloway, Fred Froeba, and Jack Palmer.
Edward B. Marks Music Corp.
Introduced by Cab Calloway.

Just a Dream
Words and music by Big Bill Broonzy.
Leeds Music Corp.
Blues, introduced by Big Bill Broonzy.

Just for a Thrill
Words and music by Lil Armstrong and Don Raye.
Leeds Music Corp.
Earlier version introduced in 1936 by Lil Armstrong and her
    Swing Band.

Katie Went to Haiti
Words and music by Cole Porter.
Chappell & Co., Inc.
Introduced by Ethel Merman in *Du Barry Was a Lady* (musical).
    Sung by The Pied Pipers, Jo Stafford, and Dick Haymes, with
    Tommy Dorsey and his Orchestra, in film version, 1943.

Lady's in Love with You, The
Words by Frank Loesser, music by Burton Lane.
Paramount Music Corp.
Introduced by Shirley Ross and Bob Hope, with Gene Krupa and his
    Orchestra, in *Some Like It Hot* (film).

Lamp Is Low, The
Words by Mitchell Parish, adaptation of music by Peter De Rose
    and Bert Shefter.
Éditions Max Eschig, Paris, France, 1899/Robbins Music Corp.
Adapted from Ravel's "Pavane pour Une Infante Défunte."
    Introduced by Larry Clinton and his Orchestra.

Leanin' on the Ole Top Rail
Words and music by Nick Kenny and Charles Kenny.
Leo Feist, Inc.
Introduced by Gene Autry in *Ride Tenderfoot Ride* (film, 1940).

Let's Have an Old Fashioned Christmas
Words by Larry Conley, music by Joe Solomon.
Mayfair Music Corp.

Let's Hit the Nail on the Head
Words by E. Y. Harburg, music by Harold Arlen.
Mills Music, Inc.

Let's Make Memories Tonight
Words and music by Lew Brown, Charles Tobias, Al Sherman, and
Sam H. Stept.
Chappell & Co., Inc.
Introduced by Lois January in *Yokel Boy* (musical).

Lilacs in the Rain
Words by Mitchell Parish, music by Peter De Rose.
Robbins Music Corp., 1934, 1939.
Song version of De Rose piano piece composed in 1934.

Little Red Fox, The (N'ya N'ya Ya Can't Catch Me)
Words by James V. Kern, Hy Heath, and Johnny Lange, music by
Lew Porter.
Leo Feist, Inc.
Introduced by Kay Kyser and Harry Babbitt in *That's Right —
You're Wrong* (film).

Little Sir Echo
Original words and music by Laura R. Smith and J. S. Fearis; verse
and revised arrangement by Adele Girard Marsala and Joe Mar-
sala.
Bregman, Vocco & Conn, Inc.
Popularized by Horace Heidt and his Musical Knights.

Lonesome Walls
Words by Du Bose Heyward, music by Jerome Kern.
T. B. Harms Co.
Introduced in *Mamba's Daughters* (play).

Love Never Went to College
Words by Lorenz Hart, music by Richard Rodgers.
Chappell & Co., Inc.
Introduced by Marcy Westcott and Richard Kollmar in *Too Many
Girls* (musical). Sung by Frances Langford in film version, 1940.

Low Down Rhythm in a Top Hat
Words and music by Al Donahue, Jimmy Eaton, and Terry Shand.
Shapiro, Bernstein & Co., Inc.
Theme song of Al Donahue and his Orchestra.

Lydia, the Tattooed Lady
Words by E. Y. Harburg, music by Harold Arlen.
Leo Feist, Inc.
Introduced by Groucho Marx in *At the Circus* (film).

Mama Yo Quiero, see I Want My Mama.

Man and His Dream, A
Words by Johnny Burke, music by James V. Monaco.
Anne-Rachel Music Corp.
Introduced by Bing Crosby in *The Star Maker* (film).

Mene, Mene, Tekel
Words and music by Harold Rome.
Florence Music Co., Inc.
Introduced by Dorothy Harrison in *Pins and Needles* (revue).

Merry Old Land of Oz, The
Words by E. Y. Harburg, music by Harold Arlen.
Leo Feist, Inc.
Introduced by Singer's Midgets in *The Wizard of Oz* (film).

Mile after Mile
Words by Charles Alan and Buddy Bernier, music by Kurt Weill.
De Sylva, Brown & Henderson, Inc.
Introduced in *Railroads on Parade,* musical pageant at New York
    World's Fair.

Moon Love
Words and music by Mack David, Mack Davis, and
    André Kostelanetz.
Famous Music Corp .
Adapted from Tchaikovsky's "Symphony, No. 5," Second Movement.

Moonlight Serenade
Words by Mitchell Parish, music by Glenn Miller.
Robbins Music Corp.
Earlier version, written by Miller while with Ray Noble's Orchestra,
    entitled "Now I Lay Me Down To Weep," with lyrics by Edward
    Heyman. Theme song of Glenn Miller and his Orchestra and of
    Tex Beneke and his Orchestra.

My Last Goodbye
Words and music by Eddy Howard.
Bourne Co.
Introduced by Dick Jurgens and his Orchestra, vocal by
    Eddy Howard.

My Prayer (English-French)
Words and adaptation of music by Jimmy Kennedy, music by
    Georges Boulanger.
The Peter Maurice Music Co., Ltd., London, England/Shapiro,
    Bernstein & Co., Inc.
Adapted from Boulanger's short composition for violin, "Avant de
    Mourir." Vocal version introduced by Vera Lynn. Introduced in
    United States by Sammy Kaye and his Orchestra. Revived in 1956
    with best-selling record by The Platters (Mercury).

My Twilight Dream
Words and adaptation of music by Lew Sherwood and Eddy Duchin.
Robbins Music Corp.
Based on Chopin's "Nocturne in E-flat." Introduced by and theme
  song of Eddy Duchin and his Orchestra.

My Wubba Dolly
Words and music by Kay Werner and Sue Werner.
American Academy of Music, Inc.
Best-selling record by Ella Fitzgerald (Decca).

Non-Stop Flight
Music by Artie Shaw.
Lincoln Music Corp.
Swing instrumental, introduced by Artie Shaw and his Orchestra.

Oh, You Crazy Moon
Words by Johnny Burke, music by James Van Heusen.
M. Witmark & Sons.
First song of team of Burke and Van Heusen. Introduced by
  Tommy Dorsey and his Orchestra.

Old Fashioned Tune Always Is New, An
Words and music by Irving Berlin.
Irving Berlin Music Corp.
Introduced by Rudy Vallée in *Second Fiddle* (film).

Old Mill Wheel
Words and music by Benny Davis, Milton Ager, and Jesse Greer.
Advanced Music Corp.

One-Two-Three-Kick
Words by Al Stillman, music by Xavier Cugat.
Larry Spier, Inc.
Introduced by Xavier Cugat and his Orchestra.

Ooh! What You Said
Words by Johnny Mercer, music by Hoagy Carmichael.
Edwin H. Morris & Co., Inc.
Introduced by Mitzi Green and The Modernaires in *Walk with
  Music* (musical, 1940).

Our Love
Words and music by Larry Clinton, Buddy Bernier, and
  Bob Emmerich.
Chappell & Co., Inc.
Adapted from Tchaikovsky's "Romeo and Juliet Fantasie Overture."
  Introduced by Larry Clinton and his Orchestra.

Over the Rainbow
Words by E. Y. Harburg, music by Harold Arlen.
Leo Feist, Inc.
Introduced by Judy Garland in *The Wizard of Oz* (film). Academy
    Award-winning song, 1939. Hummed by Elizabeth Hartman in *A
    Patch of Blue* (film, 1965).

Pastel Blue, see Why Begin Again, 1943.

Peace Brother
Words by Eddie De Lange, music by Jimmy Van Heusen.
Bregman, Vocco & Conn, Inc.
Introduced by The Deep River Boys in *Swingin' the Dream*
    (musical).

Perfidia, see 1941.

Portrait of the Lion
Music by Edward Kennedy "Duke" Ellington.
American Academy of Music, Inc.
Dedicated to Willie "The Lion" Smith. Introduced by Duke Ellington
    and his Orchestra.

Put Your Little Foot Right Out
Words and adaptation of music by Larry Spier.
Larry Spier, Inc.
Adapted from "Varsovienne," a French folk-dance melody.
    Introduced by Ann Sheridan in *San Antonio* (film, 1945).

Riverboat Shuffle, see 1925.

Rumba Jumps, The
Words by Johnny Mercer, music by Hoagy Carmichael.
Edwin H. Morris & Co., Inc.
Introduced by Frances Williams and The Modernaires in
    Walk with Music (musical, 1940).

Run, Rabbit, Run (English)
Words by Noel Gay and Ralph Butler, music by Noel Gay.
Noel Gay Music Co., Ltd., London, England/Mills Music, Inc.
Introduced in London in *The Little Dog Laughed* (musical).

Says My Heart
Words by Frank Loesser, music by Burton Lane.
Famous Music Corp.
Introduced by Harriet Hilliard, with Harry Owens and his
    Orchestra, in *Cocoanut Grove* (film, 1938).

Scatterbrain
Words and music by Johnny Burke, Frankie Masters, Kahn Keene, and Carl Bean.
Bregman, Vocco & Conn, Inc.
Introduced by and theme song of Frankie Masters and his Orchestra. Performed by Kay Kyser and his Orchestra in *That's Right — You're Wrong* (film).

See What the Boys in the Back Room Will Have, see The Boys in the Back Room.

Sent for You Yesterday (and Here You Come Today)
Words and music by William "Count" Basie, Ed Durham, and James Rushing.
Bregman, Vocco & Conn, Inc.
Introduced and best-selling record by Count Basie and his Orchestra, vocal by Jimmy Rushing (Decca).

Serenade to Sweden
Music by Edward Kennedy "Duke" Ellington.
Robbins Music Corp.
Swing instrumental, introduced by Duke Ellington and his Orchestra.

Seven Twenty in the Books
Words by Harold Adamson, music by Jan Savitt and Johnny Watson.
Robbins Music Corp.
Introduced by Jan Savitt and his Orchestra.

She Had To Go and Lose It at the Astor
Words and music by Don Raye and Hugh Prince.
Leeds Music Corp.
Introduced by Johnny Messner and his Orchestra.

Shoot the Sherbet to Me, Herbert
Words and music by Ben Homer.
MCA, Inc.

Sing a Song of Sunbeams
Words by Johnny Burke, music by James V. Monaco.
Anne-Rachel Music Corp.
Introduced by Bing Crosby in *East Side of Heaven* (film).

Sing My Heart
Words by Ted Koehler, music by Harold Arlen.
De Sylva, Brown & Henderson, Inc.
Introduced by Irene Dunne in *Love Affair* (film).

Six Lessons from Madame La Zonga
Words and music by Charles Newman and James Monaco.
Bregman, Vocco & Conn, Inc.
Introduced by Jimmy Dorsey and his Orchestra, vocal by Helen
O'Connell. Featured in *Six Lessons from Madame La Zonga* (film,
1941).

So Long (It's Been Good To Know Yuh)
Words and music by Woody Guthrie.
Folkways Music Publishers, Inc., 1939, 1950.
Introduced by Woody Guthrie. Revived in 1950 with best-selling
record by The Weavers (Decca).

Some Other Spring
Words by Arthur Herzog, Jr., music by Irene Kitchings.
Edward B. Marks Music Corp.
Introduced by Billie Holiday.

Something I Dreamed Last Night
Words by Herb Magidson and Jack Yellen, music by Sammy Fain.
De Sylva, Brown & Henderson, Inc.
Introduced by Ella Logan in *George White's Scandals of 1939*
(revue).

Something To Live For
Words and music by Edward Kennedy "Duke" Ellington and
Billy Strayhorn.
American Academy of Music, Inc.
First collaboration between Ellington and Strayhorn. Introduced by
Duke Ellington and his Orchestra, vocal by Jean Eldridge.

Song of the Metronome, The
Words and music by Irving Berlin.
Irving Berlin Music Corp.
Introduced by The Brian Sisters and children's chorus in
Second Fiddle (film).

South American Way
Words by Al Dubin, music by Jimmy McHugh.
Harms, Inc.
Introduced by Ramon Vinay, The Hylton Sisters, Della Lind, and
Carmen Miranda in *Streets of Paris* (revue). Sung by Miss Mi-
randa in *Down Argentine Way* (film, 1940).

South of the Border (Down Mexico Way) (English)
Words and music by Jimmy Kennedy and Michael Carr.
The Peter Maurice Music Co., Ltd., London, England/Shapiro,
Bernstein & Co., Inc.
Introduced by Gene Autry during tour of England. Best-selling
record by Shep Fields and his Rippling Rhythm (Bluebird).

Sparkling Blue Eyes, also known as **Sparkling Brown Eyes**
Words and music by Billy Cox.
Dixie Music Publishing Co.
Best-selling record in 1954 by Webb Pierce (Decca).

Sparkling Brown Eyes, see **Sparkling Blue Eyes.**

Stairway to the Stars
Words by Mitchell Parish, music by Matt Malneck and
Frank Signorelli.
Robbins Music Corp.
Based on a theme from "Park Avenue Fantasy," instrumental composition published in 1935. Introduced by Paul Whiteman and his
Orchestra.

Starlit Hour, The
Words by Mitchell Parish, music by Peter De Rose.
Robbins Music Corp.
Best-selling records in 1940 by Ella Fitzgerald (Decca) and
Glenn Miller and his Orchestra (Victor).

Start the Day Right
Words and music by Charles Tobias, Al Lewis, and Maurice Spitalny.
Harms, Inc.
Introduced by Bing Crosby and Connee Boswell.

Strange Enchantment
Words by Frank Loesser, music by Frederick Hollander.
Famous Music Corp.
Introduced by Dorothy Lamour in *Man about Town* (film).

Strange Fruit
Words and music by Lewis Allan.
Edward B. Marks Music Corp.
Anti-lynching song, introduced by Billie Holiday.

Swingin' the Blues
Music by William "Count" Basie and Ed Durham.
Bregman, Vocco & Conn, Inc.
Introduced by Count Basie and his Orchestra.

'Taint What You Do (It's the Way That Cha Do It)
Words and music by Sy Oliver and James "Trummy" Young.
Leeds Music Corp.
Introduced by Jimmie Lunceford and his Orchestra.

Tara's Theme
Music by Max Steiner.
Remick Music Corp., 1941.
A theme from *Gone with the Wind* (film, 1939). Published but not until 1941, in a folio, *Piano Miniatures.* Lyrics for song version, entitled "My Own True Love," written by Mack David in 1954.

Teeter Totter Tessie
Words by Morgan Lewis, music by Nancy Hamilton.
Chappell & Co., Inc.
Introduced by Gene Kelly and Grace McDonald in *One for the Money* (revue).

Tell Me You're Mine (Italian)
English words by Ronnie Vincent, Italian words by U. Bertini, music by D. Vasin.
S. A. Edizioni Suvini-Zerboni, Italy/Capri Music Corp.
Original Italian title, "Per un Bacio d'Amore." Best-selling record in 1953 by The Gaylords (Mercury).

That Lucky Fellow, also known as That Lucky Lady
Words by Oscar Hammerstein II, music by Jerome Kern.
T. B. Harms Co.
Introduced by Robert Shackleton, and reprised as "That Lucky Lady" by Grace McDonald, in *Very Warm for May* (musical).

That Lucky Lady, see That Lucky Fellow.

That Sentimental Sandwich
Words by Frank Loesser, music by Frederick Hollander.
Famous Music Corp.
Introduced by Dorothy Lamour, Eddie "Rochester" Anderson, and Phil Harris in *Man about Town* (film).

That Sly Old Gentleman (from Featherbed Lane)
Words by Johnny Burke, music by James V. Monaco.
Anne-Rachel Music Corp.
Introduced by Bing Crosby in *East Side of Heaven* (film).

There'll Always Be an England (English)
Words and music by Ross Parker and Hughie Charles.
Irwin Dash Music Co., Ltd., London, England/Gordon V. Thompson, Ltd.
Introduced in England by Billy Cotton and his Orchestra. Introduced on records in United States by The Band of the Coldstream Guards (Victor).

Things That Might Have Been
Words and music by Bob Miller.
Leeds Music Corp.
Introduced by Roy Acuff.

This Is It
Words by Dorothy Fields, music by Arthur Schwartz.
Chappell & Co., Inc.
Introduced by Ethel Merman in *Stars in Your Eyes* (musical).

This Night (Will Be My Souvenir)
Words by Gus Kahn, music by Harry Warren.
Bregman, Vocco & Conn, Inc./Leo Feist, Inc.
Introduced in *Honolulu* (film).

Three Little Fishies (Itty Bitty Poo)
Words and music by Saxie Dowell.
Anne-Rachel Music Corp.
Nonsense song, introduced by Hal Kemp and his Orchestra.

Tomorrow Night
Words by Sam Coslow, music by Will Grosz.
Bourne Co.
Best-selling record in 1948 by Lonnie Johnson (King).

Tootin' through the Roof
Music by Edward Kennedy "Duke" Ellington.
Robbins Music Corp.
Swing instrumental, introduced by Duke Ellington and his
    Orchestra.

Traffic Jam
Music by Teddy McRae and Artie Shaw.
Lincoln Music Corp.
Swing instrumental, introduced by Artie Shaw and his Orchestra.

Truck Drivers (Blues)
Words and music by Ted Daffan.
Dixie Music Publishing Co.
Introduced by Moon Mullican.

Turn On the Old Music Box
Words by Ned Washington, music by Leigh Harline.
Bourne Co.
Introduced instrumentally in *Pinocchio* (cartoon film, 1940).

Two Blind Loves
Words by E. Y. Harburg, music by Harold Arlen.
Leo Feist, Inc.
Introduced by Kenny Baker and Florence Rice in *At the Circus*
    (film).

U.S. Air Force, The (The Wild Blue Yonder)
Words and music by Major Robert M. Crawford.
Carl Fischer, Inc.
Official Air Force song. Known earlier under titles, "Army Air
    Corps" and "Nothing'll Stop the Air Corps Now." Featured in
    Air Corps-sponsored *Winged Victory* (revue, 1943).

Undecided
Words by Sid Robin, music by Charles Shavers.
Leeds Music Corp.
Introduced by Chick Webb and his Orchestra, vocal by Ella Fitzgerald. Revived in 1951 with best-selling record by The Ames Brothers (Coral).

Vagabond Dreams
Words by Jack Lawrence, music by Hoagy Carmichael.
Paramount Music Corp.

Wanderlust
Music by Edward Kennedy "Duke" Ellington and Johnny Hodges.
American Academy of Music, Inc.
Introduced by Duke Ellington and his Orchestra.

(We're Gonna Hang Out) The Washing on the Siegfried Line (English)
Words and music by Jimmy Kennedy and Michael Carr.
The Peter Maurice Music Co., Ltd., London, England/Shapiro, Bernstein & Co., Inc.
Popularized in England by Flanagan and Allen, comedy team.

Well All Right! (Tonight's the Night)
Words and music by Frances Faye, Don Raye, and Dan Howell (pseudonym for David Kapp).
Leeds Music Corp.
Best-selling record by The Andrews Sisters (Decca).

Well, Did You Evah?
Words and music by Cole Porter.
Chappell & Co., Inc.
Introduced by Betty Grable and Charles Walters in *Du Barry Was a Lady* (musical). Sung by Frank Sinatra and Bing Crosby in *High Society* (film, 1957).

We'll Meet Again (English)
Words and music by Ross Parker and Hughie Charles.
Irwin Dash Music Co., Ltd., London, England/World Music, Inc.
Introduced by and identified with Vera Lynn. Sung by Miss Lynn on soundtrack of *Dr. Strangelove or: How I Learned To Stop Worrying and Love the Bomb* (film, 1964).

We're Gonna Hang Out the Washing on the Siegfried Line, see (We're Gonna Hang Out) The Washing on the Siegfried Line.

We're Off To See the Wizard
Words by E. Y. Harburg, music by Harold Arlen.
Leo Feist, Inc.
Introduced by Judy Garland, Bert Lahr, Jack Haley, and Ray Bolger in *The Wizard of Oz* (film).

What's New?
Words by Johnny Burke, music by Bob Haggart.
M. Witmark & Sons.
Introduced in 1938 as instrumental, entitled "I'm Free," by Bob Crosby and his Orchestra. Theme song of Billy Butterfield and his Orchestra.

When Winter Comes
Words and music by Irving Berlin.
Irving Berlin Music Corp.
Introduced by Rudy Vallée in *Second Fiddle* (film).

Where Was I?
Words by Al Dubin, music by W. Franke Harling.
Remick Music Corp.
Introduced in *'Til We Meet Again* (film, 1940). Best-selling records in 1940 by Charlie Barnet and his Orchestra (Bluebird) and Jan Savitt and his Orchestra (Decca).

Who Are We To Say (Obey Your Heart)
Words by Gus Kahn, music by Sigmund Romberg.
Leo Feist, Inc.
Introduced by Nelson Eddy in *Girl of the Golden West* (film, 1938).

Wishing (Will Make It So)
Words and music by B. G. De Sylva.
De Sylva, Brown & Henderson, Inc.
Introduced by Irene Dunne in *Love Affair* (film). Nominated for Academy Award, 1939. Best-selling record by Glenn Miller and his Orchestra.

Woodchopper's Ball
Music by Woody Herman and Joe Bishop.
Leeds Music Corp.
Introduced by Woody Herman and his Orchestra.

Yes, My Darling Daughter
Words and music by Jack Lawrence.
Leo Feist, Inc.
Adapted from Ukrainian folk song. Introduced by Gracie Barrie in *Crazy with the Heat* (revue, 1941). Best-selling record by Dinah Shore (Bluebird).

You Are My Flower
Words and music by A. P. Carter.
Peer International Corp.
Introduced by The Carter Family. Revived in 1964 with best-selling record by Lester Flatt and Earl Scruggs (Columbia).

You Taught Me To Love Again
Words by Charles Carpenter, music by Tommy Dorsey and
  Henri Woode.
Larry Spier, Inc.
Introduced by Tommy Dorsey and his Orchestra, vocal by
  Jack Leonard.

You're a Lucky Guy
Words by Sammy Cahn, music by Saul Chaplin.
M. Witmark & Sons.

Yours for a Song
Words by Billy Rose and Ted Fetter, music by Dana Suesse.
Robbins Music Corp.
Introduced by Morton Downey at New York World's Fair in
  Billy Rose's Aquacade (revue).

List of Titles

A

About a Quarter to Nine, 1935.
Accent on Youth, 1935.
According to the Moonlight, 1935.
Actions Speak Louder Than Words, 1931.
Adios, 1931.
Address Unknown, 1939.
Adorable, 1933.
Afraid To Dream, 1937.
After All Is Said and Done, 1932.
After All You're All I'm After, 1933.
After Sundown, 1933.
After Twelve o'Clock, 1932.
After You, 1932, 1937.
Ah, but Is It Love?, 1933.
Ah Still Suits Me, see I Still Suits Me, 1936.
Ah, the Moon Is Here, 1933.
Ain't-cha Glad?, 1933.
Alabama Barbecue, 1936.
Alabamy Home, 1937.
Alibi Baby, 1937.
All at Once, 1937.
All Dark People, 1937.
All Dressed Up (Spic and Spanish), 1939.
All God's Chillun Got Rhythm, 1937.
All I Do Is Dream of You, 1934.
All I Remember Is You, 1939.
All in Fun, 1939.
All My Life, 1936.
All of Me, 1931.
All the King's Horses, 1930.

All the Things You Are, 1939.
All This and Heaven Too, 1939.
All through the Night, 1934.
All You Want To Do Is Dance, 1937.
All-American Girl, 1932.
Allá En El Rancho Grande, see El Rancho Grande, 1934.
Allegheny Al, 1937.
Alligator Crawl, 1937.
Alone, 1935.
Alone at a Table for Two, 1935.
Alone Together, 1932.
Always and Always, 1937.
Always in All Ways, 1930.
Am I Gonna Have Trouble with You?, 1936.
Am I in Love?, 1937.
Am I Proud, 1939.
Am I Wasting My Time?, 1932.
Amber Tresses Tied with Blue, 1932.
Anatole (of Paris), 1939.
And Love Was Born, 1932.
And the Angels Sing, 1939.
And Then Some, 1935.
Angel in Disguise, 1939.
Animal Crackers in My Soup, 1935.
Annie Doesn't Live Here Anymore, 1933.
Any Old Time, 1930.
(I Would Do) Anything for You, 1932.
Anything Goes, 1934.
Apple for the Teacher, An, 1939.
April in My Heart, 1938.

294

April in Paris, 1932.
Apurksady, 1938.
Are You Havin' Any Fun?, 1939.
Are You Makin' Any Money?, 1933.
Are You My Love?, 1936.
Army Air Corps Song, see The U.S. Air Force (The Wild Blue Yonder), 1939.
Around the Corner, 1930.
As Long As I Live, 1934.
As Time Goes By, 1931.
As You Desire Me, 1932.
At a Perfume Counter (on the Rue de la Paix), 1938.
At Long Last Love, 1938.
At the Balalaika, 1939.
At the Close of a Long, Long Day, 1932.
At the Codfish Ball, 1936.
At the Roxy Music Hall, 1938.
At Your Beck and Call, 1938.
At Your Command, 1931.
A-Tisket A-Tasket, 1938.
Au Revoir, Pleasant Dreams, 1930.
Auf Wiedersehn, My Dear, 1932.
Autumn in New York, 1934.
Awake in a Dream, 1936.
Azure, 1937.

B

Babalú, 1939.
Babes in Arms, 1937.
Baby, Don't Tell on Me, 1939.
Baby, Take a Bow, 1934.
Baby When You Ain't There, 1932.
Baby's Birthday Party, 1930.
Bach Goes to Town, 1938.
Back Bay Shuffle, 1939.
Back to Back, 1939.
Balboa, 1936.
Ballad in Blue, 1935.
Barrelhouse Music, 1935.
Be a Good Scout, 1938.
Be a Good Sport, 1937.
Be Still, My Heart!, 1934.
Beat of My Heart, The, 1934.
Beautiful Girl, 1933.
Beautiful Lady in Blue, A, 1935.
Beautiful Love, 1931.

Beautiful Texas, 1933.
Because, Because, 1931.
Beer Barrel Polka (Roll Out the Barrel), 1939.
Begging for Love, 1931.
Begin the Beguine, 1935.
(I've Got) Beginner's Luck, 1937.
Bei Mir Bist Du Schön (Means That You're Grand), 1937.
Believe It, Beloved, 1934.
Beloved, 1934.
Bench in the Park, A, 1930.
Bend Down Sister, 1931.
Bess, You Is My Woman, 1935.
Best Wishes, 1932.
Betty Co-Ed, 1930.
Between a Kiss and a Sigh, 1938.
Between 18th and 19th on Chestnut Street, 1939.
Between the Devil and the Deep Blue Sea, 1931.
Between You and Me, 1939.
Bewildered, 1938.
Beyond the Blue Horizon, 1930.
Bidin' My Time, 1930.
Big Apple, The, 1937.
Big Chief De Sota, 1936.
Big John's Special, 1934.
Biggest Aspidastra in the World, The, 1938.
Black Butterfly, 1937.
Black Eyed Susan Brown, 1933.
Black Jazz, 1932.
Black Moonlight, 1933.
Blah-Blah-Blah, 1931.
Blame It on My Last Affair, 1939.
Blame It on My Youth, 1934.
Blame It on the Danube, 1937.
Blame It on the Rhumba, 1936.
Blossoms on Broadway, 1937.
Blow, Gabriel, Blow, 1934.
Blue Again, 1930.
Blue and Disillusioned, 1938.
Blue and Sentimental, 1939.
Blue Evening, 1939.
Blue Feeling, 1934.
Blue Hawaii, 1937.
Blue Hours, 1933.
Blue Interlude, 1934.
Blue Is the Night, 1930.

Titles

Blue Lament (Cry for Me), 1934.
Blue Light, 1938.
Blue Lou, 1935.
Blue Moon, 1934.
Blue Nightfall, 1939.
Blue Orchids, 1939.
Blue Prairie, 1936.
Blue Prelude, 1933.
Blue Rain, 1939.
Blue Rhythm Fantasy, 1936.
Blue September, 1937.
Blue, Turning Gray over You, 1930.
Blue Venetian Waters, 1937.
Blue Yodel No. 8, see Mule Skinner Blues, 1931.
Bluebird of Happiness, 1934.
Blues in My Heart, 1931.
Blues Serenade, A, 1935.
Bob White (Whatcha Gonna Swing Tonight?), 1937.
Body and Soul, 1930.
Bojangles of Harlem, 1936.
Bolero at the Savoy, 1939.
Boo-Hoo!, 1937.
Boomps-a-Daisy, 1939.
Boulevard of Broken Dreams, The, 1933.
Boy Meets Horn, 1939.
Boy! What Love Has Done to Me, 1930.
Boys in the Back Room, The, 1939.
Brazil, 1939.
Breakfast Ball, 1934.
Breakin' In a Pair of Shoes, 1935.
Breeze (That's Bringin' My Honey Back to Me), The, 1934.
(There's a) Bridle Hangin' on the Wall, 1936.
Broadway Jamboree, 1937.
Broadway Rhythm, 1935.
Broadway's Gone Hawaii, 1937.
Broadway's Gone Hill Billy, 1934.
Broken Record, The, 1935.
Brother, Can You Spare a Dime?, 1932.
Buddie, Beware, 1934.
Buds Won't Bud, 1937.
Business in F, 1931.
But Definitely, 1936.

But in the Morning, No!, 1939.
But Not for Me, 1930.
But Where Are You, 1936.
Button Up Your Heart, 1930.
By a Waterfall, 1933.
By Myself, 1937.
By Special Permission (of the Copyright Owners I Love You), 1931.
By Strauss, 1936.
(In the Gloaming) By the Fireside, 1932.
By the River Sainte Marie, 1931.
By the Sycamore Tree, 1931.
Bye Bye Baby, 1936.
Bye Bye Blues, 1930.

C

Cabin in the Cotton, 1932.
Calico Days, 1933.
Call Me Darling (Call Me Sweetheart, Call Me Dear), 1931.
Camel Hop, 1938.
Can I Forget You?, 1937.
Can This Be Love, 1930.
Can't We Talk It Over, 1931.
Caravan, 1937.
Careless, 1939.
Carioca, 1933.
Carry Me Back to the Lone Prairie, 1934.
Casa Loma Stomp, 1931.
Cathedral in the Pines, 1938.
Cattle Call, The, 1934.
Cavernism, 1935.
C'est Pas Comme Ca, (It's Not Like That), 1931.
Chain Store Daisy, 1937.
Champagne Waltz, The, 1934.
Change Partners, 1938.
Change Your Mind, 1935.
Chant of the Weed, 1932.
Chapel Bells, 1938.
Charlie Cadet, 1931.
Chasing Shadows, 1935.
Cheek to Cheek, 1935.
Cheerful Little Earful, 1930.
Cherokee, 1938.

Chew-Chew-Chew (Chew Your Bubble Gum), 1939.
Chime Bells, 1934.
Chimes of Arcady, 1938.
Christopher Columbus, 1936.
Cigarettes, Cigars, 1931.
Cinderella, Stay in My Arms, 1938.
Cinderella's Fella, 1933.
Circus on Parade, The, 1935.
Ciribiribin (They're So in Love), 1939.
Clarinet Lament, 1936.
Close, 1937.
Close to Me, 1936.
Close Your Eyes, 1933.
Clouds, 1935.
Clouds Will Soon Roll By, The, 1932.
Cockeyed Mayor of Kaunakakai, 1935.
Cocktails for Two, 1934.
Cocoanut Grove, 1938.
Coffee in the Morning (and Kisses in the Night), 1933.
College Rhythm, 1934.
College Swing, 1938.
Come On In, 1939.
Come Out of the Kitchen, Mary Ann, 1930.
Come to Me, 1931.
Come Up and See Me Sometime, 1933.
Comes Love, 1939.
Concentratin' (on You), 1931.
Concert in the Park, 1939.
Confession, 1931.
Confidentially, 1938.
Contented, 1932.
Continental, The, 1934.
Cooking Breakfast for the One I Love, 1930.
Cool Water, 1936.
Copper-Colored Gal, 1936.
Corrine, Corrina, 1932.
Cosi Cosa, 1935.
Cottage for Sale, A, 1930.
Could Be, 1938.
Could You Use Me, 1930.
Count Your Blessings, 1933.
Cowboy and the Lady, The, 1938.

Cowboy from Brooklyn, 1938.
Crazy Feet, 1930.
Crazy People, 1932.
Creole Rhapsody, 1931.
Crescendo in Blue, 1939.
Crosby, Columbo and Vallée, 1931.
Cross Patch, 1936.
Cross-Eyed Kelly (from Penn-syl-van-eye-ay), 1934.
Cry, Baby, Cry, 1938.
Cryin' for the Carolines, 1930.
Cuban Love Song, 1931.
Cuban Pete, 1936.
Cuckoo in the Clock, 1939.
Curly Top, 1935.
Cute Little Things You Do, The, 1931.

D

Dames, 1934.
Dance, My Darlings, 1935.
Dancing in the Dark, 1931.
Dancing on the Ceiling (He Dances on My Ceiling), 1930.
Dancing under the Stars, 1937.
Dancing with Tears in My Eyes, 1930.
Danger — Love at Work, 1937.
Dark Night, 1930.
(When It's) Darkness on the Delta, 1932.
Darling, Je Vous Aime Beaucoup, 1936.
Darn That Dream, 1939.
Daughter of Peggy O'Neil, The, 1930.
Day In — Day Out, 1939.
Day You Came Along, The, 1933.
Daybreak Express, 1934.
Daydreaming (All Night Long), 1938.
Dearest Love, 1938.
Dedicated to You, 1936.
Deep Forest, 1933.
Deep in a Dream, 1938.
Deep Purple, 1934.
Delishious, 1931.
Diavalo, 1935.
Did I Remember?, 1936.

Did You Ever Get Stung?, 1938.
Did You Ever See a Dream Walking?, 1933.
Did Your Mother Come from Ireland?, 1936.
Diminuendo in Blue, 1937.
Ding-Dong! The Witch Is Dead, 1939.
Dinner at Eight, 1933.
Dinner for One Please, James, 1935.
Dinner Music for a Pack of Hungry Cannibals, 1938.
Dipsy Doodle, The, 1937.
Dixieland Band, 1935.
Do I Love You?, 1939.
Do the New York, 1931.
Do You Wanna Jump, Children?, 1938.
Do Your Duty, 1933.
Dodging a Divorcee, 1935.
Does Your Heart Beat for Me?, 1936.
Dog Town Blues, 1938.
Doin' the Suzi-Q, 1936.
Doin' the Uptown Lowdown, 1933.
Doing the Reactionary, 1937.
Donkey Serenade, The, 1937.
Don't Ask Me Why, 1931.
Don't Be That Way, 1938.
Don't Blame Me, 1933.
Don't Cross Your Fingers, Cross Your Heart, 1938.
(Shipmates Forever) Don't Give Up the Ship, 1935.
Don't Let It Bother You, 1934.
Don't Let That Moon Get Away, 1938.
Don't Let Your Love Go Wrong, 1934.
Don't Say Goodbye If You Love Me, 1937.
Don't Say Goodnight, 1934.
Don't Send My Boy to Prison, 1930.
Don't Tell Her What's Happened to Me, 1930.
Don't Tell Your Folks, 1930.
Don't Worry 'bout Me, 1939.
Don't You Miss Your Baby, 1939.
Double Check Stomp, 1930.

Double Trouble, 1935.
Down by the River, 1935.
Down in the Depths, on the Ninetieth Floor, 1936.
Down South Camp Meetin', 1935.
Down the Old Ox Road, 1933.
Down the River of Golden Dreams, 1930.
Down t'Uncle Bill's, 1934.
Down Where Banjos Were Born, 1934.
Down with Love, 1937.
Draggin' My Heart Around, 1931.
Dream a Little Dream of Me, 1931.
Dream of You, 1934.
Dream Sweetheart, 1932.
Dreamy Hawaiian Moon, 1938.
Drop Me Off in Harlem, 1933.
Drummin' Man, 1939.
Drums in My Heart, 1931.
Duerme, 1936.
Dusk in Upper Sandusky, 1937.
Dusk on the Desert, 1937.
Dust, 1930, 1938.
(Oh Suzanna) Dust Off That Old Pianna, 1935.
Dusty Road, 1935.

E

Eadie Was a Lady, 1932.
Earful of Music, An, 1934.
Early Bird, 1936.
East of the Sun (and West of the Moon), 1934.
East Side of Heaven, 1939.
Easter Parade, 1933.
Easy Come, Easy Go, 1934.
Easy To Love, 1936.
Ebony Rhapsody, 1934.
Echo of Spring, 1935.
Echoes of Harlem, 1936.
Eeny, Meeny, Meiny, Mo, 1935.
Egyptian Ella, 1931.
(Allá En) El Rancho Grande (My Ranch), 1934.
Eleven More Months and Ten More Days, 1930.
Elizabeth, 1931.
Emaline, 1934.

Embraceable You, 1930.
Empty Saddles, 1936.
Ending with a Kiss, 1934.
España Cani, 1932.
Especially for You, 1938.
Evenin', 1934.
Every Now and Then, 1935.
Every Tub, 1938.
Everybody Sing, 1937.
Everything I Have Is Yours, 1933.
Ev'ry Day, 1934.
Ev'ry Day a Holiday, 1939.
Ev'ryone Says "I Love You," 1932.
Exactly Like You, 1930.
Experiment, 1933.

F

F.D.R. Jones, 1938.
Fair and Warmer, 1934.
Faithful Forever, 1939.
Falling in Love Again (Can't
    Help It), 1930.
Falling in Love with Love, 1938.
Falling in Love with You, 1930.
Fancy Meeting You, 1936.
Far, Far Away, 1938.
Fare Thee Honey, Fare Thee Well,
    1938.
Fare Thee Well Annabelle, 1934.
Fare-Thee-Well to Harlem, 1934.
Farewell, My Lovely, 1935.
Farewell to Arms, 1933.
Farewell to Dreams, 1937.
Fatal Fascination, 1935.
Feelin' High, 1934.
Ferdinand the Bull, 1938.
Fidgety Joe, 1939.
Fiesta, 1931.
Fifi, 1937.
Fine and Dandy, 1930.
Fine Romance, A, 1936.
First Time I Saw You, The, 1937.
First You Have Me High (Then
    You Have Me Low), 1935.
Fit As a Fiddle, 1932.
Flat Foot Floogie, The, 1938.
Flirtation Walk, 1934.
Flowers for Madame, 1935.
Flyin' Home, 1939.

Flying Down to Rio, 1933.
Foggy Day, A, 1937.
Folks Who Live on the Hill, The,
    1937.
Follow in My Footsteps, 1937.
Follow Your Heart, 1936.
Fool in Love, A, 1933.
Football Freddy (My Collegiate
    Man), 1930.
For All We Know, 1934.
For Dancers Only, 1937.
For No Rhyme or Reason, 1938.
For You, 1930.
Forty-Second Street, 1932.
Four Little Angels of Peace, 1938.
"Free and Easy," The, 1930.
Frenesi, 1939.
Friendly Moon, 1936.
Friendship, 1939.
Frisco Flo, 1936.
Froggy Bottom, 1930.
From Alpha to Omega, 1938.
From Now On, 1938.
From the Top of Your Head to the
    Tip of Your Toes, 1935.
Fun To Be Fooled, 1934.
Funnies, The, 1933.
Funny Old Hills, The, 1938.

G

Gal from Joe's, The, 1939.
Gamblin' Polka Dot Blues, 1932.
Garden of the Moon, 1938.
Gather Lip Rouge While You May,
    1933.
Gaucho Serenade, The, 1939.
Gay Ranchero, A, 1936.
Gee! but You're Swell, 1936.
Georgia on My Mind, 1930.
Get Happy, 1930.
Get Out of Town, 1938.
Get Thee behind Me Satan, 1936.
Getting Some Fun out of Life,
    1937.
(I Don't Stand) A Ghost of a
    Chance (with You), 1932.
Gimme a Pigfoot, 1933.
Gin Mill Blues, 1938.

Girl at the Ironing Board, The, 1934.

Girl Friend of the Whirling Dervish, The, 1938.

Girl on the Police Gazette, The, 1937.

Girl Trouble, 1930.

Give a Broken Heart a Break, 1935.

Give Him the Oo-La-La, 1939.

Give It Back to the Indians, 1939.

Give Me a Moment Please, 1930.

Give Me Liberty or Give Me Love, 1933.

Glad To Be Unhappy, 1936.

Gloomy Sunday, 1936.

Glory of Love, The 1936.

Go Home and Tell Your Mother, 1930.

Go into Your Dance, 1935.

God Bless America, 1939.

God's Country, 1938.

Goin' to Heaven on a Mule, 1934.

Gold Digger's Song, see We're in the Money, 1933.

Gone, 1936.

"Gone with the Wind," 1937.

Good Evening Friends, 1931.

Good for Nothin' (but Love), 1939.

Good for You, Bad for Me, 1930.

Good Mornin', 1937.

Good Morning, 1939.

Good Morning Blues, 1938.

Good Morning Glory, 1933.

Good Night Little Girl of My Dreams, 1933.

Good Night Lovely Little Lady, 1934.

Good Old Fashioned Cocktail (with a Good Old Fashioned Girl), A, 1935.

Good-bye, 1935.

Good-bye Blues, 1932.

Good-bye Jonah, 1937.

Goodbye, Little Dream, Goodbye, 1936.

Goodnight Irene, 1936.

Goodnight, My Love, 1936.

Goodnight Sweetheart, 1931.

Goody Goodbye, 1939.

Goody-Goody, 1936.

Goofus, 1930.

Got a Bran' New Suit, 1935.

Got a Date with an Angel, 1931.

Got a Man on My Mind (Worryin' Away), 1930.

Got a Pair of New Shoes, 1937.

Got My Mind on Music, 1937.

Got the Bench, Got the Park (but I Haven't Got You), 1931.

Got the Jitters, 1934.

Got the South in My Soul, 1932.

Granada, 1932.

Great Indoors, The, 1930.

Great Speckled Bird, The, 1937.

Greatest Mistake of My Life, 1937.

Green Eyes, 1931.

Grievin', 1939.

Guilty, 1931.

Guy What Takes His Time, A, 1933.

Gypsy in Me, 1934.

Gypsy in My Soul, The, 1937.

Gypsy without a Song, 1938.

H

Ha-cha-cha, 1934.

Half Caste Woman, 1931.

Half Moon on the Hudson, 1937.

Hallelujah, I'm a Bum, 1933.

Handful of Keys, 1933.

Hands across the Table, 1934.

Hang Your Heart on a Hickory Limb, 1939.

Hangin' Around with You, 1930.

Hangin' on the Garden Gate (Sayin' Good Night), 1930.

Happy As the Day Is Long, 1933.

Happy Feet, 1930.

Happy, I Am Happy, 1934.

Harbor Lights, 1937.

Harlem on My Mind, 1933.

Harlem Speaks, 1933.

Harmony in Harlem, 1938.

Haunting Me, 1934.

Have a Heart, 1931.

Have a Little Faith in Me, 1930.

Have Mercy, 1939.

Have You Ever Been Lonely (Have You Ever Been Blue?), 1933.

Have You Forgotten?, 1932.
Have You Got Any Castles, Baby?, 1937.
Have You Met Miss Jones?, 1937.
Havin' a Ball, 1937.
Havin' Myself a Time, 1938.
Hawaiian War Chant, 1936.
He Ain't Got Rhythm, 1937.
He Hasn't a Thing except Me, 1936.
He Was Too Good to Me, 1930.
Head over Heels in Love, 1936.
Headin' Home, 1935.
Hear My Song, Violetta, 1938.
Heart and Soul, 1938.
Heart Is Quicker Than the Eye, The, 1936.
Heartaches, 1931.
Heat Wave, 1933.
Heaven Can Wait, 1939.
Heaven Help This Heart of Mine, 1937.
Heaven in My Arms, 1939.
Heavenly Party, A, 1938.
Heigh-Ho (The Dwarfs' Marching Song), 1938.
Hello! Beautiful!, 1931.
Hello, My Lover, Good-bye, 1931.
Hello Stranger, 1938.
Help Yourself to Happiness, 1931.
Here Come the British (Bang! Bang!), 1934.
(Lookie, Lookie, Lookie) Here Comes Cookie, 1935.
Here Comes the Sun, 1930.
Here Goes (a Fool), 1934.
Here Lies Love, 1932.
Here's Love in Your Eye, 1936.
Here's to Romance, 1935.
Hey, Babe, Hey! (I'm Nuts about You), 1936.
Hey, Good Looking, 1939.
Hey, What Did the Bluebird Say?, 1936.
Hey, Young Fella, Close Your Old Umbrella, 1933.
High and Low (I've Been Looking for You), 1931.
High Society Blues, 1930.
High, Wide and Handsome, 1937.

Hillbilly from Tenth Avenue, 1938.
Hittin' the Bottle, 1930.
Hobo on Park Avenue, 1935.
Hold Me, 1933.
Hold Tight — Hold Tight (Want Some Sea Food Mama), 1939.
Hold Your Man, 1933.
Home (When Shadows Fall), 1931.
Home Town, 1937.
Honestly, 1933.
Honeymoon Hotel, 1933.
Hong Kong Blues, 1939.
Honky Tonk Train, 1939.
Honolulu, 1939.
(I'm in Love with) The Honorable Mr. So and So, 1939.
Hoops, 1931.
Hooray for Captain Spaulding, 1930.
Hooray for Hollywood, 1937.
Hooray for Love, 1935.
Hooray for Spinach, 1939.
Horse with the Dreamy Eyes, The, 1937.
Hot Pretzels, 1938.
Hottentot Potentate, The, 1935.
Hour of Parting, 1931.
House Is Haunted (by the Echo of Your Last Goodbye), The, 1934.
House Jack Built for Jill, The, 1936.
How about It?, 1931.
How Can You Tell an American?, 1938.
How Could We Be Wrong, 1933.
How Could You?, 1937.
How Deep Is the Ocean?, 1932.
How Long Will It Last?, 1931.
How Strange, 1939.
How To Win Friends and Influence People, 1938.
How Was I To Know, 1934.
Howdja Like To Love Me, 1938.
How'm I Doin'? (Hey, Hey!), 1932.
How's Chances, 1933.
How's Your Romance?, 1932.
Huckleberry Duck, 1939.
Hundred Years from Today, A, 1933.

Titles

Hurry Home, 1938.
Hut Sut Song, 1939.

I

I Ain't Lazy, I'm Just Dreaming, 1934.
I Am Only Human After All, 1930.
I Am So Eager, 1932.
I Am the Words, You Are the Melody, see (I Am the Words), You Are the Melody, 1930.
I Apologize, 1931.
I Believe in Miracles, 1934.
I Built a Dream One Day, 1935.
I Can Dream, Can't I?, 1937.
I Can't Be Bothered Now, 1937.
I Can't Believe It's True, 1932.
I Can't Escape from You, 1936.
I Can't Face the Music (without Singing the Blues), 1938.
I Can't Get Started, 1935.
I Can't Remember, 1933.
I Concentrate on You, 1939.
I Could Use a Dream, 1937.
I Couldn't Believe My Eyes, 1935.
I Cover the Waterfront, 1933.
I Didn't Know What Time It Was, 1939.
I Don't Know Why (I Just Do), 1931.
I Don't Want To Make History (I Just Want To Make Love), 1936.
I Double Dare You, 1937.
I Dream Too Much, 1935.
I Fall in Love with You Every Day, 1938.
I Feel a Song Comin' On, 1935.
I Feel Like a Feather in the Breeze, 1935.
I Found a Dream, 1935.
I Found a Million Dollar Baby (in a Five and Ten Cent Store), 1931.
I Get a Kick out of You, 1934.
I Get Along without You Very Well (except Sometimes), 1939.
I Go for That, 1938.
I Got Love, 1935.
I Got Plenty o' Nuttin', 1935.

I Got Rhythm, 1930.
I Gotta Right To Sing the Blues, 1932.
I Guess It Had To Be That Way, 1933.
I Hadn't Anyone till You, 1938.
I Happen To Like New York, 1931.
I Have Eyes, 1938.
I Have the Room Above, 1936.
I Heard, 1932.
I Hit a New High, 1937.
I Hope Gabriel Likes My Music, 1935.
I Hum a Waltz, 1937.
I Just Couldn't Take It, Baby, 1933.
I Keep Remembering (Someone I Should Forget), 1930.
I Know Now, 1937.
I Let a Song Go Out of My Heart, 1938.
I Like Mountain Music, 1933.
I Like the Likes of You, 1933.
I Like To Recognize the Tune, 1939.
I Live the Life I Love, 1937.
I Love a Parade, 1931.
I Love Louisa, 1931.
I Love To Rhyme, 1938.
I Love To Sing-a, 1936.
I Love To Walk in the Rain, 1938.
I Love To Whistle, 1938.
I Love You So Much, 1930.
I Loves You Porgy, 1935.
I Married an Angel, 1938.
I Mean To Say, 1930.
I Must See Annie Tonight, 1938.
I Never Had a Chance, 1934.
I Never Knew Heaven Could Speak, 1939.
I Only Have Eyes for You, 1934.
I Played Fiddle for the Czar, 1932.
I Poured My Heart into a Song, 1939.
I Saw Her at Eight o'Clock, 1935.
I Saw Stars, 1934.
I Say It's Spinach, 1932.
I See Two Lovers, 1934.
I See Your Face before Me, 1937.

I Sold My Heart to the Junk Man, 1935.

I Still Believe in You, 1930.

I Still Get a Thrill (Thinking of You), 1930.

I Still Love To Kiss You Goodnight, 1937.

I Still Suits Me, 1936.

I Surrender, Dear, 1931.

I Thought about You, 1939.

I Used To Be Color Blind, 1938.

I Wake Up Smiling, 1933.

I Wanna Be in Winchell's Column, 1937.

I Wanna Be Loved, 1932.

I Wanna Go Back to Bali, 1938.

I Wanna Go to the Zoo, 1936.

I Want a Little Girl, 1930.

I Want a Man, 1931.

I Want My Mama, 1939.

I Want To Be a Cowboy's Sweetheart, 1936.

I Want To Be with You, 1932.

I Want To Go Home, 1938.

I Want To Ring Bells, 1933.

I Want You for Christmas, 1937.

I Want You for Myself, 1931.

I Want You — I Need You, 1933.

I Was Doing All Right, 1938.

I Was Lucky (C'etait Ecrit), 1935.

I Watch the Love Parade, 1931.

I Went to a Marvelous Party, 1939.

I Wish I Were Aladdin, 1935.

I Wish I Were in Love Again, 1937.

I Wish I Were Twins (So I Could Love You Twice As Much), 1934.

I Wished on the Moon, 1935.

I Woke Up Too Soon, 1934.

I Won't Dance, 1935.

I Would Do Anything for You, see (I Would Do) Anything for You, 1932.

I Wouldn't Change You for the World, 1931.

I Wouldn't Trade the Silver in My Mother's Hair (for All the Gold in the World), 1932.

I'd Be Lost without You, 1936.

I'd Rather Be Right, 1937.

I'd Rather Drink Muddy Water, 1936.

I'd Rather Lead a Band, 1936.

I'd Rather Listen to Your Eyes, 1935.

If, 1934.

If Dreams Come True, 1934.

If I Became the President, 1930.

If I Didn't Care, 1939.

If I Forget You, 1933.

If I Had a Million Dollars, 1934.

If I Had My Life To Live Over, 1939.

If I Knew Then (What I Know Now), 1939.

If I Love Again, 1932.

If I Only Had a Brain (Scarecrow Dance), 1939.

If I Should Lose You, 1935.

If I Were King, 1930.

If It's the Last Thing I Do, 1937.

If It's True, 1933.

If My Heart Could Only Talk, 1937.

If the Moon Turns Green, 1935.

If There Is Someone Lovelier Than You, 1934.

If You Love Me, 1936.

If You Were in My Place (What Would You Do?), 1938.

If You Were Mine, 1935.

If You're a Viper, 1938.

I'll Be Faithful, 1933.

I'll Be Glad When You're Dead, You Rascal You, see (I'll Be Glad When You're Dead), You Rascal You, 1931.

I'll Be Hard To Handle, 1933.

I'll Be Seeing You, 1938.

I'll Dream Tonight, 1938.

I'll Follow My Secret Heart, 1934.

I'll Keep On Loving You, 1939.

I'll Love You in My Dreams, 1931.

I'll Never Be the Same, 1932.

I'll Never Have To Dream Again, 1932.

I'll Never Say "Never Again" Again, 1935.

I'll Never Smile Again, 1939.

I'll Pray for You, 1939.

I'll Sing You a Thousand Love Songs, 1936.
I'll Still Belong to You, 1930.
I'll String Along with You, 1934.
I'll Take an Option on You, 1933.
I'll Take Romance, 1937.
I'll Tell the Man in the Street, 1938.
Ill Wind (You're Blowin' Me No Good), 1934.
Illegitimate Daughter, The, 1931.
I'm a Black Sheep Who's Blue, 1934.
I'm a Hundred Percent for You, 1934.
I'm Afraid the Masquerade Is Over, see (I'm Afraid) The Masquerade Is Over, 1938.
I'm All Dressed Up with a Broken Heart, 1931.
I'm Alone, 1932.
I'm an Old Cow Hand (from the Rio Grande), 1936.
I'm Bubbling Over, 1937.
I'm Building Up to an Awful Let-Down, 1935.
I'm Checking Out Goombye, 1939.
I'm Confessin' (That I Love You), 1930.
I'm Crazy 'bout My Baby (and My Baby's Crazy 'bout Me), 1931.
I'm Down in the Dumps, 1933.
I'm Feelin' Blue ('Cause I Got Nobody), 1930.
I'm Feelin' Like a Million, 1937.
I'm Gettin' Sentimental over You, 1932.
I'm Getting Myself Ready for You, 1930.
I'm Glad for Your Sake (but I'm Sorry for Mine), 1938.
I'm Glad I Waited, 1930.
I'm Gonna Lock My Heart (and Throw Away the Key), 1938.
I'm Gonna Move on the Outskirts of Town, 1937.
I'm Gonna Sit Right Down and Write Myself a Letter, 1935.
I'm Happy about the Whole Thing, 1939.

I'm Hummin' — I'm Whistlin' — I'm Singin', 1934.
I'm in a Dancing Mood, 1936.
I'm in the Market for You, 1930.
I'm in the Mood for Love, 1935.
I'm Keepin' Company, 1931.
I'm Laughin', 1934.
I'm Livin' in a Great Big Way, 1935.
I'm Making Hay in the Moonlight, 1932.
I'm No Angel, 1933.
I'm on a See-Saw, 1934.
I'm One of God's Children (Who Hasn't Got Wings), 1931.
I'm Playing with Fire, 1932.
I'm Popeye the Sailor Man, 1934.
I'm Prayin' Humble, 1938.
I'm Putting All My Eggs in One Basket, 1936.
I'm Satisfied, 1933.
I'm Shooting High, 1935.
I'm Sitting High on a Hilltop, 1935.
I'm So Weary of It All, 1938.
I'm Sorry Dear, 1931.
I'm Sorry for Myself, 1939.
I'm the Echo (You're the Song That I Sing), 1935.
I'm Thinking Tonight of My Blue Eyes, 1930.
I'm Thru with Love, 1931.
I'm Wishing, 1937.
I'm with You!, 1931.
I'm Yours, 1930.
In a Blue and Pensive Mood, 1934.
In a Little Dutch Kindergarten (Down by the Zuider Zee), 1937.
In a Little Gypsy Tearoom, 1935.
In a Little Hula Heaven, 1937.
In a Moment of Weakness, 1939.
In a Sentimental Mood, 1935.
In a Shanty in Old Shanty Town, 1932.
In an Eighteenth Century Drawing Room, 1939.
In Egern on the Tegern See, 1932.
In Other Words, Seventeen, 1939.
In the Chapel in the Moonlight, 1936.

In the Dark, 1931.

In the Evening (When the Sun Goes Down), 1935.

In the Heart of the Dark, 1939.

In the Merry Month of Maybe, 1931.

In the Middle of a Kiss, 1935.

In the Mood, 1939.

In the Park in Paree, 1933.

In the Shade of the New Apple Tree, 1937.

In the Still of the Night, 1937.

In the Valley of the Moon, 1933.

In Your Own Quiet Way, 1936.

In-Between, 1938.

Indian Summer, 1939.

Inka Dinka Doo, 1933.

Into My Heart, 1930.

Is I in Love? I Is, 1932.

Is It True What They Say about Dixie?, 1936.

Is That Religion?, 1930.

Is That the Way To Treat a Sweetheart?, 1938.

Ise A-Muggin', 1936.

Island in the West Indies, 1935.

Isle of Capri, 1934.

Isn't It a Pity?, 1932.

Isn't It Romantic?, 1932.

Isn't Love the Grandest Thing?, 1935.

Isn't This a Lovely Day, 1935.

It Ain't Necessarily So, 1935.

It Don't Mean a Thing (If It Ain't Got That Swing), 1932.

It Happened in Monterey, 1930.

It Isn't Fair, 1933.

It Looks Like Rain in Cherry Blossom Lane, 1937.

It Makes No Difference Now, 1939.

It Must Be True (You Are Mine, All Mine), 1930.

It Must Be You, 1930.

It Must Have Been a Dream, 1935.

It Never Was You, 1938.

It Seems Like Old Times, 1937.

It Seems To Be Spring, 1930.

It Takes Two To Make a Bargain, 1935.

It Was a Night in June, 1933.

It Was So Beautiful, 1932.

It Was Written in the Stars, 1939.

It's a Blue World, 1939.

It's a Great Life (If You Don't Weaken), 1930.

It's a Lonesome Old Town When You're Not Around, 1930.

It's a Lovely Day Tomorrow, 1939.

It's a Low Down Dirty Shame, 1938.

It's a Sin To Tell a Lie, 1936.

It's a Wonderful World, 1939.

It's About Time, 1932.

It's an Old Southern Custom, 1935.

It's Dark on Observatory Hill, 1934.

It's D'Lovely, 1936.

It's Easy To Remember, 1935.

It's Every Girl's Ambition, 1931.

It's Funny to Everyone but Me, 1934, 1939.

It's Got To Be Love, 1936.

It's Love I'm After, 1936.

It's On, It's Off, 1937.

It's Only a Paper Moon, 1933.

It's Only a Shanty in Old Shanty Town, see In a Shanty in Old Shanty Town, 1932.

It's Over Because We're Through, 1932.

It's Raining Sunbeams, 1937.

It's Sunday Down in Caroline, 1933.

It's Swell of You, 1937.

It's the Animal in Me, 1934.

It's the Darndest Thing, 1931.

It's the Dreamer in Me, 1938.

It's the Girl, 1931.

It's the Natural Thing To Do, 1937.

It's the Talk of the Town, 1933.

It's Wearin' Me Down, 1932.

I've a Strange New Rhythm in My Heart, 1937.

I've Gone Romantic on You, 1937.

I've Got a Crush on You, 1930.

I've Got a Date with a Dream, 1938.

I've Got a Feelin' You're Foolin', 1935.

I've Got a Pocketful of Dreams, 1938.

I've Got a Pocketful of Sunshine, 1935.

I've Got an Invitation to a Dance, 1934.

I've Got Beginner's Luck, see (I've Got) Beginner's Luck, 1937.

I've Got Five Dollars, 1931.

I've Got My Eyes on You, 1939.

I've Got My Fingers Crossed, 1935.

I've Got My Love To Keep Me Warm, 1937.

I've Got the World on a String, 1932.

I've Got To Be a Rug Cutter, 1937.

I've Got To Be There, 1932.

I've Got To Get Hot, 1935.

I've Got To Pass Your House To Get To My House, 1933.

I've Got To Sing a Torch Song, 1933.

I've Got You on My Mind, 1932.

I've Got You under My Skin, 1936.

I've Had My Moments, 1934.

I've Hitched My Wagon to a Star, 1937.

I've Taken a Fancy to You, 1937.

I've Told Every Little Star, 1932.

J

Jalousie, see Jealousy, 1931.
Jazz Cocktail, 1932.
Jazz Nocturne, 1931.
Jazz Pizzicato, 1939.
Jazznocracy, 1934.
Jealous of You, 1933.
Jealousy, 1931.
Jeepers Creepers, 1938.
Jeep's Blues, 1938.
Jiminy Cricket, 1939.
Jimmie Brown, the Newsboy, 1931.
Jimmy Had a Nickel, 1933.
Jitter Bug, 1934.
Jitterbug, The, 1939.
Jockey on the Carousel, The, 1935.
Joe Hill, 1938.
John Silver, 1939.
Johnny One Note, 1937.

John's Idea, 1939.
Joint Is Jumpin', The, 1937.
Jolly Tar and the Milkmaid, The, 1937.
Jonny, 1933.
Joobalai, 1938.
Joseph! Joseph!, 1938.
Josephine, 1937.
Jubilee, 1937.
Judy, 1934.
Jumpin' at the Woodside, 1938.
Jumpin' Jive, 1939.
June in January, 1934.
Jungle Drums, 1930.
Jungle Fever, 1934.
Junk Man, 1934.
Just a Dream, 1939.
Just a Gigolo, 1930.
Just a Little Closer, 1930.
Just a Mood, 1937.
Just a Quiet Evening, 1937.
Just an Echo in the Valley, 1932.
Just an Idea, 1930.
Just Another Rhumba, 1937.
Just Because, 1937.
Just Because You're You, 1932.
Just for a Thrill, 1939.
Just Friends, 1931.
Just Let Me Look at You, 1938.
Just Like in a Story Book, 1930.
Just Once around the Clock, 1935.
Just One More Chance, 1931.
Just One of Those Things, 1935.

K

Kathleen Mine, 1931.
Katie Went to Haiti, 1939.
Katinkitschka, 1931.
Keep On Doin' What You're Doin', 1934.
Keep Romance Alive, 1934.
Keep Young and Beautiful, 1933.
Keepin' Myself for You, 1930.
Keeping Out of Mischief Now, 1932.
Key to My Heart, The, 1931.
Kickin' the Gong Around, 1931.
Kinda Like You, 1932.
Kind'a Lonesome, 1938.

King's Horses (and the King's Men), The, 1930.
Kiss To Build a Dream On, A, 1935.
Kiss Waltz, The, 1930.
Kitty from Kansas City, 1930.
Knock, Knock, Who's There?, 1936.

L

La Cucaracha, 1934.
Lady in Red, The, 1935.
Lady Is a Tramp, The, 1937.
Lady Must Live, A, 1931.
Lady of Spain, 1931.
Lady, Play Your Mandolin, 1930.
Lady's in Love with You, The, 1939.
Lambeth Walk, 1937.
Lamp Is Low, The, 1939.
Lamp on the Corner, The, 1938.
Lamplight, 1934.
Las Alteñitas, see A Gay Ranchero, 1936.
Last Night I Dreamed of You, 1937.
Last Night When We Were Young, 1936.
Last Round-Up, The, 1933.
Laugh and Call It Love, 1938.
Laughing at Life, 1930.
Laughing Irish Eyes, 1936.
Lawd, You Made the Night Too Long, 1932.
Lazy Lou'siana Moon, 1930.
Lazy Rhapsody, 1932.
Lazy River, 1931.
Lazybones, 1933.
Leanin' on the Ole Top Rail, 1939.
Leaning on the Lamp Post, 1937.
Learn To Croon, 1933.
Let 'Em Eat Cake, 1933.
Let Me Sing and I'm Happy, 1930.
Let Yourself Go, 1936.
Let's All Sing Like the Birdies Sing, 1932.
Let's Begin, 1933.
Let's Call a Heart a Heart, 1936.
Let's Call It a Day, 1932.

Let's Call the Whole Thing Off, 1937.
Let's Dance, 1935.
Let's Face the Music and Dance, 1936.
Let's Fall in Love, 1933.
Let's Fly Away, 1930.
Let's Get Together, 1934.
Let's Give Love Another Chance, 1937.
Let's Go Bavarian, 1933.
Let's Have an Old Fashioned Christmas, 1939.
Let's Have Another Cup of Coffee, 1932.
Let's Hit the Nail on the Head, 1939.
Let's K-nock K-nees, 1934.
Let's Make Memories Tonight, 1939.
Let's Put Our Heads Together, 1936.
Let's Put Out the Lights (and Go to Sleep), 1932.
Let's Say Goodbye, 1932.
Let's Step Out, 1930.
Let's Take a Walk around the Block, 1934.
Lies, 1931.
Life Goes to a Party, 1937.
Life Is a Song (Let's Sing It Together), 1935.
Life Is Just a Bowl of Cherries, 1931.
Life's a Dance, 1937.
Lights Are Low, (the Music Is Sweet), The, 1934.
Lights of Paris, 1931.
Lights Out, 1935.
Like a Bolt from the Blue, 1934.
Like Ordinary People Do, 1930.
Lilacs in the Rain, 1939.
Linda, 1930.
Listen My Children and You Shall Hear, 1937.
Little Bit Independent, A, 1935.
Little Brown Gal, 1935.
Little Dutch Mill, 1934.
Little Girl, 1931.
Little Girl Blue, 1935.

Little Joe from Chicago, 1938.
Little Kiss at Twilight, 1938.
Little Lady Make Believe, 1936.
Little Man, You've Had a Busy Day, 1934.
Little Old Lady, 1936.
Little Red Fox, The (N'ya N'ya Ya Can't Catch Me), 1939.
Little Rock Getaway, 1938.
Little Sir Echo, 1939.
Little Skipper from Heaven Above, A, 1936.
Little Street Where Old Friends Meet, A, 1932.
Little Things in Life, The, 1930.
Little Things You Used To Do, The, 1935.
Little White Gardenia, A, 1935.
Little White Lies, 1930.
(Let Me) Live and Love Tonight, 1934.
Livin' in the Sunlight — Lovin' in the Moonlight, 1930.
Living on Velvet, 1935.
Lonely, 1930.
Lonely Heart, 1933.
Lonely Lane, 1933.
Lonesome Me, 1932.
Lonesome Nights, 1934.
Lonesome Walls, 1939.
'Long about Midnight, 1934.
Looking at You, 1930.
Looking in the Window, Thinking of You, 1930.
Lorelei, 1932.
Lost, 1936.
Lost and Found, 1938.
Lost in a Fog, 1934.
Lost in Meditation, 1938.
Lost in Your Arms, 1932.
Lotus Blossom, see Marahuana, 1934.
Louise, Louise Blues, 1934.
Louisiana Hayride, 1932.
Love and a Dime, 1935.
Love and Kisses, 1935.
Love Bug Will Bite You (If You Don't Watch Out), The, 1937.
Love Came into My Heart, 1931.
Love for Sale, 1930.

Love in Bloom, 1934.
Love Is a Dancing Thing, 1935.
Love Is Here To Stay, 1938.
Love Is Just around the Corner, 1934.
Love Is Like a Song, 1930.
Love Is Like That (What Can You Do?), 1931.
Love Is Never out of Season, 1937.
Love Is Sweeping the Country, 1931.
Love Is the Sweetest Thing, 1933.
Love Is the Thing, 1933.
Love Is Where You Find It, 1938.
Love Letters in the Sand, 1931.
Love Like Ours, A, 1938.
Love Locked Out, 1933.
Love Me, 1934.
Love Me Forever, 1935.
Love Me, Love My Pekinese, 1936.
Love Me Tonight, 1932; also see Yours, 1937.
Love Never Went to College, 1939.
Love Passes By, 1935.
Love Songs of the Nile, 1933.
Love Thy Neighbor, 1934.
Love Walked In, 1938.
Love Will Tell, 1936.
Love, You Funny Thing, 1932.
Loveliness of You, The, 1937.
Lovely, 1933.
Lovely Lady, 1935.
Lovely One, 1937.
Lovely To Look At, 1935.
Lover, 1933.
Low Down Rhythm in a Top Hat, 1939.
Low-Down Lullaby, 1934.
Luckiest Man in the World, 1932.
Lucky Fella, 1933.
Lucky Seven, 1930.
Lullaby in Rhythm, 1938.
Lullaby of Broadway, 1935.
Lullaby of the Leaves, 1932.
Lulu's Back in Town, 1935.
Lydia, the Tattooed Lady, 1939.

M

Mad about the Boy, 1935.
Mad Dogs and Englishmen, 1931.

Mademoiselle in New Rochelle, 1930.

Magnolias in the Moonlight, 1936.

Make a Wish, 1937.

Mama Don't Want No Peas an' Rice an' Cocoanut Oil, 1931.

Mama Inez, 1931.

Mama Yo Quiero, see I Want My Mama, 1939.

Man and His Dream, A, 1939.

Man from the South (with a Big Cigar in His Mouth), The, 1930.

Man on the Flying Trapeze, The, 1933.

Manhattan Merry-Go-Round, 1936.

Many Happy Returns of the Day, 1931.

Marahuana, 1934.

March of Time, The, 1930.

March Winds and April Showers, 1935.

Marching Along Together, 1933.

Maria, 1938.

Maria Elena, 1933.

Maria, My Own, 1931.

Marta, 1931.

Mary's Idea, see Just an Idea, 1930.

Masquerade, 1932.

(I'm Afraid) The Masquerade Is Over, 1938.

May I?, 1934.

May I Have the Next Romance with You?, 1936.

Maybe, 1935.

Maybe It's Because (I Love You Too Much), 1933.

Me!, 1931.

Me and Marie, 1935.

Me and the Moon, 1936.

Me, Myself and I (Are All in Love with You), 1937.

Meet Miss America, 1935.

Meet the Beat of My Heart, 1938.

Melody from the Sky, A, 1936.

Memories of You, 1930.

Mene, Mene, Tekel, 1939.

Merrily We Live, 1938.

Merry Old Land of Oz, The, 1939.

Merry-Go-Round, 1935.

Merry-Go-Round Broke Down, The, 1937.

Message from the Man in the Moon, A, 1937.

Mia Cara (My Dear), 1930.

Mickey Mouse's Birthday Party, 1936.

Midnight in Paris, 1935.

Mighty Like the Blues, 1938.

Mile after Mile, 1939.

Milk Cow Blues, 1934.

Milkmen's Matinee, The, 1936.

Mimi, 1932.

Mine, 1933.

Minnie the Moocher (The Ho De Ho Song), 1931.

Minnie the Moocher's Wedding Day, 1932.

Mirabelle (Lover of My Dreams), 1931.

Miss Brown to You, 1935.

Miss Otis Regrets (She's Unable To Lunch Today), 1934.

(Thank You So Much), Missus Lowsborough-Goodby, 1934.

Mist over the Moon, 1938.

Mister and Missus Fitch, 1932.

Mr. and Mrs. Is the Name, 1934.

Mr. Bluebird, 1935.

Mister Deep Blue Sea, 1936.

Mister Freddie Blues, 1936.

Mr. Ghost Goes To Town, 1936.

Mr. Paganini, see (If You Can't Sing It) You'll Have To Swing It, 1936.

Mrs. Worthington (Don't Put Your Daughter on the Stage), 1935.

Moanin' in the Mornin', 1937.

Moment I Saw You, The, 1930.

Moments Like This, 1938.

Mon Ami, My Friend, 1936.

Mood Indigo, 1931.

Mood That I'm In, The, 1937.

Moon Country (Is Home to Me), 1934.

Moon Got in My Eyes, The, 1937.

Moon Is Low, The, 1930.

Moon Love, 1939.

Moon of Manakoora, The, 1937.

Moon over Miami, 1935.

Titles

Moon Song (That Wasn't Meant for Me), 1932.
Moon Was Yellow, The, 1934.
Moonburn, 1935.
Moonglow, 1934.
Moonlight and Pretzels, 1933.
Moonlight and Shadows, 1936.
Moonlight on the Campus, 1937.
Moonlight on the Colorado, 1930.
(There Ought To Be a) Moonlight Saving Time, 1931.
Moonlight Serenade, 1939.
Moonstruck, 1933.
More Than Ever, 1930.
Most Beautiful Girl in the World, The, 1935.
Most Gentlemen Don't Like Love, 1938.
Moten Swing, 1933.
Mother, the Queen of My Heart, 1933.
Muchacha, 1933.
Mule Skinner Blues, 1931.
Music Goes 'Round and Around, The, 1935.
Music in My Heart, 1935, 1937.
Music in the Night (and Laughter in the Air), 1936.
Music, Maestro, Please!, 1938.
Music Makes Me, 1933.
Music, Music Everywhere (but Not a Song in My Heart), 1932.
Mutiny in the Nursery, 1938.
My Baby Just Cares for Me, 1930.
My Cousin in Milwaukee, 1932.
My Dancing Lady, 1933.
My Darling, 1932.
My Dreams Have Gone with the Wind, 1937.
My Extraordinary Gal, 1931.
My Fine Feathered Friend, 1937.
My First Impression of You, 1937.
My Funny Valentine, 1937.
My Future Just Passed, 1930.
My Happiness, 1933.
My Hat's on the Side of My Head, 1933.
My Heart and I, 1935.
My Heart Belongs to Daddy, 1938.
My Heart Is an Open Book, 1935.

My Heart Is Singing, 1936.
My Heart Is Taking Lessons, 1938.
My Heart Is Unemployed, 1938.
My Ideal, 1930.
My Kingdom for a Kiss, 1936.
My Last Affair, 1936.
My Last Goodbye, 1939.
My Little Buckaroo, 1937.
My Love, 1933.
My Love Is Young, 1936.
My Lover, 1932.
My Mad Moment, 1930.
My Man's Gone Now, 1935.
My Mom, 1932.
My Moonlight Madonna, 1933.
My Old Flame, 1934.
My Own, 1938.
My Prayer, 1939.
My Reverie, 1938.
My Romance, 1932, 1935.
My Shawl (Ombo), 1934.
My Silent Love, 1932.
My Song, 1931.
My Twilight Dream, 1939.
My Very Good Friend, the Milkman, 1935.
My Walking Stick, 1938.
My Wubba Dolly, 1939.
Mysterious Mose, 1930.

N

Nasty Man, 1934.
Neath the Silv'ry Moon, 1932.
Needle in a Haystack, A, 1934.
Never Again, 1938.
Never Gonna Dance, 1936.
Never in a Million Years, 1937.
Nevermore, 1934.
Nevertheless, 1931.
New Deal Rhythm, 1933.
New Faces, 1937.
New Love Is Old, A, 1931.
New Moon Is over My Shoulder, A, 1934.
New Mule Skinner Blues, see Mule Skinner Blues, 1931.
New O'leans, 1935.
New Orleans, 1932; also see New O'leans, 1935.

310

New Sun in the Sky, 1931.
Nice Work If You Can Get It, 1937.
Night and Day, 1932.
Night Is Filled with Music, The, 1938.
Night Is Young and You're So Beautiful, The, 1936.
(There Was a) Night on the Water, 1934.
Night Owl, 1933.
Night Was Made for Love, The, 1931.
Nightfall, 1936.
Nightmare, 1937.
Nina Rosa, 1930.
(There Is) No Greater Love, 1936.
No More Love, 1933.
No! No! a Thousand Times No!, 1934.
No Regrets, 1936.
No Strings (I'm Fancy Free), 1935.
Nobody Makes a Pass at Me, 1937.
Nobody's Darlin' but Mine, 1935.
Noche de Ronda, 1935.
Non-Stop Flight, 1939.
Not for All the Rice in China, 1933.
Now, 1936.
Now I'm a Lady, 1935.
Now It Can Be Told, 1938.
Now or Never, 1936.
Now That You're Gone, 1931.
Now You're in My Arms, 1931.
Now's the Time To Fall in Love (Potatoes Are Cheaper — Tomatoes Are Cheaper), 1931.

O

O, Heart of Love, 1936.
Object of My Affection, The, 1934.
Occidental Woman, 1936.
Of Thee I Sing, 1931.
Oh Bess, Oh Where's My Bess, 1935.
Oh, Diogenes!, 1938.
Oh, Donna Clara, 1931.
Oh How I Long To Belong to You, 1932.

Oh! Ma-Ma (The Butcher Boy), 1938.
Oh Mo'nah!, 1931.
Oh, My Goodness!, 1936.
Oh, the Rio Grande, 1936.
Oh, You Crazy Moon, 1939.
Okay Toots, 1934.
Ol' Man Mose, 1938.
(There's Something about an) Old Fashioned Girl, 1930.
Old Fashioned Tune Always Is New, An, 1939.
Old Flame Never Dies, An, 1937.
Old Folks, 1938.
Old King Cole, 1937.
Old Man Harlem, 1933.
Old Man of the Mountain, The, 1932.
Old Mill Wheel, 1939.
Old Spinning Wheel, The, 1933.
Old Straw Hat, An, 1938.
Old Water Mill, An, 1934.
Ole Faithful, 1934.
On a Little Street in Singapore, 1938.
On a Roof in Manhattan, 1932.
On a Sunday Afternoon, 1935.
On Account of I Love You, 1931.
On Accounta I Love You, 1934.
On and On and On, 1933.
On Revival Day, 1931.
On the Beach at Bali-Bali, 1936.
On the Bumpy Road to Love, 1938.
On the Good Ship Lollipop, 1934.
On the Sentimental Side, 1938.
On the Sunny Side of the Rockies, 1937.
On the Sunny Side of the Street, 1930.
On the Trail, 1933.
On Treasure Island, 1935.
On with the Dance, 1937.
On Your Toes, 1936.
Once in a Blue Moon, 1934.
Once in a Lifetime, 1934.
Once in a While, 1937.
One Big Union for Two, 1937.
(I'd Love To Spend) One Hour With You, 1932.
One Minute to One, 1933.

Titles

One Moment Alone, 1931.
One More Dance, 1932.
One More Hour of Love, 1931.
One More Waltz, 1930.
One Morning in May, 1933.
One Never Knows, Does One?, 1936.
One Night of Love, 1934.
One o'Clock Jump, 1938.
One Rose (That's Left in My Heart), The, 1936.
One Song, 1937.
One, Two, Button Your Shoe, 1936.
One-Two-Three-Kick, 1939.
Oodles of Noodles, 1933.
Ooh That Kiss, 1931.
Ooh! What You Said, 1939.
Oooh! Look-a-There, Ain't She Pretty?, 1933.
Orchid to You, An, 1933.
Orchids in the Moonlight, 1933.
Oregon Trail, The, 1935.
Organ Grinder, The, 1932.
Organ Grinder's Swing, 1936.
Our Big Love Scene, 1933.
Our Love, 1939.
Our Penthouse on Third Avenue, 1937.
Our Song, 1937.
Ours, 1936.
Out in the Cold Again, 1934.
Out in the Great Open Spaces, 1932.
Out of Nowhere, 1931.
Out of Space, 1934.
Outside of You, 1935.
Over and Over Again, 1935.
Over Somebody Else's Shoulder (I Fell in Love with You), 1934.
Over the Rainbow, 1939.
Overnight, 1930.
Ozarks Are Calling Me Home, The, 1936.

P

P.S. I Love You, 1934.
Page Miss Glory, 1935.
Panamania, 1935.
Panic Is On, The, 1936.
Paper Doll, 1930.

Paradise, 1931.
Paradise Isle, 1937.
Pardon My Southern Accent, 1934.
Paris in the Spring, 1935.
Parlez-moi d'Amour, see Speak to Me of Love, 1932.
Party's Over Now, The, 1932.
Pastel Blue, 1939.
Patty Cake, Patty Cake (Baker Man), 1938.
Pavanne, 1938.
Peace Brother, 1939.
Peach Picking Time Down in Georgia, 1933.
Peanut Vendor, The, 1932.
Peckin', 1937.
Pennies from Heaven, 1936.
Penny Serenade, 1938.
Penthouse Serenade (When We're Alone), 1931.
Perfidia, 1939.
Peter Piper, 1936.
Pettin' in the Park, 1933.
Physician, The, 1933.
Piccolino, The, 1935.
Pick Yourself Up, 1936.
Picture Me without You, 1936.
Picture of Me without You, A, 1935.
Pig Got Up and Slowly Walked Away, The, 1933.
Play, Fiddle, Play, 1932.
Play, Orchestra, Play, 1935.
Play to Me, Gypsy, 1934.
Please, 1932.
Please Be Kind, 1938.
Please Believe Me, 1935.
Please Don't Talk about Me When I'm Gone, 1930.
Please Forgive Me, 1938.
Please Handle with Care, 1932.
Please Pardon Us, We're in Love, 1937.
Poinciana (Song of the Tree), 1936.
Poor Pierrot, 1931.
Pop! Goes Your Heart, 1934.
Popcorn Man, 1937.
Porter's Love Song to a Chambermaid, A, 1930.

Portrait of the Lion, 1939.
Posin', 1937.
Powerhouse, 1937.
Practising Up on You, 1930.
Prelude to a Kiss, 1938.
Prisoner of Love, 1931.
Public Melody Number One, 1937.
Put On an Old Pair of Shoes, 1935.
Put Your Little Arms around Me, 1931.
Put Your Little Foot Right Out, 1939.
Puttin' on the Ritz, 1930.
Pyramid, 1938.

Q

Quaker City Jazz, 1937.
Queer Notions, 1933.
Quiérme Mucho, see Yours, 1937.
Quiet Night, 1936.

R

Ragamuffin Romeo, 1930.
Rain, 1934.
Rain on the Roof, 1932.
Rain, Rain, Go Away!, 1932.
Rainbow on the River, 1936.
Rainy Day, A, 1932.
Raisin' the Rent, 1933.
Rap Tap on Wood, 1936.
Reaching for the Moon, 1930.
Reckless, 1935.
Red Apple, 1932.
Red Headed Woman Makes a Choo Choo Jump Its Track, A, 1935.
Red, Hot and Blue, 1936.
Red Sails in the Sunset, 1935.
Reefer Man, 1932.
Regency Rakes, 1934.
Remember Me?, 1937.
Remember My Forgotten Man, 1933.
Reminiscing in Tempo, 1935.
Rendezvous with a Dream, 1936.
Rhythm and Romance, 1935.
(If I Had) Rhythm in My Nursery Rhymes, 1935.
Rhythm Lullaby, 1935.

Rhythm of the Rain, 1935.
Rhythm of the Raindrops, 1934.
(Listen to the) Rhythm of the Range, 1938.
Rhythm Saved the World, 1936.
Ride, Tenderfoot, Ride, 1938.
Ridin' Around in the Rain, 1934.
Ridin' High, 1936.
Right Guy for Me, The, 1938.
Right Somebody To Love, The, 1936.
Ring Dem Bells, 1930.
Riptide, 1934.
Rise 'n Shine, 1932.
River Stay 'Way from My Door, 1931.
Riverboat Shuffle, 1939.
Robins and Roses, 1936.
Rock and Roll, 1934.
Rock It for Me, 1938.
Rockin' Chair, 1930.
Rockin' in Rhythm, 1931.
Rogue Song, The, 1930.
Roll Along Covered Wagon, 1934.
Roll Along Kentucky Moon, 1932.
Roll Along Prairie Moon, 1935.
Roll 'Em, 1937.
Roll On, Mississippi, Roll On, 1931.
Rollin' Plains, 1937.
Room with a View, A, 1938.
Rosalie, 1937.
Rose in Her Hair, The, 1935.
Roses Are Forget-Me-Nots, 1930.
Roses in December, 1937.
Roses in the Rain, 1934.
Rosetta, 1935.
Rug Cutter's Swing, 1934.
Rumba Jumps, The, 1939.
Run, Rabbit, Run, 1939.
Running between the Raindrops, 1931.

S

Saddest Tale, 1935.
Sail Along, Silv'ry Moon, 1937.
Sail On, Little Girl, Sail On, 1934.
Sailboat in the Moonlight, 1937.
Sailor Beware, 1935.
Sailors' Chanty (Lady Fair), see

Sittin' on a Log (Pettin' My Dog), 1933.
Six Lessons from Madame La Zonga, 1939.
Sixty Seconds Got Together, 1938.
Skeleton in the Closet, 1936.
Skippy, 1930.
Skrontch, 1937.
Slap That Bass, 1937.
Slaughter on Tenth Avenue, 1936.
Slave Song, The, see Until the Real Thing Comes Along, 1936.
Sleepy Head, 1934.
(By the) Sleepy Lagoon, 1930.
Sleepy Town Express, 1930.
Slippery Horn, 1933.
Slumming on Park Avenue, 1937.
Small Fry, 1938.
(You Know It All) Smarty, 1937.
Smile, Darn Ya, Smile, 1931.
Smile for Me, 1932.
Smoke Dreams, 1936.
Smoke Gets in Your Eyes, 1933.
Smoke Rings, 1933.
Smokin' Reefers, 1932.
Snake Charmer, The, 1937.
Snowball, 1933.
Snuggled on Your Shoulder (Cuddled in Your Arms), 1931.
So At Last It's Come to This, 1932.
So Beats My Heart for You, 1930.
So Do I, 1932, 1936.
So Help Me, 1934.
So Help Me (If I Don't Love You), 1938.
So Long (It's Been Good To Know Yuh), 1939.
So Rare, 1937.
So What?, 1932.
Soft Lights and Sweet Music, 1932.
Solitude, 1934.
Solomon, 1933.
Some Other Spring, 1939.
Somebody Changed the Lock on My Door, 1936.
Somebody Else Is Taking My Place, 1937.
Somebody from Somewhere, 1931.
Somebody Loves You, 1932.
Somebody Ought To Be Told, 1935.

Someday I'll Find You, 1930.
Someday My Prince Will Come, 1937.
Someone Stole Gabriel's Horn, 1932.
Someone To Care For, 1932.
Something Had To Happen, 1933.
Something I Dreamed Last Night, 1939.
Something New Is in My Heart, 1935.
Something To Do with Spring, 1932.
Something To Live For, 1939.
Something To Remember You By, 1930.
Somewhere in Old Wyoming, 1930.
Song Is You, The, 1932.
Song of the Blacksmith, Clang, Clang, Clang, 1934.
Song of the Dawn, 1930.
Song of the Marines, The (We're Shovin' Right Off Again), 1937.
Song of the Metronome, The, 1939.
Song of the Open Road, 1935.
Song of the Woodman, 1936.
Soon, 1930, 1935.
Sophia, see Wake Up, Brother, and Dance, 1937.
Sophisticated Lady, 1933.
Sophisticated Swing, 1936.
Sous les Toits de Paris (Under a Roof in Paree), 1931.
South, 1930.
South American Joe, 1934.
South American Way, 1939.
South of the Border (Down Mexico Way), 1939.
South Rampart Street Parade, 1938.
Sparkling Blue Eyes, 1939.
Sparkling Brown Eyes, see Sparkling Blue Eyes, 1939.
Speak to Me of Love, 1932.
Speaking Confidentially, 1935.
Speaking of Love, 1932.
Speaking of the Weather, 1936.
Spreadin' Rhythm Around, 1935.
Spring Again, 1938.
Spring Is Here, 1938.

315

Titles

Stairway to the Stars, 1939.
Stand Up and Cheer, 1934.
Star Fell Out of Heaven, A, 1936.
Stardust on the Moon, 1937.
Starlit Hour, The, 1939.
Stars Fell on Alabama, 1934.
Stars in My Eyes, 1936.
Start the Day Right, 1939.
Stately Homes of England, The, 1938.
Stay As Sweet As You Are, 1934.
Stay on the Right Side, Sister, 1933.
Stealin' Apples, 1936.
Steppin' into Swing Society, 1938.
Stiff Upper Lip, 1937.
Stompin' at the Savoy, 1936.
Stompy Jones, 1934.
Stop Beatin' 'Round the Mulberry Bush, 1938.
Stop! You're Breakin' My Heart, 1937.
Stormy Weather, 1933.
Straight from the Shoulder (Right from the Heart), 1934.
Strange As It Seems, 1932.
Strange Enchantment, 1939.
Strange Fruit, 1939.
Strange Interlude, 1932.
Stranger in Paree, 1938.
Street of Dreams, 1932.
Street Scene, 1933.
Study in Brown, 1937.
Stuff Is Here (and It's Mellow), The, 1935.
Such Is Life, Such Is Love, 1931.
Suddenly, 1934.
Sugar Plum, 1935.
Summer Night, 1936.
Summertime, 1935.
Sunday in the Park, 1937.
Sunrise Serenade, 1938.
Supper Time, 1933.
Susie Sapple, 1937.
Swamp-Fire, 1935.
(Up on Top of a Rainbow) Sweepin' the Clouds Away, 1930.
Sweet and Hot, 1930.
Sweet and Lovely, 1931.
Sweet As a Song, 1937.

Sweet Heartache, 1937.
Sweet Is the Word for You, 1937.
Sweet Jennie Lee, 1930.
Sweet Leilani, 1937.
Sweet Madness, 1933.
Sweet Sixty-Five, 1937.
Sweet Someone, 1937.
Sweetheart Darlin', 1933.
Sweethearts Forever, 1932.
Swing, Brother, Swing, 1936.
Swing High, Swing Low, 1937.
Swing Is Here To Stay, 1937.
Swing Me an Old Fashioned Song, 1938.
Swingin' in a Hammock, 1930.
Swingin' the Blues, 1939.
Swingin' the Jinx Away, 1936.
Swingtime in the Rockies, 1936.
Swingy Little Thingy, 1933.
Symphony in Riffs, 1935.

T

Tabu, 1931.
'Taint What You Do (It's the Way That Cha Do It), 1939.
Take a Lesson from the Lark, 1934.
Take a Number from One to Ten, 1934.
Take and Take and Take, 1937.
Take It Easy, 1935.
Take Me Back to Manhattan, 1930.
Take Me Back to My Boots and Saddle, 1935.
Take Me for a Buggy Ride, 1933.
Take Me in Your Arms, 1932.
Take My Heart (and Do with It What You Please), 1936.
Takes Two To Make a Bargain, 1935.
Taking Care of You, 1935.
Taking Off, 1931.
Tango Della Gelosia, see Jealous of You, 1933.
Tara's Theme, 1939.
Teeter Totter Tessie, 1939.
Tell Me That You Love Me, 1935.
Tell Me Why You Smile, Mona Lisa, 1932.
Tell Me with a Love Song, 1931.

316

Tell Me You're Mine, 1939.
Temptation, 1933.
Ten Cents a Dance, 1930.
Ten Pins in the Sky, 1938.
Tender Is the Night, 1935.
Texas Tornado, 1936.
Thank You for a Lovely Evening, 1934.
Thank Your Father, 1930.
Thanks, 1933.
Thanks a Million, 1935.
Thanks for Ev'rything, 1938.
Thanks for the Memory, 1937.
Thanksgivin', 1932.
That Certain Age, 1938.
That Foolish Feeling, 1936.
That Lucky Fellow, 1939.
That Lucky Lady, see That Lucky Fellow, 1939.
That Moment of Moments, 1935.
That Old Feeling, 1937.
That Sentimental Sandwich, 1939.
That Silver Haired Daddy of Mine, 1932.
That Sly Old Gentleman (from Featherbed Lane), 1939.
That Week in Paris, 1938.
That's Life I Guess, 1936.
That's Love, 1934.
That's My Desire, 1931.
That's What I Hate about Love, 1932.
That's What I Want for Christmas, 1935.
That's What You Think, 1935.
That's Why Darkies Were Born, 1931.
Them There Eyes, 1930.
Then, 1935.
Then I'll Be Tired of You, 1934.
(If It Isn't Pain) Then It Isn't Love, 1935.
Then You've Never Been Blue, 1935.
There Goes My Heart, 1934.
There Is No Greater Love, see (There Is) No Greater Love, 1936.
There Isn't Any Limit to My Love, 1936.

There Ought To Be a Moonlight Saving Time, see (There Ought To Be a) Moonlight Saving Time, 1931.
There'll Always Be a Lady Fair, 1936.
There'll Always Be an England, 1939.
There's a Bluebird at My Window, 1933.
There's a Boat Dat's Leavin' Soon for New York, 1935.
There's a Boy in Harlem, 1938.
There's a Cabin in the Pines, 1933.
There's a Far Away Look in Your Eye, 1938.
There's a Gold Mine in the Sky, 1937.
There's a Home in Wyomin', 1933.
There's a House in Harlem for Sale, 1934.
There's a Little Bit of You in Every Love Song, 1933.
There's a Lull in My Life, 1937.
There's a Small Hotel, 1936.
There's No Two Ways about It, 1936.
There's Nothing Too Good for My Baby, 1931.
There's Nothing Wrong in a Kiss, 1930.
There's Nowhere To Go but Up, 1938.
There's So Much More, 1931.
There's Something about a Soldier, 1933.
There's Something about an Old Fashioned Girl, see (There's Something about an) Old Fashioned Girl, 1930.
There's Something about an Old Love, 1938.
There's Something in the Air, 1936.
There's That Look in Your Eyes, 1936.
These Foolish Things (Remind Me of You), 1935.
They All Laughed, 1937.
They Call Me Sister Honky Tonk, 1933.

Titles

They Can't Take That Away from Me, 1937.
They Say, 1938.
Thief in the Night, 1935.
Things Are Looking Up, 1937.
Things I Want, The, 1937.
Things That Might Have Been, 1939.
Thinking of You, 1936.
This Can't Be Love, 1938.
This Is It, 1939.
This Is My Night To Dream, 1938.
This Is Our Last Night Together, 1934.
This Is the Missus, 1931.
This Is the Night, 1932.
This Little Piggie Went to Market, 1933.
This Never Happened Before, 1937.
This Night (Will Be My Souvenir), 1939.
This Time It's Love, 1935.
This Year's Kisses, 1937.
This'll Make You Whistle, 1936.
Three Little Fishes (Itty Bitty Poo), 1939.
Three Little Words, 1930.
Three on a Match, 1932.
Three's a Crowd, 1932.
Thrill Is Gone, The, 1931.
Thrill of a Lifetime, 1937.
Through the Years, 1931.
Throw Another Log on the Fire, 1933.
Thru the Courtesy of Love, 1936.
Till the Real Thing Comes Along, see Until the Real Thing Comes Along, 1936.
Time on My Hands (You in My Arms), 1930.
Tiny Little Fingerprints, 1935.
Ti-Pi-Tin, 1938.
Tired of It All, 1934.
To Love You and To Lose You, 1936.
To You Sweetheart, Aloha, 1936.
Tom Thumb's Drum, 1932.
Tomorrow, 1938.
Tomorrow Is Another Day, 1937.
Tomorrow Night, 1939.

Tonight Is Mine, 1934.
Tonight Will Live, 1938.
Tony's Wife, 1933.
Too Beautiful for Words, 1934.
Too Good for the Average Man, 1936.
Too Late, 1931.
Too Marvelous for Words, 1937.
Toodle-oo, So Long, Good-Bye, 1931.
Tootin' through the Roof, 1939.
Top Hat, White Tie and Tails, 1935.
Top of the Town, 1936.
Torch Song, The, 1931.
Tormented, 1936.
Touch of God's Hand, The, 1936.
Touch of Your Hand, The, 1933.
Touch of Your Lips, The, 1936.
Toy Trumpet, The, 1937.
Traffic Jam, 1939.
Train Whistle Blues, 1930.
Tramps at Sea, 1932.
Travelin' Blues, 1931.
Travelin' Light, 1937.
Trav'lin All Alone, 1930.
Treat Me Rough, 1930.
Triplets, 1937.
Truck Drivers (Blues), 1939.
Truckin', 1935.
True, 1934.
True Confession, 1937.
Trust in Me, 1934.
Try a Little Tenderness, 1932.
Try To Forget, 1931.
Try To See It My Way, 1934.
Tumbling Tumbleweeds, 1934.
Turn Off the Moon, 1937.
Turn On the Old Music Box, 1939.
Turn Out the Light, 1932.
Tutti-Frutti, 1938.
Twentieth Century Blues, 1931.
Twenty Million People, 1932.
Twenty One Years, 1931.
Twilight in Turkey, 1937.
Twilight on the Trail, 1936.
Twinkle in Your Eye, A, 1938.
Twinkle, Twinkle, Little Star, 1936.
Two Blind Loves, 1939.
Two Bouquets, 1938.
Two Cigarettes in the Dark, 1934.

Two for Tonight, 1935.

Two Hearts in Three-Quarter Time, 1930.

Two Little Blue Little Eyes, 1931.

Two Loves Have I, 1931.

Two Sleepy People, 1938.

Two Tickets to Georgia, 1933.

Two Together, 1935.

Typical Self-Made American, A, 1930.

U

U.S. Air Force, The (The Wild Blue Yonder), 1939.

Umbrella Man, The, 1938.

Undecided, 1939.

Under a Blanket of Blue, 1933.

Under a Roof in Paree, see Sous les Toits de Paris, 1931.

Under Your Spell, 1934.

Underneath the Arches, 1933.

Underneath the Harlem Moon, 1932.

Unless, 1934.

(It Will Have To Do) Until the Real Thing Comes Along, 1936.

Until Today, 1936.

V

Vagabond Dreams, 1939.

Very Thought of You, The, 1934.

Vieni, Vieni, 1937.

Viper's Drag, 1934.

Vol Vist Du Gaily Star, 1938.

W

W.P.A. Blues, 1936.

Wabash Moon, 1931.

Wacky Dust, 1938.

Wagon Wheels, 1933.

Wah-Hoo!, 1936.

Wail of the Reefer Man, The, 1932.

Wail of the Winds, 1935.

Waitin' at the Gate for Katy, 1934.

Wake Up and Live, 1937.

Wake Up and Sing, 1936.

Wake Up, Brother, and Dance, 1937.

Walk Right In, 1930.

Walkin' My Baby Back Home, 1930.

Waltz down the Aisle, 1934.

Waltz in Swingtime, 1936.

Waltz Was Born in Vienna, A, 1936.

Waltz You Saved for Me, The, 1930.

Waltzing in a Dream, 1932.

Waltzing Mathilda, 1936.

Wanderlust, 1939.

War Dance for Wooden Indians, 1938.

Was I To Blame for Falling in Love with You, 1930.

Was It Rain?, 1937.

Was That the Human Thing To Do, 1931.

(We're Gonna Hang Out) The Washing on the Siegfried Line, 1939.

Wasn't It Beautiful While It Lasted?, 1930.

Water under the Bridge, 1933.

'Way Back Home, 1935.

Way Out West (on West End Avenue), 1937.

Way You Look Tonight, The, 1936.

We Just Couldn't Say Good-bye, 1932.

We Saw the Sea, 1936.

We Will Always Be Sweethearts, 1932.

Weekend of a Private Secretary, The, 1938.

Well All Right! (Tonight's the Night), 1939.

We'll Be the Same, 1931.

Well, Did You Evah?, 1939.

We'll Make Hay While the Sun Shines, 1933.

We'll Meet Again, 1939.

We're Gonna Hang Out the Washing on the Siegfried Line, see (We're Gonna Hang Out) The Washing on the Siegfried Line, 1939.

We're in the Money (The Gold Digger's Song), 1933.

Titles

We're Off To See the Wizard, 1939.
We're Working Our Way through College, 1937.
Were You Foolin'?, 1934.
Were Your Ears Burning, Baby?, 1934.
What a Beautiful Beginning, 1937.
What a Diff'rence a Day Made, 1934.
What a Life Trying To Live without You, 1932.
What a Little Moonlight Can Do, 1934.
What a Perfect Combination, 1932.
What a Wonderful World, 1935.
What Can You Do with a Man?, 1938.
What Can You Say in a Love Song?, 1934.
What Goes On Here in My Heart, 1938.
What Good Is Love, 1937.
What Have You Got That Gets Me?, 1938.
What Is That Tune?, 1938.
What Is There To Say, 1933.
What More Can I Ask?, 1933.
What Shall I Do?, 1938.
What Will I Tell My Heart, 1937.
Whatever It Is I'm Against It, 1933.
What's Good about Goodnight?, 1938.
What's New?, 1939.
What's the Reason (I'm Not Pleasin' You)?, 1935.
What's the Use of Getting Sober, 1938.
What's Your Story, Morning Glory?, 1938.
When a Gypsy Makes His Violin Cry, 1935.
When a Woman Loves a Man, 1930, 1934.
When Did You Leave Heaven, 1936.
When He Comes Home to Me, 1934.
When I Grow Too Old To Dream, 1935.
When I Grow Up, 1935.

When I Take My Sugar to Tea, 1931.
When I'm the President, 1931.
When I'm with You, 1936.
When It's Harvest Time in Peaceful Valley, 1930.
When It's Lamp Lightin' Time in the Valley, 1933.
When It's Round-up Time in Heaven, 1936.
When It's Sleepy Time down South, 1931.
When Lights Are Low, 1936.
When Love Comes Your Way, 1933.
When Love Is Young, 1937.
When My Dreamboat Comes Home, 1936.
When My Ship Comes In, 1934.
(Oh, How I'll Miss You) When Summer Is Gone, 1937.
When the Bloom Is on the Sage, 1930.
When the Moon Comes over the Mountain, 1931.
When the Spring Is in the Air, 1932.
When the Sun Goes Down, 1935.
When They Played the Polka, 1938.
When Tomorrow Comes, 1933.
When We're Alone, see Penthouse Serenade, 1931.
When Winter Comes, 1939.
When You Are Dancing the Waltz, 1936.
When You Were a Smile on Your Mother's Lips (and a Twinkle in Your Daddy's Eye), 1934.
When Your Hair Has Turned to Silver (I Will Love You Just the Same), 1930.
When Your Lover Has Gone, 1931.
When Yuba Plays the Rhumba on the Tuba, 1931.
Where Am I? (Am I in Heaven?), 1935.
Where Are the Songs We Sung?, 1938.
Where Are You?, 1936.
Where Can He Be?, 1931.
Where Have We Met Before?, 1932.

Where Have You Been?, 1930.
Where Have You Been All My
    Life, 1936.
Where in the World, 1938.
Where or When, 1937.
Where the Blue of the Night (Meets
    the Gold of the Day), 1931.
Where the Lazy River Goes By,
    1936.
Where Was I?, 1939.
Where You Go, I Go, 1932.
Which Side Are You On, 1932.
Whiffenpoof Song, The, 1936.
While a Cigarette Was Burning,
    1938.
While Hearts Are Singing, 1931.
Whispers in the Dark, 1937.
Whistle While You Work, 1937.
Whistling Boy, The, 1937.
Whistling in the Dark, 1931.
White Dove, The, 1930.
White Heat, 1934.
White Jazz, 1933.
Who Are We To Say (Obey Your
    Heart), 1939.
Who Cares? (So Long As You
    Care for Me), 1931.
Who Knows?, 1937.
Who Minds about Me?, 1936.
Whole Darned Thing's for You,
    The, 1930.
Who's Afraid of Love, 1936.
Who's Afraid of the Big Bad
    Wolf, 1933.
Who's Your Little Whoozis?, 1931.
Whose Big Baby Are You, 1935.
Why Can't This Night Go On
    Forever, 1933.
Why Dance?, 1931.
Why Did You Do It?, 1937.
Why Do I Dream Those Dreams,
    1934.
Why Do You Pass Me By, 1936.
Why Dream?, 1935.
Why Not String Along with Me?,
    1938.
Why Should I Care?, 1937.
Why Shouldn't I, 1935.
Why Stars Come Out at Night,
    1935.

Wild Honey, 1934.
Will You Marry Me Tomorrow,
    Maria?, 1937.
Will You Remember Me?, 1938.
Willow Weep for Me, 1932.
Winter Wonderland, 1934.
Wintergreen for President, 1931.
Wishing (Will Make It So), 1939.
With a Banjo on My Knee, 1936.
With a Feather in Your Cap, 1933.
With a Smile and a Song, 1937.
With All My Heart, 1935.
With Every Breath I Take, 1934.
With My Eyes Wide Open, I'm
    Dreaming, 1934.
With Plenty of Money and You,
    1936.
(I'm Still without a Sweetheart)
    With Summer Coming On, 1932.
With You on My Mind, 1938.
Without a Word of Warning, 1935.
Without Love, 1930.
Without That Certain Thing, 1933.
Without Your Love, 1937.
Woman Is a Sometime Thing, A,
    1935.
Wonder Bar, 1934.
Woodchopper's Ball, 1939.
Wooden Soldier and the China
    Doll, The, 1932.
Words Are in My Heart, The, 1935.
Words without Music, 1936.
World Is Mine (Tonight), The,
    1935.
World Owes Me a Living, The,
    1934.
Worried Man Blues, 1935.
Would You, 1936.
Would You Like To Take a Walk?
    (Sump'n Good'll Come from
    That), 1930.
Wouldja for a Big Red Apple,
    see Red Apple, 1932.
Wrap Your Troubles in Dreams (and
    Dream Your Troubles Away),
    1931.
Wrappin' It Up (The Lindy Glide),
    1934.
Wynken, Blynken and Nod, 1938.

Titles

Y

Yam, The, 1938.
Yancey Special, 1938.
Yearning for Love, 1936.
Yes, My Darling Daughter, 1939.
Yesterdays, 1933.
You, 1936.
You and I Know, 1937.
You and the Night and the Music, 1934.
You Are My Flower, 1939.
You Are My Lucky Star, 1935.
You Are So Lovely and I'm So Lonely, 1935.
(I Am the Words), You Are the Melody, 1930.
You Are Too Beautiful, 1932.
You Better Go Now, 1936.
You Brought a New Kind of Love to Me, 1930.
You Call It Madness (but I Call It Love), 1931.
You Came Along (from Out of Nowhere), see Out of Nowhere, 1931.
You Can Depend on Me, 1932.
You Can Make My Life a Bed of Roses, 1932.
You Can't Have Everything, 1937.
You Can't Pull the Wool over My Eyes, 1936.
You Can't Stop Me from Dreaming, 1937.
You Can't Stop Me from Lovin' You, 1931.
You Couldn't Be Cuter, 1938.
You Didn't Have To Tell Me — I Knew It All the Time, 1931.
You Do the Darndest Things, Baby, 1936.
You Dropped Me Like a Red Hot Penny, 1936.
You Forgot Your Gloves, 1931.
You Go to My Head, 1938.
You Gotta Be a Football Hero (To Get Along with the Beautiful Girls), 1933.
You Gotta S-M-I-L-E To Be H-A-Double P-Y, 1936.

You Have Cast Your Shadow on the Sea, 1938.
You Have Everything, 1937.
You Have Taken My Heart, 1933.
You Hit the Spot, 1935.
You Leave Me Breathless, 1938.
You Let Me Down, 1935.
You Must Have Been a Beautiful Baby, 1938.
You Never Know, 1938.
You Oughta Be in Pictures, 1934.
(I'll Be Glad When You're Dead), You Rascal You, 1931.
You Said It, 1931.
You Showed Me the Way, 1937.
You Stayed Away Too Long, 1936.
You Taught Me To Love Again, 1939.
You Took the Words Right Out of My Heart, 1937.
You Took the Words Right Out of My Mouth, 1935.
You Try Somebody Else (We'll Be Back Together Again), 1931.
You Turned the Tables on Me, 1936.
You Were There, 1935.
You Will Remember Vienna, 1930.
You'll Be Mine in Apple Blossom Time, 1931.
(If You Can't Sing It) You'll Have To Swing It, 1936.
Young and Healthy, 1932.
Your Feet's Too Big, 1936.
Your Head on My Shoulder, 1934.
Your Mother's Son-in-Law, 1933.
Your Smiles, Your Tears, 1930.
You're a Builder-Upper, 1934.
You're a Heavenly Thing, 1935.
You're a Lucky Guy, 1939.
You're a Natural, 1938.
You're a Sweet Little Headache, 1938.
You're a Sweetheart, 1937.
You're All I Need, 1935.
You're an Angel, 1935.
You're an Old Smoothie, 1932.
You're As Pretty As a Picture, 1938.
You're Blasé, 1932.

You're Devastating, 1933.
You're Driving Me Crazy (What Did I Do?), 1930.
You're Everywhere, 1932.
You're Getting To Be a Habit with Me, 1932.
You're Gonna Lose Your Gal, 1933.
You're in Love, 1932.
You're Just a Dream Come True, 1931.
You're Laughing at Me, 1937.
You're Lucky to Me, 1930.
You're Mine, You!, 1933.
You're My Everything, 1931.
You're My Past, Present and Future, 1933.
You're My Thrill, 1935.
You're Not the Kind, 1936.
You're Not the Only Oyster in the Stew, 1934.
You're Simply Delish, 1930.
You're Slightly Terrific, 1936.
You're So Desirable, 1938.
You're Such a Comfort to Me, 1933.

You're the Cure for What Ails Me, 1936.
You're the One, 1930.
You're the One I Care For, 1930.
You're the Only Star (in My Blue Heaven), 1938.
You're the Top, 1934.
Yours, 1937.
Yours and Mine, 1937.
Yours for a Song, 1939.
Yours Is My Heart Alone, 1931.
You've Got Everything, 1933.
You've Got Me Crying Again, 1933.
You've Got Me in the Palm of Your Hand!, 1932.
You've Got Something, 1936.
You've Got Something There, 1937.
You've Got What Gets Me, 1932.
You've Gotta Eat Your Spinach, Baby, 1936.

Z

Zing Went the Strings of My Heart, 1935.

List of Publishers

This is a list of the publishers of the songs in Volume 4 of *Popular Music*. Publishers which are members of the American Society of Composers, Authors and Publishers or whose catalogs are available under ASCAP license are indicated by the designation, ASCAP. Publishers which have granted performing rights to Broadcast Music, Inc. are designated by the notation, BMI.

A

Advanced Music Corp. (ASCAP)
488 Madison Avenue
New York, New York 10022

Fred Ahlert Music Corp. (ASCAP)
15 East 48th Street
New York, New York 10017

Ahlert-Burke Corp. (ASCAP)
15 East 48th Street
New York, New York 10017

Alamo Music, Inc. (ASCAP)
241 West 72nd Street
New York, New York 10023

Allison's Music, Inc. (ASCAP)
c/o Mr. Allie Wrubel
535 South Curson Avenue
Los Angeles, California 90036

American Academy of Music, Inc. (ASCAP)
1619 Broadway
New York, New York 10019

American Division of Elvis Presley Music, Inc.
and Rumbalero Music, Inc. (BMI)
241 West 72nd Street
New York, New York 10023

Anne-Rachel Music Corp. (ASCAP)
241 West 72nd Street
New York, New York 10023

Arko Music Corp. (ASCAP)
c/o Edwin H. Morris & Co., Inc.
31 West 54th Street
New York, New York 10019

B

Irving Berlin Music Corp. (ASCAP)
1290 Avenue of the Americas
New York, New York 10019

Bibo Music Publishers, Inc. (ASCAP)
2444 Wilshire Boulevard
Santa Monica, California 90403

Bourne Co. (ASCAP)
136 West 52nd Street
New York, New York 10019

Bregman, Vocco & Conn, Inc. (ASCAP)
1619 Broadway
New York, New York 10019

Brenner Music, Inc. (BMI)
241 West 72nd Street
New York, New York 10023

Broadway Music Corp. (ASCAP)
Suite 1920
135 West 50th Street
New York, New York 10020

Joe Burke Music Co. (ASCAP)
15 East 48th Street
New York, New York 10017

Burke & Van Heusen, Inc. (ASCAP)
Suite 901
250 West 57th Street
New York, New York 10019

C

Irving Caesar (ASCAP)
1619 Broadway
New York, New York 10019

325

Capri Music Corp. (BMI)
145 West 45th Street
New York, New York 10036

Carmichael Music Publications, Inc. (ASCAP)
119 West 57th Street
New York, New York 10019

Chappell & Co., Inc. (ASCAP)
609 Fifth Avenue
New York, New York 10017

Ched Music Co. (ASCAP)
c/o Mr. Charles Tobias
1650 Broadway
New York, New York 10019

Commander Publications (ASCAP)
1610 North Argyle Avenue
Hollywood, California 90028

Crisscott Music Co. (ASCAP)
10807 Wellworth Avenue
Los Angeles, California 90024

Cromwell Music, Inc. (ASCAP)
Suite 2160
10 Columbus Circle
New York, New York 10019

D

Charles N. Daniels, Inc. (ASCAP)
241 West 72nd Street
New York, New York 10023

De Sylva, Brown & Henderson, Inc. (ASCAP)
609 Fifth Avenue
New York, New York 10017

Dixie Music Publishing Co. (BMI)
57 Third Avenue
New York, New York 10003

Dorsey Bros. Music, Inc. (ASCAP)
33 West 60th Street
New York, New York 10023

Duchess Music Corp. (BMI)
445 Park Avenue
New York, New York 10022

E

Elar Music Corp. (ASCAP)
 c/o Chappell & Co., Inc.
 609 Fifth Avenue
 New York, New York 10017

Elbee Music Co.
 c/o De Sylva, Brown & Henderson, Inc.
 609 Fifth Avenue
 New York, New York 10017

Exeter Music, Inc. (ASCAP)
 Suite 2160
 10 Columbus Circle
 New York, New York 10019

F

Famous Music Corp. (ASCAP)
 1501 Broadway
 New York, New York 10036

Leo Feist, Inc. (ASCAP)
 1350 Avenue of the Americas
 New York, New York 10019

Carl Fischer, Inc. (ASCAP)
 c/o Mr. Frank H. Connor, President
 62 Cooper Square
 New York, New York 10003

Fred Fisher Music Co., Inc. (ASCAP)
 1619 Broadway
 New York, New York 10019

Flojan Music Publishing Co. (ASCAP)
 42 Lafayette Place
 Woodmere, New York 11598

Florence Music Co., Inc. (ASCAP)
 609 Fifth Avenue
 New York, New York 10017

Charles Foley, Inc. (ASCAP)
 156 West 44th Street
 New York, New York 10036

Folkways Music Publishers, Inc. (BMI)
 Suite 2160
 10 Columbus Circle
 New York, New York 10019

Forster Music Publishers, Inc. (ASCAP)
216 South Wabash Avenue
Chicago, Illinois 60604

Sam Fox Publishing Co., Inc. (ASCAP)
1841 Broadway
New York, New York 10023

Frank Music Corp. (ASCAP)
119 West 57th Street
New York, New York 10019

G

Gem Music Corp. (ASCAP)
c/o Mr. Barney Young
Post Office Box 340
Radio City Station
New York, New York 10019

General Music Publishing Co., Inc. (ASCAP)
53 East 54th Street
New York, New York 10022

Gershwin Publishing Corp. (ASCAP)
609 Fifth Avenue
New York, New York 10017

Gladys Music, Inc. (ASCAP)
241 West 72nd Street
New York, New York 10023

H

Hallmark Music Co., Inc. (ASCAP)
626 North Rodeo Drive
Beverly Hills, California 90210

Harms, Inc. (ASCAP)
488 Madison Avenue
New York, New York 10022

T. B. Harms Co. (ASCAP)
609 Fifth Avenue
New York, New York 10017

Holliday Publications (ASCAP)
319 Lee Avenue
Yonkers, New York 10705

I

International Pauline Corp. (ASCAP)
45 West 56th Street
New York, New York 10019

J

Jewel Music Publishing Co., Inc. (ASCAP)
1619 Broadway
New York, New York 10019

K

Irving Kahal Music, Inc. (ASCAP)
c/o A. Halsey Cowan, Esq.
1740 Broadway
New York, New York 10019

Gus Kahn Music Co. (ASCAP)
6223 Selma Avenue
Hollywood, California 90028

L

La Salle Music Publishers, Inc. (ASCAP)
1619 Broadway
New York, New York 10019

Laursteed Music, Inc. (ASCAP)
c/o Edward Traubner & Co., Inc.
Suite 501
132 South Rodeo Drive
Beverly Hills, California 90212

Leeds Music Corp. (ASCAP)
445 Park Avenue
New York, New York 10022

Samuel M. Lerner Publications (ASCAP)
1857 North Wilton Place
Hollywood, California 90028

Edgar Leslie (ASCAP)
59 West 46th Street
New York, New York 10036

Lincoln Music Corp. (ASCAP)
c/o Mr. Abner Silver
Suite 203
160 Central Park South
New York, New York 10019

John Jacob Loeb Co. (ASCAP)
42 Lafayette Place
Woodmere, New York 11598

M

MCA, Inc. (ASCAP)
445 Park Avenue
New York, New York 10022

Magidson Music Co., Inc. (ASCAP)
10464 Lindbrook Drive
Los Angeles, California 90024

Malneck Music (ASCAP)
508 North Elm Drive
Beverly Hills, California 90210

Edward B. Marks Music Corp. (BMI)
136 West 52nd Street
New York, New York 10019

Marlo Music Corp. (ASCAP)
c/o Mr. David W. Katz
Attention: Mr. P. Plumer
10 East 40th Street
New York, New York 10016

Marlong Music Corp. (ASCAP)
11 Park Place
New York, New York 10007

The Peter Maurice Music Co., Ltd. (ASCAP)
101 West 55th Street
New York, New York 10019

Mayfair Music Corp. (ASCAP)
31 West 54th Street
New York, New York 10019

Miller Music Corp. (ASCAP)
1350 Avenue of the Americas
New York, New York 10019

Mills Music, Inc. (ASCAP)
1619 Broadway
New York, New York 10019

Morley Music Co., Inc. (ASCAP)
31 West 54th Street
New York, New York 10019

Edwin H. Morris & Co., Inc. (ASCAP)
31 West 54th Street
New York, New York 10019

Morro Music Corp. (BMI)
Suite 1531-2
250 West 57th Street
New York, New York 10019

Movietone Music Corp. (ASCAP)
1841 Broadway
New York, New York 10023

Musical Works (ASCAP)
77 West Washington Street
Chicago, Illinois 60602

N

Al J. Neiburg, Music Publisher (ASCAP)
321 West 78th Street
New York, New York 10024

New Dawn Music Corp. (ASCAP)
609 Fifth Avenue
New York, New York 10017

New World Music Corp. (ASCAP)
488 Madison Avenue
New York, New York 10022

Northern Music Corp. (ASCAP)
c/o MCA, Inc.
445 Park Avenue
New York, New York 10022

P

Paramount Music Corp. (ASCAP)
1501 Broadway
New York, New York 10036

Peer International Corp. (BMI)
1619 Broadway
New York, New York 10019

Photo Play Music Co., Inc. (ASCAP)
c/o Mr. Allan Betzenberger, President
117 Fourth Street
Sladington, Pennsylvania 18080

Piedmont Music Co., Inc. (ASCAP)
136 West 52nd Street
New York, New York 10019

R

Record Music Publishing Co. (ASCAP)
Room 605
1650 Broadway
New York, New York 10019

Regent Music Corp. (BMI)
1619 Broadway
New York, New York 10019

Remick Music Corp. (ASCAP)
488 Madison Avenue
New York, New York 10022

Harry Revel Music Corp. (ASCAP)
155 West 68th Street
New York, New York 10023

Robbins Music Corp. (ASCAP)
1350 Avenue of the Americas
New York, New York 10019

Robert Music Corp. (ASCAP)
Suite 901
1650 Broadway
New York, New York 10019

J. Russel Robinson, Inc. (ASCAP)
18 East 48th Street
New York, New York 10017

Rytvoc, Inc. (ASCAP)
39 West 54th Street
New York, New York 10019

S

Scarsdale Music Corp. (ASCAP)
666 Fifth Avenue
New York, New York 10019

G. Schirmer, Inc. (ASCAP)
609 Fifth Avenue
New York, New York 10017

Shapiro, Bernstein & Co., Inc. (ASCAP)
666 Fifth Avenue
New York, New York 10019

Al Sherman Music Co. (ASCAP)
Apartment 305
700 South Hobart Boulevard
Los Angeles, California 90005

Sherwin Music, Inc. (ASCAP)
c/o Mr. Robert Mellin
Room 901
1650 Broadway
New York, New York 10019

Shubert Music Publishing Corp. (ASCAP)
c/o Mr. Syd Goldberg
488 Madison Avenue
New York, New York 10022

George Simon, Inc. (ASCAP)
c/o Larry Shayne Music, Inc.
Room 516
1619 Broadway
New York, New York 10019

Skidmore Music Co., Inc. (ASCAP)
666 Fifth Avenue
New York, New York 10019

Southern Music Publishing Co., Inc. (ASCAP)
1619 Broadway
New York, New York 10019

Sovereign Music Corp. (ASCAP)
c/o Mr. Al Lewis
22 East 49th Street
New York, New York 10017

Larry Spier, Inc. (ASCAP)
Suite 408
1650 Broadway
New York, New York 10019

Spina Music (ASCAP)
2233 Vista Del Mar Place
Hollywood, California 90028

T

Tempo Music, Inc. (ASCAP)
52 West 58th Street
New York, New York 10019

Gordon V. Thompson, Ltd.
32 Alcorn Avenue
Toronto 7, Ontario
Canada

Tobey Music Corp. (ASCAP)
1650 Broadway
New York, New York 10019

V

Venus Music Corp. (ASCAP)
Room 404
1619 Broadway
New York, New York 10019

Jerry Vogel Music Co., Inc. (ASCAP)
121 West 45th Street
New York, New York 10036

W

Warock Corp. (ASCAP)
39 West 54th Street
New York, New York 10019

Webster Music Corp. (ASCAP)
c/o Edward Traubner & Co., Inc.
Suite 501
132 South Rodeo Drive
Beverly Hills, California 90212

Westpar Music Corp. (BMI)
1330 Avenue of the Americas
New York, New York 10019

Whiting Music Corp. (ASCAP)
Room 502
1619 Broadway
New York, New York 10019

Williamson Music, Inc. (ASCAP)
609 Fifth Avenue
New York, New York 10017

M. Witmark & Sons (ASCAP)
488 Madison Avenue
New York, New York 10022

Words & Music, Inc. (ASCAP)
8th Floor
17 West 60th Street
New York, New York 10023

World Music, Inc. (ASCAP)
18 East 48th Street
New York, New York 10017

Y

The Vincent Youmans Co., Inc. (ASCAP)
Suite 404
157 West 57th Street
New York, New York 10019

Victor Young Publications, Inc. (ASCAP)
609 Fifth Avenue
New York, New York 10017

About the Editor

Nat Shapiro is Co-Editor of two standard jazz works, *Hear Me Talkin' to Ya* and *The Jazz Makers;* a frequent contributor to periodicals in the United States and abroad; and a prolific annotator of record albums. For two decades, he has been active in the creation, promotion, and production of popular music as press agent, artists' representative, editor, music publisher, and artists and repertoire director. He has produced and co-produced popular, classical, folk, jazz, and spoken word recordings in the United States, France, England, Holland, Germany, Italy, Spain, Argentina, Brazil, and Mexico with such artists as Lotte Lenya, Marlene Dietrich, Yves Montand, Mahalia Jackson, Michel Legrand, Miles Davis, Juliette Greco, and Barbra Streisand. Recently instrumental in bringing about the productions of two outstanding musical projects, the "folk-rock" musical, *Hair,* and *Jacques Brel Is Alive and Well and Living in Paris,* he is currently involved in the preparation of two Broadway musicals. He is also working on a long-range project, a "nostalgic history" of American popular songs, as well as on the subsequent volumes of *Popular Music.*